THE BIOGRAPHICAL DICTIONARY OF SCIENTISTS

Chemists

THE BIOGRAPHICAL DICTIONARY OF SCIENTISTS

Chemists

General Editor
David Abbott PhD

BLOND EDUCATIONAL

First published in Great Britain in 1983 by
Frederick Muller Limited, Alexandra Road,
Wimbledon, London SW19 7JZ.

Blond Educational is an imprint of Frederick
Muller Limited

Biographical dictionary of scientists.
   2. Chemists
   1. Scientists – Biography
   I. Abbott, David
   509'.2'2   Q141

ISBN 0-584-70000-8

Made and printed in Great Britain by
Butler & Tanner Ltd, Frome and London

Contents

Acknowledgements

Many people are involved in the creation of a major new series of reference books. The General Editor and the publishers are grateful to all of them and wish to thank particularly the contributing authors: Gareth Ashurst; Jim Bailey; Mary Basham; Alan Bishop; William Cooksey; David Cowey; Patricia Nash; Valerie Neal; Mary Sanders; Robert Smith and David Ward. Our thanks are also due to the contributing consultant: Martin Sherwood; to Bull Publishing Consultants Ltd, whose experience in the development of reference books has made a significant contribution to the series: John Clark; Martyn Page and Sandy Shepherd; and to Mick Saunders for his artwork.

Historical introduction

Chemistry seems to have originated in the countries of Egypt and Mesopotamia several thousand years before Christ. Certainly by about 3000 BC the Egyptians had produced the copper–tin alloy known as bronze, by heating the ores of copper and tin together, and this new material was soon common enough to be made into tools, ornaments, armour and weapons. The Ancient Egyptians were also skilled at extracting juices and infusions from plants, and pigments from minerals, which they used in the embalming and preserving of their dead. By 600 BC the Greeks were also becoming a settled and prosperous people with leisure time in which to think. They began to turn their attention to the nature of the Universe and to the structure of its materials. They were thus the first to study the subject we now call chemical theory. Aristotle (384–322 BC) proposed that there were four elements - earth, air, fire and water - and that everything was a combination of these four. They were thought to possess the following properties: earth was cold and dry, air was hot and moist, fire was hot and dry, and water was cold and moist. The idea of the four elements persisted for 2,000 years. The Greeks also worked out, at least hypothetically, that matter ultimately consisted of small indivisible particles, *atomos* - the origin of our word atom.

From the Egyptians and the Greeks comes *khemeia*, alchemy and eventually chemistry as we know it today. The source of the word *khemeia* is debatable, but it is certainly the origin of the word chemistry. It may derive from the Egyptians' word for their country (*Khem*, meaning the black land). It may come from the Greek word *khumos* (the juice of a plant), so that *khemeia* is "the art of extracting juices"; or from the Greek *cheo* (I pour or cast), which refers to the activities of the metal workers. Whatever its origin, the art of *khemeia* soon became akin to magic and was feared by the ordinary people. One of the greatest aims of the subject involved the attempts to transform base metals such as lead and copper into silver or gold. From the four-element theory, it seemed that it should be possible to perform any such change, if only the proper technique could be found.

The Arabs and alchemy

With the decline of the Greek empire *khemeia* was not pursued and little new was added to the subject until it was embraced by the increasingly powerful Arabs in the seventh century AD. Then for five centuries *al-kimiya*, or alchemy, was in their hands. The Arabs drew many ideas from the *khemeia* of the Greeks, but they were also in contact with the Chinese - for example, the idea that gold possessed healing powers came from China. They believed that "medicine" had to be added to base metals to produce gold, and it was this medicine that was to become the philosopher's stone of the later European alchemists. The idea that not only could the philosopher's stone heal "sick" or base metals, but that it could also act as the elixir of life, was also originally Chinese. The Arab alchemists discovered new classes of chemicals such as the caustic alkalis (from the Arabic *al-qaliy*) and they improved technical procedures such as distillation.

Western Europe had its first contact with the Islamic world as a result of the Crusades. Gradually the works of the Arabs - handed down from the Greeks - were translated into Latin and made available to European scholars in the twelfth and thirteenth centuries. Many men spent their lives trying in vain to change base metals into gold; and many alchemists lost their heads for failing to supply the promised gold. Throughout the fifteenth to seventeenth centuries their symbolism became more and more complex. In 1689 the preparation of silver chloride, by dissolving metallic silver in nitric acid and then adding hydrochloric acid, was described like this:

Recipe ☽ , in Ω ☉ solve, cum Ω ⊖ precipitata, filtra. ☽ = Moon = silver (the same symbols were used for the metals and their associated planets), ☉ = nitre, ⊖ = mineral acid, and Ω = spirit.

A new era in chemistry began with the researches of Robert Boyle (1627–1691), who carried out many experiments on air. These experiments were the beginning of a long struggle to find out what air had to do with burning and breathing. From Boyle's time onwards, alchemy became chemistry and it was realized that there was more to the subject than the search for the philosopher's stone.

Chemistry as an experimental science

During the 1700s the phlogiston theory gained popularity. It went back to the alchemists' idea that combustible bodies lost something when they burned. Metals were thought to be composed of a calx (different for each) combined with phlogiston, which was the same in all metals. When a candle burned in air, phlogiston was given off. It was believed that combustible objects were rich in phlogiston and what was left after combustion possessed no phlogiston and would therefore not burn. Thus wood possessed phlogiston but ash did not; when metals rusted, it was considered that the metals contained phlogiston but that its rust or calx did not. By 1780 this theory was almost universally accepted by chemists. Joseph Priestley (1733-1804) was a supporter of the theory and in 1774 he had succeeded in obtaining from mercuric oxide a new gas which was five or six times purer than ordinary air. It was, of course, oxygen but Priestley called it "dephlogisticated air" because a smouldering splint of wood thrust into an atmosphere of this new gas burst into flames much more readily than it did in an ordinary atmosphere. He took this to mean that the gas must be without the usual content of phlogiston, and was therefore eager to accept a new supply.

It was Antoine Lavoisier (1743-1794) who put an end to the phlogiston theory by working out what was really happening in combustion. He repeated Priestley's experiments in 1775 and named the dephlogisticated air oxygen. He realized that air was not a single substance but a mixture of gases, made up of two different gases in the proportion of 1 to 4. He deduced that one-fifth of the air was Priestley's dephlogisticated air (oxygen), and that it was this part only that combined with rusting or burning materials and was essential to life. Oxygen means "acid-producer" and Lavoisier thought, erroneously, that oxygen was an essential part of all acids. He was a careful experimenter and user of the balance, and from his time onwards experimental chemistry was concerned only with materials that could be weighed or otherwise measured. All the "mystery" disappeared and Lavoisier went on to work out a logical system of chemical nomenclature, much of which has survived to the present day.

Early in the nineteenth century many well-known chemists were active. Claude Berthollet (1748-1822) worked on chemical change and composition, and Joseph Gay-Lussac (1778-1850) studied the volumes of gases that take part in chemical reactions. Others included Berzelius, Cannizzaro, Avogadro, Davy, Dumas, Kolbe, Wöhler and Kekulé. The era of modern chemistry was beginning.

Atomic theory and new elements

An English chemist, John Dalton (1766-1844), founded the atomic theory in 1803 and in so doing finally crushed the belief that the transmutation to gold was possible. He realized that the same two elements can combine with each other in more than one set of proportions, and that the variation in combining proportions gives rise to different compounds with different properties. For example, he determined that one part (by weight) of hydrogen combined with eight parts of oxygen to form water, and if it was assumed (incorrectly) that a molecule of water consisted of one atom of hydrogen and one atom of oxygen, then it was possible to set the mass of the hydrogen atom arbitrarily at 1 and call the mass of oxygen 8 (on the same scale). In this way Dalton set up the first table of atomic weights (now called relative atomic masses), and although this was probably his most important achievement, it contained many incorrect assumptions. These errors and anomalies were researched by Jöns Berzelius (1779-1848), who found that for many elements the atomic weights were not simple multiples of that of hydrogen. For many years, oxygen was made the standard and set at 16.000 until the mid-twentieth century, when carbon ($= 12.000$) was adopted. Berzelius suggested representing each element by a symbol consisting of the first one or two letters of the name of the element (sometimes in Latin) and these became the chemical symbols of the elements as still used today.

At about the same time, in 1808, Humphry Davy (1778-1829) was using an electric current to obtain from their oxides elements that had proved to be unisolatable by chemical means: potassium, sodium, magnesium, barium and calcium. His assistant, Michael Faraday (1791-1867), was to become even better known in connection with this technique, electrolysis. By 1830, more than 50 elements had been isolated; chemistry had moved a long way from the four elements of the Ancient Greeks, but their properties seemed to be random. In 1829 the German chemist Johann Döbereiner (1780-1849) thought that he had observed some slight degree of order. He wondered if it was just coincidence that the properties of the element bromine seemed to lie between those of chlorine and iodine, but he went on to notice a similar gradation of properties in the triplets calcium, strontium and barium and with sulphur, selenium and tellurium. In all of these examples, the atomic weight of the element in the middle of the set was about half way between the atomic weights of the other two elements. He called these groups "triads", but because he was unable to find any other such groups, most chemists remained unimpressed by his discovery. Then in 1864 John Newlands (1837–1898) arranged the elements in order of their increasing atomic weights and found that if he wrote them in horizontal rows, and started a new row with every eighth element, similar elements tended to fall in the same vertical columns. Döbereiner's three sets of triads were among them. Newlands called this his "Law of Octaves" by analogy with the repeating octaves in music. Unfortunately there were many places in his chart where obviously dissimilar elements fell together and so it was generally felt that Newland's similarities were not significant but probably only coincidental. He did not have his work published.

In 1862 a German chemist, Julius Lothar Meyer (1830–1895), looked at the volumes of certain fixed weights of elements, and talked of atomic volumes. He plotted the values of these for each element against its atomic weight, and found that there were sharp peaks in the graph at the alkali metals – sodium, potassium, rubidium and caesium. Each part of the graph between the peaks corresponded to a "period" or horizontal row in the table of the elements, and it became obvious where Newlands had gone wrong. He had assumed that each period contained only seven elements; in fact the later periods had to be longer than the earlier ones. By the time Meyer published his findings, he had been anticipated by the Russian chemist Dmitri Mendeleyev (1834–1907), who in 1869 published his version of the Periodic Table, which was more or less as we have it today. He had the insight to leave gaps in his table for three elements which he postulated had not yet been discovered, and was even able to predict what their properties would be. Chemists were sceptical, but within 15 years all three of the "missing" elements had been discovered and their properties were found to agree with Mendeleyev's predictions.

The beginnings of physical chemistry

Until the beginning of the nineteenth century, the areas covered by the subjects of chemistry and physics seemed well-defined and quite distinct. Chemistry studied changes where the molecular bonding structure of a substance was altered, and physics studied phenomena in which no such change occurred. Then in 1840 physics and chemistry merged in the work of Germain Hess (1802–1850). It had been realized that heat – a physical phenomenon – was produced by chemical reactions such as the burning of wood, coal and oil, and it was gradually becoming clear that all chemical reactions involved some sort of heat transfer.

Hess showed that the quantity of heat produced or absorbed when one substance was changed into another was the same no matter by which chemical route the change occurred, and it seemed likely that the law of conservation of energy was equally applicable to chemistry and physics. Thermochemistry had been founded and work was able to begin on thermodynamics. Most of this research was done in Germany and it was Wilhelm Ostwald (1853–1932), towards the end of the nineteenth century, who was responsible for physical chemistry developing into a discipline in its own right. He worked on chemical kinetics and catalysis in particular, but was the last important scientist to refuse to accept that atoms were real – there was at that time still no direct evidence to prove that they existed. Other contemporary chemists working in the new field of physical chemistry included Jacobus van't Hoff (1852–1911) and Svante Arrhenius (1859–1927). Van't Hoff studied solutions and showed that molecules of dissolved substances behaved according to rules analogous to those that describe the behaviour of gases. Arrhenius carried on the work which had been begun by Davy and Faraday on solutions that could carry an electric current. Faraday had called the current-carrying particles "ions", but nobody had worked out what they were. Arrhenius suggested that they were atoms or groups of atoms which bore either a positive or a negative electric charge. His theory of ionic dissociation was used to explain many of the phenomena in electrochemistry.

Towards the end of the nineteenth century, mainly as a result of the increasing interest in the physical side of chemistry, gases came under fresh scrutiny and some errors were found in the law that had been proposed three centuries earlier by Robert Boyle. Henri Regnault (1810–1878), James Clerk Maxwell (1831–1879) and Ludwig Boltzmann (1844–1906) had all worked on the behaviour of gases, and the kinetic theory of gases had been derived. Taking all their findings into account, Johannes van der Waals (1837–1923) arrived at an equation that related pressure, volume and temperature of gases and made due allowance for the sizes of the different gas molecules and the attractions between them. By the end of the century William Ramsay (1852–1916) had begun to discover a special group of gases – the inert or rare gases – which have a valency (oxidation state) of zero and which fit neatly into the Periodic Table between the halogens and the alkali metals.

Organic chemistry becomes a separate discipline

Meanwhile the separate branches of chemistry were emerging and organic substances were being distinguished from inorganic ones. In 1807 Berzelius had proposed that substances such as olive oil and sugar, which were products of living organisms, should be called organic, whereas sulphuric acid and salt should be termed inorganic. Chemists at that time had realized that organic substances were easily converted into inorganic substances by heating or in other ways, but it was thought to be impossible to reverse the process and convert inorganic substances into organic ones. They believed in Vitalism - that somehow life did not obey the same laws as did inanimate objects and that some special influence, a "vital force", was needed to convert inorganic substances into organic ones. Then in 1828 Friedrich Wöhler (1800-1882) succeeded in converting ammonium cyanate (an inorganic compound) into urea. In 1845 Adolf Kolbe (1818-1884) synthesized acetic acid, squashing the Vitalism theory for ever. By the middle of the nineteenth century organic compounds were being synthesized in profusion; a new definition of organic compounds was clearly needed, and most organic chemists were working by trial and error. Nevertheless there was a teenage assistant of August von Hofmann (1818-1892), called William Perkin (1838-1907), who was able to retire at the age of only 35 because of a brilliant chance discovery. In 1856 he treated aniline with potassium chromate, added alcohol, and obtained a beautiful purple colour, which he suspected might be a dye (later called aniline purple or mauve). He left school and founded what became the synthetic dyestuffs industry.

Then in 1861 the German chemist Friedrich Kekulé (1829-1886) defined organic chemistry as the chemistry of carbon compounds and this definition has remained, although there are a few carbon compounds (such as carbonates) which are considered to be part of inorganic chemistry. Kekulé suggested that carbon had a valency of four, and proceeded to work out the structures of simple organic compounds on this basis. These representations of the structural formulae showed how organic molecules were generally larger and more complex than inorganic molecules. There was still the problem of the structure of the simple hydrocarbon benzene, C_6H_6, until 1865 when Kekulé suggested that rings of carbon atoms might be just as possible as straight chains. The idea that molecules might be three-dimensional came in 1874 when Van't Hoff suggested that the four bonds of the carbon atom were arranged tetrahedrally. If these four bonds are connected to four different types of groups, the carbon atom is said to be asymmetric and the compound shows optical activity - its crystals or solutions rotate the plane of polarized light.

Viktor Meyer (1848-1897) proposed that certain types of optical isomerism could be explained by bonds of nitrogen atoms. Alfred Werner (1866-1919) went on to demonstrate that this principle also applied to metals such as cobalt, chromium and rhodium, and succeeded in working out the necessary theory of molecular structure, known as co-ordination theory. This new approach allowed there to be structural relationships within certain fairly complex inorganic molecules, which were not restricted to bonds involving ordinary valencies. It was to be another 50 years before enough was known about valency for both Kekulé's theory and Werner's to be fully understood, but by 1900 the idea was universally accepted that molecular structure could be represented satisfactorily in three dimensions.

Kekulé's work gave the organic chemist scope to alter a structural formula stage by stage, to convert one molecule into another, and modern synthetic organic chemistry began. Richard Willstätter (1872-1942) was able to work out the structure of chlorophyll and Heinrich Wieland (1877-1957) determined the structures of steroids. Paul Karrer (1889-1971) elucidated the structures of the carotenoids and other vitamins and Robert Robinson (1886-1975) tackled the alkaloids - he worked out the structures of morphine and strychnine. The alkaloids have found medical use as drugs, as have many other organic compounds. The treatment of disease by the use of specific chemicals is known as chemotherapy and was founded by the bacteriologist Paul Ehrlich (1854-1915). The need for drugs to combat disease and infection during World War II spurred on research, and by 1945 the antibiotic penicillin, first isolated by Howard Florey (1898-   ) and Ernst Chain (1906-   ), was being produced in quantity. Other antibiotics such as streptomycin and the tetracyclines soon followed.

Some organic molecules contain thousands of atoms; some, such as rubber, are polymers and others, such as haemoglobin, are proteins. Synthetic polymers have been made which closely resemble natural rubber; the leader in this field was Wallace Carothers (1896-1937), who also invented Nylon. Karl Ziegler (1898-1973) and Giulio Natta (1903-   ) worked out how to prevent branching during polymerization, so that plastics, films and fibres can now be made more or less to order. Work on the make-up of proteins had to wait for the development of chemical techniques such as chromatography (by Mikhail Tswett (1872-1919) and by Archer Martin (1910-   ) and Richard Synge (1914-   )) and electrophoresis (Arne Tiselius (1902-1971)). In the forefront of molecular biological research are Frederick Sanger (1918-   ), John Kendrew

(1917–   ) and Max Perutz (1914–   ). One technique that has been essential for their work is X-ray diffraction, and for the background to this development we have to return to the area of research between chemistry and physics at the beginning of the present century.

Modern atomic theory

Ever since Faraday had proposed his laws of electrolysis, it had seemed likely that electricity might be carried by particles. The physicist Ernest Rutherford (1871–1937) decided that the unit of positive charge was a particle quite different from the electron, which was the unit of negative charge, and in 1920 he suggested that this fundamental positive particle be called the proton. In 1895 Wilhelm Röntgen (1845–1923) discovered X-rays, but other radiation components – alpha and beta rays – were found to be made up of protons and electrons. In about 1902 it was proved, contrary to all previous ideas, that radioactive elements changed into other elements, and by 1912 the complicated series of changes of these elements had been worked out. In the course of this research, Frederick Soddy (1877–1956) realized that there could be several atoms differing in mass but having the same properties. They were called isotopes and we now know that they differ in the number of neutrons which they possess, although the neutron was not to be discovered until 1932, by the physicist James Chadwick (1891–1974).

Rutherford evolved the theory of the nuclear atom, which suggested that sub-atomic particles made up the atom, which had until that time been considered to be indivisible. The question now was, how did the nuclear atom of one element differ from that of another? In 1909 Max von Laue (1879–1960) began a series of brilliant experiments. He established that crystals consist of atoms arranged in a geometric structure of regularly repeating layers, and that these layers scatter X-rays in a set pattern. In so doing, he had set the scene for X-ray crystallography to be used to help to work out the structures of large molecules for which chemists had not been able to determine formulae.

In 1913 the young scientist Henry Moseley (1887–1915) found that there were characteristic X-rays for each element and that there was an inverse relationship between the wavelength of the X-ray and the atomic weight of the element. This relationship depended on the size of the positive charge on the nucleus of the atom, and the size of this nuclear charge is called the atomic number. Mendeleyev had arranged his Periodic Table, by considering the valencies of the elements, in sequence of their atomic weights, but the proper periodic classification is by atomic numbers. It was now possible to predict exactly how many elements were still to be discovered. Since the proton is the only positively charged particle in the nucleus, the atomic number is equal to the number of protons; the neutrons contribute to the mass but not to the charge. For example, a sodium atom, with an atomic number of 11 and an atomic weight (relative atomic mass) of 23, has 11 protons and 12 neutrons in its nucleus.

Isotopes and biochemistry

The new electronic atom was also of great interest to organic chemists. It enabled theoreticians such as Christopher Ingold (1893–1970) to try to interpret organic reactions in terms of the movements of electrons from one point to another within a molecule. Physical chemical methods were being used in organic chemistry, founding physical organic chemistry as a separate discipline. Linus Pauling (1911–   ), a chemist who was to suggest in the 1950s that proteins and nucleic acids possessed a helical shape, worked on the wave properties of electrons, and established the theory of resonance. This idea was very useful in establishing that the structure of the benzene molecule possessed "smeared out" electrons and was a resonance hybrid of the two alternating double bond/single bond structures. The concept of atomic number was clarified by Francis Aston (1877–1945) with the mass spectrograph. This instrument used electric and magnetic fields to deflect ions of identical charge by an extent that depended on their mass – the greater the mass of the ion, the less it was deflected. He found for instance that there were two kinds of neon atoms, one of mass 20 and one of mass 22. The neon-20 was ten times as common as the neon-22, and so it seemed reasonable that the atomic weight of the element was 20.2 – a weighted average of the individual atoms and not necessarily a whole number. In some cases, the weighted average (atomic weight) of a particular atom may be larger than that for an atom of higher atomic number. This explains the relative positions of iodine and tellurium in the Periodic Table, which Mendeleyev had placed correctly without knowing why.

In 1931 Harold Urey (1893–1981) discovered that hydrogen was made up of a pair of isotopes, and he named hydrogen-2 deuterium. In 1934 it occurred to the physicist Enrico Fermi (1901–1954) to bombard uranium (element number 92, the highest atomic number known at that time) in order to see whether he could produce any elements of higher atomic numbers. This approach was pursued by Glenn Seaborg

(1912–   ) and the transuranium elements were discovered, going up from element 94 to 104 but becoming increasingly difficult to form and decomposing again more rapidly with increasing atomic number.

The area between physics and chemistry has been replaced by a common ground where atoms and molecules are studied together with the forces that influence them. The boundary between chemistry and biology has also become less well defined and is now a scene of intense activity, with the techniques of chemistry being applied successfully to biological problems. Electron diffraction, chromatography and radioactive tracers have all been used to help to discover what living matter is composed of, although it is possible that these investigations in biology are only now at the stage that atomic physics was at the beginning of this century. It was Lavoisier who said that life is a chemical function, and perhaps the most important advance of all is towards understanding the chemistry of the cell.

Alder, Kurt (*1902–1958*), was a German organic chemist who with Otto Diels (1876–1954) developed the diene synthesis, a fundamental process that has become known as the Diels–Alder reaction. It is used on organic chemistry to synthesize cyclic (ring) compounds, including many that can be made into plastics and others - which normally occur only in small quantities in plants and other natural sources - that are the starting materials for various drugs and dyes. This outstanding achievement was recognized by the award of the 1950 Nobel Prize in Chemistry jointly to Alder and Diels.

Alder was born on 10 July 1902 in the industrial town of Königshütte (Krolewska Huta) in Upper Silesia, which was then part of Germany (it is now in Poland). He was the son of a schoolteacher and began his education in his home town. When the region became part of Poland at the end of World War I, the Alder family moved to Berlin. There Kurt Alder finished his schooling and went on to study chemistry, first at the University of Berlin and later at Kiel, where he worked under Otto Diels. Alder became a chemistry reader at Kiel in 1930 and a professor in 1934, but two years later he began a four-year period in industry as Research Director of I. G. Farben at Leverkusen on the northern outskirts of Cologne. He returned to academic life in 1940 as Professor and Director of the Chemical Institute at the University of Cologne, where he remained for the rest of his life. He died in Cologne on 20 June 1958.

The first report of the diene synthesis, stemming from work in Diels' laboratory at Kiel, was made in 1928. The Diels–Alder reaction involves the adding of an organic compound that has two double bonds separated by a single bond (called a conjugated diene) to a compound with only one, activated double bond (termed a dienophile). A common example of a conjugated diene is butadiene (but-1,2:3,4-diene) and of a dienophile is maleic anhydride (*cis*-butenedioic anhydride). These two substances react readily to form the bicyclic compound tetrahydrophthalic anhydride (cyclohexene-1:2-dicarboxylic anhydride) - one of the reactions originally reported by Diels and Alder in 1928:

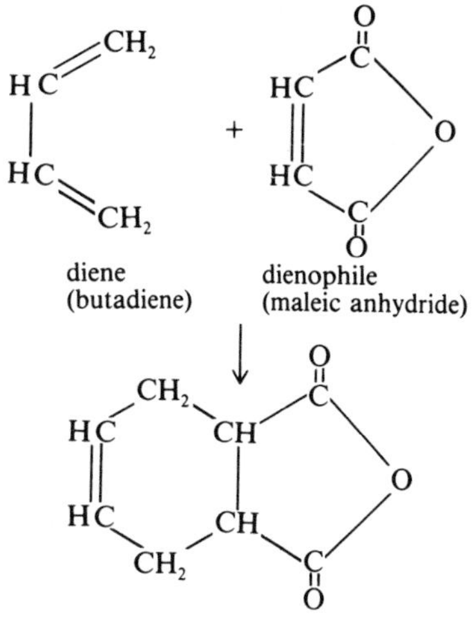

diene
(butadiene)

dienophile
(maleic anhydride)

Diels-Alder adduct
(tetrahydrophthalic anhydride)

Azo-diesters, general formula $RCO_2.N:N.CO_2R$, also act as dienophiles in the reaction, as can other unsaturated acids and their esters. With a cyclodiene, the synthesis yields a bridged cyclic compound:

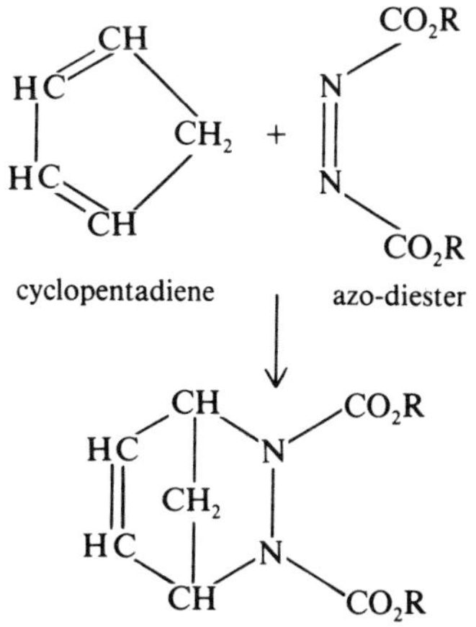

cyclopentadiene

azo-diester

adduct

One or two reactions of this type had been reported in the early 1900s, but Diels and Alder were the first to recognize its widespread and general nature. They also demonstrated the ease with which it takes place and the high yield of the product - two vitally important factors for successful organic synthesis. In association with

Diels, and later with his own students, Alder continued to study the general conditions of the diene synthesis and the overall scope of the method for synthetic purposes. In his Nobel Prize address, Alder listed more than a dozen different dienes of widely differing structure that participate in the reaction. He also showed that the reaction is equally general with respect to dienophiles, provided that their double bonds are activated by a nearby group such as carboxyl, carbonyl, cyano, nitro or ester. Many of the compounds studied were prepared for the first time in Alder's laboratory.

Alder was a particularly able stereochemist, and he showed that the diene addition takes place at double bonds with a *cis* configuration - i.e., where the two groups substituting the double bond are both on the same side of it, as opposed to the *trans* isomer, with the groups on opposite sides:

cis configuration
(maleic acid)

trans configuration
(fumaric acid)

That is why maleic acid (*cis*-butenedicarboxylic acid) reacts whereas its isomer fumaric acid (*trans*-butenedicarboxylic acid) does not. The stereospecific nature of the Diels–Alder reaction has thus become useful in structural studies for the detection of conjugated double bonds.

The bridged ring, or bicyclic, compounds formed by using cyclic dienes (such as cyclopentadiene, above) are closely related to many naturally occuring organic compounds such as camphor and pinene, which belong to the group known as terpenes. The diene synthesis stimulated and made easier the understanding of this important group of natural products by providing a means of synthesizing them. Indeed, the ease with which the reaction takes place suggests that it may be the natural biosynthetic pathway. It has been found to be relevant in connection with quinone (vitamin K) - whose synthetic analogues are used to stimulate blood clotting - and anthraquinone type dyes now used universally. Many other commercial products have been

made possible by Alder's work, including drugs, insecticides, lubricating oils, synthetic rubber and plastics. He made a great contribution to synthetic organic chemistry at a time when it was effecting a great transition in industry and science.

Andrews, Thomas (*1813–1885*), was an Irish physical chemist, best known for postulating the idea of critical temperature and pressure from his experimental work on the liquefaction of gases, which demonstrated the continuity of the liquid and gaseous states. He also studied heats of chemical combination and was the first to establish the composition of ozone, proving it to be an allotrope of oxygen.

Andrews was born in Belfast on 19 December 1813, the son of a linen merchant. He attended five universities (acting on the advice of a physician friend of his father), beginning at the age of 15 at the University of Glasgow; after only a year there he published two scientific papers. Then in 1830 he went to Paris where, like his contemporary Louis Pasteur (1822–1895), he studied under the French organic chemist Jean Baptiste Dumas. He also became acquainted with several famous scientists of that time, including Joseph Gay-Lussac and Henri Becquerel. He returned to Ireland, but to Trinity College Dublin, and went from there via Belfast to Edinburgh. In 1835 he graduated from Edinburgh as a qualified doctor and surgeon, with a thesis on the circulation and properties of blood.

Even while following his medical studies, Andrews continued to experiment in chemistry, although he declined professorships in that subject at both the Richmond School of Medicine and at the Park Street School of Medicine, Dublin, preferring to devote his time to the private medical practice he had established in Belfast. He did, however, lecture on chemistry for a few hours each week at the Royal Belfast Academical Institution. It was during this time that he began work on a study of the heats of chemical combination, and in 1844 his paper on the thermal changes that accompany the neutralization of acids by bases won him the Medal of the Royal Society (of which he became a Fellow five years later). By this time he was one of the leading scientific figures in the British Isles. In 1845 he was appointed Vice-President designate of the projected Queen's College, Belfast, in order that he might contribute to its foundation and philosophy, and in 1849 he became its Professor of Chemistry. He held both posts until 1879, when ill-health forced his retirement. He died in Belfast six years later, on 26 November 1885.

Andrews' research was concentrated into three

main channels: the heat of chemical combination, ozone, and changes in physical state. He was only one of many mid-nineteenth century investigators of thermochemistry: his Russian contemporary Germain Hess was carrying out similar experiments at St Petersburg. Andrews' chief contribution was the direct determination of heats of neutralization and of formation of halides (chlorides, bromides and iodides), but the law of constant heat summation was finally worked out by and is now named after Hess.

Before Andrews began to study ozone, it was postulated that the gas was either a "compound" of oxygen or that it was an oxide of hydrogen that contained a larger proportion of oxygen than does water. Andrews proved conclusively that ozone is an allotrope of oxygen, that from whatever source it is "one and the same body, having identical properties and the same constitution, and is not a compound body but oxygen in an altered or allotropic condition". Ozone is triatomic, with molecules represented by the formula O_3.

Many other scientists had tried to explain the relationship between gases and liquids, but none had really come to grips with the fundamentals. It is for his meticulous experimental work in this area that Andrews is best remembered. He constructed elaborate equipment in which he initially investigated the liquefaction of carbon dioxide, exploring the state of the substance (gas or liquid) over a wide range of temperatures and pressures. By 1869 he had concluded that if carbon dioxide is maintained at any temperature above 30.9°C, it cannot be condensed into a liquid by any pressure no matter how great. This discovery of a

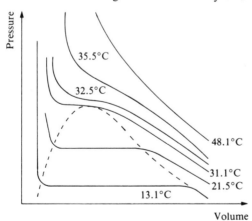

Pressure-volume isotherms for carbon dioxide. The critical temperature is 30·9°C and the critical pressure 72·8 atmospheres. At temperatures and pressure corresponding to the region under the dotted curve, carbon dioxide is a liquid (the isotherm is a horizontal line).

critical temperature (or critical point) soon enabled other workers – such as Raoul Pictet (1846–1929) in Geneva and Louis Cailletet (1832–1913) in France, both of whom independently in 1877 liquefied oxygen – to liquefy gases that had previously been thought to be "non-condensible", the so-called permanent gases. Hydrogen, nitrogen and air were also liquefied by applying pressure to the gases once they had been cooled to below their critical temperatures. Andrews also worked out sets of pressure-volume isotherms at temperatures above and below the critical temperature, and brought a sense of order to what had previously been a chaotic branch of physical chemistry.

Arrhenius, Svante August (*1859–1927*), was a Swedish physical chemist who first explained that in an electrolyte (a solution of a chemical dissolved in water) the dissolved substance is dissociated into electrically charged ions. The electrolyte conducts electricity because the ions migrate through the solution. Although later modified, Arrhenius' theory of conductivity in solutions has stood the test of time. It was a major contribution to physical chemistry, ultimately acknowledged by the award to Arrhenius of the 1903 Nobel Prize in Chemistry.

Arrhenius was born in Uppsala on 19 February 1859, the son of a surveyor and estate manager who was also a supervisor at the local university. He was a brilliant student, entering Uppsala University at the age of 17 to study chemistry, physics and mathematics. After graduating in 1878, he stayed to write his doctorial thesis, but became dissatisfied with the teaching at Uppsala and went to Stockholm to study solutions and electrolytes under Erik Edlund (1819–1888).

In 1884 he submitted his thesis, which contained the basis of the dissociation theory of electrolytes (although he did not at that time use the term dissociation), together with many other novel theories which aroused only suspicion and doubt in his superiors. The largely theoretical document was not welcomed by the academics, who were devoted experimentalists; Arrhenius later boasted that he had never performed an exact experiment in his life and preferred to take a general view of relationships from the results of many approximate experiments. The thesis (written in French) was awarded only a fourth class, the lowest possible pass, but Arrhenius sent copies of it to several eminent chemists, including Friedrich Wilhelm Ostwald (at Riga), Rudolf Clausius (Bonn), Lothar Meyer (Tübingen) and Jacobus Van't Hoff (Amsterdam). Ostwald's offer to Arrhenius of an academic appointment moderated the scepticism of the Uppsala authorities, who finally offered him a position and, later, a travelling fellowship. This enabled him to spend some time with other scientists working in the same field, such as Friedrich Kohlrausch and Hermann Nernst at Würzburg, Ludwig Boltzmann at Graz and Jacobus van't Hoff, whose solution theories paralleled that of Arrhenius.

In 1891 Arrhenius was offered a professorship at Giessen in Germany as successor to Justus von Liebig, but he declined in preference for an appointment at the Royal Institute of Technology in Stockholm. Four years later he became professor of physics at a time when his work was attracting the attention of scientists throughout Europe, if not in his native Sweden - his election to the Swedish Academy of Sciences had to wait another six years until 1901 (the same year in which Van't Hoff was awarded the first Nobel Prize in Chemistry). He again declined a German professorship, in Berlin, in 1905 and took instead the specially created post of Director of the Nobel Institute of Physical Chemistry (Stockholm), where he remained until shortly before his death on 2 October 1927.

The Arrhenius theory of electrolytes (1887) is concerned with the formation, number and speed of ions in solution. The key to the theory is the behaviour of the dissolved substance (solute) and the liquid (solvent), both of which are capable of dissociating into ions. It postulates that there is an equilibrium between undissociated solute molecules and its ions, whose movement or migration can conduct an electric current through the solution. Its chief points may be summarized as follows:

(a) An electrolytic solution contains free ions (i.e., dissociation takes place even if no current is passed through the solution).

(b) Conduction of an electric current through such a solution depends on the number and speed of migration of the ions present.

(c) In a weak electrolyte, the degree of ionization (dissociation) increases with increasing dilution.

(d) In a weak electrolyte at infinite dilution, ionization is complete.

(e) In a strong electrolyte, ionization is always incomplete because the ions impede each other's migration; this interference is less in dilute solutions of strong electrolytes.

Apart from (e), regarding strong electrolytes (a difficulty not resolved until the work of Peter Debye and Erich Hückel in the 1920s), Arrhenius' theory is still largely accepted.

In another notable achievement, Arrhenius adapted Van't Hoff's work on the colligative properties of non-electrolyte solutions. He found that solutions of salts, acids and bases - electrolytes - possess greater osmotic pressures, higher vapour pressures and lower freezing points than Van't Hoff's calculated values but explained the discrepancies in terms of ionic dissociation by taking into account the number of solute ions (as opposed to molecules) present. In 1889 Arrhenius suggested that a molecule will take part in a chemical reaction on collision only if it has a higher than average energy - that is, if it is activated. As a result, the rate of a chemical reaction is proportional to the number of activated molecules (not to the total number of molecules, or concentration) and can be related to the activation energy.

After 1905 Arrhenius widened his research activities. For example, he applied the laws of theoretical chemistry to physiological problems (particularly immunology); once again initial criticism was replaced by universal acceptance. With N. Ekholm he published papers on cosmic physics concerning the Northern Lights, the transport of living matter ("spores") through space from one planet to another, and the climatic changes of the Earth over geological time - pointing out the "greenhouse effect" brought about by carbon dioxide in the atmosphere. Arrhenius became more and more respected by the world of science and was much sought after for meetings, lectures and discussions throughout the world. In his latter years he had to rise at 4 am in order to maintain his scientific activities, and this consistent hard work probably contributed to his death at the age of 68.

Aston, Francis William (*1877-1945*), was a British chemist and physicist who developed the mass spectrograph, which he used to study atomic masses and to establish the existence of isotopes. For his unique contribution to analytic chemistry and the study of atomic theory he was awarded the 1922 Nobel Prize in Chemistry.

Aston was born on 1 September 1877 at Harbourne, Birmingham, the son of a merchant. He went to school at Malvern College, where he excelled at mathematics and science, and then to Mason College (which later became the University of Birmingham) to study chemistry. There from 1898 to 1900 he studied optical rotation with P. F. Frankland (1858-1946). Aston then left academic life for three years to work with a firm of brewers, although during his spare time he continued to experiment with discharge tubes. He returned to Mason College in 1903 to study gaseous discharges, before moving in 1909 to the Cavendish Laboratory, Cambridge, where J.J. Thomson was also investigating positive rays from discharge tubes. Thomson and Aston examined the effects of electric and magnetic fields on positive rays, showing that the rays were deflected

– one of the basic principles of the mass spectrograph.

Aston's researches were interrupted by World War I, during which he worked at the Royal Aircraft Establishment, Farnborough, on the treatment of aeroplane fabrics using dopes (lacquers). He escaped injury in 1914 after crashing in an experimental aircraft. After the war he returned to Cambridge and improved his earlier equipment, and the mass spectrograph was born. He went on to refine the instrument and apply it to a study of atomic masses and isotopes. Aston continued to live and work in Cambridge, where he died on 20 November 1945.

Between 1910 and 1913, Thomson and Aston showed that the amount of deflection of positive rays in electric and magnetic fields depends on their mass. The deflected rays were made to reveal their positions by aiming them at a photographic plate. Thomson was seeking evidence for an earlier theory of William Crookes that the non-integral atomic mass of neon (20.2) was caused by the presence of two very similar but different atoms. Each was expected to have a whole-number atomic mass, but their mixture would result in an "average" non-integral value. The Cambridge scientists found that the two paths of deflected positive rays from a neon discharge tube were consistent with atomic masses of 20 and 22. Aston attempted to fractionate neon and in 1913 made a partial separation by repeatedly diffusing the gas through porous pipeclay.

Aston's first improvement to the apparatus, made in 1919, caused the positive-ray deflections by both electric and magnetic fields to be in the same plane. The image produced on the photographic plate became known as a mass spectrum, and the instrument itself as a mass spectrograph.

Its principle is relatively simple. A beam of positive ions is produced by an electric discharge tube (in which a high voltage is passed between electrodes in a glass tube containing rarefied gas), which has holes in its cathode to let the accelerated ions pass through. The beam passes between a pair of electrically charged plates, whose electric field deflects the moving ions according to their charge-to-mass ratio, e/m (where e is the charge on the ion – usually 1 or 2 – and m is its mass). Lighter ions are deflected most, whereas those of largest mass are deflected least. The now separate ion streams then pass through a magnetic field arranged at right-angles to the electric field, which deflects them still further in the same plane. The streams strike a photographic plate, where they expose a series of lines that constitute the mass spectrum. The position of a line depends on the ion's mass, and its intensity depends on the relative abundance of the ion in the original positive-ion beam.

The work with neon established that two spectral lines are produced on the plate, one about nine times darker (on a positive print) than the other. Calculation showed that these correspond to two types of ions of atomic masses 20 and 22. There are nine times as many of the former as of the latter, giving a weighted average atomic mass of about 20.2 (the value originally reported in 1898 by William Ramsay and Morris Travers, the discoverers of neon). Aston stated that there must be two kinds of neon atoms which differ in mass but not in chemical properties, i.e. that naturally occurring neon gas consists of two isotopes.

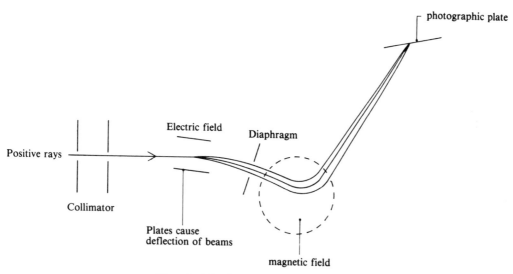

The principle of Aston's mass spectrograph.

Over the next few years Aston examined the isotopic composition of more than 50 elements. Most were found to have isotopes - tin has ten - with atomic masses that are whole numbers (integers). In 1920, using the first mass spectrograph, he determined the mass of a hydrogen atom and found it to be 1 per cent greater than a whole number (1.01). (Twelve years later in the United States Harold Urey discovered deuterium, an isotope of hydrogen with mass 2.) With an improved spectrograph, accurate to 1 part in 10,000, Aston confirmed that some other isotopes also show small deviations from the whole-number rule. The slight discrepancy is the packing fraction. (For example, the particles that make up four atoms of hydrogen are the same as those in one atom of helium, but in helium they are "packed" and have 1 per cent less mass. This mass defect is now known to be the source of the thermonuclear energy released during the fusion of hydrogen to form helium.)

Aston's interests also included astronomy, particularly observations of the Sun and its eclipses. His knowledge of photography made him a valuable member of the expeditions that studied eclipses in Sumatra (1925), Canada (1932) and Japan (1936). But Aston will be remembered for his development of the mass spectrograph, which became an essential tool in the study of nuclear physics and later found application in the determination of the structures of organic compounds.

Avogadro, Amedeo, Conte de Quaregna (*1776-1856*), was an Italian scientist who shares with his contemporary Claud Berthollet (1748-1822) the honour of being one of the founders of physical chemistry. Although he was a professor of physics, he acknowledged no boundary between physics and chemistry and based most of his findings on a mathematical approach. Principally remembered for the hypothesis subsequently known as Avogadro's Law (which states that, at a given temperature, equal volumes of all gases contain the same number of molecules), he gained no recognition for his achievement during his lifetime. He lived in what was a scientific backwater, with the result that his writings received scant examination or regard from the leading authorities of his day.

Avogadro was born in Turin on 9 June 1776. He began his career in 1796 by obtaining a doctorate in law and for the next three years practised as a lawyer. In 1800 he began to take private lessons in mathematics and physics, made impressive progress and decided to make the natural sciences his vocation. He was appointed as a demonstrator at the Academy of Turin in 1806 and

Professor of Natural Philosophy at the College of Vercelli in 1809, and when in 1820 the first professorship in mathematical physics in Italy was established at Turin, Avogadro was chosen for the post. Because of the political turmoil at that time the position was subsequently abolished, but calmer times permitted its re-establishment in 1832 and two years later Avogadro again held the appointment. He remained at Turin until his retirement in 1850. When he died there on 9 July 1856 his European contemporaries still regarded him as an incorrigibly self-deluding provincial professor of physics.

In 1809 Joseph Gay-Lussac had discovered that all gases, when subjected to an equal rise in temperature, expand by the same amount. Avogadro therefore deduced (and announced in 1811) that at a given temperature all gases must contain the same number of particles per unit volume. He also made it clear that the gas particles need not be individual atoms but might consist of molecules, the term he introduced to describe combinations of atoms. No previous scientists had made this fundamental distinction between the atoms of a substance and its molecules.

Using his hypothesis Avogadro provided the theoretical explanation of Gay-Lussac's law of combining volumes. It had already been observed that the electrolysis of water (to form hydrogen and oxygen) produces twice as much hydrogen (by volume) as oxygen. He reasoned that each molecule of water must contain hydrogen and oxygen atoms in the proportion of 2 to 1. Also, because the oxygen gas collected weighs eight times as much as the hydrogen, oxygen atoms must be 16 times as heavy as hydrogen atoms. It also follows from Avogadro's hypothesis that a molar volume of any substance (i.e., the volume whose mass is one gram molecular weight) contains the same number of molecules. This quantity, now known as Avogadro's number or constant, is equal to 6.02252×10^{23}.

Leading chemists of the day paid little attention to Avogadro's hypothesis, with the result that the confusion between atoms and molecules and between atomic weights and molecular weights continued for nearly 50 years. In 1858, only two years after Avogadro's death, his fellow Italian Stanislao Cannizzaro showed how the application of Avogadro's hypothesis could solve many of the major problems in chemistry. At the Karlsruhe Chemical Congress of 1860 Avogadro's 1811 paper was read again to a much wider and more receptive audience of distinguished scientists. One of the most impressed was the young German chemist Julius Lothar Meyer. He found this final establishment of order in place of conflicting theories one of the great stimuli that eventually led him in 1870 to produce his most detailed exposition of the periodic law. A year later his namesake Viktor Meyer used Avogadro's law as his principal yardstick in theoretically explaining the nature of vapour density.

It is interesting to analyse why such a fundamental and potentially useful work as Avogadro's lay fallow for nearly half a century. Various factors contributed to the delay. To begin with, Avogadro did not support his hypothesis with an impressive display of experimental results. He never acquired, nor did he deserve, a reputation for accurate experimental work; his contemporaries did not therefore regard him as a brilliant theoretician, merely as a careless experimenter. Also Avogadro extended his hypothesis to solid elements – and lacking experimental evidence he relied on analogy. So that whereas he was correct in considering molecules of oxygen and hydrogen to be diatomic, he had little justification for making a similar assumption about carbon and sulphur. His speculative treatment of metals in the vapour state (in his second paper of 1814) did little to advance his cause, revealing an excess of theorizing at the cost of attention to detail.

Furthermore, Avogadro's idea of a diatomic molecule was at odds with the dominant dualistic outlook of Jöns Berzelius. According to the principles of electrochemistry, two atoms of the same element would have similar electric charges and therefore repel rather than attract each other (to form a molecule). During the 50 years after Avogadro's original hypothesis most activity was being devoted to organic chemistry, whose analysis and classification was based chiefly on weights, not volumes. And even when Avogadro's work was translated and published, it tended to appear in obscure journals, perhaps as a result of his modesty and his geographical isolation from the mainstream of the chemistry of his time.

B

Baekeland, Leo Hendrik (*1863–1944*), was a Belgian-born American industrial chemist famous for the invention of Bakelite, the first commercially successful thermosetting plastic resin.

Baekeland was born in Ghent on 14 November 1863. He was a brilliant pupil at school and at the age of only 16 won a scholarship to the University of Ghent, from which he graduated in 1882. Two years later, still aged only 21, he was awarded his

doctorate after studying electrochemistry at Charlottenburg Polytechnic. In 1887 he became Professor of Physics and Chemistry at the University of Bruges, and in 1888 returned to Ghent as Assistant Professor of Chemistry. The next year he got married and then went on a tour of the United States for his honeymoon, with financial help from a travelling scholarship. He decided to settle in the United States and took a job as a photographic chemist, setting up as a consultant in his own laboratory in New York City in 1891.

He returned briefly to Europe in 1900 to study at the Technische Hochschule at Charlottenburg. His development of Bakelite came after he had gone back to the United States and was announced in 1909, the year in which he founded the General Bakelite Corporation, later to become part of the Union Carbide and Carbon Company. He continued his chemical researches and in 1924 was elected President of the American Chemical Society. He died in Beacon, New York, on the 23 February 1944.

Baekeland's first chemical invention was a type of photographic printing paper, which he called Velox, which could be developed under artificial light. He began manufacturing it in 1893 at Yonkers, New York, and in 1899 George Eastman's Kodak Corporation bought the invention and the manufacturing company (the Nepera Chemical Co) from Baekeland for one million dollars.

Johann Baeyer had discovered the resin formed by the condensation reaction between formaldehyde (methanal) and phenol in 1871, and in the early 1900s Baekeland began to investigate it as a possible substitute for shellac. He could find no solvent for the resin, but discovered that it can be produced in a hard, machinable form that can also be moulded by casting under heat and pressure. On initial heating the material melts (becomes plastic) and then sets extremely hard and will not melt on further heating. Bakelite is a good insulator, and soon found use in the manufacture of electrical fittings such as plugs and switches. The General Bakelite Corporation merged with two other companies in 1922 and seven years later was incorporated into the Union Carbide group.

Baeyer, Johann Friedrich Wilhelm Adolf von (*1835–1917*), was a German organic chemist famous for developing methods of synthesis, the best known of which is his synthesis of the dye indigo. His major contribution to the science was acknowledged by the award of the 1905 Nobel Prize in Chemistry.

Baeyer was born in Berlin on 31 October 1835, the son of the Prussian general Johann Jacob von

Baeyer, who later became head of the Berlin Geodetic Institute. He began his university career at Heidelberg in 1853 where he studied chemistry under Robert Bunsen and Friedrich Kekulé. He gained his PhD at Berlin in 1858 after working in the laboratory of August Hofmann, and two years later took an appointment as a teacher at a technical school in Berlin. He became Professor of Chemistry at the University of Strasbourg in 1872 and three years later was appointed to succeed Justus von Liebig as Professor of Chemistry at Munich, where he stayed for the rest of his career. He died at Starnberg, near Munich, on 20 August 1917.

Baeyer began his researches in the early 1860s with studies of uric acid, which led in 1863 to the discovery of barbituric acid, later to become the parent substance of a major class of hypnotic drugs. In 1865 he turned his attention to dyes. His student Karl Graebe (1841–1927) synthesized alizarin in 1868 (at the same time as William Perkin), and in 1871 Baeyer discovered phenolphthalein and fluorescein. He also found the resinous condensation product of phenol and formaldehyde (methanal), which Leo Baekeland later developed into the thermosetting plastic Bakelite.

In 1883 Baeyer determined the structure of indigo by reducing it to indole using powdered zinc. He had already (1880) devised a method for its synthesis, which was more lengthy than the commercial method later used when synthetic indigo began to be manufactured in 1890. In 1888 he carried out the first synthesis of a terpene.

His work with ring compounds and the highly unstable polyacetylenes led him to consider the effects of carbon-carbon bond angles on the stability of organic compounds. He concluded that the more a bond is deformed away from the ideal tetrahedral angle, the more unstable it is – known as Baeyer's strain theory. It explains why rings with five or six atoms are much more common, and stable, than those with fewer or more atoms in the ring. He also noticed that the aromatic character of the six-carbon benzene and its analogues is lost on reduction and saturation of the carbon atoms.

Bartlett, Neil (*1932–*), is a British-born chemist who achieved fame by preparing the first compound of one of the rare gases, previously thought to be totally inert and incapable of reacting with anything.

Bartlett was born in Newcastle-upon-Tyne on 15 September 1932. He attended the University of Durham, gaining his PhD in 1957. A year later he took an appointment at the University of British Columbia, Canada, and in 1966 became Professor of Chemistry at Princeton in the United States. In 1969 he moved to a similar position at the University of California, Berkeley.

In Canada in the early 1960s Bartlett was working with the fluorides of the platinum metals. He prepared platinum hexafluoride, PtF_6, and found that it is extremely reactive. It reacts with oxygen, for example, to form the ionic compound $O_2^+ PtF_6^-$. In 1962 he reacted platinum hexafluoride with xenon, the heaviest of the stable rare gases, and obtained xenon platinofluoride (xenon fluoroplatinate, $XePtF_6$), the first chemical compound of a rare gas. Other compounds of xenon followed, including xenon fluoride (XeF_4) and xenon oxyfluoride ($XeOF_4$). Other chemists soon made compounds of krypton and radon. It is for this reason that this and other modern books use the term "rare gases" to describe the helium group of elements, not the former terms "inert gases" or "noble gases", for inert or noble they no longer are, due to the pioneer work of Bartlett.

Barton, Derek Harold Richard (*1918–*), is a British organic chemist whose chief work concerns the stereochemistry of natural compounds. He showed that their biological activity often depends on the shapes of their molecules and the positions and orientations of key functional groups. For this achievement he shared the 1969 Nobel Prize in Chemistry with the Norwegian Odd Hassel (1897–).

Barton was born in Gravesend on 8 September 1918. He was educated at Tonbridge School and graduated from Imperial College, London, in 1940, gaining a PhD in organic chemistry two years later. He has held various professorships: at Birkbeck College, London (1953–1955), Glasgow (1955–1970) and Imperial College, London (1970–1978). In 1978 he became Emeritus Professor of Organic Chemistry at the University of London, the same year that he was appointed Director of the Institute for the Chemistry of Natural Substances at Gif-sur-Yvette in France. He was knighted in 1972.

While lecturing in the United States at Harvard between 1949 and 1950, Barton studied the different rates of reaction of certain steroids and their triterpenoid isomers (substances with the same composition but differing in the way their atoms are joined and arranged in space). He deduced that the difference in the spatial orientation of their functional groups accounts for their behaviour, and so developed a new field in organic chemistry which became known as conformational analysis. Barton realized that in a complex system where the conformation is fixed, the reactivity of a given group depends on whether it is attached to the main molecule in an axial or an equatorial position. He discovered important correlations between the chemical reactivity and conformation of various groups in steroids and terpenes (which are structurally very similar).

Barton went on to examine many natural products, including phenols. For example, in 1956 he challenged the generally accepted structure of the substance known as Plummerer's ketone,

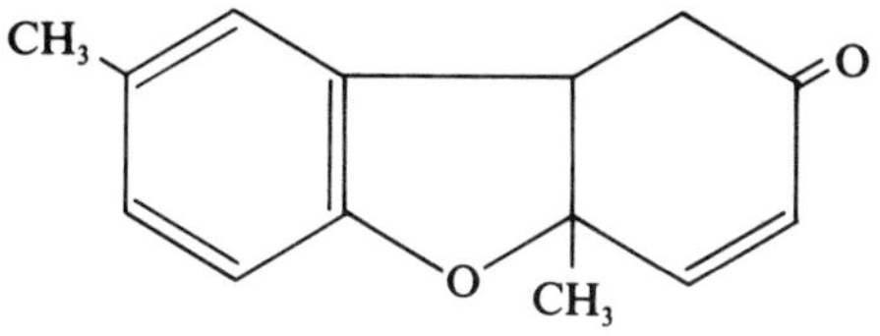

original proposal

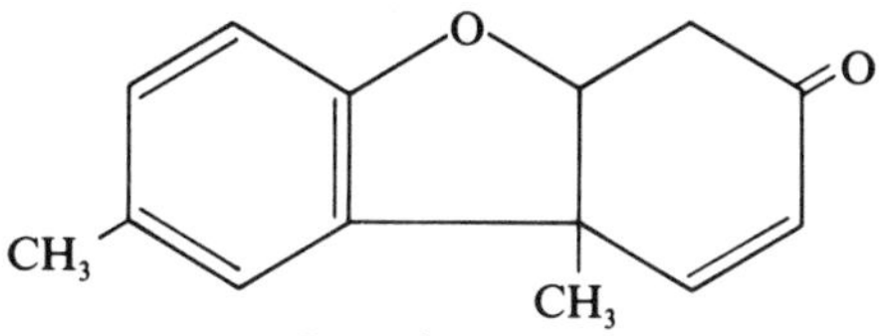

Barton's structure

showing how it could be formed by the oxidative coupling of two phenolic residues:

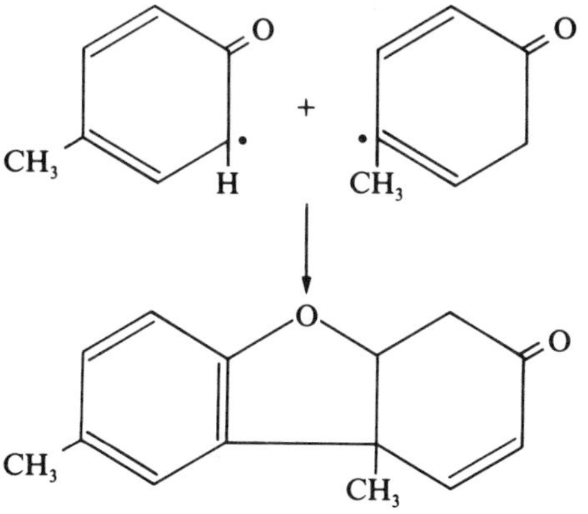

He realized the biosynthetic importance of this reaction, concluding that the structures of many phenols and alkaloids could be explained and predicted. He devised new ways of preparing oxy-radicals and studied various natural products that contain the dienone group, predicting that if a hydrogen atom of the same molecule is spatially orientated near to a generated oxy-radical, intermolecular elimination of the hydrogen atom is preferred.

Barton also studied photochemical routes and unravelled the complex transformations that take place during photolysis. In 1959 (at Cambridge, Massachusetts) he devised a simple synthesis of the naturally occurring hormone aldosterone. He also worked on the antibiotics tetracycline and penicillin. He has thus contributed greatly to the study of natural products and their formation, and has enabled a rational interpretation to be made of much stereochemical information.

Bergius, Friedrich Karl Rudolf (*1884–1949*), was a German industrial chemist famous for developing a process for the catalytic hydrogenation of coal to convert it into useful hydrocarbons such as petrol and lubricating oil. For this achievement he shared the 1931 Nobel Prize in Chemistry with Carl Bosch (1874–1940).

Bergius was born in Goldschmieden, near Breslau, Silesia (now in Poland), on 11 October 1884, the son of the owner of a chemical factory. He studied chemistry at the universities of Breslau and Leipzig, gaining his doctorate in 1907. He did postdoctorial research with Herman Walther Nernst at Berlin and then at Karlsruhe Technische Hochschule with Fritz Haber, who introduced him to high-pressure reactions. From 1909 he was Professor of Chemistry at the Technische Hochschule in Hannover. He then founded a private research laboratory in Hannover and in 1914 went to work for Goldschmidt AG in Essen, where he remained until the end of World War II in 1945. He lived for a while in Austria, then went to Spain, before finally settling in Argentina in 1948, where he held an appointment as a technical adviser to the government. He died in Buenos Aires on 30 March 1949.

In 1912 Bergius worked out a pilot scheme for using high pressure, high temperature and a catalyst to hydrogenate coal dust or heavy oil to produce paraffins (alkanes) such as petrol and kerosene. The commercial process went into production in the mid-1920s, and became important to Germany during World War II as an alternative source of supply of petrol and aviation fuel. The process yielded nearly 1 tonne of petrol from 4.5 tonnes of coal. He also discovered a method of producing sugar and alcohol from simple substances made by breaking down the complex molecules in wood; the rights to the process were purchased by the German government in 1936. He continued this work in Argentina, and found a way of making fermentable sugars and thus cattle food from wood.

Berthelot, Pierre Eugène Marcelin (*1827–1907*), was a French chemist best known for his work on organic synthesis and in thermochemistry.

Berthelot was born in Paris on 27 October 1827, the son of a doctor. At first he studied medicine at the Collège de France, graduating in 1851; he then took up the study of chemistry. He worked at the Collège as assistant to his former tutor, Antoine Balard, under Jean Baptiste Dumas and Henri Regnault, gaining his doctorate in 1854 for a thesis on the synthesis of natural fats, which extended the work of Michel Chevreul. From 1859 to 1865 he was Professor of Organic Chemistry at the École Supérieur de Pharmacie and in 1865 he returned to the Collège de France to take up a similar appointment, which he retained until his death. In 1870/1871, during the siege of Paris in the Franco-Prussian War, he was consulted about the defence of the capital and became President of the Scientific Defence Committee, and supervised the manufacture of guns and explosives. Thereafter he took an increasing part in politics. He became Inspector of Higher Education in 1876, President of the Committee on Explosives in 1878, a Senator in 1881, and Minister for Public Instruction in 1886; he was Foreign Minister from 1895 to 1896. In 1889 he succeeded Louis Pasteur as Secretary of the French Academy of Sciences. He died in Paris on 18 March 1907, on the same day as his wife.

All of Berthelot's early research concerned organic synthesis. He first studied alcohols, showing in 1854 that glycerol is a triatomic alcohol; he combined it with fatty (aliphatic) acids to make fats, including fats that do not occur naturally. This work provided increasing justification for the view that organic chemistry deals with all the compounds of carbon (including Berthelot's synthetic fats) and not just compounds formed and found in nature. He continued his research by investigating sugars, which he identified as being both alcohols and aldehydes. Using crude but effective methods he also synthesized many simple organic compounds, including methane, methyl alcohol (methanol), formic acid (methanoic acid), ethyl alcohol (ethanol), acetylene (ethyne) and benzene; he also made naphthalene and anthracene. His work during the 1850s was summed up in his book *Chimie organique fondée sur la synthèse* (1860).

Berthelot began his studies of thermochemistry in 1864. Parallelling the work of Germain Hess he measured the heat changes during chemical reactions, inventing the bomb calorimeter to do so and to study the speeds of explosive reactions. He introduced the term exothermic to describe a reaction that evolves heat, and endothermic for a reaction that absorbs heat. In 1878 he published *Mécanique chemique* followed by *Thermochimie* (1897), which put the science of thermochemistry on a firm footing.

In 1883 Berthelot established an experimental farm at Meudon, on the south-west of Paris. He discovered that some plants can absorb atmospheric nitrogen, investigated the action of nitrifying bacteria, and began to determine the details of the nitrogen cycle. But Berthelot was not a theorist; he was at his best carrying out practical work in the laboratory, and even led the opposition to the theory of atoms and molecules championed by Stanislao Cannizzaro in the early 1860s.

Berthollet, Claude Louis (*1748–1822*), was a French chemist with a wide range of interests, the most significant of which concerned chemical reactions and the composition of the products of such reactions. He proposed that reactivity depends on the masses of the reactants (similar to the modern law of mass action) but that the composition of the product or products can vary, depending on the proportions of the reacting substances (contrary to the law of definite proportions). He was a champion of his contemporary Antoine Lavoisier – although not of his political views – and had a desire to put science at the service of man's practical needs.

Berthollet was born of French parents on 9 December 1748 (six years to the day after Karl Scheele) in the then Italian region of Savoy. In 1768 he qualified as a physician at the University of Turin, moving to Paris four years later to study chemistry under Pierre Macquer (1718–1784) while continuing his medical studies, receiving his French qualification in 1778. While private physician to Mme de Montesson in the household of the duc d'Orléans he carried out research in the laboratory at the Palais Royale.

After the death of Macquer in 1784 Berthollet was appointed inspector of dyeworks and director of the Gobelins tapestry factory. In 1787 he collaborated with Lavoisier on the publication of *Méthode de Nomenclature Chemique*, which incorporated the principles of the "new chemistry" of Lavoisier. He taught chemistry to Napoleon and went with him to Egypt in 1798. There he observed the high concentration of sodium carbonate (soda) by Lake Natron on the edge of the desert. He reasoned that, under the prevailing physical conditions, sodium chloride in the upper layer of soil had reacted with calcium carbonate from nearby limestone hills – the beginning of his theory that chemical affinities are affected by physical conditions, in this case the heat and high concentration of calcium carbonate. He became a senator in 1804 but ten years later voted against Napoleon, and after the Reformation he became a count. Berthollet died on 6 November 1822 at Arcueil, near Paris.

Berthollet's proposal that chemical compounds do not have a constant composition brought him into conflict with Louis Proust, who in 1799 put forward his law of definite proportions (which states that "all pure samples of the same chemical compound contain the same elements combined together in the same proportions by weight"). It turned out that Berthollet's severe (but non-acrimonious) criticisms of Proust were based on imprecise distinctions between compounds, solutions and mixtures, as well as on the inaccurate analyses of impure compounds. For example, he suggested that lead and oxygen could combine in almost any proportion, but it is now known that he was making and analysing mixtures of various lead oxides. Although the controversy between Berthollet and Proust ended mainly in Proust's favour, Berthollet's views were not entirely wrong, although at that time they were based on false evidence. Non-stoichiometric compounds (also called Berthollide compounds), with a variable composition, have been studied since 1930. For example, it is now believed that lattice deficiencies in iron can account for ferrous sulphide - iron (II) sulphide, FeS - with compositions that vary between $FeS_{1.00}$ and $FeS_{1.14}$ (or $Fe_{1.00}S$ and $Fe_{0.88}S$).

Berthollet also found himself disagreeing with Lavoisier, and would not concur with the theory that all acids contain oxygen. In this he was correct, but shared with Carl Scheele the false assumption that chlorine was not an element but consists of oxygenated hydrochloric acid. He did, however, introduce the use of chlorine as a bleaching agent (which led him to devise a volumetric analytical method for estimating the chlorine content of a bleaching solution by titration against a standard solution of indigo). Berthollet also investigated chlorates, suggesting that the oxidizing properties of potassium chlorate could make it a replacement for potassium nitrate in gunpowder and so produce a more powerful explosive. A public demonstration of this idea in 1778 resulted in disaster and the deaths of some of the onlookers.

In other wide-ranging studies Berthollet devised a method of smelting iron and making steel; he correctly determined the compositions of ammonia, prussic (hydrocyanic) acid and sulphuretted hydrogen (hydrogen sulphide); and he made various discoveries in organic chemistry. On balance, Berthollet was right more often than he was wrong - and even when he was wrong, his arguments with Proust and Lavoisier stimulated chemical thought, ultimately to the benefit of the science.

Berzelius, Jöns Jakob (*1779–1848*), was a Swedish chemist, one of the founders of the science in its modern form. He contributed to atomic theory, devised chemical symbols, determined atomic weights, and discovered or had a hand in the discovery of several new elements. He became renowned as a teacher and gained a reputation as a world authority; such was his influence that other scientists were wary of contradicting him. Indeed the obstinacy with which he clung to his own theories, especially in later life, may well have retarded progress in some areas despite his many magnificent achievements, particularly in theoretical chemistry.

Berzelius was born on 20 August 1779 at Väversunda, Östergötland, of an ancient Swedish family that had long associations with the church. His father, a teacher at the gymnasium in nearby Linköping, died when Berzelius was only four years old and his mother remarried a pastor, Anders Ekmarck. Berzelius and his sister were brought up with the five Ekmarck children and educated by their step-father and by private tutors. When in 1788 his mother also died, the nine-year-old Berzelius moved again to live with a maternal uncle. He attended his father's old school but quarrelled with his cousins and six years later left the family to become a tutor on a nearby farm, where he developed a strong interest in collecting and classifying flowers and insects. He had been destined for the priesthood, but decided in 1796 to study natural sciences and medicine at Uppsala University.

Berzelius had to interrupt his studies to earn some money. His step-brother aroused in him an interest in chemistry, but he received little encouragement at the university and began to experiment on his own. In the summer of 1800 he was introduced to Hedin, the chief physician at the Medivi mineral springs, and began his first scientific work - an analysis of the mineral content of the water. Hedin also secured for Berzelius the unpaid post of assistant to the Professor of Medicine and Pharmacy at the College of Medicine in Stockholm, and when the professor died in 1807 Berzelius was given the post. The College became an independent medical school, the Karolinska Institute, in 1810, the same year that Berzelius was appointed President of the Swedish Academy of Sciences. On his wedding day in 1835 he was made a baron by the King of Sweden, in recognition of his status as the most influential chemist of the era. Berzelius died on 7 August 1848.

As an experimenter Berzelius was meticulous. Papers he published between 1810 and 1816 describe the preparation, purification and analysis of about 2,000 chemical compounds. In the course of this work he improved many existing methods and developed new techniques. Quantitative analysis on such a broad scale established beyond doubt Dalton's atomic theory and Proust's law of definite proportions. It also laid the foundation of Berzelius' determination of the

17

atomic weights of the 40 elements known at that time – a prodigious task in which he was aided by the work of several contemporaries, such as Eilhard Mitscherlich (isomorphism), Pierre Dulong and Alexis Petit (specific heats), and Joseph Gay-Lussac (combining volumes); Mitscherlich and Dulong were his former students. In common with other scientists of the time, Berzelius rejected Avogadro's hypothesis, which led him to confuse some atomic weights and molecular weights. Nevertheless most of the atomic weights in the table he published in 1828 closely correspond to the modern accepted values.

His dealing with such a variety of elements and compounds led Berzelius to simplify chemical symbols. Alchemists had used an elaborate pictorial presentation, and John Dalton had devised a system based on circular symbols that could be

Berzelius also made his mark in the discovery of new elements. With the German chemist Wilhelm Hisinger he found cerium in 1803. In 1815 he believed that he had isolated a second new element from a mineral specimen and named it thorium. Subsequent experiments revealed that the "element" could be broken down into yttrium and phosphorus. His disappointment was softened by his discovery of selenium in 1818, silicon in 1824, and in 1829 a fourth new element, extracted from its ore by reduction with potassium, which he called thorium.

Several chemical terms in use today were coined by Berzelius. He noted that some reactions appeared to work faster in the presence of another substance which itself did not appear to change, and postulated that such a substance contained a "catalytic force". Platinum, for example, was well

	Alchemists	Dalton	Berzelius
Phosphorus			P
Sulphur			S
Iron (ferrum)			Fe
Hydrogen	unknown		H
Oxygen	unknown		O
Water			H^2O later H_2O

combined to represent compounds. Berzelius discarded both of these and introduced the notation still used today, in which letters (sometimes derived from Latin names) represent the elements and combined, with numbers if necessary, constitute the chemical formulae of compounds.

The invention of the voltaic cell at the beginning of the nineteenth century opened up a new field of research – electrochemistry. Berzelius' work in this area, although by no means as comprehensive as that of Humphry Davy, lent support to his dualistic theory, which stated that compounds consist of electrically and chemically opposed parts. He considered the parts to be stable groups of atoms, which he called "radicals". Although Berzelius' extension of the theory was later proved to be incorrect, it did contain the basis of the modern theory of ionic compounds.

endowed with such a force because it was capable of speeding up reactions between gases. Although he appreciated the nature of catalysis, Berzelius was unable to give any real explanation of the mechanism.

In the early nineteenth century it became apparent that elements could be grouped by similar chemical properties. Chlorine, bromine and iodine formed such a grouping. Each of these elements could be found as salts in sea water, consequently Berzelius invented the name "halogens" (salt formers) to collectively describe the family. The other two halogens were isolated later – fluorine by Henri Moissan in 1886 and astatine by Emilio Segrè in 1940.

A different branch of chemistry, concerned with substances derived from living things, was capturing the interest of scientists of the day. Berzelius referred to this new sphere as "organic chemistry" and expounded the belief that organic compounds arose from the operation of a "vital force" in the living cell; synthesis was therefore impossible. Then in 1828 Friedrich Wöhler (previously a student of Berzelius) prepared the organic compound urea from the inorganic salt ammonium cyanate. With great reluctance Berzelius eventually abandoned his vital force theory.

The word "isomerism" was also introduced by Berzelius, to describe substances that have the same chemical composition but different physical properties. He encountered the phenomenon when working with the salts of racemic and tartaric acids. Later Mitscherlich showed that, of the two, only tartarates rotate the plane of polarized light (are optically active); in 1848 Louis Pasteur resolved the racemates, which are an equimolecular mixture of two optically active tartarates (and have given their name to all such combinations, which are now known as racemic mixtures).

Throughout his career Berzelius recognized the importance to chemical progress of disseminating information. His *Textbook of Chemistry*, first published in 1803, was received with acclaim and was soon accepted as the definitive work for students of the time. In addition to publishing numerous research papers of his own, he collated the work of other chemists and acted as editor of an annual review of chemistry which was published between 1821 and 1849.

Black, Joseph (*1728–1799*), was a Scottish chemist and physicist, remembered for his discovery of carbon dioxide (which he called "fixed air") and for his work on latent heats. He is classed with Henry Cavendish and Antoine Lavoisier as one of the pioneers of modern chemistry.

Black was born in Bordeaux, France, on 16 April 1728. His father was from Belfast, but of Scottish descent, and was working in Bordeaux in the wine trade. Black went to Belfast to be educated, and then on to Glasgow University to study natural sciences and medicine. He moved to Edinburgh in 1751 to finish his studies, gaining his doctor's degree in 1754. Two years later he took over from William Cullen, his chemistry teacher at Glasgow, and was also offered the Chair in Anatomy. He soon changed this position for that of Professor of Medicine, and also practised as a physician. In 1766 he again followed Cullen as the Professor of Chemistry at Edinburgh University. Black died on 10 November 1799.

In Black's doctorate, he described investigations in "causticization" and indicated the existence of a gas distinct from common air, which he detected using a balance. He was therefore the founder of quantitative pneumatic chemistry and preceded Antoine Lavoisier in his experiments. In a more detailed account of his work, published in 1756, Black described how carbonates (which he called mild alkalis) become more alkaline (are causticized) when they lose carbon dioxide, whereas the taking up of carbon dioxide reconverts caustic alkalis into mild alkalis. Black identified "fixed air" (carbon dioxide) but did not pursue this work. He also discovered that it behaves like an acid; is produced by fermentation, respiration and the combustion of carbon; and had guessed that it is present in the atmosphere. He also discovered the bicarbonates (hydrogen carbonates). From 1760 onwards, most of his experimental work was in physics.

Bloch, Konrad Emil (*1912–*), is a German-born American biochemist whose best known work has been concerned with the biochemistry and metabolism of fats (lipids), particularly reactions involving cholesterol.

His research into the biosynthesis of cholesterol has produced a better understanding of this complex substance, whose presence in the human body is of supreme importance but whose excess is thought to be dangerous. For his work on the mechanism of cholesterol and fatty acid metabolism he shared the 1964 Nobel Prize in Medicine with Feodor Lynen.

Bloch was born on 21 January 1912 at Niesse, Germany, and educated at the Munich Technische Hochschule, from which he graduated as a chemical engineer in 1934. In 1936 he emigrated to the United States where two years later he received his doctorate in biochemistry from Columbia University. Bloch became an American citizen in 1944 while serving on the faculty of the Columbian University College of Physicians and Surgeons. He joined the staff of the University of Chicago in 1946 and became Professor of Biochemistry there in 1952. He moved to a similar position at Harvard two years later and in 1956 became a member of the National Academy of Sciences.

Cholesterol, the most abundant sterol in animal tissue, was discovered in 1812 and is now one of the best known (and commonest) steroids in the human body. It occurs either free or as esters of fatty acids, being found in practically all tissues but most abundant in the brain, nervous tissue and adrenal glands and, to a lesser extent, in the liver, kidneys and skin. Its name arose because of its occurrence in gall-stones (from the Greek for "bile solid"). Cholesterol has the molecular formula $C_{27}H_{46}O$ and, like most steroids, a structure based on phenanthrene:

Structural formula of cholesterol.

It is important to the body because it is a component of all cell membranes and is the metabolic precursor of many compounds with various physiological functions, including vitamin D, cortisone and the male and female sex hormones.

In the early 1940s Bloch took the first steps that were to lead to today's extensive knowledge of cholesterol. Working first with David Rittenberger and later with Henry Little, he demonstrated that carbon atoms of carbon-labelled acetate (ethanoate) fed to rats was incorporated into cholesterol in the animals' livers. Using acetic acid (ethanoic acid) labelled with deuterium he showed for the first time that it is this acid, a compound having only two carbon atoms, which is the major precursor of cholesterol. This discovery was the first of a long series that elucidated the biological synthesis of the steroid. Later, using acetic acid labelled at one carbon atom with radioactive carbon-14, Bloch demonstrated which of the 27 carbon atoms in cholesterol is derived from each of the two carbon atoms of acetic acid.

The overall conversion of acetic acid to cholesterol requires 36 distinct chemical transformations, which occur in various tissues but principally in the liver. The route begins with the conversion of three molecules of acetic acid to form a five-carbon compound and carbon dioxide. Then six of the five-carbon compounds combine to form the long-chain unsaturated 30-carbon compound squalene which, after cyclization, forms langesterol: the langesterol is finally converted to cholesterol.

Bloch's work undoubtedly paved the way to the successful tracing of the numerous metabolic changes that take place in the biosynthesis of cholesterol. It has important applications to medicine, because it is now thought that high levels of cholesterol in the bloodstream can cause it to be deposited on the inner walls of arteries (arteriosclerosis), where it narrows the vessels and increases the chances of blood clotting.

Boyle, Robert (*1627–1691*), was an English natural philosopher and one of the founders of modern chemistry. He is best remembered for the law named after him which states that, at a constant temperature, the volume of a given mass of gas varies inversely as the pressure upon it. He was instrumental in the founding of the Royal Society and a pioneer in the use of experiment and the scientific method.

Boyle was born on 25 January 1627 in Lismore Castle, Ireland, the fourteenth child and seventh son of the Earl of Cork. He learned to speak French and Latin as a child and was sent to Eton College at the early age of eight. In 1641 he visited Italy, returning to England in 1644. He joined a group known as the Invisible College, whose aim was to cultivate the "new philosophy" and which met at Gresham College, London, and in Oxford, where Boyle went to live in 1654. The Invisible College became, under a charter granted by Charles II in 1663, the Royal Society of London for Improving Natural Knowledge, and Boyle was a member of its first council. (He was elected President of the Royal Society in 1680, but declined the office.) He moved to London in 1668 where he lived with his sister for the rest of his life. He died there on 30 December 1691.

Boyle's most active research was carried out while he lived in Oxford. By careful experiments he established Boyle's law. He determined the density of air and pointed out that bodies alter in weight according to the varying buoyancy of the atmosphere. He compared the lower strata of the air to a number of sponges or small springs which are compressed by the weight of the layers of air above them. In 1660 these findings were published in a book, shortened title *The Spring of Air*, and gave us the word elastic in its present meaning.

A year later Boyle published *The Sceptical Chymist* in which he criticized previous researchers for thinking that salt, sulphur and mercury were the "true principles of things". He advanced towards the view that matter is ultimately composed of "corpuscles" of various sorts and sizes, capable of arranging themselves into groups, and that each group constitutes a chemical substance. He successfully distinguished between mixtures and compounds and showed that a compound can have very different qualities from those of its constituents.

Also in about 1660 Boyle studied the chemistry of combustion, with the assistance of his pupil Robert Hooke (1635–1703). They proved using an air pump that neither charcoal nor sulphur burns when strongly heated in a vessel exhausted of air, although each inflames as soon as air is re-admitted. Boyle then found that a mixture of either substance with saltpetre (potassium nitrate) catches fire even when heated in a vacuum and concluded that combustion must depend on something common to both air and saltpetre. Further experiments involved burning a range of combustible substances in a bell-jar of air enclosed over water. But it was left to Joseph Priestley in 1774 to discover the component of air that vigorously supports combustion, which three years later Antoine Lavoisier named oxygen.

The term analysis was coined by Boyle and many of the reactions still used in qualitative work were known to him. He also introduced certain plant extracts, notably litmus, for the indication of acids and bases. In 1667 he was the first to study the phenomenon of bioluminescence, when he showed that fungi and bacteria require air (oxygen) for luminescence, becoming dark in a vacuum and luminescing again when air is re-admitted. In this he drew a comparison between a glowing coal and phosphorescent wood, although oxygen was still not known and combustion not properly understood. Boyle also seems to have been the first to construct a small portable box-type camera obscura in about 1665. It could be extended or shortened like a telescope to focus an image on a piece of paper stretched across the back of the box opposite the lens.

In 1665 Boyle published the first account in England of the use of a hydrometer for measuring the density of liquids. The instrument he described is essentially the same as those in use today. He can also be credited with the invention of the first match. In 1680 he found that by coating coarse paper with phosphorus, fire was produced when a sulphur-tipped splint was drawn through a fold in the treated paper. Boyle experimented in physiology, although "the tenderness of his nature" prevented him from performing actual dissections! He also carried out experiments in the hope of changing one metal into another, and was instrumental in obtaining in 1689 the repeal of the statute of Henry IV against multiplying gold and silver.

Besides being a busy natural philosopher, Boyle was interested in theology and in 1665 would have received the provostship of Eton had he taken orders. He learned Hebrew, Greek and Syriac in order to further his studies of the scriptures, and spent large sums on biblical translations. He founded the Boyle Lectures for proving the Christian religion against "notorious infidels such as atheists, theists, pagans, Jews and Mahommedans" (but made the proviso that controversies between Christians were not to be mentioned).

Boyle accomplished much important work in physics, with Boyle's law, the role of air in propagating sound, the expansive force of freezing water, the refractive powers of crystals, the density of liquids, electricity, colour, hydrostatics and so on. But his greatest fondness was researching in chemistry, and he was the main agent in changing the outlook from an alchemical to a chemical one. He was the first to work towards removing the mystique and making chemistry into a pure science. He questioned the basis of the chemical theory of his day and taught that the proper object of chemistry was to determine the compositions of substances. His great merit as a scientific investigator was that he carried out the principles of Bacon, although he did not consider himself to be a follower of him or any other teacher. After his death, his natural history collections passed as a bequest to the Royal Society.

Bredig, Georg (*1868–1944*), was a German physical chemist who contributed to a wide range of subjects within his discipline but is probably best known for his work on colloids and catalysts.

Bredig was born on 1 October 1868 in Glogau, Lower Silesia (now Głogow, Poland). After qualifying he went to work as an assistant in the laboratory of the great German chemist Friedrich Ostwald in Leipzig, and it was there that he did much of his significant work. He held a series of academic appointments in physical chemistry: at Heidelberg, Germany (1901-1910); Zurich, Switzerland (1910); and from 1911 at the Karlsruhe Hochschule, Germany. He went to the United States in 1940, and died in New York City on 24 April 1944.

While working with Ostwald, Bredig collaborated with him on the accumulation of experimental data with which to validate Ostwald's dilution law (which states that, for a binary electrolyte, the equilibrium constant K_c of a chemical reaction has the same value at all dilutions). The equilibrium constant depends not on the dilution, but on the chemical nature of the particular acid or base. Ostwald confirmed the law for 250 acids, and Bredig provided the comparable data for 50 bases.

The variation in the relative atomic mass (atomic weight) of lead from various sources, the transition metals (on which he worked with Jacobus Van't Hoff), and catalytic action formed other areas of his research. Bredig also supervised overseas chemistry students, such as the British chemist Nevil Sidgewick.

In the field of catalysis Bredig's particular study was the catalytic action of colloidal platinum and the "poisoning" of catalysts by impurities. His most important contribution was a method of preparing colloidal solutions (lyophobic sols) using an electric arc, which he devised in 1898.

There are two ways of producing particles of colloidal size: larger particles can be broken down (dispersed) or smaller particles can be made to aggregate. Bredig's arc method is a dispersion technique. An electric arc is struck between metal electrodes immersed in a suitable electrolyte – for example, platinum, gold or silver electrodes in distilled water containing an alkali. The colloidal particles are thought to be produced mainly by rapid condensation of the vapour of the arc, and they may be in the form of the metal or its oxide. A later extension of the method developed by Theodor Svedburg in the early 1900s uses an alternating current and produces sols of greater purity.

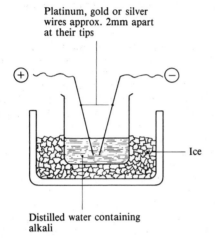

Platinum, gold or silver wires approx. 2mm apart at their tips

Ice

Distilled water containing alkali

Brönsted, Johannes Nicolaus (*1879-1947*), was a Danish physical chemist whose work in solution chemistry, particularly electrolytes, resulted in a new theory of acids and bases.

Brönsted was born on 22 February 1879 in Varde, Jutland, the son of a civil engineer. He was educated at local schools before going to study chemical engineering at the Technical Institute of the University of Copenhagen in 1897. He graduated two years later and then turned to chemistry, in which he qualified in 1902. After a short time in industry, he was appointed an assistant in the university's chemical laboratory in 1905, becoming Professor of Physical and Inorganic Chemistry in 1908. In his later years he turned to politics, being elected to the Danish parliament in 1947. He died on 17 December in that year, before he could take his seat.

Brönsted's early work was wide ranging, particularly in the fields of electrochemistry, the measurement of hydrogen ion concentrations, amphoteric electrolytes, and the behaviour of indicators. He discovered a method of eliminating potentials in the measurement of hydrogen ion concentrations, and devised a simple equation that connects the activity and osmotic coefficients

of an electrolyte, and another that relates activity coefficients to reaction velocities. From the absorption spectra of chromic – chromium (III) – salts he concluded that strong electrolytes are completely dissociated, and that the changes of molecular conductivity and freezing point that accompany changes in concentration are caused by the electrical forces between ions in solution. He related the stages of ionization of polybasic acids to their molecular structure, and the specific heat capacities of steam and carbon dioxide to their band spectra. In 1912 he published work with Herman Nernst on the specific heat capacities of steam and carbon dioxide at high temperatures. Two years later he laid the foundations of the theory of the infra-red spectra of polyatomic molecules by introducing the so-called valency force-field. Brönsted also applied the newly developed quantum theory of specific heat capacities to gases, and published papers about the factors that determine the pH and fertility of soils.

In 1887 Svante Arrhenius had proposed a theory of acidity that explained its nature on an atomic level. He defined an acid as a compound that could generate hydrogen ions in aqueous solution, and an alkali as a compound that could generate hydroxyl ions. A strong acid is completely ionized (dissociated) and produces many hydrogen ions, whereas a weak acid is only partly dissociated and produces few hydrogen ions. Conductivity measurements confirm the theory, as long as the solutions are not too concentrated.

In 1923 Brönsted published (simultaneously with Thomas Lowry in Britain) a new theory of acidity which has certain important advantages over that of Arrhenius. Brönsted defined an acid as a proton donor and a base as a proton acceptor. The definition applies to all solvents, not just water. It also explains the different behaviour of pure acids and acids in solution. Pure dry liquid sulphuric acid or acetic (ethanoic) acid does not change the colour of indicators nor react with carbonates or metals. But as soon as water is added, all of these reactions occur.

In Brönsted's scheme, every acid is related to a conjugate base, and every base to a conjugate acid. When hydrogen chloride dissolves in water, for example, a reaction takes place and an equilibrium is established:

$$HCl + H_2O \rightleftharpoons H_3O^+ + Cl^-$$

Acid 1   Base 2   Acid 2   Base 1

HCl is an acid for the forward reaction, but the hydroxonium ion (H_3O^+) is an acid in the reverse reaction; it is the conjugate acid (acid 2) of water (base 2). Similarly, the chloride ion (Cl^-, base 1) accepts protons in the reverse reaction to form its conjugate acid (HCl, acid 1). In this theory acids are not confined to neutral species or positive ions. For example, the negatively charged hydrogen sulphate ion can behave as an acid:

$$HSO_4^-(aq) + H_2O(1) \rightleftharpoons H_3O^+ + SO_4^{2-}(aq)$$

It donates a proton to form the hydroxonium ion.

Buchner, Eduard (*1860-1917*), was a German organic chemist who discovered non-cellular alcoholic fermentation of sugar - that is, that the active agent in the reaction is an enzyme contained in yeast, and not the yeast cells themselves. For this achievement he was awarded the 1907 Nobel Prize in Chemistry.

Buchner was born in Munich on 20 May 1860, of an old Bavarian family of scholars. His father was a professor of forensic medicine and obstetrics, as well as being editor of a medical journal. When Buchner graduated from the Realgymnasium he served in the field artillery before going to study chemistry at the Munich Technische Hochschule. His studies were again interrupted - for financial reasons this time - and he spent four years working in the canneries of Munich and Mombach. In 1884, with the assistance of his elder brother Hans, a bacteriologist, he resumed his academic training in the organic section of the chemical laboratory of the Bavarian Academy of Sciences in Munich, where he worked under Johann von Baeyer.

While he was studying chemistry, Buchner also worked in the Institute for Plant Physiology under the Swiss botanist Karl von Nägeli (1817-1891). He obtained his doctorate in 1888 and was appointed teaching assistant to von Baeyer at the Privatdozent. In 1893 he succeeded Theodor Curtius (1857-1928) as head of the section for analytical chemistry at the University of Kiel and became Associate Professor there in 1895. Later professorships included appointments at Tübingen (1896), Berlin (1898), Breslau (1909) and Würzburg (1911). In 1914 he served in the German army as a Captain in the ammunition supply unit and was promoted to Major in 1916. He was recalled to Würzburg to teach for a short time but returned to the front in Romania on 11 August 1917. He was killed by a grenade four days later at Focşani.

It was while Buchner was working at the Institute for Plant Physiology that he first became interested in the problems of alcoholic fermentation, and in his first paper (1886) he came to the conclusion that Louis Pasteur was wrong in his contention that the absence of oxygen was a necessary prerequisite for fermentation. In 1858 Moritz Traube had proposed that all fermentations were caused by what he termed "ferments" - definite chemical substances which he thought

were related to proteins and produced by living cells; in 1878 Willy Kühne (1837-1900) called these substances enzymes. Many researchers, including Pasteur, had tried to liberate the fermentation enzyme from yeast.

In 1893 Buchner and his elder brother found that the cells of micro-organisms were disrupted when they were ground with sand. After yeast had been treated in this way, it was possible to use a hydraulic press to squeeze out a yellow viscous liquid, free from cells. The Buchners were using the liquid for pharmaceutical studies (not for experiments on fermentation) and wished to add a preservative to it. As the juice was being used in experiments on animals, antiseptics could not be used and so Buchner added a thick sugar syrup to stop any bacterial action. He fully expected the sugar to act as a preservative, as it usually does, but to his surprise it had the opposite effect and carbon dioxide was produced. Thus the sugar had fermented, producing carbon dioxide and alcohol, in the same way as if whole yeast cells had been present. He named the enzyme concerned zymase.

Invertase, another enzyme of yeast, has been known since 1860 but zymase is different in that it is less stable to heat and catalyses a more complex reaction. Buchner was fortunate that he chose the correct type of yeast. It was soon realized that the conversion of sugar into alcohol by means of yeast juice is a series of stepwise reactions, and that zymase is really a mixture of several enzymes. It was to be 40 years before the process was fully understood, through the work of Arthur Harden (1865-1940), Otto Meyerhof (1884-1951) and others.

Buchner's other main research concerned aliphatic diazo compounds. Between 1885 and 1905 he published 48 papers that dealt with the synthesis of nitrogenous compounds, especially pyrazole. He also synthesized cycloheptane compounds.

Bunsen, Robert Wilhelm (*1811-1899*), was a German chemist who pioneered the use of the spectroscope to analyse chemical compounds. Using the technique, he discovered two new elements, rubidium and caesium. He also devised several pieces of laboratory apparatus, although he probably played only a minor part (if any) in the invention of the Bunsen burner.

Bunsen was born on 31 March 1811 at Göttingen, son of a librarian and linguistics professor at the local university. He studied chemistry there and at Paris, Berlin and Vienna, gaining his PhD in 1830. He was appointed professor at the Polytechnic Institute of Kassel in 1836, and subsequently held chairs at Marburg (1838) and

Breslau (1851) before becoming Professor of Experimental Chemistry at Heidelberg in 1852. He remained there until he retired. Bunsen never married, and ten years after retiring he died, on 16 August 1899.

Bunsen's first significant work, begun in 1837, was on cacodyl compounds, unpleasant and dangerous organic compounds of arsenic; a laboratory explosion cost Bunsen the sight of one eye and he nearly died of arsenic poisoning. He did, however, stimulate later researches into organometallic compounds by his student, the British chemist Edward Frankland. In 1841 he devised the Bunsen cell, 1.9-volt carbon-zinc primary cell which he used to produce an extremely bright electric arc light. He then (1844) invented a grease-spot photometer to measure brightness (by comparing a light source of known brightness with that being investigated). His contribution to the improvement of laboratory instruments and techniques gave rise also to the Bunsen ice calorimeter, which he developed in 1870 to measure the heat capacities of substances that were available in only small quantities.

Bunsen's first work in inorganic chemistry made use of his primary cell. Using electrolysis, he was the first to isolate metallic magnesium, and demonstrate the intense light produced when the metal is burned in air. But his major contribution was the analysis of the spectra produced when metal salts (particularly chlorides) are heated to incandescence in a flame, a technique first advocated by the American physicist David Alter (1807–1891). Working with Gustav Kirchhoff (1824–1887) in about 1860, Bunsen observed "new" lines in the spectra of minerals which represented the elements rubidium (which has a prominent red line) and caesium (blue line). Other workers using the same technique soon discovered several other new elements.

The Bunsen burner, probably used to heat the materials for spectroscopic analysis, seems to have been designed by Peter Desdega, Bunsen's technician. Gas (originally coal gas, but any inflammable gas can be used) is released from a jet at the base of a chimney. A hole or holes at the base of the chimney are encircled by a movable collar, which also has holes. Rotation of the collar controls the amount of air admitted at the base of the chimney; the air-gas mixture burns at the top. With the air holes closed, the gas burns with a luminous, sooty flame. With the air holes open, the air-gas mixture burns with a hot, non-luminous flame (and makes a characteristic roaring sound).

C

Calvin, Melvin (*1911–*), is an American chemist who worked out the biosynthetic pathways involved in photosynthesis, the process by which green plants use the energy of sunlight to convert water and carbon dioxide into carbohydrates and oxygen. For this achievement he was awarded the 1961 Novel Prize in Chemistry.

Calvin was born of Russian immigrant parents on 8 April 1911 in St Paul, Minnesota. He graduated from Michigan College of Mining and Technology in 1931 and was awarded his PhD by the University of Minnesota in 1935. For the next two years he did research at the University of Manchester, England, and then returned to the United States as an Instructor at the University of California. He remained there, becoming Assistant Professor (1941), Associate Professor (1945), Professor (1947) and finally University Professor of Chemistry (1971).

Calvin began work on photosynthesis in 1949,

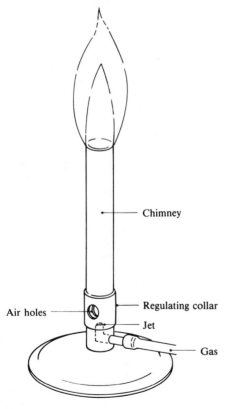

The Bunsen burner.

Chimney

Air holes

Regulating collar

Jet

Gas

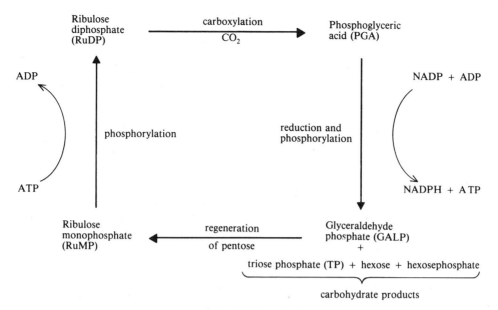

The Calvin cycle.

using radioactive carbon-14 as a tracer to investigate the conversion of carbon dioxide into starch. It was already known that there were two interdependent processes: the light reaction, in which a plant "captured" energy from sunlight, and the dark reaction (which proceeds in the absence of light), during which carbon dioxide and water combine to form carbohydrates such as sugar and starch. Calvin studied the latter reaction in a single-celled green alga called *Chlorella*. He showed that there is in fact a cycle of reactions (now called the Calvin cycle) in which the key step is the enzyme-catalysed carboxylation of the phosphate ester of a pentose (5-carbon) sugar, ribulose diphosphate (RuDP), to form the 3-carbon phosphoglyceric acid (PGA). This acid is then reduced to the 3-carbon glyceraldehyde phosphate (GALP), with the formation also of triose phosphate (TP) and hexose and its phosphate. The reduction and phosphorylation of PGA involves a reducing agent, NADPH, and the energy-rich compound adenosine triphosphate, ATP, which are derived from the photochemical light reaction. Finally, another enzyme catalyses the generation of ribulose monophosphate (RuMP) which a second ATP-induced phosphorylation reconverts to ribulose diphosphate (RuDP). The sequence of reactions is also called the reductive pentose phosphate cycle.

Cannizzaro, Stanislao (*1826-1910*), was an Italian chemist who, through his revival of Avogadro's hypothesis, laid the foundations of modern atomic theory. He is also remembered for an organic reaction named after him, the decomposition of aromatic aldehydes into a mixture of the corresponding acid and alcohol.

Cannizzaro was born on 13 July 1826 in Palermo. He studied chemistry at the universities of Palermo, Naples and Pisa, where in 1845 he became assistant to Raffaele Piria (1815-1865) who worked on salicin (preparing salicylic acid) and glucosides. In 1848 Cannizzaro joined the artillery to fight in the Sicilian Revolution, was condemned to death, but in 1849 escaped to Marseilles and went on to Paris. There he worked with Michel Chevreul (1786-1889, who was aged 103 when he died) and F. Cloëz (1817-1883). In 1851 he synthesized cyanamide by treating an ether solution of cyanogen chloride with ammonia, and in the same year became Professor of Physics and Chemistry at the Technical Institute of Alessandria, Piedmont. It was there that he discovered the Cannizzaro reaction. He was appointed Professor of Chemistry at Genoa University in 1855, followed by professorships at Palermo (1861-1871) and Rome. He became a Senator in 1871 and eventually Vice-President, pursuing his interest in scientific education. He died in Rome on 10 May 1910.

Cannizzaro's reaction involves the teatment of an aromatic aldehyde with an alcoholic solution of potassium hydroxide. The aldehyde undergoes simultaneous oxidation and reduction to form an alcohol and a carboxylic acid:

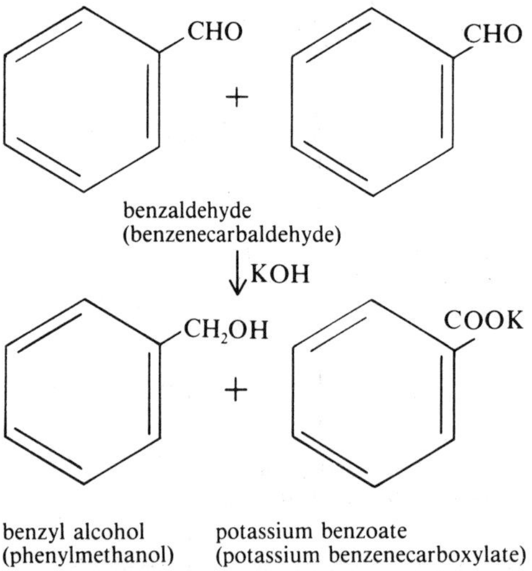

benzaldehyde
(benzenecarbaldehyde)

↓ KOH

benzyl alcohol   potassium benzoate
(phenylmethanol)   (potassium benzenecarboxylate)

It is an example of a dismutation or disproportionation reaction, and finds many uses in synthetic organic chemistry. Cannizzaro also investigated the natural plant product santonin, used as a vermifuge, which he showed was related to naphthalene.

His greatest contribution to chemistry was made in 1858 when he revived Avogadro's hypothesis and insisted on a proper distinction between atomic and molecular weights (relative atomic and molecular masses). The pamphlet he published was distributed at the Chemical Congress at Karlsruhe in 1860. Cannizzaro pointed out that once the molecular weight of a (volatile) compound had been determined from a measurement of its vapour density, it was necessary only to estimate, within limits, the atomic weight of one of its elemental components. Then by investigating a sufficient number of compounds of that element, the chances were that at least one of them would contain only one atom of the element concerned, so that its equivalent weight (atomic weight divided by valency) would correlate with

its atomic weight. Despite objections by a group of French chemists led by Sainte-Claire Deville (who studied abnormal vapour densities of substances such as ammonium chloride and phosphorus pentachloride, and were reluctant to account for these in terms of thermal dissociation), Cannizzaro's proposal was soon widely accepted.

Cannizzaro's contribution to atomic theory paved the way for later work on the periodic law and on an understanding of valency. The Royal Society recognized its significance with the award in 1891 of its Copley Medal.

Carothers, Wallace Hume (*1896–1937*), was an American organic chemist who did pioneering work on the development of commercial polymers, producing nylon (a polyamide) and neoprene (a polybutylene, one of the first synthetic rubbers).

Carothers was born on 27 April 1896 in Burlington, Iowa, the son of a teacher. He attended schools in Des Moines, graduating from the North High School in 1914. His further studies were in accountancy and clerical practice at his father's college in Des Moines, until he entered Tarkio College, Missouri, in 1915 and specialised in chemistry. He later gained higher degrees in organic chemistry from the University of Illinois and Harvard, where he was appointed in 1926. In 1928 he accepted the post as head of organic chemistry research at the Du Pont research laboratory in Wilmington, Delaware. For his fundamental work on polymers he was elected to the US National Academy of Sciences in 1931. Carothers suffered from periods of depression which became more prolonged and severe as he grew older. He was deeply affected by the death of his sister in 1936, the same year in which he married. A few months later, on 29 April 1937, he committed suicide in Philadelphia, Pennsylvania.

Carothers began his work on polymerization

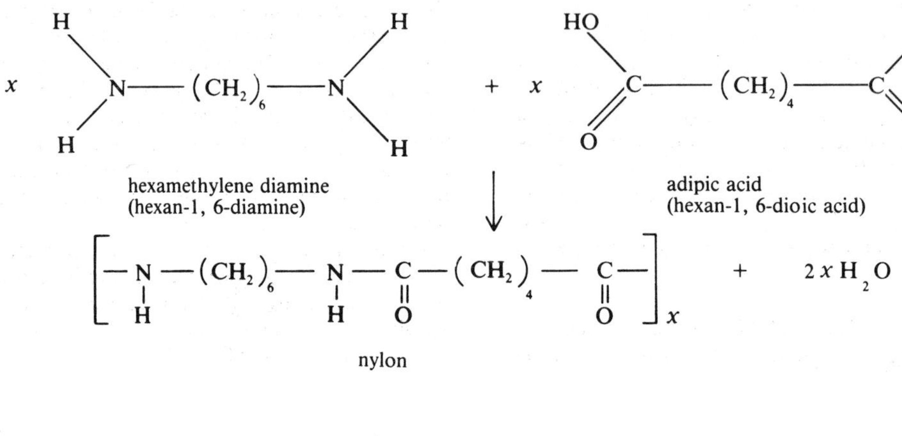

hexamethylene diamine
(hexan-1, 6-diamine)

adipic acid
(hexan-1, 6-dioic acid)

nylon

and the structures of high molecular weight substances while at Harvard. Then at Du Pont's he carried out studies on linear condensation polymers, which culminated in 1931 with the development of nylon and neoprene. Much of his research effort was directed at producing a polymer that could be drawn out into a fibre. His first successful experiments involved polyesters formed from trimethylene glycol (propan-1, 3-diol) and octadecane dicarboxylic acid (octadecan-1, 18-dioic acid). But for finer fibres with enough strength (emulating silk) he turned to polyamides. Early attempts, made by heating amino-caproic acid (hexan-6-amino-1-oic acid), resulted in an unstable product containing ring compounds. The first polymer to be called nylon (strictly the trade-name Nylon 66) was made by heating hexamethylene diamine (hexan-1, 6-diamine) and adipic acid (hexan-1, 6-dioic acid). The product is a linear chain polymer which can be cold drawn after extrusion through spinnerets to orientate the molecules parallel to each other so that lateral hydrogen bonding takes place. The resultant nylon fibres are strong and have a characteristic lustre.

Carothers also worked on synthetic rubbers. His monomer was chlorobutadiene (but-2-chloro-1, 3-diene), which he first had to make by treating vinylacetylene (but-1-en-3-yne) with hydrogen chloride:

also carried out fundamental experiments concerning electricity and gravitation.

Cavendish was born on 10 October 1731 in Nice, France, the first son of Lord Charles Cavendish and Lady Anne Grey, the daughter of the Duke of Kent. His uncle was the third Duke of Devonshire. His mother died when he was two years old and he was sent to school at Dr Newcome's Academy in Hackney, London, and then in 1749 attended Peterhouse College at Cambridge University. He left there in 1753 without a degree – a not unusual practice at that time – and spent the rest of his life privately in London living as a recluse and shunning most social contact. He was, however, an active participant in the scientific community and attended all meetings of the Royal Society. But he remained shy and retiring, had an abhorrence of women and never married, and died alone in London on 2 February 1810.

Little is known of Cavendish's work until the late 1760s, when he began experimenting with "facticious airs" (gases that can be produced by the chemical treatment of solids or liquids). He studied "fixed air" (carbon dioxide) produced by mixing acids and bases; "inflammable air" (hydrogen) generated by the action of acids on metals; and the "airs" produced during decay and fermentation. He measured the specific gravities of hydrogen and carbon dioxide, comparing them with that of "common" (i.e. atmospheric) air.

$$H_2C = CH - C \equiv CH \quad + \quad HCl \quad \longrightarrow \quad H_2C = \underset{\underset{Cl}{|}}{C} - \underset{\underset{H}{|}}{C} = CH_2$$

vinylacetylene
(but-1-en-3-yne)

chlorobutadiene
(but-2-chloro-1, 3-diene)

$$\left[- CH_2 - \underset{\underset{Cl}{|}}{C} = \underset{\underset{H}{|}}{C} - CH_2 - \right]_x$$

neoprene

Using a peroxide catalyst, the chloro compound polymerizes readily by a free radical mechanism to form neoprene. This polymer, first produced commercially in 1932, is resistant to heat, light and most solvents. In the years that followed, a whole range of useful polymers of the nylon and neoprene types were produced.

Cavendish, Henry (*1731–1810*), was a British natural philosopher whose main interests lay in the fields of chemistry and physics. His chief experimental work concerned gases, although he

In 1783 Cavendish found that the composition of the atmosphere is the same in different locations and at different times. He also found that a small fraction of "common air" seems to be inert – a hundred years later William Ramsay was to show that this inert gas is mainly argon. A year later Cavendish demonstrated that water is produced when hydrogen burns in air, thus proving that water is a compound and not an element as had been suggested by early Greek scientists. By sending electric sparks through "common air" he caused the nitrogen in it to combine with oxygen.

When the gas produced was dissolved in water it produced nitric acid. He also showed that "calcareous earth" dissolves in water containing carbon dioxide, to form what is now known as calcium bicarbonate. He distinguished between the two oxides of arsenic, demonstrating that one contains more oxygen than does the other.

During the 1770s Cavendish worked on electricity, anticipating much of the later researches of Michael Faraday and Charles Coulomb, but his results remained unknown until they were published by James Clerk Maxwell in 1879. His other experiments in physics concerned heat and gravitation, including his classic determination of the gravitational constant and the mass of the Earth.

Cavendish was a great scientist, honoured by the naming of the Cavendish Laboratories at Cambridge University in his memory. His contributions are notable for their value and diversity, and had he allowed all of his results to be published, the rate of advancement of science would undoubtedly have been greatly accelerated. He stands today as one of the giants of modern science.

Chardonnet, Louis-Marie-Hilaire Bernigaud, Comte de (*1839-1924*), was a French industrial chemist who invented rayon, the first type of artificial silk. He also worked on nitrocellulose (gun cotton).

Chardonnet was born into an aristocratic family on 1 May 1839 at Besançon, Doubs. He trained first as a civil engineer at the École Polytechnique, Paris, and then went to work under Louis Pasteur, who was studying diseases in silkworms. This inspired Chardonnet to seek an artificial replacement for soil which he first patented in 1884. Five years later, at the Paris Exposition, he was awarded the Grand Prize for his invention. He opened his first factory, the Societé de la Soie de Chardonnet, at Besançon in 1889 and in 1904 he built a second factory at Sarvar in Hungary. He died in Paris on 12 March 1924 at the age of 85.

Chardonnet began his experiments in 1878 but it took six years before he had produced a satisfactory fibre. He prepared nitrocellulose (mainly cellulose tetranitrate) by treating a pulp made from mulberry leaves - the food plant of silkworms - with mixed nitric and sulphuric acids. The cellulose compound was dissolved in a mixture of ether and alcohol and the hot viscous solution forced through fine capillary tubes into cold water. The warm threads were stretched and dried in heated air.

The original nitrocellulose fibre was extremely inflammable, and Chardonnet continued working to produce a fireproof version. By 1889 he had developed rayon, so-called because the brightness of the material was thought to resemble the emission of the sun's rays. He later was able to make 35-40 denier threads (denier is the weight in grams of 9,000 m of yarn) of tensile strength equivalent to that of natural silk.

Rayon was the first man-made fibre to come into common use. It was, admittedly, only modified cellulose but it pointed the way to the totally synthetic fibres developed about 50 years later by Wallace Carothers and others. Today the term rayon is generally used for all types of fibres made from cellulose, although is most often applied to viscose yarns. The cellulose is usually derived from cotton or wood pulp.

As well as his development of artificial fibres, Chardonnet also spent some time working for the French government on the production of gun cotton, the original smokeless powder for cartridges and shells which exploits the material's high inflammability - the very feature that Chardonnet had to eliminate from his textile fibre. He also made minor contributions to studies of the absorption of ultraviolet light, telephony, and the behaviour of eyes of birds.

Chevreul, Michel Eugène (*1786-1889*), was a French organic chemist who in a long lifetime devoted to scientific research studied a wide range of natural substances, including fats, sugars and dyes.

Chevreul was born in Angers on 31 August 1786, the son of a surgeon. He went to Paris in 1803 when he was 17 years old to study chemistry at the Collège de France under Louis Vauquelin. He became an assistant to Antoine Fourcroy (1783-1791) in 1809 and a year later took up an appointment as an assistant at the Musée d'Histoire Naturelle. He was Professor of Physics at the Lycée Charlemagne from 1813 until 1830, when he returned to the Musée as Professor of Chemistry, succeeding his old tutor Vauquelin. In 1824 he was made a Director of the dyeworks associated with the Gobelins Tapestry Factory, and in 1864 he became Director for life of the Musée d'Histoire Naturelle. He died, aged 103, in Paris on 8 April 1889.

Chevreul's earliest research under Vauquelin was on indigo, a subject he was to return to later. He began his studies of fats in 1809 by first decomposing soaps (which at that time were made exclusively by the action of alkali on animal fats). By treating soaps with hydrochloric acid he obtained and identified various fatty acids, including stearic, palmitic, oleic, caproic and valeric acids. He thus realized that the soap-making process is the treatment of a glyceryl ester of fatty acids (i.e., a fat) with an alkali to form fatty acid salts (i.e., soap) and glycerol.

Soap-making (saponification):

glyceryl stearate + sodium hydrox- → sodium stearate + glycerol
                          ide
(fat)   (alkali)   (soap)

Chevreul's acid hydrolysis:

sodium stearate + hydrochloric acid → stearic acid + sodium chloride
(soap)   (acid)   (fatty acid)   (salt)

One of the most useful of the newly discovered acids was stearic acid, and in 1825 Chevreul and Joseph Gay-Lussac patented a process for making candles from stearin (crude stearic acid), providing a cleaner and less odorous alternative to tallow candles. Chevreul determined the purity of fatty acids by measuring their melting points, and constancy of melting point soon became a criterion of purity throughout preparative and analytical organic chemistry. He also investigated natural waxy substances, such as spermaceti, lanolin and cholesterol (which did not yield fatty acids on treatment with hydrochloric acid).

During the many years he was working with fats Chevreul also studied other natural compounds. In 1815 he isolated grape sugar (glucose) from the urine of a patient suffering from diabetes mellitus. At the Gobelin dyeworks he discovered haematoxylin in the reddish-brown dye logwood and quercitrin in yellow oak; he also prepared the colourless reduced form of indigo. His interest in the creation of the illusion of continuous colour gradation by using massed small monochromatic dots (as in an embroidery or tapestry) later influenced the Pointillistes and Impressionist painters.

Cori, Carl Ferdinand (*1896–*), and **Cori, Gerty Theresa** (*1896–1957*), husband and wife, Czech-born American biochemists who worked out the biosynthesis and degradation of glycogen, the carbohydrate stored in the liver and muscles. For this achievement they were jointly awarded the 1947 Nobel Prize in Physiology and Medicine, which they shared with the Argentinian biochemist Bernardo Houssay (1887–).

Carl Cori was born on 5 December 1896 in Prague, then in Austria-Hungary. He was educated in Austria at the Trieste Gymnasium, and graduated in 1920 with a medical degree from the University of Prague. It was while he was a medical student that he met and married his classmate Gerty Radnitz. She was also born in Prague, on 15 August 1896, entered the medical school in 1914 and graduated in the same year as her hus-

band. After having spent several years in war-torn Austria – Carl Cori was in the Austrian army during World War I – they emigrated to the United States in 1922 and became American citizens six years later.

From 1922–1931 Carl Cori was a biochemist at the State Institute for Study of Malignant Diseases at Buffalo, New York. In 1931 he was appointed Professor of Biochemistry at Washington University School of Medicine in St Louis, Missouri. In the same year his wife became Fellow and Research Associate in Pharmacology and Biochemistry there, a position she held until 1947. Gerty Cori died in St Louis on 26 October 1957. Carl Cori remained at St Louis until 1967, when he took up the appointment of Biochemist at Massachusetts General Hospital, Harvard Medical School, Boston.

It was during the 1930s that the Coris began their researches on glycogen. Its basic structure was known; it is a polysaccharide, a highly branched sugar molecule composed of several hundred glucose molecules linked by glycosidic bonds. Any excess food in an animal's diet is stored as glycogen or fat, and in times of shortage the animal makes use of these reserves. Glycogen is broken down in the muscles into lactic acid (2-hydroxypropanoic acid), as worked out by Otto Meyerhof (1884–1951) about 20 years earlier, which when the muscles rest is reconverted to glycogen. The Coris set out to determine exactly how these changes take place.

It was tempting to assume that glycogen broke down into separate glucose molecules. But this hydrolysis would involve a loss of energy, which would have to be re-supplied for the conversion back to glycogen. Gerty Cori found a new substance in muscle tissue, glucose-1-phosphate, now known as Cori ester. Its formation from glycogen involves only a small amount of energy change, so that the balance between the two substances can easily be shifted in either direction. The second step in the reaction chain involves the conversion of glucose-1-phosphate into glucose-6-phosphate. Finally this second phosphate is changed to fructose-1,6-diphosphate, which is eventually converted to lactic acid. The first set of reactions from glycogen to glucose-6-phosphate

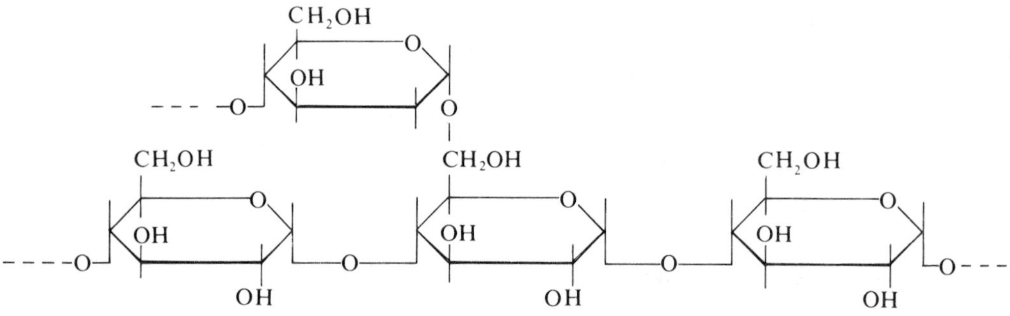

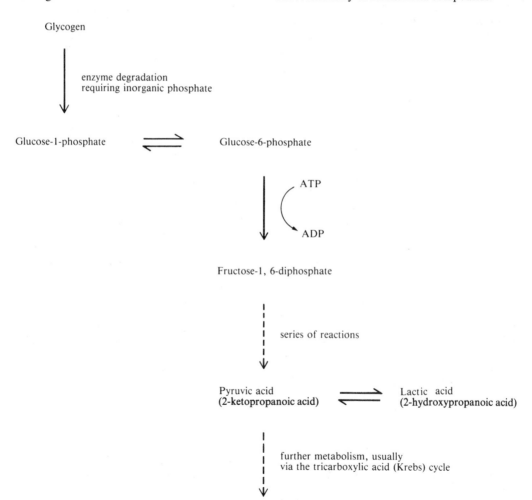

Part of glycogen molecule.

is now termed glycogenolysis; the second set, from glucose-6-phosphate to lactic acid, is referred to as glycolysis.

The whole sequence can be set out in the form of a diagram:

Cornforth, John Warcup (*1917–   *), is an Australian organic chemist who shared the 1975 Nobel Prize in Chemistry with the Swiss biochemist Vladimir Prelog for his work on the stereochemistry of biochemical compounds.

Glycogen

↓ enzyme degradation
requiring inorganic phosphate

Glucose-1-phosphate ⇌ Glucose-6-phosphate

↓ ATP ↘ ADP

Fructose-1, 6-diphosphate

⇣ series of reactions

Pyruvic acid
(2-ketopropanoic acid) ⇌ Lactic acid
(2-hydroxypropanoic acid)

⇣ further metabolism, usually
via the tricarboxylic acid (Krebs) cycle

The metabolism of glycogen.

Cornforth was born on 7 September 1917 in Sydney, Australia. He began his academic training at the University of Sydney and then went to Oxford University, where he obtained his doctorate in 1941. For the next five years he worked with Robert Robinson, who 30 years earlier had worked in Sydney and who was to receive the 1947 Nobel Chemistry Prize for his work on plant alkaloids. At about this time Cornforth's hearing began to deteriorate and he was soon totally deaf. He worked for the British Medical Research Council from 1946 until 1962, when he became Director of the Milstead Laboratory of Chemical Enzymology, Shell Research Ltd. He remained there until 1975, when he accepted a professorship at the University of Sussex; he had previously been an Associate Professor at Warwick University (1965-1971) and Visiting Professor at Sussex (1971-1975).

In his researches, Cornforth studied enzymes, trying to determine specifically which group of hydrogen atoms in a biologically active compound is replaced by an enzyme to bring about a given effect. He painstakingly developed techniques to pinpoint a specific hydrogen component by using the element's three isotopes - normal hydrogen (^1H), deuterium (^2H) and tritium (^3H). Each isotope has a different speed of reaction and, by careful observation and many experiments, Cornforth was able to identify precisely which hydrogen atom was affected by enzyme action. He was able, for example, to establish the orientation of all the hydrogen atoms in the cholesterol molecule.

Coulson, Charles Alfred (*1910-1974*), was a British theoretical chemist whose major contribution to the science was his molecular orbital theory and the concept of partial valency. He also worked - and held professorships - in physics and mathematics and published hundreds of papers on topics as diverse as pure mathematics and the effects of radiation on bacteria.

Coulson was born in Dudley, Yorkshire, on 13 December 1910, one of twin sons. His family moved to Bristol in 1920 and he went to Clifton College, from which he won an open scholarship to Trinity College, Cambridge, in 1928. He graduated in mathematics three years later. He was awarded a research scholarship, and later an open scholarship, and worked with Lennard Jones, the first holder of the Chair in Theoretical Chemistry. It was then that he was introduced to wave mechanics and quantum theory, to which he was to devote himself so successfully for much of his career. He remained at Cambridge until 1938, when he got married and took up an appointment as Senior Lecturer in Mathematics at the University of Dundee. In 1930 he had adopted deep Christian beliefs that were to lead him to become a pacifist; for many years he was chairman of the charity Oxfam (1965-1971).

In Dundee, Coulson taught and carried out research. His first book, *Waves* (1941), ran to seven editions and is still in worldwide use. In 1945 he moved to Oxford University to join the Physical Chemistry Laboratory as a "theoretician", and soon became also a mathematics lecturer. Two years later he accepted the chair of Theoretical Physics at King's College, London. His second book, *Electricity*, was published in 1948 and was another immediate success.

In 1952 came the appearance of his third best seller, *Valence*. In the same year he returned to Oxford as a Professor of Mathematics. But he continued to teach chemistry and physics, beginning his famous summer schools in 1955. In 1963 he became Curator of the Mathematics Institute (where he started the first university computing department), and was appointed its President in 1971. He further demonstrated his versatility by becoming Oxford's first Professor of Theoretical Chemistry. He died suddenly in 1974 from an illness that had begun some years earlier.

Coulson's great contribution to chemistry was the way in which he influenced thinking about forces in molecules. Since J.J. Thomson's discovery of the electron and Ernest Rutherford's of the atomic nucleus, it had been obvious that chemical bonds must involve electrons, but nobody fully understood what form this involvement takes. The quantum theory of the time showed how electrons occupy energy levels in atoms, but it gave no real help with molecular forces. In the 1920s wave mechanics began to revolutionize the subject, but Erwin Schrödinger's famous wave equation becomes hopelessly complicated in all but the simplest cases. Coulson used powerful methods of approximation and computation to obtain some solutions of the wave equation for molecular systems.

The molecular orbital theory that Coulson developed is an extension of atomic quantum theory and deals with "allowed" states of electrons in association with two or more atomic nuclei, treating a molecule as a whole. He was thus able to explain properly phenomena such as the structure of benzene and other conjugated systems, and invoked what he called partial valency to account for the bonding in such compounds as diborane - neither of which could be accounted for by the alternative valence bond system proposed by Linus Pauling and others.

Practical applications of Coulson's molecular orbital theory have included the prediction of

'Classical' (Kekulé) structure of benzene with alternate double and single carbon— carbon bonds which would not be equivalent.

Molecular orbital structure of benzene with six equivalent bonds; each carbon atom has three complete bonds and two partial bonds to complete its valency of four.

Diborane depicted with full and partial bonds.

new aromatic systems and accurate forecasting of bond lengths and angles.

Coulson also contributed significantly to the understanding of the solid state (particularly metals), such as the structure of graphite and its "compounds". He developed many mathematical techniques for solving chemical and physical problems while retaining the capacity to produce simple, intuitive models of the systems he was studying, and the ability to formulate these models in manipulatable mathematical terms.

Crookes, William (*1832–1919*), was a British chemist and physicist who, in a scientific career lasting more than 50 years, made many fundamental contributions to both sciences. One of his major achievements in chemistry was the discovery of the element thallium. He never held a senior academic post, and carried out most of his researches in his own laboratory.

Crookes was born in London on 17 June 1832, the eldest of the sixteen children of a tailor and businessman. Little is known of his early education but in 1848 he began a chemistry course at the new Royal College of Chemistry under August von Hofmann, who later made him a junior assistant, promoting him to Senior Assistant in 1851. Crookes' only academic posts were as Superintendent of the Meteorological Department at the Radcliffe Observatory, Oxford (1854–1855), and Lecturer in Chemistry at Chester Training College (1855–1856). He left Chester after only one year, dissatisfied at being unable to carry out original research and after having inherited enough money to make him financially independent.

He returned to London and became secretary of the London Photographic Society and editor of its *Journal* in 1858. The following year he set up a chemical laboratory at his London home and founded as sole manager and editor the weekly *Chemical News*, which covered all aspects of theoretical and industrial chemistry and which he edited until 1906. He carried out also experiments in physics, particularly on spectroscopy and electric discharges in gases, and invented the radioscope and the spinthariscope (for detecting alpha-rays). He was knighted in 1897 and made a Member of the Order of Merit in 1910. He died in London on 4 April 1919.

One of Crookes' earliest pieces of chemical research concerned the preparation and properties of potassium selenocyanate (potassium cyanoselenate (VI)), which he made using selenium isolated from 5kg of waste from a German sulphuric acid works. Then in 1861, while examining selenium samples by means of a spectroscope – the method newly developed by Robert Bunsen and Gustav Kirchhoff – Crookes observed a transitory green line in the spectrum and attributed it to a new element which he called thallium (from the Greek *thallos*, meaning a budding shoot). Over the next few years he determined the properties of thallium and its compounds; using thallium nitrate and a specially constructed sensitive balance he measured thallium's atomic weight (relative atomic mass) as 203.715 ± 0.0365 (modern value: 204.39).

In the 1880s Crookes studied the phosphorescent spectra of rare earth minerals, principally substances containing yttrium and samarium. He made the first references to what Frederick Soddy was to call isotopes. While experimenting with radium, he devised the spinthariscope. The instrument consists of a screen coated with zinc sulphide at the end of a tube fitted with a low-powered lens. When alpha-particles emitted from a radioactive source (such as radium) hit the screen they produce a small flash of light.

Crookes' interests continued to widen. Topics covered by his publications included chemical analysis; the manufacture of sugar from sugar-beet; dyeing and printing of textiles; oxidation of platinum, iridium and rhodium; use of carbolic acid (phenol) as an antiseptic in the treatment of diseases in cattle; the origin and formation of diamonds in South Africa; and the use of artificial fertilizers and their manufacture from atmospheric nitrogen. Crookes was never afraid of pursuing an idea counter to the trend of contemporary opinion. For several years, for example, he was very interested in spiritualism and published several papers that described experiments undertaken by a medium. To many of his scientific colleagues this was akin to heresy!

Curie, Marie (*1867-1934*), was a Polish-born French scientist who, with her husband **Pierre Curie** (*1859-1906*), was an early investigator of radioactivity. The Curies discovered the radioactive elements polonium and radium, for which achievement they shared the 1903 Nobel Prize in Physics with Henri Becquerel. Madame Curie went on to study the chemistry and medical applications of radium, and was awarded the 1911 Nobel Prize in Chemistry in recognition of her work in isolating the pure metal.

Madame Curie's Polish maiden name was Manya Skłodowska. She was born in Warsaw on 7 November 1867, at a time when Poland was under Russian domination after the unsuccessful revolt of 1863. Her parents were teachers and soon after Manya was born - their fifth child - they lost their teaching posts and had to take in boarders. Their young daughter worked long hours helping with the meals, but nevertheless won a medal for excellence at the local High School, where the examinations were held in Russian. No higher education was available so Manya took a job as a governess, sending part of her savings to Paris to help to pay for her elder sister's medical studies. Her sister qualified and married a fellow doctor in 1891 and Manya went to join them in Paris. She entered the Sorbonne and studied physics and mathematics, graduating top of her class. In 1894 she met the French chemist Pierre Curie and they were married the following year.

Pierre Curie was born in Paris on 15 May 1859, the son of a doctor. He was educated privately and at the Sorbonne, becoming an assistant there in 1878. He discovered the piezoelectric effect and, after being appointed head of the laboratory of the École de Physique et Chimie, went on to study magnetism and formulate Curie's law (which states that magnetic susceptibility is inversely proportional to absolute temperature). In 1895 he discovered the Curie point, the critical temperature at which a paramagnetic substance become ferromagnetic. In the same year he married Manya Skłodowska.

From 1896 the Curies worked together on radio-activity, building on the results of Wilhelm Röntgen (who had discovered X-rays) and Henri Becquerel (who had discovered that similar rays are emitted by uranium salts). Madame Curie discovered that thorium also emits radiation and found that the mineral pitchblende was even more radioactive than could be accounted for by any uranium and thorium content. The Curies then carried out an exhaustive search and in July 1898 announced the discovery of polonium, followed in December of that year with the discovery of radium. They eventually prepared 1 gram of pure radium chloride - from 8 tonnes of waste pitchblende from Austria. They also established that beta-rays (now known to consist of electrons) are negatively charged particles.

In 1906 Pierre Curie was run down and killed by a horse-drawn carriage. Marie took over his post at the Sorbonne, becoming the first woman to teach there, and concentrated all her energies into research and caring for her daughters (one of whom, Irène, was to later marry Frédéric Joliot and become a famous scientist and Nobel prizewinner). In 1910 with André Debierne (1874-1949), who in 1899 had discovered actinium in pitchblende, she isolated pure radium metal.

At the outbreak of World War I in 1914 Madame Curie helped to equip ambulances with X-ray equipment, which she drove to the front lines. The International Red Cross made her head of its Radiological Service. Assisted by Irène Curie and Martha Klein at the Radium Institute she held courses for medical orderlies and doctors, teaching them how to use the new technique. By the late 1920s her health began to deteriorate: continued exposure to high-energy radiation had given her leukaemia. She entered a sanatorium at Haute Savoie and died there on 4 July 1934, a few months after her daughter and son-in-law, the Joliot-Curies, had announced the discovery of artifical radioactivity.

Throughout much of her life Marie Curie was poor and the painstaking radium extractions were carried out in primitive conditions. The Curies refused to patent any of their discoveries, wanting them freely to benefit everyone. The Nobel prize-money and other financial rewards were used to finance further research. One of the outstanding applications of their work has been the use of radiation to treat cancer, one form of which cost Marie Curie her life.

D

Dalton, John (*1766-1844*), was an English chemist, one of the founders of atomic theory. Some of his proposals have since proved to be incorrect, but his chief contribution was that he channelled the thinking of contemporary scientists along the correct lines, particularly in his method of using established facts to explain a new phenomenon.

Dalton was born in the village of Eaglesfield near Cockermouth in Cumbria on or about 6 September 1766. He was the third of six children of a weaver, who was a devout Quaker and did not register the date of his son's birth. Dalton attended the village Quaker school and by the age of 12 was running it. He later became headmaster of a school in Kendal, before taking up a post in 1793 to teach mathematics and natural philosophy in Manchester. Dalton was largely self-taught, his Quaker beliefs excluding him from attending Oxford or Cambridge universities (at that time open only to members of the Church of England).

Even before he moved to Manchester, a wealthy Quaker friend, the blind philosopher John Gough, had stimulated in Dalton an interest in meteorology and for 57 years (beginning in 1787) he kept a diary of observations about the weather. He gave lectures on this subject to the Manchester Literary and Philosophical Society, of which he became honorary Secretary and later President. He determined that the density of water varies with temperature, reaching a maximum at 42.5°F (i.e. 6.1°C; the modern value of this temperature is 4°C). He also lectured about colour blindness, a condition he shared with his brother and which for a time was known as Daltonism. He resigned his lectureship in Manchester in 1799 in order to pursue his own researches, working as a private tutor to make a living. He did, however, remain as the Society's Secretary and was given accommodation in a house they bought for him. This house, still containing many of Dalton's records, was destroyed in a bombing raid in 1940 during World War II. He was awarded a government pension of £150 in 1833, which was doubled three years later. He died in Manchester on 27 July 1844.

From his interest in the weather, atmosphere and gases in general, Dalton in 1803 proposed his law of partial pressures (which states that, in a mixture of gases, the total pressure is the sum of the pressures that each component would exert if it alone occupied the same volume). He also studied the variation of a gas's volume with temperature, concluding (independently of Joseph Gay-Lussac) that all gases have the same coefficient of thermal expansion. Gaseous diffusion and the solubility of gases in water were also the subjects of his experiments.

The work on the absorption of gases led Dalton to formulate his atomic theory – he considered that gases must be made up of particles that can somehow occupy spaces between the particles that make up water, and that in a mixture of gases the different particles must intermingle rather than separate into layers depending on their density. When presented in his book *New System of Chemical Philosophy* (1808), the idea that atoms of different elements have different weights was supported by a list of atomic weights and his newly devised system of chemical symbols. Combinations of element symbols could be made to represent compounds.

Many of the atomic weights (confused with equivalent weights) were incorrect, for example oxygen =8 and carbon=6, but a pattern had been established, introducing order to a science that was hitherto little more than a collection of facts.

Taking into account later work, Dalton's atomic theory may be summarized as follows:
(a) Matter cannot be subdivided indefinitely, because each element consists of indivisible particles called atoms.
(b) The atoms of the same element are alike in every respect, having the same weight (mass), volume and chemical properties; atoms of different elements have different properties.
(c) In chemical combinations of different elements, atoms join together in simple definite numbers to form compound atoms (now called molecules).

His formula for water - one hydrogen atom combined with one oxygen atom - was wrong, although he was more fortunate with carbon monoxide ("carbonic oxide") and carbon dioxide ("carbonic acid"). But nevertheless he did bring a sort of order to the existing chaos, and provided a foundation for several generations of scientists. Several years later Jöns Berzelius was to supersede Dalton's system with the chemical symbols and formulae still used today.

Throughout his life Dalton retained his Quaker habits and dress, and new acquaintances were often taken aback by his appearance. He continued to keep his diary, which eventually ran to 200,000 entries. He distrusted the results of other workers, preferring to rely on his own experiences. As he grew older he became almost a recluse, with few friends and deeply involved in his pursuit of knowledge. And although he shunned fame and glory, he became famous even outside the realms of science. When his coffin stood on public display in Manchester Town Hall, more than 40,000 people filed past to pay their respects.

Davy, Humphry (*1778-1829*), was an English chemist who is best known for his discovery of the elements sodium and potassium and for inventing a safety lamp for use in mines.

Davy was born on 17 December 1778 at Penzance, Cornwall, the son of well-to-do parents. He was educated in Penzance and, from 1793, in Truro, where he studied classics. But his father died a year later and, to help to support the family, the young Davy became apprenticed to a Penzance surgeon-apothecary, J. Bingham Borlase. His interest in chemistry began in 1797 through reading Antoine Lavoisier's *Traité Elémentaire*, and by 1799 he was working on the therapeutic uses of gases as an assistant at the Pneumatic Institute in Bristol.

Following Alessandro Volta's announcement in 1800 of the voltaic cell, Davy began his researches in electrochemistry. He moved to the Royal Institution in London in 1801, where he became influenced by Count Rumford and Henry Cavendish. He was knighted by the Prince Regent in 1812 and three days later married a wealthy widow named Jane Apreece. In 1813 he took on Michael Faraday as a laboratory assistant, who accompanied him on a tour of Europe. When he returned in 1815 Davy designed his miner's safety lamp, which would burn safely even in an explosive mixture of air and fire damp (methane). He did not patent the lamp, a fact that was to lead to an acrimonious claim to priority by the steam locomotive engineer George Stephenson. Davy was created a baronet in 1818 and two years later he succeeded the botanist Joseph Banks (1743–1820) as President of the Royal Society. He took seriously ill in 1827 and went abroad in 1828 to try to improve his health. He settled in Rome in early 1829 but suffered a heart attack and died in Geneva, Switzerland, on 29 May of that year.

While Davy was working in Bristol (1799) he prepared nitrous oxide (dinitrogen monoxide) by heating ammonium nitrate. He investigated the effects of breathing the gas, showing that it causes intoxication (although it was to be another 45 years before the gas was used as a dental anaesthetic). His early experiments on electrolysis of aqueous solutions (from 1800) led Davy to suggest its large-scale use in the alkali industry. He theorized that the mechanism of electrolysis could be explained in terms of species that have opposite electric charges, which could be arranged on a scale of relative affinities - the foundation of the modern electrochemical series. The climax of this work came in 1807 with the isolation of sodium and potassium metal by the electrolysis of their fused salts. Later, after consultation with Jöns Berzelius, he also isolated calcium, strontium, barium and magnesium. His intensive study of the alkali metals provided proof of Lavoisier's idea that all alkalis contain oxygen. In 1808 he first isolated boron, by heating borax with potassium.

Davy also initially supported Lavoisier's contention that oxygen is present in all acids. But in 1810, after doing quantitative analytical work with muriatic acid (hydrochloric acid) he disproved this hypothesis. He went on to show that its oxidation product, oxymuriatic acid (discovered in 1774 by Karl Scheele), is an element, which he named chlorine. He explained its bleaching action and later prepared two of its oxides and chlorides of sulphur and phosphorus. He also suggested that the element common to all acids is hydrogen, not oxygen.

Davy was reluctant to accept the atomic theory of his contemporary John Dalton, but in the face of mounting evidence finally concurred and attempted to apply the laws of definite and multiple proportions to various compounds. He determined the "proportional weights" (relative atomic masses), of various elements, including chlorine at 33.9 (actual value 35.5), oxygen 15 (16), potassium 40.5 (39.1) and sulphur 30 (32).

The safety lamp of 1815 was designed after a series of laboratory experiments on explosive mixtures. Davy showed that a flame continued to burn safely in such a mixture if it is surrounded by a fine metal mesh to dissipate heat, if only a narrow air inlet is used, and if the air inside the lamp is diluted with an unreactive gas such as carbon dioxide.

Numerous other achievements can be attributed to this great scientist. Davy introduced a chemical approach to agriculture, the tanning industry and mineralogy; he designed an arc lamp for illumination, an electrolytic process for the desalination of sea water, and a method of cathodic protection for the copper-clad ships of the day by connecting them to zinc plates. But his genius has been described as erratic. At his best he was a scientist of great perception, a prolific laboratory worker and a brilliant lecturer. At other times he was unsystematic, readily distracted and prone to hasty decisions. He was never trained as a chemist, and consequently his excellence in qualitative work was not always matched by quantitative skills. He sought and won many scientific honours, which he then jealously guarded, even going so far in 1824 as trying to oppose the election of his protégé Michael Faraday to the Royal Society.

Debye, Peter Joseph Willem (*1884-1966*), was a Dutch-born American physical chemist who in a long career made many important contributions to the science. He was awarded the 1936 Nobel Prize in Chemistry for his work on dipole moments and molecular structure.

Debye was born on 24 March 1884 at Maastricht in the Netherlands. From 1900 to 1905 he went to school at the Technische Hochschule over the border in Aachen, Germany, where he qualified as an electrical engineer. He then became assistant to Arnold Sommerfeld (1868-1951) at the University of Munich, gaining his PhD in 1910. The next few years saw a remarkable progress from one distinguished post to another, starting in Zurich (1910) where he succeeded Albert Einstein as Professor of Theoretical Physics and culminating, via Utrecht (1912) and Göttingen (1914), in a return to Zurich in 1920 as Professor of Experimental Physics and Director of the Physics Institute. By 1927 Debye moved to Leipzig, where he took over from Friedrich Ostwald,

and in 1934 he went to Berlin to supervise the building of the Kaiser Wilhelm Institute of Physics, which he renamed the Max Planck Institute.

In the late 1930s Debye found himself in difficulties with the Nazi authorities in Germany – mainly because of his Dutch nationality. He was lecturing at Cornell University in the United States in 1940 when Germany invaded the Netherlands, whereupon he accepted the post of professor and head of the chemistry department at Cornell. He became an American citizen in 1946 and formally retired in 1952, although he remained active until his death at the age of 82 on 2 November 1966 at Ithaca, New York.

Debye's first major contribution was a modification of Einstein's theory of specific heats to include compressibility and expansivity, leading to the expressions for specific heat capacities, $C_v = aT^3$ etc., as T approaches absolute zero. The "Debye extrapolation" incorporating these terms acknowledges the action of intermolecular forces. His studies of dielectric constants led to the explanation of their temperature dependence and of their importance in the interpretation of dipole moments as indicators of molecular structure. The unit of dielectric constant is now called the debye.

While he was at Göttingen in 1916, Debye followed on the work of Max von Laue and the Braggs on X-ray crystallography. He showed that the thermal motion of the atoms in a solid affects the X-ray interfaces and explained (using his specific heat theories) the temperature dependence of X-ray intensities. This work provided the basis for his observation with Paul Scherrer (1890-1969) that randomly orientated particles can produce X-ray diffraction patterns of a characteristic kind. Thus the need for comparatively large single crystals was avoided and powder X-ray diffraction analysis – now called the Debye-Scherrer method – became a new and versatile analytical tool.

At Zurich, Debye's work was dominated by his interest in electrolysis and the extension in 1923 of Svante Arrhenius' theory of ionization developed by himself and Erich Hückel. The Debye-Hückel theory compares the ordering of ions in solution to the situation in the crystalline state and postulates (a) that ionization is complete in a strong electrolyte and (b) that each ion is surrounded by a cluster of ions of opposite charge. The extent of this ordering is determined by the equilibrium between thermal motion and interionic forces. Also at Zurich, Debye used the quantum theory to derive a quantitative interpretation of the Compton effect (the small change in wavelength that occurs when an X-ray is scattered by collision with an electron). This laid the foundation for other researchers' work on electron diffraction.

In the 1930s Debye moved on to a study of the scattering of light by solutions. He showed that sound waves in a liquid can behave like a diffraction grating and developed techniques in turbidimetry which led to useful molecular weight determinations for polymers. In the last phase of his researches Debye pursued his interest in polymers, investigating their behaviour in terms of viscosity, diffusion and sedimentation, and he was involved in studies of synthetic rubber.

Debye was an excellent teacher as well as a brilliant experimentalist. But perhaps the outstanding feature of his long career was the very clear thinking that enabled him to persist with incomplete or inadequate theories until he had derived important generalizations.

Diels, Otto (*1876-1954*), was a German organic chemist who many fundamental discoveries, including (with Kurt Alder) the diene synthesis or Diels–Alder reaction. He shared with Alder the 1950 Nobel Prize in Chemistry.

Diels was born in Hamburg on 23 January 1876 into a talented academic family. His father Hermann Diels (1848-1922) was Professor of Classical Philology at Berlin University and his brothers Paul and Ludwig became professors of, respectively, philology and botany. During his school years Otto Diels became interested in chemistry and carried out a series of experiments with his brother Ludwig. In 1895 he went to his father's university to study chemistry under the great organic chemist Emil Fischer, obtaining his doctorate in 1899. He continued research as Fischer's assistant and became a lecturer in 1904. He moved to the Chemical Institute of the then Royal Friedrich Wilhelm University in 1914 and two years later was invited by the Christian Albrecht University in Kiel to serve as Director of their Chemical Institute, where he remained for 32 years until he retired.

Diels married in 1909 and had three sons and two daughters; two of his sons were killed on the eastern front near the end of World War II. After the destruction of his Institute by enemy action during the war, Diels planned to retire in 1945 but was persuaded to stay on to help with its rebuilding. He finally retired in 1948, and died in Kiel on 7 March 1954.

In 1906, while working in Berlin, Diels discovered carbon suboxide (tricarbon dioxide), which he prepared by dehydrating malonic acid (propandioic acid) with phosphorus pentoxide (phosphorus(V) oxide):

$$O = C - CH_2 - C = O \xrightarrow{P_2O_5}$$
$$\qquad | \qquad\qquad\quad |$$
$$\qquad OH \qquad\qquad OH$$

malonic acid
(propandioic acid)

$$O = C = C = C = O \quad + \quad 2H_2O$$

carbon suboxide
(tricarbon dioxide)

A year later he published the first edition of his textbook of organic chemistry (*Einführung in die organische Chemie*) which, because of its scope and clarity, became one of the most popular books of its kind.

Diels' investigation of the nature and structure of the biologically important compound cholesterol began as early as 1906. He isolated pure cholesterol from gall-stones and converted it to "Diels acid". But it was not until 1927 that he successfully dehydrogenated cholesterol (by the drastic process of heating it with selenium at 300°C) to produce "Diels hydrocarbon". This substance was later shown to be 3′methyl-1,2-cyclopentanophenanthrene ($C_{18}H_{16}$), an aromatic hydrocarbon closely related to the skeletal structure of all steroids, of which cholesterol is one. In 1935 he synthesized the $C_{18}H_{16}$ compound and showed it to be identical with Diels hydrocarbon. This work proved to be a turning point in the understanding of the chemistry of cholesterol and other steroids, although it was not until about 1955 that its structure was completely known.

cholesterol

$$\xrightarrow[300°C]{Se}$$

Diels hydrocarbon
(3′-methyl-1, 2-cyclopentanophenanthrene)

Working with his assistant Kurt Alder, Diels spent much of the rest of his life developing the diene synthesis, which first achieved success in 1928 when they combined cyclopentadiene with maleic anhydride (*cis*-butenedioic anhydride) to form a complex derivative of phthalic anhydride. Generally, conjugated dienes (compounds with two double bonds separated by a single bond) react with dienophiles (compounds with one double bond activated by a neighbouring substituent such as a carbonyl or carboxyl group) to form a six-membered ring. For example, butadiene (but-1,3-diene) reacts with acrolein (prop-2-en-1-al) to give tetrahydrobenzaldehyde (cyclohex-4-en-1-carbaldehyde):

$$CH_2 = CH - CH = CH_2 \quad + \quad CH_2 = CH - CHO$$

butadiene
(but-1, 3-diene)

acrolein
(prop-2-en-1-al)

$$\longrightarrow$$

tetrahydrobenzaldehyde
(cyclohex-4-en-1-carbaldehyde)

Applications of the Diels–Alder synthesis are numerous throughout organic chemistry and it is of great importance because many reactions of this type occur easily at low temperatures and give good yields.

Diels was considered always to be a reserved man, but one with a good sense of humour, and he was liked and respected by his students who enjoyed his well planned lectures and experimental demonstrations.

Dulong, Pierre Louis (*1785–1838*), was a French chemist, best known for his work with Alexis Petit that resulted in Dulong and Petit's law which states that, for any element, the product of its specific heat and atomic weight is a constant, a quantity they termed the atomic heat. In modern terms, the product of the specific heat capacity of an element (expressed in joules per gram per kelvin) and the relative atomic mass is about 25.

Dulong was born on or about 12 February 1785 in Rouen. He studied at the École Polytechnique in Paris, training initially as a doctor. He married young and had to take a teaching post to keep his family and finance his research; one such (1811) was at the École Normale and another (1813) was at the École Veterinaire at Alfort. He returned to Paris in 1820 to become Professor of Chemistry at the Faculté des Sciences, moving back to the École Polytechnique, becoming its Director of Studies in 1830. He was elected to the physics section of the French Academy of Sciences in 1823. He died in Paris on or about 18 July 1838.

During Dulong's early work in chemistry he was an assistant to Claude Berthollet, and he studied the oxalates of calcium, strontium and barium. In 1811 he discovered the explosive compound nitrogen trichloride, an accident with which cost him a finger and the sight in one eye. He resolved the contemporary dispute among chemists about the composition of phosphorus and phosphoric acids, identifying two new acids in the process. In 1815 he began working with Alexis Petit, and at first they applied their researches to the problem of measuring heat. They determined the absolute coefficient expansion of mercury, so improving the accuracy of mercury thermometers. They then explored the laws of cooling in a vacuum, work later extended by Josef Stefan (1835–1893).

Then in 1818 Dulong and Petit began studying the specific heat capacity of elements, measuring this quantity for sulphur and 12 metals. When they multiplied each result by the elements atomic weight (relative atomic mass), they obtained values that were in close agreement with each other. They showed that an element's specific heat capacity is inversely proportional to its relative atomic mass (Dulong and Petit's law). Its chief application was in the estimation of the atomic weights of new elements.

After Petit died in 1820, Dulong continued to work on specific heat capacities, publishing his findings in 1829. He concluded that, under the same conditions of temperature and pressure, equal volumes of all gases evolve or absorb the same quantity of heat when they are suddenly expanded or compressed to the same fraction of their original volumes. He also deduced that the accompanying temperature changes are inversely proportional to the specific heat capacities of the gases at constant volume. He also collaborated with the French physicist Dominique Arago (1786–1853) on a study of the pressure of steam at high temperatures. In this rather hazardous research working at pressures up to 27 atmospheres, their results were in agreement with Boyle's law. Dulong's last paper on the heats of chemical reaction was published in 1838 after his death.

Dumas, Jean Baptiste André (*1800-1884*), was a French chemist who made contributions to organic analysis and synthesis, and to the determination of atomic weights through the measurement of vapour densities.

Dumas was born on or about 19 July 1800 in Alais (now Alès), Gard. He was educated at the local college and intended to enter the navy, but changed his mind after the overthrow of Napoleon I and became instead apprenticed to an apothecary, also in Alais. But he soon moved to Geneva, Switzerland, and in 1816 was working in the laboratory of a pharmacist there (who was investigating plant extracts). He studied also under the Swiss physicist Pierre Prévost (1751-1839) and the botanist Augustin Candolle (1778-1841), and in 1822 accepted an invitation from Alexander von Humboldt to go to Paris, where he took up an appointment at the École Polytechnique and held the Chair in Chemistry at the Lyceum (later Athenaeum), succeeding André Ampère. The following year he became a lecturing assistant to the French chemist Louis Thénard (1777-1857) at the École Polytechnique, whom he succeeded as Professor of Chemistry in 1835. Following the political upheavals of 1848 Dumas abandoned much of his scientific work for politics and public office. He served under Napoleon III as Minister of Agriculture and Commerce, Minister of Education, and Master of the Mint. After the deposition of Napoleon in 1871, Dumas left politics. He died in Cannes on 11 April 1884.

While he was an 18-year-old in Geneva, Dumas was involved in the study of the use of iodine to treat goitre (endemic in Switzerland at that time). Then under Prévost he - unsuccessfully - investigated the physiological effects of digitalis. They also studied blood and showed that urea is present in the blood of animals from which the kidneys have been removed, proving that one of the functions of the kidneys is to remove urea from the blood, not to produce it.

In 1826 Dumas began working on atomic theory. He determined the molecular weights of many substances by measuring their vapour densities and concluded that "in all elastic fluids observed under the same conditions, the molecules are placed at equal distances" - that is, they are present in equal numbers.

His important work on the theory of substitution in organic compounds was inspired at a soirée at the Tuilleries when the candles gave off irritating fumes. The candle wax had been bleached with chlorine, some of which had been retained and during combustion was converted to hydrogen chloride. Dumas soon proved by experiments that organic substances treated with chlorine retain it in combination, and proposed that the chlorine had displaced hydrogen, atom for atom. He studied the action of chlorine on alcohol (ethanol) to produce chloral (trichloroethanal), which he decomposed with alkali to give chloroform (trichloromethane) and formic acid (methanoic acid). He also chlorinated acetic acid (ethanoic acid) to give trichloracetic acid (trichlorethanoic acid), thus proving his theory of substitution. He had shown that atoms of apparently opposite electrical charge had replaced each other, in opposition to the dualistic theory of organic chemistry proposed by Jöns Berzelius, who in 1830 was at the height of his fame and influence.

Together with the Belgian chemist Jean Stas (1813-1891), who was at that time his student, Dumas investigated the action of alkalis on alcohols and ethers, which led to a study of the acids produced by the oxidation of alcohols.

In 1833 Dumas worked out an absolute method for the estimation of the amount of nitrogen in an organic compound - which still forms the basis of modern methods of analysis. The nitrogen in a sample of known weight is eliminated in gaseous form and estimated by direct measurement. The sample is heated with cupric oxide (copper(II) oxide) and oxidized completely in a stream of carbon dioxide; the gaseous products of combustion are passed over a heated copper spiral and the nitrogen collected in a gas burette over concentrated potassium hydroxide solution.

Also with Stas, in 1849 he revised the atomic weight (relative atomic mass) of carbon to 12 (from Berzelius' value of 12.24). He went on to correct the atomic weights of 30 elements - half the total number known at that time - referring to the hydrogen value as 1. With Milne Edwards he investigated the way in which bees convert sugar to fat (wax). His last papers were on alcoholic fermentation (1872) and on the occlusion of oxygen in silver (1878).

Eigen, Manfred (*1927-*), is a German physical chemist who shared the 1967 Nobel Prize in Chemistry with Ronald Norrish and George Porter for his work on the study of fast reactions in liquids.

Eigen was born in Bochum, Ruhr, on 9 May 1927, the son of a musician. He was educated at

Göttingen University and on his eighteenth birthday, one day after the formal ending of World War II, he was drafted to do military service with an anti-aircraft artillery unit. He later returned to Göttingen, gained his doctorate in 1951, and worked as a research assistant there for the next two years. In 1953 he moved to the Max Planck Institute for Physical Chemistry, becoming a research fellow (1958), head of the Department of Biochemical Kinetics (1962), and eventually Director of the Institute.

Eigen studied fast reaction kinetics by disturbing the equilibria in liquid systems using short changes of temperature, pressure or electric field (whereas Norrish and Porter had used flashes of light to disturb equilibria in gaseous systems). He investigated particularly very fast biochemical reactions that take place in the body, trying to discover how rapidly reactions proceed among the working molecules of life and how a particular sequence of chemical units could come about by chance in the time available. With his colleague Ruthild Winkler he tried to relate chance and chemistry in processes that could have led to the origin of life on Earth. They questioned how molecules with the right kind of properties might form and what would be the simplest combination of molecules that could survive and evolve into the first primitive organisms. Eigen theorized that in the "primeval soup" of the early Earth, cycles of chemical reactions would have occurred, one reproducing nucleic acids (which possess information but have a very limited chemical function) and one reproducing proteins (which ensured chemical function and reproduction of the information contained in the nucleic acids). He postulated that eventually a number of the nucleic acid cycles and proteins would have come to coexist and form a "hypercycle". By natural selection the best hypercycle would have eventually caused the first organism to evolve – a chance set of molecules coming together in a single drop – providing a possible theory of the chemical transition from non-life to life.

Emeléus, Harry Julius (*1903–*   ), is a British chemist who made wide-ranging investigations in inorganic chemistry, studying particularly nonmetallic elements and their compounds.

Emeléus was born in London on 22 June 1903. He attended Hastings Grammar School and Imperial College, London. After graduation he went to Karlsruhe University where he met several of the German exponents of preparative inorganic chemistry. From 1929 to 1931 he worked at Princeton University in the United States, and it was there that he met and married Mary Catherine Horton. He returned to Imperial College to continue his researches and in 1945 became Professor of Inorganic Chemistry at Cambridge University, where he remained until he retired in 1970.

Emeléus began his researches during his first period at Imperial College with a study of the phosphorescence of white phosphorus, showing that the glow was caused by the slow oxidation of phosphorus(III) oxide formed in a preliminary non-luminous oxidation. He also studied the inhibition of the glow by organic vapours. His work continued with spectrographic investigations of the phosphorescent flames of carbon disulphide, ether (ethoxyethane), arsenic, sulphur and the phosphorescence of phosphorus(V) oxide illuminated with ultraviolet light. The results provided new information about the mechanisms of combustion reactions.

While at Princeton Emeléus worked on the photosensitization by ammonia of the polymerization of ethene (ethylene), the photochemical interaction of amines and ethene, and the photochemistry of the decomposition of amines and their reaction with carbon monoxide. This phase of his work, on chemical kinetics, helped to prepare him for the great career in chemistry that lay ahead.

On his return to Imperial College he began investigating the hydrides of silicon, especially the kinetics of the oxidation of mono-, di- and trisilane. He also studied the isotopic composition of water from different sources. He developed a very accurate method of measuring densities and showed that naturally occurring water exhibits a small variation in deuterium content, and that distillation, freezing and adsorption methods can all effect some degree of separation of the two isotopic forms. Continuing his work on silicon hydrides, he prepared tetrasilane, Si_4H_{10} (the silicon analogue of butane), by treating magnesium silicide with dilute hydrochloric acid, and went on to produce alkyl and aryl derivatives of the silanes. In 1938 Emeléus and John Anderson published *Modern Aspects of Inorganic Chemistry*.

When Emeléus moved to Cambridge in 1945 he started studying the halogen fluorides. He showed that the much sought after trifluoroidomethane, CIF_3 – the key to many synthetic processes – can be made by reacting iodine(V) fluoride with carbon(IV) iodide. He prepared polyhalides of potassium and demonstrated that bromine(III) fluoride could be used as a nonaqueous solvent in the study of acid/base reactions. In 1949 he prepared organometallic fluorides of mercury and went on to make various derivatives containing the methylsilyl group, CH_3SiH_2-. By 1959 he was working with the fluorides of vanadium, niobium, tantalum and tungsten and much of his research in the 1960s concerned the fluoralkyl derivatives of metals. He summarized much of his work in *The Chemistry of Fluorine and its Compounds* (1969).

Eméléus received many honours but remains an extremely modest man, never claiming that the results of his work were of outstanding significance. But his influence on inorganic chemistry since 1945 has been enormous.

Fajans, Kasimir (*1887–1975*), was a Polish-born American chemist, best known for his work on radioactivity and isotopes and for formulating rules that help to explain valence and chemical bonding.

Fajans was born in Warsaw on 27 May 1887. He was educated at Leipzig, Heidelberg (where he gained his PhD in 1909), Zurich and Manchester. From 1911 to 1917 he worked at the Technische Hochschule at Karlsruhe, and between 1917 and 1935 he held appointments at the Munich Institute of Physical Chemistry, where he rose from Assistant Professor to be the Director. In 1936 he emigrated to the United States and served as a professor at the University of Michigan, Ann Arbor. He became an American citizen in 1942. He died, aged 88, on 18 May 1975.

In 1913 Fajans formulated, simultaneously with but independently of Frederick Soddy, the theory of isotopes – that is, elements that have the same atomic number but different atomic weights (relative atomic masses). He showed that uranium-X_1 (itself a decay product by alpha-ray emission of uranium-238) disintegrates by beta-ray emission into uranium-X_2, which he called "brevium" on account of its short half-life; this latter isotope then undergoes further beta-decay to form uranium-234. An alpha particle is a helium nucleus ($^4_2$He), consisting of two protons and two neutrons; its loss from an element's nucleus results in a different element that is 4 mass units lighter and two less in atomic number. A beta-particle is an electron so that its emission, on the other hand, results in an element of the same mass number but with an atomic number larger by 1. Thus the decay of uranium-238 by emitting first an alpha-particle and then two beta-particles should produce a new uranium isotope 4 mass units lighter: uranium-234. Fajans and Soddy were the first to explain this and other radioactive processes in terms of transitions between various isotopes.

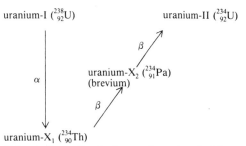

Fajans' scheme for the decay of uranium-I with modern symbols added. Uranium-X_1 and uranioum-X_2 are actually isotopes of thorium and protactinium. The half-lives of the four isotopes are:

$$^{238}_{92}U = 4\cdot49 \times 10^9 \text{ years}$$
$$^{234}_{90}Th = 24\cdot1 \text{ days}$$
$$^{234}_{91}Pa = 1\cdot18 \text{ minutes}$$
$$^{234}_{92}U = 2\cdot48 \times 10^5 \text{ years}$$

Fajans' work in inorganic chemistry was equally important. He formulated two rules to account for the well-known diagonal similarities between elements in the Periodic Table in terms of the ease of formation of covalencies and electrovalencies (ionic valencies). The first rule states that covalencies are more likely to be formed as the number of electrons to be removed or donated increases, so that highly charged ions are rare or impossible. The removal (or donation) of a second electron must overcome the effect of charge due to the removal (or donation) of the first, and so on for each successive electron. As the number of electrons increases, the work required soon becomes impossibly great for chemical forces, and covalencies result instead.

Fajans' second rule states that electrovalencies are favoured by large cations and small anions. In a large atom, the outer electrons are farther from the attractive force of the positive nucleus and hence are more easily removed to form cations. In a small atom, on the other hand, an electron added to form an anion can approach more closely to the positive field of the nucleus and is therefore more strongly held than in a large anion.

The operation of the first rule in passing from Group I to Group II of the Periodic Table is approximately balanced by the effect of the second rule in passing from the first period to the second period. The most obvious examples of diagonal similarity are the following:

Lithium, for example, shows its similarity to magnesium in all those points that emphasize its difference from sodium.

In an extension of his work on radioactivity Fajans estimated the ages of minerals from Norway, by measuring the percentages of lead, the end-product of radioactive decay. In 1919 he did research on the energies of hydration of ions. Thermochemistry, theory of chemical forces, light absorption and photochemistry are other areas in which he became an authority.

Faraday, Michael (*1791-1867*), was an English chemist and physicist, one of the world's greatest scientists in terms of the range, diversity and fundamental nature of his achievements. This article deals primarily with his contributions to chemistry, among the most important of which were the discovery of benzene and the formulation of his laws of electrolysis.

Faraday was born in Newington, Surrey, on 22 September 1791, one of the ten children of a blacksmith who had moved there from Yorkshire. He had no formal education and at the age of 14 was apprenticed to a bookbinder. He attended Humphry Davy's lectures at the Royal Institution and sent a bound copy of his lecture notes to the great man with a request for a job. When he was 21, Faraday found himself being taken on as Davy's laboratory assistant. From 1813 to 1815 he accompanied Davy on a scientific tour of Europe. He continued to serve his scientific apprenticeship as an analytical chemist, and in 1825 was made Director of the Royal Institution Laboratory, four years after he had married Sarah Barnard who, like Faraday, was a member of the dissident Christian sect called the Sandemanians.

In 1826 he began his Royal Institution Christmas Lectures for young people – which have continued in essence to the present day. Towards the end of the 1830s his faith failed and for several years he suffered from mental derangement. He became a recluse in his personal life, although by 1844 he was back working at the Institution. Finally in the 1860s his mental powers declined, and he ended his days in a house placed at his disposal by Queen Victoria. He died in London on 25 August 1867.

Faraday's first serious chemical discoveries were made in 1820, when he prepared the chlorides of carbon - C_2Cl_6 from ethane and C_2Cl_4 from ethylene (ethene) – substitution reactions that anticipated the work a few years later by Jean Baptiste Dumas. In 1823 Faraday produced liquid chlorine by heating crystals of chlorine hydrate ($Cl_2.8H_2O$) in an inverted U-tube, one limb of which was heated and the other placed in a freezing mixture (liquefaction resulted because of the high pressure of the gas cooled below its relatively high critical temperature). He then liquefied other gases, including sulphur dioxide, hydrogen sulphide, nitrous oxide (dinitrogen monoxide), chlorine dioxide, cyanogen and hydrogen bromide. After the production of liquid carbon dioxide in 1835, Faraday used this coolant to liquefy such gases as ethylene (ethene), phosphine, silicon tetrafluoride and boron trifluoride.

In the same year (1835) he made his greatest contribution to organic chemistry, the isolation of benzene from gas oils. He also worked out the empirical formula of naphthalene and prepared various sulphonic acids – later to have great importance in the industries devoted to dyestuffs and detergents. It was also at about this time that Faraday demonstrated the use of platinum as a catalyst and showed the importance in chemical reactions of surfaces and inhibitors – again foreshadowing a huge area of modern chemical industry.

Also during the 1830s Faraday turned his attention to the electrical nature of matter. His researches, summed up in Faraday's laws of electrolysis, established the link between electricity and chemical affinity, one of the most fundamental concepts in science. It was Faraday who coined the terms anode, cathode, cation, anion, electrode and electrolyte. He postulated that during the electrolysis of an aqueous electrolyte, positively-charged cations move towards the negatively-charged cathode and negatively-charged anions migrate to the positively-charged anode. At each electrode the ions are discharged according to the following rules:

(a) the quantity of a substance produced is proportional to the amount of electricity passed;
(b) the relative quantities of different substances produced by the same amount of electricity are proportional to their equivalent weights (i.e. the relative atomic mass divided by the oxidation state or valency).

A faraday of electricity (96,500 coulombs, where 1 coulomb is 1 ampere flowing for 1 second) liberates a gram equivalent weight of any substance – i.e., a mole divided by the oxidation state of the element concerned. For example, 1 faraday liberates $63.5 \div 2 = 31.75$ grams of copper, $108 \div 1 = 108$ grams of silver, $1 \div 1 = 1$ gram of hydrogen, or $16 \div 2 = 8$ grams of oxygen.

In physics, Faraday's chief work concerned the magnetic effects of electric currents, which led him to the discovery of electromagnetic induction (the working principle of the induction coil, transformer, dynamo and electric motor). He also studied the fields of permanent magnets, distinguishing between diamagnetic and paramagnetic substances and establishing field theory. In the late 1830s he defined an electric current in terms of its effect on the molecules that make up insulators, conductors and electrolytes.

Faraday was a gifted teacher and excellent lecturer; one of his books for children, *The Chemical History of a Candle*, is still in print. He received many honours, most of which he accepted diffidently to preclude any charge of vanity, which would have been strictly against his religious principles; for example he declined a knighthood and the Presidency of the Royal Society. He did, however, value his election to fellowship of the Royal Society; the only sour note was that professional jealousy motivated Humphry Davy, his former mentor, to cast the single vote against Faraday's election.

Fischer, Emil (*1852–1919*), was a German organic chemist who analysed and synthesized many biologically important compounds. He was awarded the 1902 Nobel Prize in Chemistry for his work on the synthesis of sugars and purine compounds.

Fischer was born in Euskirchen, near Bonn, on 9 October 1852, the son of a merchant. After leaving school he acceded to his father's wishes and joined the family business, but later left and in 1871 entered the University of Bonn to study chemistry under Friedrich Kekulé. The following year he went to Strasbourg and graduated from the university there in 1874 with a doctoral thesis which was supervised by Johann von Baeyer. He continued his studies at Munich where he became an unpaid lecturer in 1878 and (paid) Assistant Professor in 1879. He then held professorships at Erlangen (1882), Würzburg (1885) and finally Berlin (1892). Before his last move he married Agnes Gerlach. His wife died young but they had three sons, the eldest of whom, Hermann, also became a distinguished organic chemist; two sons were killed in World War I. Fischer suffered a serious

coupled with the death of his sons, led him to commit suicide on 15 July 1919.

Fischer's early research, carried out with his cousin Otto Fischer, concerned the dye rosaniline and similar compounds, which they showed have a structure related to that of triphenylmethane. In 1875 Fischer discovered phenylhydrazine, but it was not until 1884 that he found it formed bright yellow crystalline derivatives with carbohydrates, a key reaction in the study of sugars. The derivatives are known as osazones, and Fischer obtained the same osazone from three different sugars – glucose, fructose and mannose – demonstrating that all three have the same structure in the part of their molecules unaffected by phenylhydrazine. He went on to determine the structures of the 12 possible stereoisomers of glucose, the important group of sugars known collectively as hexoses. The naming of carbohydrates is a complicated process based on the chemical origin (D or L) and optical activity (+ or −) of the compound. Fischer based his nomenclature on dextro-rotatory (+) glyceraldehyde and called this the D series. It was only the advent of X-ray analysis that confirmed that Fischer's arbitrarily assigned configurations are correct.

From about 1882 he began working on a group of compounds that included uric acid and caffeine. Fischer realized that they were all related to a hitherto unknown substance which he called purine. Over the next few years he synthesized about 130 related compounds, one of which was the first synthetic nucleotide, a biologically important phosphoric ester of a compound made from a purine-type molecule and a carbohydrate. These studies led to the synthesis of powerful hypnotic drugs derived from barbituric acids, including in 1903 5,5-diethyl barbituric acid which became widely used as a sedative.

purine   uric acid   caffeine   barbituric acid   5, 5-diethylbarbituric acid (Veronal)

bout of mercury poisoning (during a brief incursion into inorganic chemistry) and from the equally serious effects of phenylhydrazine poisoning. He contracted cancer and this fact,

In 1885 experiments with phenylhydrazine led to what is known as Fischer's indole synthesis, in which he heated a phenylhydrazone with an acid catalyst to produce a derivative of indole:

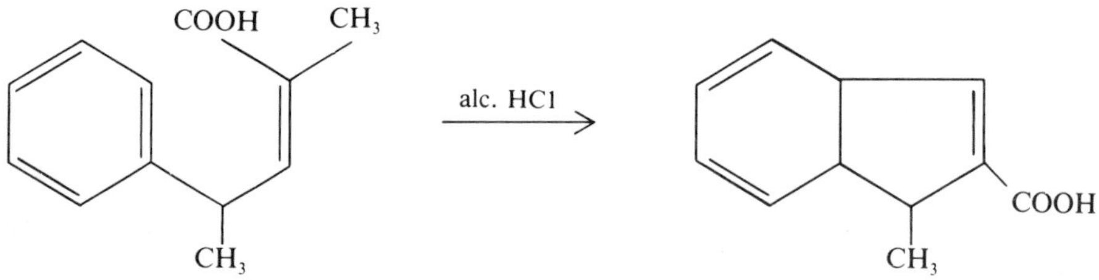

COOH CH₃

alc. HC1 →

COOH

CH₃

CH₃

derivative of 1-methylphenylhydrazone

indole derivative

Indole itself cannot, however, be obtained by this method.

Fischer's investigations into the chemistry of proteins began in 1899. He synthesized the amino acids ornithine (1,4-diaminopentanoic acid) in 1901, serine (1-hydroxy-2-aminobutanoic acid) in 1902 and the sulphur-containing cystine in 1908. He then combined amino acids to form polypeptides, the largest of which – composed of 18 amino acid residues – had a molecular weight of 1,213. Later work included a study of tannins, which he carried out with the assistance of his son Hermann.

Fischer was involved with many aspects and branches of organic chemistry. He was a man of considerable insight, as exemplified by his description of the action of enzymes as a lock and key mechanism in which the enzyme model fits exactly onto the molecule with which it reacts. But he did not consider himself to be a theoretician; he believed in, and used, the synthetic methods of the practical organic chemist.

Fischer, Ernst Otto (*1918–*), and **Wilkinson, Geoffrey** (*1921–*), are inorganic chemists who shared the 1973 Nobel Prize in Chemistry for their pioneering work, which they carried out independently, on the organometallic compounds of the transition metals.

Fischer was born in Munich on 10 November 1918, the son of Professor Karl T. Fischer. He was educated at the Munich Technical University, from which he gained a Diploma in Chemistry in 1949 and a doctorate in 1952. He remained at Munich, becoming successively Associate Professor (1957), Professor (1959) and finally Professor and Director of Inorganic Chemistry (1964).

Wilkinson was born on 14 July 1921 and educated at Todmorden Grammar School. In 1939 he obtained a scholarship to Imperial College, London, and from 1943 to 1946 worked as a Junior Scientific Officer for the Atomic Energy Division of the National Research Council in Canada. He then took up various appointments in the United States: at the Radiation Laboratory at Berkeley, California (1946-1950); in the Chem-

istry Department of the Massachusetts Institute of Technology (1950-1951); and Assistant Professor (1951-1956) and Professor (1956-1978) at Harvard. In 1978 he became the Sir Edward Frankland Professor of Inorganic Chemistry at the University of London, working at Imperial College. Wilkinson was knighted in 1976.

In about 1830 a Danish pharmacist described the compound $PtCl_2.C_2H_4$, which is now known to exist as a dimer with chloride bridges. This and the ion $[C_2H_4PtCl_3]^-$ were the first known organometallic derivatives of the transition metals. In 1951, both Fischer and Wilkinson read an article in the journal *Nature* about a puzzling synthetic compound called ferrocene. Working independently, they came to the conclusion that each molecule of ferrocene consists of a single iron atom sandwiched between two five-sided carbon rings – an organometallic compound. A combination of chemical and physical studies, finally confirmed by X-ray analysis, showed that the compound's structure is as shown in the diagram. In the ferrocene molecule, the two symmetrical five-membered rings are staggered with respect to each other, but in the corresponding ruthenium compound (called ruthenocene) they are eclipsed.

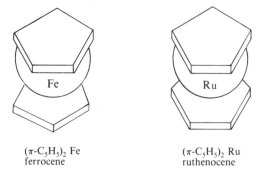

$(\pi\text{-}C_5H_5)_2$ Fe
ferrocene

$(\pi\text{-}C_5H_5)_2$ Ru
ruthenocene

Structures of ferrocene and ruthenocene.

With this work came the general realization that transition metals can bond chemically to carbon, and other ring systems were then studied. The hydrocarbon cyclopentadiene behaves as a weak acid and with various bases forms salts containing the symmetrical cyclopentadienide ion $C_5H_5^-$. It also forms "sandwich" compounds and like other ring systems that behave in this way has the "aromatic" sextet of (six) electrons. All of the elements of the first transition series have now been incorporated into molecules of this kind and all except that of manganese have the ferrocene-type structure. Only ferrocene, however, is stable in air, the others being sensitive to oxidation in the order (of decreasing stability) nickel, cobalt, vanadium, chromium, titanium. The cationic species behaves like a large monopositive ion; $(\pi - C_5H_5)Co^+$ is particularly stable.

The recognition of the "sandwich" concept initiated a vast amount of research, not only on cyclopentadienyl derivatives but on similar systems with four-, six-, seven- and even eight-membered carbon rings. All of this work was stimulated by the revolutionary explanation by Fischer and Wilkinson of the previously unknown way in which metals and organic compounds can combine.

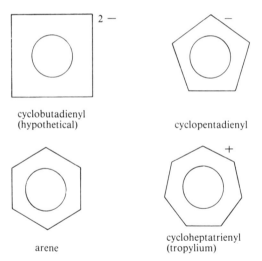

cyclobutadienyl
(hypothetical)

cyclopentadienyl

arene

cycloheptatrienyl
(tropylium)

'Aromatic' ring compounds that might form transition metal organometallic compounds.

Fischer, Hans (*1881–1945*), was a German organic chemist who is best known for his determinations of the molecular structures of three important biological pigments: haemoglobin, chlorophyll and bilirubin. For his work on haemoglobin he was awarded the 1930 Nobel Prize in Chemistry.

Fischer was born in Höchst-am-Main, near Frankfurt, on 27 July 1881, the son of a chemical manufacturer. He studied chemistry at the University of Marburg, gaining his doctorate in 1904. He then went to the University of Munich to study medicine, qualifying as a doctor in 1908.

He became a research assistant to his namesake Emil Fischer at the University of Berlin, before taking up an appointment as Professor of Medical Chemistry at the University of Innsbruck in 1915 as successor to Adolf Windaus (1876–1959). Three years later he held a similar post at Vienna, before taking over from Heinrich Wieland at the Munich Technische Hochschule in 1921 as Professor of Organic Chemistry. Towards the end of World War II in 1945 Fischer's laboratories were destroyed in an Allied bombing raid and in a fit of despair, like Emil Fischer before him, he committed suicide. He died in Munich on 31 March 1945.

In 1921 Fischer began investigating haemoglobin, the oxygen-carrying, red colouring matter in blood. He concentrated on haem, the iron-containing non-protein part of the molecule, and showed that it consists of four pyrrole rings (five-membered heterocyclic rings containing four carbon atoms and one nitrogen atom) surrounding a single iron atom. By 1929 he had elucidated the complete structure and synthesized haem.

He then turned his attention to chlorophyll, the green colouring matter in plants that Richard Willstätter had isolated in 1910. He found that its structure is similar to that of haem, with a group of substituted porphins surrounding an atom of magnesium. This work occupied Fischer for much of the 1930s, after which he began to study the bile pigments, particularly bilirubin (the pigment responsible for the colour of the skin of patients suffering from jaundice). He showed that the bile acids are degraded porphins and by 1944 had achieved a complete synthesis of bilirubin. He also investigated the yellow plant pigment carotene, the precursor of vitamin A.

Fischer, Hermann Otto Laurenz (*1888–1960*), was a German organic chemist whose chief contribution to the science concerned the synthetic and structural chemistry of carbohydrates, glycerides and inositols.

Fischer was born on 8 December 1888 in Würzburg, Bavaria, the eldest of the three sons of Emil Fischer, who at that time was Professor of Organic Chemistry at the local university. The early death of his mother brought him and his two brothers into closer contact with their illustrious father. The two younger brothers went on to study medicine, while Hermann followed his father into organic chemistry.

Fischer began his undergraduate career at Cambridge University in 1907, but had to return to Germany the following year for military training. After a brief period in Berlin, he started his doctorial research work at Jena University under Ludwig Knorr. In 1912 he returned to the Chemical Institute of Berlin University to continue research with his father. Two years later the outbreak of World War I interrupted his research. Both his brothers were killed in the war and his father committed suicide in 1919 soon after Hermann returned to Berlin.

In 1922 Fischer married Ruth Seckels, and they had a daughter and two sons. With the rise of Adolf Hitler the Fischers left Berlin in 1932 and went to Basle in Switzerland. Then in 1937 he moved to the Banting Institute in Toronto, Canada, where he stayed until his final move to the United States in 1948 to the Biochemistry Department of the University of California at Berkeley. He became Chairman of the Department and Emeritus Professor before retiring in 1956. Fischer died on 9 March 1960.

While working with Knorr at Jena, Fischer separated the keto and enol tautomers of acetylacetone (pentan-2,4-dione) by low-temperature crystallization. Then in Berlin his father (Emil Fischer), who was investigating tannins, assigned him the task of synthesizing some of the naturally occurring depsides (a depside is a condensation product formed from two hydroxy-aromatic acid molecules). He succeeded in producing various didepsides and diorsellinic acids.

Between 1920 and 1932 Fischer pursued two main lines of research. One was the study of quinic acid (tetrahydroxycyclohexanecarboxylic acid). By 1921 he had made various derivatives, but it was not until 1932 that he finally worked out its exact structure. The other research during this period dealt with the difficult chemistry of the trioses glyceraldehyde and dihydroxyacetone (2,3-dihydroxy-propanal and 1,3-dyhydroxypropanone) and the related two-, three- and four-carbon compounds. The crowning achievement of this work was the preparation by his assistant Erich Baer of DL-glyceraldehyde-3-phosphate.

Baer accompanied Fischer to Basle in 1932 and there they developed a practical method for the preparation of the enantiomorphous acetonated glyceraldehydes. They were able to make D-fructose and D-sorbose almost entirely free from their isomers D-psicose and D-tagatose using the aldol reaction between unsubstituted D-glyceraldehyde and its ketonic isomer, dihydroxyacetone.

While at Basle Fischer continued to collaborate with Gerda Dangschat (who had remained at Berlin) on structural and configurational studies of shikimic acid (first isolated in 1885). By a series of degradation reactions they converted shikimic acid into 2-deoxy-D-arabino-hexonic acid, which finally located the position of the double bond in the former (proving it to be 3,4,5-trihydroxycyclohexene-1-carboxylic acid).

From 1937, at the Canadian Banting Institute, Fischer extended his work on glyceraldehydes to

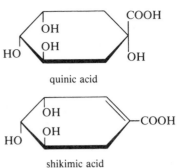

quinic acid

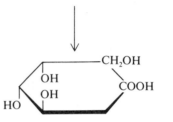

shikimic acid
(3, 4, 5-trihydroxycyclohexene-1-carboxylic acid)

2-deoxy-D-arabino-hexanoic acid
(3, 4, 5, 6-tetrahydroxyhexanoic acid)

glycerides (esters of glycerol, i.e. propan-1,2,3-triol). He prepared the first optically pure α-monoglycerides and α-glycerophosphoric acids (glycerol-1-phosphates) and demonstrated the action of lipase enzymes on these biologically important substances.

Despite the intervention of World War II and the separation of Berlin and Toronto, Fischer and Dangschat continued their work on the inositols (hexahydroxycyclohexanes). They succeeded in establishing the configuration of myo-inositol and showed its relationship to D-glucose.

At Berkeley, Fischer carried on research into the inositols and other carbohydrates. He described the 12 years in California as the most

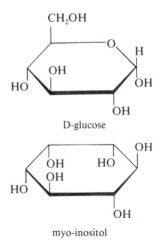

D-glucose

myo-inositol

pleasant in his life. His warm and friendly personality made him many friends there and among distinguished scientists throughout the world.

Flory, Paul John (1910–   ), is an American polymer chemist who was awarded the 1974 Nobel Prize in Chemistry for his investigations of synthetic and natural macromolecules. With Wallace Carothers he developed nylon, the first synthetic polyamide, and the synthetic rubber neoprene.

Flory was born on 19 June 1910 at Sterling, Illinois. He graduated from Manchester College, Indiana, in 1931 and gained his PhD from Ohio State University three years later. He then embarked on a career as an industrial research chemist, working at the Du Pont Experimental Station in Wilmington, Delaware (with Carothers) from 1934 to 1938 and at the Esso Laboratory Standard Oil Development Company in Elizabeth, New Jersey (1940–1943), before becoming Director of Fundamental Research at the Goodyear Tire and Rubber Company (1943–1948). He had held a research associateship at Cincinnati for three years between 1940 and 1943, and in 1948 he again took up an academic post as Professor of Chemistry at Cornell University. He remained there until 1956 when he became Executive Director of Research at the Mellon Institute, Pittsburgh. In 1961 he was made Professor of Chemistry at Stamford University where he remained, eventually becoming Emeritus Professor.

Flory pioneered research into the constitution and properties of substances made up of giant molecules, such as rubbers, plastics, fibres, films and proteins. He showed the importance of understanding the sizes and shapes of these flexible molecules in order to be able to relate their chemical structures to their physical properties. In addition to developing polymerization techniques, he discovered ways of analysing polymers. Many of these substances are able to increase the lengths of their component molecular chains and Flory found that one extending molecule can stop growing and pass on its growing ability to another molecule.

Working with Carothers he prepared the polyamide Nylon 66 by heating a mixture of adipic acid (hexan-1,6-dioic acid) and hexamethylene diamine (hexan-1,6-diamine). They made Nylon 6 from caprolactam, showing it to be a polymer of the type $-[-CO(CH_2)_5NH-]_n-$. Neoprene was made by polymerizing chloroprene (but-2-chloro-1,3-diene), and was soon followed by other synthetic rubbers made by polymerization and co-polymerization of various butenes. Flory's later researches looked for and found similarities between the elasticity of natural organic tissues – such as ligaments, muscles and blood vessels – and synthetic and natural plastic materials.

Freundlich, Herbert Max Finlay (*1880–1941*), was a German physical chemist, best known for his extensive work on the nature of colloids, particularly sols and gels.

Freundlich was born in Berlin-Charlottenburg on 28 January 1880, the son of a German father and a Scottish mother. Shortly after his birth the family moved to Biebrich, where his father had been made director of an iron foundry. At school Freundlich studied classics and showed a great aptitude for music, but by the time he left the Gymnasium in 1898 he had opted for a career in science. In that same year he went to the University of Munich for a preliminary science course, then specialized in chemistry when he moved to the University of Leipzig. His thesis on the precipitation of colloidal solutions by electrolysis gained him a doctorate in 1903.

From 1903 to 1911 he assisted Friedrich Ostwald at his Leipzig Institute for Analytical and Physical Chemistry. He then became Professor of Physical Chemistry at the Technische Hochschule in Brunswick. At the outbreak of World War I in 1914 he was declared unfit for military service, so went to the Kaiser Wilhelm Institut in Berlin-Dahlem where he worked (under Fritz Haber) on the use of charcoal in gas masks. In 1919 he became the head of the institute's section devoted to colloid chemistry. He had married his first wife Marie Mann in 1908, but she died in 1917 during childbirth. Six years later he married Hella Gilbert.

Freundlich resigned his position when Adolf Hitler came to power in 1933 and went to Britain where, sponsored by Imperial Chemical Industries (ICI), he worked at University College, London. Later, in 1938, he went to the United States and took up the appointment of Distinguished Service Professor of Colloid Chemistry at the University of Minnesota. He died in Minnesota on 30 March 1941.

While he was at Leipzig, Freundlich formulated what has become known as Freundlich's adsorption isotherm, which concerns the accumulation of molecules of a solution at a surface. It can be expressed as $x/m = (kc)^{1/n}$, where x and m are the masses of material adsorbed and adsorbent, respectively, c is the equilibrium concentration of the solution, and k and n are constants.

Freundlich's other researches were devoted to all aspects of colloid science. He investigated colloid optics, the scattering of light by dispersed particles of various shapes. He studied the electrical properties of colloids, since electrostatic charges are largely responsible for holding colloidal dispersions in place.

He also carried out a major series of investigations on mechanical properties such as viscosity and elasticity, and studied the behaviour of certain systems under other types of mechanical forces. For example, he introduced the term thixotropy to describe the behaviour of gels, the jelly-like colloids that show many strange properties intermediate between those of liquids and solids. One modern industrial application of this work has been the development of non-drip paints.

Freundlich was very much a chemist and was not particularly interested in formulating long mathematical equations to explain or justify his practical results. In his later years he was particularly interested in the commercial use of colloids in the rubber and paint industries.

Friedel, Charles (*1832-1899*), was a French organic chemist and mineralogist, best remembered for his part in the discovery of the Friedel-Crafts reaction. Throughout his career, he successfully combined his interests in chemistry and minerals.

Friedel was born on 12 March 1832 in Strasbourg. He was educated locally (where he studied under Louis Pasteur) and at the Sorbonne in Paris. He qualified in both chemistry and mineralogy and in 1856 was made curator of the collection of minerals at the École des Mines. In 1871 he became an instructor at the École Normale and from 1876 was Professor of Mineralogy at the Sorbonne. Following the death of Charles Adolphe Wurtz in 1884 he became also Professor of Organic Chemistry and Director of Research, a post he held until he died at Montaubin on 20 April 1899.

Friedel's dual interests gave him a wide-ranging field for research, which he covered with great success. He made extensive inroads into the mysteries of the various alcohols, a subject that had received little attention until then. In 1871, working with R.D. da Silva, he synthesized glycerol (propantriol) from propylene (propene). Friedel met and became friends with the American chemist James Mason Crafts (1839-1917), who arrived in Paris having spent a year doing postgraduate studies in Germany. Crafts returned to the United States to take up a professorship at Cornell University, but went back to Paris in 1874 and began carrying out research with Friedel.

In 1877 they discovered the Friedel-Crafts reaction, which uses aluminium chloride as a catalyst to facilitate the addition of an alkyl halide (halogenoalkane) to an aromatic compound. The reaction has proved to be extremely useful in

organic synthesis and is now employed extensively in the industrial preparation of triphenylamine dyes.

From 1879 to 1887 Friedel concentrated on the attempted synthesis of minerals, including diamonds, using heat and pressure. He established the similarity in properties between carbon and silicon and therefore the similarity in structure of

Examples of Friedel-Crafts reactions.

their long-chain polymeric compounds. This work paved the way for a better understanding of silica minerals and the use of silicates in industry.

Funk, Casimir (*1884-1967*), was a Polish-born American biochemist who is best known for his researches on dietary requirements, particularly of vitamins (a term derived from vitamines – Funk's original name for them). He was the first to isolate nicotinic acid (also called niacin, one of the B vitamins) and his work did much to further studies of nutritional requirements.

Funk was born in Warsaw on 23 February 1884, the son of a prominent dermatologist. An able student, he was educated at the University of Bern, Switzerland, from which he gained his doctorate in organic chemistry in 1904, when he was still only 20 years old. He then worked at the Pasteur Institute in Paris, the Wiesbaden Municipal Hospital, the University of Berlin, and the Lister Institute in London, where he was assigned to work on beriberi. In 1915 he emigrated to the United States, where he held several industrial and university positions in New York; he became a naturalized American citizen in 1920.

In 1923 the Rockefeller Foundation supported his return to Warsaw as Director of the Biochemistry Department of the State Institute of Hygiene but, because of the country's uncertain political situation, Funk left this post in 1927 and went to Paris. In the following year he became a consultant to a pharmaceutical company and founded a privately financed research institution, the Casa Biochemica. With the German invasion of France at the outbreak of World War II in 1939, Funk abandoned this venture and returned to the United States, where he worked as a consultant to the United States Vitamin Corporation. In 1940 he became President of the Funk Foundation for Medical Research, a position he held until his death. He died in Albany, New York, on 20 November 1967.

Following the research of Frank Gowland Hopkins into what we now know to be deficiency diseases, such as beriberi and pellagra, Funk succeeded in 1911 at the Lister Institute in obtaining a concentrate that cured a pigeon disease similar to beriberi. He showed that the anti-beriberi concentrate was an amine, and in 1912 he discussed the causes of beriberi, scurvy and rickets as deficiency diseases. He also suggested that the accessory food factors needed to prevent these disorders are all amines and so he named them vitamines (vital amines). It was later discovered that not all accessory food factors are amines, and Funk's term was shortened to vitamins.

Funk continued to try to find the anti-beriberi factor for human beings and finally isolated nicotinic acid from rice polishings. But it did not cure beriberi, so he discarded it. (Later Otto Warburg discovered that nicotinic acid prevents pellagra.) In 1934 Robert Williams (1886-1965) isolated about 10 gm of the anti-beriberi factor (now known as thiamin or vitamin B_1) from 1,000 kg of rice polishings, and in 1936 Funk determined its molecular structure and developed a method of synthesizing it.

Funk also did extensive research into animal hormones, particularly male sex hormones, and into biochemistry of cancer, diabetes and ulcers. He improved the methods used for the commercial manufacture of many drugs, as well developing several new commercial products in his own laboratories.

G

Gay-Lussac, Joseph Louis (*1778-1850*), was a French chemist who pioneered the quantitative study of gases and established the link between gaseous behaviour and chemical reactions. He also made important discoveries in inorganic chemistry, often parallelling (independently) the work of Humphry Davy in England.

Gay-Lussac was born on 6 December 1778 at Saint-Léonard, Haute Vienne, the son of a judge (who was arrested in 1793 for his aristocratic sympathies). He entered the École Polytechnique in Paris in 1797 and graduated in 1800. His first interest was in engineering but in 1801 the great French chemist Claude Berthollet invited Gay-Lussac to join him as an assistant at his house in Arcueil, the meeting place of many contemporary scientists, including Pierre Laplace. From 1805 to 1806 he accompanied Alexander von Humboldt on an expedition to measure terrestrial magnetism and in 1809, a year after his marriage to Geneviève Rojet, he became Professor of Chemistry at the École and Professor of Physics at the Sorbonne. He held various government appointments, including that of superintendent of a gunpowder factory (1818) and Chief Assayer to the Mint (1829). In 1832 he was made Professor of Chemistry at the Musée National d'Histoire Naturelle. He was a member of the Chamber of Deputies for a short time in the 1830s, and was made a Peer of France in 1839. He died in Paris on 9 May 1850.

Gay-Lussac began studying gases in collaboration with Louis Thénard. In 1802 he formulated the law of expansion of gases, which states that for a given rise in temperature all gases expand by the same fraction of their volume (Jacques Charles had recognized equal expansion in 1787 but had not published his findings; nevertheless the relationship is now usually known as Charles' law). During balloon ascents in 1804, in which he established an altitude record that was to stand for 50 years, Gay-Lussac showed that the composition of air is constant up to heights in excess of 7,000 m above sea level. With Humboldt he accurately determined the proportions of hydrogen and oxygen in water, showing the volume ratio to be 2:1; they also established the existence of explosive limits in mixtures of the two gases.

His greatest achievement concerning gases came in 1808 with the formulation of Gay-Lussac's law of combining volumes, which states that gases combine in simple proportions by volume and that the volumes of the products are related to the original volumes. His examples include:

$$HCl + NH_3 \rightarrow NH_4Cl$$
$$1 \quad\quad 1 \quad\quad\quad 1$$

and

$$2CO + O_2 \rightarrow 2CO_2$$
$$2 \quad\quad 1 \quad\quad 2$$

Another fruitful area of Gay-Lussac's work with Thénard concerned the alkali metals, where they followed up the discovery of sodium and potassium by Davy by devising chemical means for producing the metals in quantity (heating fused alkalis with red-hot iron). They anticipated (by nine days) Davy's isolation of boron and independently investigated the properties of iodine, which had been discovered in 1811 by Bernard Courtois (1777-1838) but was named by Gay-Lussac in 1813. He first prepared iodine(I) chloride, ICl, and iodine(III) chloride, ICl_3. Studies of the hydrogen halides - hydrogen fluoride, hydrogen chloride and hydrogen iodide - led to the extremely important conclusion that acids need not contain oxygen (as proposed by Antoine Lavoisier) and to the naming of hydrochloric acid (previously known as muriatic acid). From his researches with Prussian blue Gay-Lussac prepared hydrogen cyanide and in 1815 discovered cyanogen, $(CN)_2$; he went on to develop the chemistry of the cyanides.

Another significant area of work was the development of volumetric analysis - which provided more evidence, if any were needed, of Gay-Lussac's quantitative approach to chemistry. In 1832 he introduced the method of estimating silver by titrating silver nitrate against sodium chloride. Later work included the analysis of vegetable and animal substances and a contribution to the manufacture of sulphuric acid, the Gay-Lussac tower, which recovers spent nitrogen oxides from the chamber process.

Gibbs, Josiah Willard (*1839-1903*), was an American scientist who laid the foundation of modern chemical thermodynamics. He devised the phase rule and formulated Gibbs' adsorption isotherm.

Gibbs was born on 11 February 1839 in New Haven, Connecticut, into an academic family. His father was Professor of Sacred Literature at the Divinity School of Yale University, and Gibbs excelled at classics at school. He attended Yale in 1854, winning prizes for Latin and mathematics before graduating in 1858 at the age of only 19. During the next five years he continued his studies by specializing in engineering and in 1863 gained the first Yale PhD in this subject for a thesis on the design of gears. He then accepted teaching posts at Yale, first in Latin and then in natural philosophy. In 1866 he patented a railway braking system.

Also in 1866 Gibbs went abroad for three years to attend lectures (mainly in physics) in Paris, Berlin and Heidelberg. In 1871, two years after his return to the United States, he was appointed Professor of Mathematical Physics at Yale, a post he retained until his death despite offers from other academic institutions. He never married but lived with his sister and her family. He died in New Haven on 28 April 1903.

Gibbs did not publish his first papers until 1873, which were preliminaries to his 300-page series *On the Equilibrium of Heterogeneous Substances* (1876-1878). In it he formulated the phase rule, which may be stated as $f = n + 2 - r$, where f is the number of degrees of freedom, n the number of chemical components, and r the number of phases - solid, liquid or gas; degrees of freedom are quantities such as temperature and pressure which may be altered without changing the number of phases. Gibbs did not explore the chemical applications of the phase rule, later done by others who came to realize its importance. In the same work he also described his concept of free energy, which can be used as a measure of the feasibility of a given chemical reaction. It is defined in terms of the enthalpy, or heat content, and entropy, a measure of the disorder of a chemical system. From this Gibbs developed the notion of chemical potential, which is a measure of how the free energy of a particular phase depends on changes in composition (expressed mathematically as the differential coefficient of the free energy with respect to the number of moles of the chemical). The fourth fundamental contribution in this extensive work was a thermodynamic analysis which showed that changes in the concentration of a component of a solution in contact with a surface occur if there is an alteration in the surface tension - the Gibbs' adsorption isotherm.

All of these very technical discoveries now form

part of the armoury of the physical chemist and thermodynamicist, together with their extension to electrochemistry and the subsequent developments of other scientists. But for many years Gibbs' work was unknown outside the United States, until it was translated into German by Friedrich Ostwald in 1891 and into French by Henri Le Châtelier in 1899.

During his teaching studies Gibbs adapted the work of the mathematicians William Hamilton (1805–1865) and Hermann Grassman (1809–1877) into a vector analysis which was both simple to use and easily applicable to physics, particularly electricity and magnetism. It was left to one of Gibbs' students, E.B. Wilson, to write a textbook on the subject, which was largely responsible for the popularization of vector analysis. Also during the 1880s Gibbs worked on the electromagnetic theory of light. From an entirely theoretical viewpoint and making very few assumptions he accounted correctly for most of the properties of light using only an electrical theory.

In his last major work, *Elementary Principles of Statistical Mechanics*, Gibbs turned his attention to heat and showed how many thermodynamic laws could be interpreted in terms of the results of the movements of enormous numbers of bodies such as molecules. His ensemble method equated the behaviour of a large number of systems at once to that of a single system over a period of time.

Gilman, Henry (*1893–*), is an American organic chemist best known for his work on organometallic compounds, particularly Grignard reagents.

Gilman was born on 9 May 1893 in Boston, Massachusetts. He grew up there and attended university in nearby Harvard, from which he graduated with top honours in 1915. After a year abroad, during which he visited academic centres in Zurich, Paris and Oxford, he returned to Harvard to continue his postgraduate studies, and gained his PhD in chemistry in 1918.

He began his career as an instructor at Harvard, but in 1919 was offered a similar post in the chemistry department at the University of Illinois. Then an assistant professorship at the newly established faculty at Iowa State University prompted another move in the same year. He became Professor of Organic Chemistry in 1923 and continued to teach at Iowa until 1947, when his vision deteriorated to such an extent that he became virtually blind.

Gilman's first paper on organometallic compounds, on Grignard reagents, was published in 1920. He went on to investigate the organic chem-

istry of 26 different metals, from aluminium, arsenic and barium through to thallium, uranium and zinc, and discovered several new types of compounds. He was the first to study organocuprates, now known as Gilman reagents, and his early work with organomagnesium compounds (Grignard reagents) led to experiments with organolithium compounds, later to play an important part in the preparation of polythene. Organogold compounds found applications in medicine.

The comprehensive study of methods of high-yield synthesis, quantitative and qualitative analysis, and uses of organometallic compounds represent only part – albeit the major one – of Gilman's research achievements. He also developed an international reputation for his work on organosilicon compounds, which again found many industrial applications. Other research interests include heterocyclic compounds, catalysis, resins, plastics and insecticides.

Glasstone, Samuel (*1897–*), is a British-born American physical chemist and nuclear technologist, probably best known as a writer of textbooks.

Glasstone was born in London on 5 March 1897. He was educated in London, attended London University, and gained his PhD in physical chemistry in 1922 and his DSc in 1926. From 1919 to 1921 he was a lecturer in physical chemistry at the university, and then held a similar position at the University of Sheffield until 1939. In that year he went to the United States to Princeton, followed by professorships at the University of Oklahoma (1942) and Boston College (1947). From 1948 he was a consultant to the US Department of Energy and in 1952 gained the concurrent post as consultant to the Los Alamos Scientific Laboratories. He also worked at the Oak Ridge National Laboratory on the operation and development of nuclear reactors.

Probably Glasstone's best known publication is his *Textbook of Physical Chemistry* (1940), for many years the principal book on the subject for undergraduates. A shorter and simpler version, *Elements of Physical Chemistry*, was later produced in collaboration with D. Lewis. In conjunction with M.C. Edlund he wrote *Elements of Nuclear Reactor Theory* (1952), and with the assistance of many of the staff of the Oak Ridge National Laboratory he published *Principles of Nuclear Reactor Engineering* (1956).

Glauber, Johann Rudolf (*1604–1670*), was a German chemist who lived at a time when chemistry was evolving as a science from the mysticism of alchemy. He prepared and sold what today would be called patent medicines and panaceas, one of which (Glauber's salt, sodium sulphate) still bears his name. He did make some genuine chemical experiments and preparations, although many of the results were misinterpreted (through ignorance) or simply ignored by his contemporaries.

Glauber was born in Karlstadt, Franconia, some time during 1604, the son of a barber. His parents died when he was young and he had little or no formal education, teaching himself and acquiring knowledge on his travels through Germany. He earned a living chiefly from selling medicines and chemicals. He lived for a while in Vienna, then in various places along the Rhine valley, before going to Amsterdam in 1648 and finally settling there in 1655 after another six-year sojourn in Germany. He designed and built a chemical laboratory in an Amsterdam house formerly occupied by an alchemist. He died in Amsterdam on or about 10 March 1670, possibly from the cumulative effects of poisonous substances with which he had worked and, no doubt, tried on himself as medicaments.

Some time about 1625 Glauber prepared hydrochloric acid by the action of concentrated sulphuric acid on common salt (sodium chloride). He found that the other product of the reaction, sodium sulphate, was a comparatively safe but efficient laxative, and could be sold as a cure-all for practically any complaint. He called it *sal mirabile* (miraculous salt), although it soon became known as Glauber's salt - and it is still the chief active ingredient of various patent medicines. A Stassfurt mineral, a double sulphate of sodium and calcium, is known as glauberite. He also prepared nitric acid by substituting saltpetre (potassium nitrate) for salt in the reaction with sulphuric acid. He made many metal chlorides and nitrates from the mineral acids. He discovered tartar emetic (antimony potassium tartrate), so-called because of its medicinal use in the days before antimony's toxicity was fully realized.

In his Amsterdam laboratory Glauber investigated and developed processes that could have industrial application, pursuing the principles he had outlined in his book *Furni Novi Philosophici* (c. 1646). Many of his experiments were carried out in secret, so that the methods or their products could be sold exclusively. He produced organic liquids containing such solvents as acetone (dimethylketone) and benzene - although he did not identify them - by reacting and distilling natural substances such as wood, wine, vinegar, vegetable oils and coal. One aim of his experiments was to improve the chemical techniques involved, and this aspect of Glauber's work was summarized in his book *Opera Omnia Chymica*, which was published in various versions between

1651 and 1661. He was conscious of the value to any country of its chemical and mineral raw materials, which he thought should be husbanded and exploited only for the good of the whole community. He outlined his views on a possible utopian future for Germany in *Teutschlands Wolfarth* (*Germany's Prosperity*).

Goldschmidt, Victor Moritz (*1888-1947*), was a Swiss-born Norwegian chemist who has been called the founding father of modern geochemistry.

Goldschmidt was born on 27 January 1888 in Zurich but moved to Norway with his family in 1900, where his father became Professor of Physical Chemists, at the University of Christiania (now Oslo). The family became Norwegian citizens in 1905. Goldschmidt completed his schooling in Christiania and continued at the university there, where he studied under the geologist Waldemar Brøgger and graduated in 1911. He was appointed Professor and Director of the Mineralogical Institute in 1914, a post he held until 1929, when he moved to Göttingen. The rise of anti-Semitism forced Goldschmidt to return to Norway in 1935, but soon World War II engulfed Europe and he had to flee again, first to Sweden and then to Britain, where he worked at Aberdeen and Rothamsted (on soil science). He returned to Norway after the end of the war in 1945, and died in Oslo on 20 March 1947.

Goldschmidt's doctoral thesis on contact metamorphism on rocks is recognized as a fundamental work in geochemistry. It set the scene for a huge programme of research on the elements, their origins and their relationships, which was to occupy him for the next 30 years. He broke new ground when he applied the concepts of Josiah Gibbs' phase rule to the colossal chemical processes of geological time, which he considered to be interpretable in terms of the laws of chemical equilibrium. The evidence of geological change over millions of years represents a series of chemical processes on a scarcely imaginable scale, and even an imperceptibly slow reaction can yield megatonnes of product over the time scale involved.

Shortage of materials during World War I led Goldschmidt to speculate further on the distribution of elements in the Earth's crust. In the next few years he and his co-workers studied 200 compounds of 75 elements and produced the first tables of ionic and atomic radii. The new science of X-ray crystallography, developed by the Braggs after Max von Laue's original discovery in 1912, could hardly have been more opportune. Goldschmidt was able to show that, given an electrical balance between positive and negative ions, the most important factor in crystal structure is ionic size. He suggested furthermore that complex natural minerals, such as hornblende $(OH)_2Ca_2Mg_5Si_8O_{22}$, can be explained by the balancing of charge by means of substitution based primarily on size. This led to the relationships between close-packing of identical spheres and the various interstitial sites available for the formation of crystal lattices. He also established the relation of hardness to interionic distances.

At Göttingen (1929) Goldschmidt pursued his general researches and extended them to include meteorites, pioneering spectrographic methods for the rapid determination of small amounts of elements. Exhaustive analysis of results from geochemistry, astrophysics and nuclear physics led to his work on the cosmic abundance of the elements and the important links between isotopic stability and abundance. Studies of terrestrial abundance reveal about eight predominant elements. Recalculation of atom and volume percentages lead to the remarkable notion that the Earth's crust is composed largely of oxygen anions (90 per cent of the volume), with silicon and the common metals filling up the rest of the space.

Goldschmidt was a brilliant scientist, with the rare ability to arrive at broad generalizations which draw together many apparently unconnected pieces of information. He also had a steely sense of humour. During his exile in Britain he carried a cyanide suicide capsule for the ultimate escape should the Germans have successfully invaded Britain. When a colleague asked for one he was told "Cyanide is for chemists; you, being a professor of mechanical engineering, will have to use the rope."

Graham, Thomas (*1805–1869*), was a British physical chemist who pioneered the chemistry of colloids, but who is best known for his studies of the diffusion of gases, the principal law concerning which is named after him.

Graham was born on 21 December 1805 in Glasgow, the son of a successful local manufacturer. His father had hoped that his son would, after leaving school, enter the Presbyterian ministry but in 1819, when he was only 14 years old, Graham enrolled at Glasgow University to study science. He later transferred to Edinburgh University and graduated in 1824. He returned to Glasgow to teach at the Mechanics Institute, which had been founded a year or two earlier by George Birkbeck for teaching craftsmen the scientific principles of their trades. In 1830 Graham became Professor of Chemistry at Anderson's College, Glasgow. He left Scotland seven years later to take up a similar position at University College, London, where he remained until

1854. In 1841 he became the first President of the Chemical Society of London, itself the first national society devoted solely to the science of chemistry. In 1855 he was appointed Master of the Royal Mint, a position once held by Isaac Newton. He died in London on 16 September 1869.

Graham's early interest was the dissolution and diffusion of gases. In 1826 he discovered that very soluble gases do not obey Henry's law (which states that solubility is proportional to the pressure of the gas). He measured the rates at which gases diffused through a porous plug of plaster-of-Paris, through narrow glass tubes, and through small holes in a metal plate. By 1831 he had formulated Graham's law of diffusion, which states that the rate of diffusion of a gas is inversely proportional to the square root of its density.

In 1829 Graham turned his attention briefly to inorganic chemistry. He studied the glow of phosphorus and observed that it was extinguished by organic vapours and various gases. He went on to examine phosphorus compounds in general, particularly phosphine and salts of the various oxyacids. He distinguished ortho-, meta- and pyrophosphates, which he prepared by fusing sodium carbonate with orthophosphoric acid. Graham had made the first detailed study of a polybasic acid.

In the 1850s, following his work on gases, Graham investigated the movement of molecules in solutions. He added crystals of a coloured chemical, such as cupric sulphate, to water and noted how long it took for the colour to spread throughout the solution. He observed that different chemicals took different times to disperse and that the dispersion rate increased with increasing temperature.

Then in 1861 he tried a technique similar to that which he had used for gases. He inserted a parchment barrier across a tank of water and added a coloured salt to the water on one side of it. He discovered that some of the coloured substance passed through the barrier. Repeating the experiment using glue or gelatin, he found that these substances did not pass through parchment. All the substances tested that could pass through also formed crystals, and Graham called this category crystalloids. Those that failed to cross the barrier did not form crystals and he called these colloids (from the Greek *kolla*, meaning glue). He distinguished between sols and gels (although he did not use these terms to describe them).

Using the same discovery, Graham developed a method of purifying colloids. The impure colloid was placed in a porous tube suspended in running water. The crystalloids (impurities) were washed away, leaving the purified colloid in the tube. He called the process dialysis, and it has since found a multitude of applications, from desalination equipment to artificial kidney machines.

Graham maintained his interest in gases, and in 1866 started a study of the occlusion of hydrogen by metals such as iron, platinum and palladium. He observed that metal foils which freely absorb gas at low temperatures become permeable to hydrogen when heated.

Grignard, François Auguste Victor (*1871–1935*), was a French organic chemist, best known for his work on organomagnesium compounds or Grignard reagents. For this work he shared the 1912 Nobel Prize in Chemistry with Paul Sabatier.

Grignard was born on 6 May 1871 in Cherbourg, the son of a sailmaker, and educated locally and at Cluny. His studies were interrupted for a year in 1892 while he did his military service (rising to the rank of corporal), after which he went to the University of Lyon and took a degree in mathematics. A former classmate then persuaded him to work in an organic chemistry laboratory under P.A. Barbier (1848–1922), where he quickly took to the new subject and began studying organomagnesium compounds, the subject of his PhD thesis in 1901. In 1905 he began lecturing in chemistry at Besançon and a year later he moved to Lyon. He was placed in charge of the organic chemistry courses at the University of Nancy in 1909, becoming a professor there in 1910. During World War I Grignard headed a department at the Sorbonne in Paris

concerned with the development of chemical warfare, going on a scientific trip to the United States in 1917. He succeeded Barbier as Professor of Chemistry at the University of Lyon in 1919, where he remained for the rest of his life. He died in Lyon on 13 December 1935.

Grignard's scientific career can be divided into three main periods. Up to 1914 he was concerned with the discovery, modifications and applications of organomagnesium compounds (Grignard reagents). During the years 1914 to 1918 he was engaged in research geared to the war effort, and afterwards he carried out a variety of researches in organic chemistry and concerned himself with chemistry education.

The general formula of a Grignard reagent is RMgX, where R is an alkyl radical, Mg is magnesium, and X is a halogen – usually chlorine, bromine or iodine. It is used to add an alkyl group (−R) to various organic molecules. Grignard made his first reagents in about 1900 by treating magnesium shavings with an alkyl halide (halogenoalkane) in anhydrous ether (ethoxyethane). The discovery made a dramatic impact on synthetic organic chemistry; by 1905, 200 publications had appeared on the topic of Grignard reagents and within another three years the total had risen to 500.

Grignard reagents added to formaldehyde (methanal) produce a primary alcohol; with any other aldehyde they form secondary alcohols, and added to ketones give rise to tertiary alcohols. They will also add to a carboxylic acid to produce first a ketone and ultimately a tertiary alcohol.

$$RMgX \quad + \quad \overset{R'}{\underset{R''}{\diagdown}} C = O \quad \longrightarrow \quad \left[R - \overset{R'}{\underset{R''}{\overset{|}{\underset{|}{C}}}} - OMgX \right] \quad \overset{H_2O}{\longrightarrow} \quad R - \overset{R'}{\underset{R''}{\overset{|}{\underset{|}{C}}}} - OH$$

ketone   tertiary alcohol

$$RMgX \quad + \quad \overset{R'}{\underset{HO}{\diagdown}} C = O \quad \longrightarrow \quad \overset{R'}{\underset{R}{\diagdown}} C = O \quad + \quad RMgX \quad \longrightarrow \quad R - \overset{R'}{\underset{R}{\overset{|}{\underset{|}{C}}}} - OH$$

carboxylic acid   ketone   tertiary alcohol

Examples of typical Grignard syntheses.

The reagents have many industrial applications, such as the production of tetraethyl lead (from ethyl magnesium bromide and lead chloride) for use as an anti-knock compound in petrol.

During World War I Grignard worked on the production of the poisonous gas phosgene (carbonyl chloride) and on methods for the rapid detection of the presence of mustard gas. After the war he started compiling his great *Traité de Chimie Organique*, a multi-volume work that began publication in 1935. He continued research, investigating the organic compounds of aluminium and mercury; he also studied the terpenes.

Haber, Fritz (*1868–1934*), was a German chemist who made contributions to physical chemistry and electrochemistry, but who is best remembered for the Haber process, a method of synthesizing ammonia by the direct catalytic combination of nitrogen and hydrogen. For this outstanding achievement he was awarded the 1918 Nobel Prize in Chemistry (presented in 1919).

Haber was born on 9 December 1868 in Breslau, Silesia (now Wrocław, Poland), the son of a dye manufacturer. He was educated at the local Gymnasium and at the universities of Berlin (under August von Hofmann) and Heidelberg (where he was a student of Robert Bunsen). He completed his undergraduate studies at the Technische Hochschule at Charlottenburg, where he carried out his first research in organic chemistry. After spending some time working for three chemical companies, he briefly entered his father's business, but after only a few months Haber returned to organic chemistry research at Jena.

He then obtained a junior post at Karlsruhe Technische Hochschule, becoming an unpaid lecturer there in 1896. He held the professorship of Physical Chemistry and Electrochemistry at Karlsruhe from 1906 until 1911, by which time his reputation had grown to such an extent that he was made Director of the newly established Kaiser Wilhelm Institute for Physical Chemistry at Berlin-Dahlem. During World War I he placed the Institute's resources in the hands of the government and, being a staunch patriot, was bitterly disappointed by Germany's defeat in 1918. Then when Adolf Hitler rose to power in 1933 even Haber's genius and patriotism could not compensate for his Jewish ancestry and he was forced to seek exile in Britain, where he worked for a few months at the Cavendish Laboratory, Cambridge. Shortly afterwards, while on holiday in Switzerland, he died of a heart attack in Basle on 29 January 1934.

During the late 1890s Haber carried out important researches in thermodynamics and electrochemistry, studying particularly electrode potentials and the processes that occur at electrodes. He was an early, but largely unsuccessful, pioneer of fuel cells in which the electric current was produced by the atmospheric oxidation of carbon or carbon monoxide. He also worked on the electrodeposition of iron, which had applications in the making of plates for printing banknotes. His work during this period culminated with the publication of two influential books: *The Theoretical Bases of Technical Electrochemistry* (1898) and *The Thermodynamics of Technical Gas Reactions* (1905).

Haber used his extensive knowledge and experience of thermodynamics in his investigations of the synthesis of ammonia by the catalytic hydrogenation of atmospheric nitrogen. Although from 1904 he made extensive free energy calculations and performed many experiments, it was not until 1909 that the process was ready for industrial development under Carl Bosch (1874–1940). Haber's early successful experiments used osmium or uranium catalysts at a temperature of 550°C (823K) and 150–200 atmospheres pressure $(1.5–2.0 \times 10^7 \, \mathrm{Nm^{-2}})$. Later industrial processes used higher pressures and slightly lower temperatures, with finely divided iron as the catalyst. The nitrogen from air was compressed with producer gas (the source of hydrogen) and the ammonia formed was removed as a solution in water. In this version it is also known as the Haber–Bosch process.

At Karlsruhe Haber continued his work in electrochemistry and in 1909 constructed the first glass electrode (which measures hydrogen ion concentration – acidity, or pH – by monitoring the electrode potential across a piece of thin glass). One of his first tasks after the outbreak of World War I in 1914 was to devise a method of producing nitric acid for making high explosives, using ammonia from the Haber process (to make blockaded Germany independent of supplies of Chile saltpetre – sodium nitrate – from South America). Later he became involved in the gas offensive and superintended the release of chlorine into the Allied trenches at Ypres. When the French later retaliated by using phosgene (carbonyl chloride, whose production was in the hands of François Grignard), Haber was given control of the German Chemical Warfare Service, with the rank of Captain, and organized the manufacture of lethal gases. He was also responsible for the training of personnel and developed an effective gas mask.

After the war Haber set himself the task of extracting gold from sea water to help to pay off the debt demanded by the Allies in reparation for the damage caused during the hostilities. Svante Arrhenius had calculated that the sea contains 8,000 million tonnes of gold. The project got as far as the fitting out of a ship and the commencement of the extraction process, but the yields were too low and the project was abandoned in 1928.

One of his most important ideas after the war was what is now known as the Born–Haber cycle. In a conversation with Max Born (1882–1970) – who also came from Breslau and who was also to go to Cambridge in 1933 – Haber suggested how various chemical energies could be calculated. He extended Born's work and expressed it in diagrammatic form.

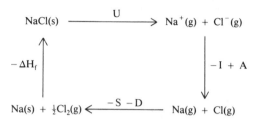

Born-Haber cycle for the formation of sodium chloride

In the diagram, U is the lattice energy of sodium chloride, I is the ionization energy of sodium (the energy necessary to remove an electron from the gaseous atom), A is the electron affinity of chlorine (the energy required to remove an electron from a gaseous negative ion), S and D are the sublimation and dissociation energies of sodium and chlorine respectively, and ΔH_f is the heat of formation of sodium chloride.

Hammick, Dalziel Llewellyn (*1887–1966*), was a British chemist whose major contributions were in the fields of theoretical and synthetic organic chemistry.

Hammick was born in West Norwood, London, the son of a businessman; when he was 12 years old his family moved to the country, which gave him a life-long interest in rural pursuits. He was educated at Whitgift School and then won a scholarship to Magdalen College, Oxford; he graduated in 1908. From Oxford he went to work in the laboratory of Otto Dimroth in Munich, where in 1910 he gained a PhD for his researches on solubility. He returned to Britain and held teaching posts at Gresham's School in Holt, Norfolk, and at Winchester College. In 1921 he returned to Oxford as a Fellow of Oriel College and a Lecturer at Corpus Christi College. He remained at Oxford until his retirement; he died there on 17 October 1966.

Hammick's research activities began at Gresham's School, where he investigated the action of sulphur dioxide on various metal oxides. At Oxford he initially continued researching inorganic substances, particularly with regard to their solubilities. He investigated the dimorphism of potassium ethyl sulphate and the ternary system comprising water, sodium sulphite and sodium hydroxide. He also studied sulphur and its compounds (such as carbon disulphide), and suggested structures for liquid sulphur and plastic sulphur (which later workers interpreted in terms of linear polymers).

By the mid-1920s, Hammick's attentions had begun to swing towards organic chemistry. In 1922 he showed that the sublimation of α-trioxymethylene results in the polymer polyoxymethylene; 40 years later this substance was to be used as a commercial polymer. In 1930 Hammick devised a rule to predict the order of substitution in benzene derivatives. Aromaticity and the role of electron attraction and donation of substituents already present in the benzene ring were not yet understood, but Hammick proposed the following useful rule for further substitution of the compound Ph-XY: "If Y is in a higher group of the periodic table than X or is in the same group (Y is of a lower mass than X), then further substitution will take place *meta* to the group XY (giving 1,3 di-substitution). In all other cases, substitution goes *ortho* or *para* (giving 1,2- or 1,4-di-substitution); the nitroso group is an exception."

Hammick spent much time investigating organic reaction rates. He studied, for example, the decarboxylation of quinaldinic acid (the alpha-, *ortho-* or 2- carboxylic acid of quinoline) by aldehydes and ketones. The reaction, now known as the Hammick reaction, is used in the synthesis of larger molecules.

quinaldinic acid

acetophenone
(methylphenylketone)

quinoline-2-phenyl-2′-ethanol

During World War II, when supplies of toluene for making explosives were short, Hammick directed his efforts at syntheses using benzene (obtained from the distillation of coal tar). Using alumina-silica catalysts, he achieved a 30 per cent conversion of benzene to toluene.

Harden, Arthur (*1865–1940*), was a British biochemist who investigated the mechanism of sugar fermentation and the role of enzymes in this process. For this work he shared the 1929 Nobel Prize in Chemistry with the German biochemist Hans von Euler-Chelpin (1873–1964).

Harden was born in Manchester on 12 October 1865, the third child of a local businessman. With his eight sisters, he was brought up in an austere non-conformist family environment. At the age of seven he attended a private school in Manchester and then from 1876 to 1881 he was at Tettenhall College, Staffordshire. From there he moved to Owen's College (now the University of Manchester) to study chemistry, graduating in 1885. In the following year he won a research scholarship to Erlangen University and was awarded his PhD in 1888 for his work on purification and properties of β-nitrosonaphthylamine.

On his return to Owen's College Harden became a lecturer and demonstrator, teaching chemistry and writing textbooks. In 1897 he became head of the chemistry section of the British Institute of Preventative Medicine, later called the Jenner Institute. In 1905 the chemistry and biology departments merged under his direction. In 1912 he was appointed Professor of Biochemistry at the University of London. His main researches were interrupted by World War I, when he turned his attention to the production of vitamins B and C as a contribution to the war effort. Harden was knighted in 1936 and died in Bourne End, Buckinghamshire, on 17 June 1940.

Harden began work on sugar fermentation in 1898, soon after joining the Jenner Institute. He used the bacterium *Bacillus coli* (now *Escherichia coli*), hoping to detect metabolic differences that would help to distinguish between the various strains. He started studying the metabolism of yeasts in 1900, three years after Eduard Buchner had produced evidence for the existence of enzymes with his experiments on cell-free alcoholic fermentation of sugar. Harden showed that the occurrence of fermentation in the cell-free yeast extract even in the absence of sugar was caused by the action of the enzyme zymase on glycogen from the disrupted cells. The extract's loss of enzymic activity on standing he demonstrated to be caused by a second enzyme, a proteolytic (protein-splitting) substance which breaks down zymase.

Harden and his co-workers then went on to show that zymase consists of at least two different substances: one heat-sensitive (probably a protein, the enzyme) and one heat-stable, which he called a co-ferment (now known as a co-enzyme). He separated the two using Thomas Graham's dialysis method, proving that the co-enzyme is not colloidal in nature. Hans von Euler-Chelpin later showed that it is diphospho-pyridine nucleotide (DPN).

So far Harden had demonstrated that the fermentation process requires three ingredients: enzyme, co-enzyme and substrate. But with only these three the reaction soon slowed down. It was accelerated, however, by the unlikely addition of phosphates. Harden discovered the hexose sugar compound hexosediphosphate in the normal reaction mixture (he later found hexosemonophosphate as well), thus proving that phosphorylation is an intermediate step in the fermentation process. This important finding stimulated great interest in intermediate metabolism, and later researchers were able to show the widespread importance of phosphate groups in many metabolic reactions.

After World War I Harden continued to investigate the details of fermentation. His approach to work always remained accurate, objective and dispassionate. In fact his unwillingness to speculate combined with a sometimes narrow approach to a problem may have hampered his researches. In later life he devoted much of his energy to launching and promoting the *Biochemical Journal* and was its editor for many years.

Haworth, Walter Norman (*1883-1950*), was a British organic chemist whose researches concentrated on carbohydrates, particularly sugars. He made significant advances in determining the structures of many of these compounds, for which he shared the 1937 Nobel Prize in Chemistry with the German organic chemist Paul Karrer, becoming the first British organic chemist to be so honoured.

Haworth was born in Chorley, Lancashire, on 19 March 1883, the son of a factory manager. He left school at the age of 14 and joined his father's linoleum works, where he became interested in the dyestuffs used in floor coverings. In spite of parental disapproval, he continued his education with a private tutor and in 1903 realized his ambition to enter the chemistry department of the University of Manchester, where he studied under William Perkin Jr. He gained his degree in 1906 and won a scholarship to Göttingen, where he did research with Otto Wallach (1847-1931). He was awarded his doctorate after only one year and returned to Manchester, gaining a DSc there in 1911 in the remarkably short time of only five years since his first degree.

Over the next few years Haworth held various university appointments - at Imperial College, London (1911-1912), St Andrews (1912-1920) and Durham (1920-1925) - before accepting a professorship at Birmingham University, where he remained until he retired in 1948, a year after he received a knighthood. He died in Birmingham on his birthday (19 March) 1950.

Haworth's lifelong interest in carbohydrates began when he was at St Andrews. There he teamed up with T. Purdie and J.C. Irvine, trying to characterize sugars by methylation of their hydroxy groups. The work was interrupted by World War I, when the laboratory was turned

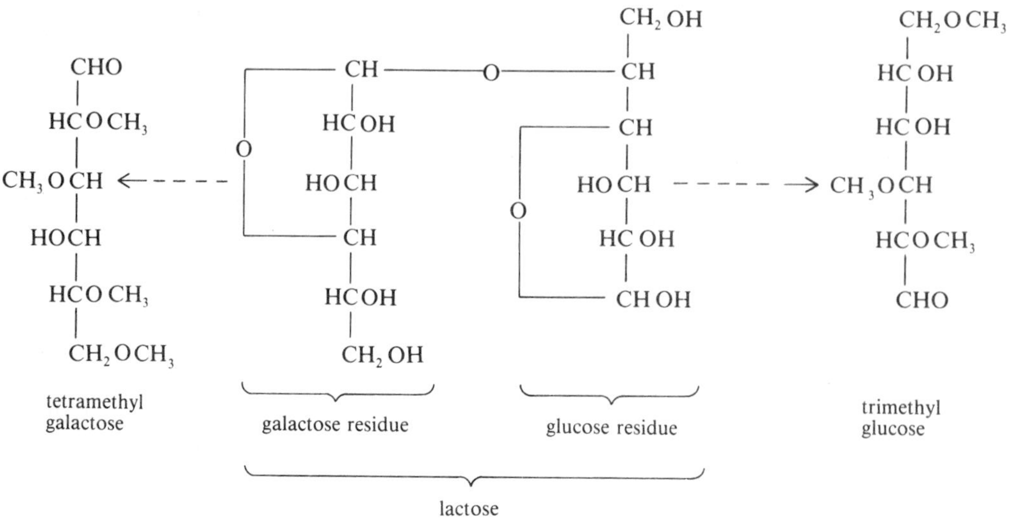

tetramethyl galactose

galactose residue

glucose residue

trimethyl glucose

lactose

over to the production of fine chemicals and drugs, which Haworth supervised. After the war he continued research, concentrating his team's efforts on the disaccharides. Again he used the technique of methylation followed by acid hydrolysis. Lactose, for example, forms an octamethyl derivative which on hydrolysis yields tetramethyl galactose and 2,3,6-trimethyl glucose, indicating the structural formula for lactose.

Later investigations suggested that the carbon atoms in hexoses usually have a ring structure and a great deal of Haworth's work at Birmingham was devoted to establishing the linkages in these rings (known as Haworth formulae). In 1926 he proposed that methyl glucose normally exists as what is now called a pyranose ring. The complex analytical procedures involved oxidation and methylation to give products that were further reacted to form simpler known substances that could be crystallized and identified. He also established that methyl glucose can have an alternative furanose structure. His book *The Constitution of the Sugars* (1929) became a standard work.

pyran   furan

β-glucopyranose   β-glucofuranose

Using their knowledge of simple sugars, Haworth's research team was able to investigate the chain structures of polysaccharides, establishing the structures of cellulose, starch and glycogen. Work on sugars led naturally to studies of vitamin C and by 1932 the whole research effort was directed to the determination of the structure and synthesis of this substance, which Haworth named ascorbic acid. The research resulted in an industrial process for synthesizing vitamin C for medical uses.

In the late 1930s Haworth studied the reactions of polysaccharides with enzymes and certain aspects of the chemistry of the hormone insulin. During World War II (1939–1945) Haworth's laboratory became a primary producer of purified uranium for the war effort, which led to work on the preparation and properties of organic fluorine compounds. Many of the workers went to the newly opened experimental stations at Oak Ridge in the United States and Chalk River in Canada.

Henry, William (*1774–1836*), was a chemist and physician, best known for his study of the solubility of gases in liquids which led to what is now known as Henry's law. He was also an early experimenter in electrochemistry, and he established that firedamp – the cause of many mining disasters – is methane.

Henry was born in Manchester on 12 December 1774. His father was a physician and industrial chemist who introduced the use of chlorine as a bleaching agent for textiles. A childhood accident affected Henry's growth and left him in poor health for the rest of his life. He went to a school run by a local clergyman and then to Manchester Academy, which was an offshoot of the famous Dissenting Academy at Warrington. (The Dissenting Institutions offered a wide curriculum containing scientific, practical and mathematical subjects, unlike the grammar schools of the time which provided an education based almost entirely on Latin.)

On leaving the Academy in 1790 Henry became secretary companion to Dr Thomas Percival, the founder of the influential Literary and Philosophical Society of Manchester. Five years later he went to Edinburgh University to study medicine, but left after a year to help his father. During this time he began his own chemical experiments, and published his first paper in 1797. He returned to Edinburgh in 1805 and graduated in medicine two years later, with a thesis on uric acid.

Henry suffered from a disorder that affected his hands and after unsuccessful surgery in 1824 he was unable to carry out chemical experiments; he returned to a study of medicine. But his continuing poor health led to severe depression and in Manchester on 2 September 1836 he committed suicide.

Henry's early chemical experiments concerned the composition of hydrogen chloride and hydrochloric acid. A series of chemistry lectures which he gave in Manchester in the winter of 1798–1799 were later published as a successful textbook *Elements of Experimental Chemistry*, which he expanded over the following 30 years and which by 1829 had run to its eleventh edition. In 1803 he published the results of his research on the solubility of gases, outlining the basis of Henry's law which in its modern form states that the mass of gas dissolved by a given volume of liquid is directly proportional to the pressure of the gas with which it is in equilibrium, provided the temperature is constant. In mathematical terms, $m = kp$, where m is the mass of gas, p the pressure exerted by the undissolved gas, and k a constant. There are many deviations from the law and it is closely obeyed only by very dilute solutions.

In 1805 Henry worked at determining the composition of ammonia. He confirmed that it contains hydrogen and nitrogen in the proportions suggested by Humphry Davy and Claude Berthollet, but showed that Davy was incorrect in his belief that it contains also oxygen, which for Davy was a necessary characteristic of all alkalis.

At the beginning of the nineteenth century coal gas was being introduced as a possible fuel for illumination. Henry worked for about 20 years on the analysis of inflammable mixtures of gases and attempted to find correlations between chemical composition and illuminative properties. During these investigations he confirmed John Dalton's results of the composition of methane and ethane, and like Dalton showed that hydrogen and carbon combine in definite proportions to form a limited number of compounds. In this work Henry made use of the catalytic properties of platinum, newly discovered by Johann Döbereiner in 1821.

After 1824 Henry returned to medical investigations and studied contagious diseases. He believed that these were spread by chemicals which could be rendered harmless by heating; he used heat to disinfect clothing during an outbreak of Asiatic cholera in 1831. By the time of Henry's death, his son W.C. Henry was already an active chemist, publishing a work in 1836 on the poisoning of platinum catalysts.

Hess, Germain Henri (1802–1850), was a Swiss-born Russian chemist, best known for his pioneering work in thermochemistry and the law of constant heat summation named after him.

Hess was born in Geneva on 7 August 1802, the son of a Swiss artist. When he was only three years old his family moved to St Petersburg (now Leningrad) to enable his father to be a tutor in a rich Moscow family and they adopted a Russian way of life. Hess became known as German Ivanovich Gess. He qualified in medicine in 1825 at the University of Dorpat, where he also received a thorough grounding in chemistry and geology. He went to Stockholm for a short time to study chemistry under Jöns Berzelius, then returned to Russia for a geological expedition to the Urals before settling in Irkutsk in a medical practice. He was elected an adjunct member of the St Petersburg Academy of Sciences in 1828 and two years later was chosen as extraordinary Academician. He then settled in St Petersburg, abandoned his medical practice, and devoted the rest of his life to chemistry.

Hess then took various academic appointments: Commissioner to plan the course in practical and Theoretical Chemistry at the St Petersburg Technological Institute (leading to a professorship there); at the Mining Institute and Chief Pedagogical Institute; and in 1838 at the Artillery School. One of his students at the Chief Pedagogical Institute was A.A. Voskressenskii, who was later to become the Professor of Chemistry and teach Dmitri Mendeleyev.

In 1834 Hess was made an Academician of the Russian Academy of Sciences. Between 1838 and 1843 he did the research in thermochemistry for which he is most famous, but then became less active in the field of chemical research, concentrating more on education and the seeking of due recognition for other workers. He was responsible, for example, for the granting of the prestigious Demidov Award to Karl Klaus for his discovery of ruthenium. In 1848 Hess's health failed, and he died in St Petersburg on 30 November 1850.

Hess pioneered in the field of thermochemistry which, in a climate concerned mainly with analysis and synthesis in organic and inorganic chemistry, had largely been left to physicists. He had previously worked in various other areas, including the prevention of endemic eye disorders, the analysis of water and minerals from various parts of Russia, the analysis of natural gas from the region of Baku, the oxidation of sugars, and the chemical properties of waxes and resins. His textbook *Fundamentals of Pure Chemistry* (1831) remained the standard work in the Russian language until Mendeleyev's books of the 1860s.

Hess's first paper on thermochemistry, on "The evolution of heat in multiple proportions", was published in 1838. Two years later he published the full text of Hess's law in both French and German, which states that the heat change in a given chemical reaction depends only on the initial and final states of the system and is independent of the path followed, provided that heat is the only form of energy to enter or leave the system. Every chemical change either absorbs or evolves heat (even if the amount is not enough to cause a measurable temperature change); reactions that absorb heat are called endothermic, those that evolve heat are termed exothermic. According to modern convention, evolved heat is negative in sign and absorbed heat is positive. The symbol ΔH denotes a change in heat content at constant pressure, the unit of heat and energy being the joule.

Suppose a substance A can be converted to substance D either directly, with a heat of reaction of w joules, or indirectly by way of substances B and C, with heats of reaction of the three stages of x, y and z joules respectively. Then

for $A \rightarrow D$, $\Delta H = -w$,
$A \rightarrow B$, $\Delta H = -x$,
$B \rightarrow C$, $\Delta H = -y$,
and $C \rightarrow D$, $\Delta H = -z$.

According to Hess's law the heat of reaction in going from A to D is the same whether the change is achieved directly or through a series of changes, and $w = x + y + z$. Heat changes can thus be added algebraically, allowing the calculation of heats of reaction that it would be impossible to measure directly by experiment. It is in modern terms merely an application of the law of conservation of energy, which was not formulated until 1842. In that year Hess proposed his second law, the law of thermoneutrality, which states that in exchange reactions of neutral salts in aqueous solution, no heat effect is observed. No explanation of this law was forthcoming until the announcement of Svante Arrhenius' theory of electrolytic dissociation in 1887.

After Hess died no other researchers carried on his work, and thermochemistry was neglected for the next decade. Investigations of heats of reaction had to be carried out all over again (by scientists such as Pierre Berthelot in France and Hans Thomsen in Denmark). Final recognition came in 1887, when Friedrich Wilhelm Ostwald began the section on thermochemistry in his *General Chemistry* textbook with a full account of Hess's work.

Hevesy, Georg von (*1885-1966*), was a Hungarian-born chemist whose main achievements were the introduction of isotopic tracers (to follow chemical reactions) and the discovery of the element hafnium. For his work on isotopes he was awarded the 1943 Nobel Prize in Chemistry. In 1959 he received the Atoms for Peace Prize.

Hevesy was born in Budapest on 1 August 1885, into a family of industrialists. He was educated there in a Roman Catholic School and then attended the Technische Hochschule in Berlin with the intention of training as a chemical engineer. But he contracted pneumonia and moved to the more agreeable climate of Freiburg. After obtaining his doctorate in 1908 he moved again to study chemistry at the Zurich Technische Hochschule, where he worked under Richard Lorenz on the chemistry of molten salts. Following yet another move to the Karlsruhe laboratories of Fritz Haber (where he investigated the emission of electrons during the oxidation of sodium/potassium alloys), Hevesy took Haber's advice and went to Manchester in 1911 to learn some of the new research techniques being developed by Ernest Rutherford, particularly those involving radioactive elements.

In 1913 Hevesy went to join Friedrich Paneth in Vienna for a short time to continue these studies and but for the outbreak of World War I in 1914 would have carried on this work with Henry Moseley at Oxford. Instead he continued his researches in Budapest and then in 1920 went to Copenhagen to work in the Institute of Physics under the guidance of Niels Bohr and Johannes Brönsted. He returned to Freiburg in 1926, only to go back to Copenhagen eight years later. In 1943, during World War II, he escaped to Sweden from the German occupation of Denmark and became a professor at the University of Stockholm, where he remained until shortly before his death. During an academic career extending over 58 years Hevesy worked in nine major research centres in seven European countries. He died at a clinic in Freiburg on 5 July 1966.

At Manchester in 1911 Rutherford set Hevesy the task of separating radioactive radium-D from a 100 kg sample of lead. After a year's work Hevesy had been unable to achieve any separation – neither could he detect any chemical differences between radium-D and lead (we now know that this was an impossible task using conventional chemical techniques because radium-D is an isotope of lead, lead-210). But he turned this similarity to advantage by mixing some pure radium-D with ordinary lead and following chemical reactions of the lead by detecting its "acquired" radioactivity. He perfected this technique while working with Paneth in Vienna (1913), using added radium-D to study the chemistry of lead and bismuth salts. This was the beginning of the use of radioactive tracers.

During his first period at Copenhagen (1920–1926), Hevesy successfully separated isotopes of mercury using fractional distillation at low pressure. During an investigation of zirconium minerals using X-rays, he and Dirk Coster in 1922 discovered hafnium (so-called after Hafnia, the latin name for Copenhagen). Continuing his interest in isotopes, he effected a method of isotopic enrichment of chlorine and potassium.

On his return to Freiburg (1926) he studied the relative abundances of elements on Earth and in the universe, basing his calculations on chemical analyses by means of X-ray fluorescence. During the early 1930s he commenced experiments with his radioactive tracer technique on biological specimens, noting, for example, the take-up of radioactive lead by plants. The production of an unstable isotope of phosphorus in 1934 enabled the first tracer studies to be made on animals. Hevesy used the isotope to trace the movement of phosphorus in the tissues of the human body. During his second stay at Copenhagen (1934–1943) he took with him a sample of heavy water (donated by Harold Urey in the United States who in 1923 had spent a year at Bohr's laboratory). Hevesy used the sample to study the mechanism of water exchange between goldfish and their surroundings and also within the human body. He then extended his experiments using potassium-42, sodium-34 and chlorine-38.

During his later years in Stockholm he continued to work on the transfer of radioactive isotopes within living material. Using radioactive calcium to label families of mice he showed that of calcium atoms present at birth about 1 in 300 are passed on to the next generation.

Heyrovský, Jaroslav (1890–1967), was a Czech chemist who was awarded the 1959 Nobel Prize in Chemistry for his invention and development of polarography, an electrochemical technique of chemical analysis.

Heyrovský was born in Prague on or about 20 December 1890, the son of a Professor of Law at Charles University, Prague. He studied chemistry, physics and mathematics at his father's university and graduated from there in 1910. He then went to University College, London, to pursue postgraduate research under William Ramsey and Frederick Donnan (1870–1956), who aroused his interest in electrochemistry. He became a demonstrator in the chemistry department in 1913. He served in a military hospital during World War I and in 1920 was appointed an assistant in the Institute of Analytical Chemistry at Prague. He subsequently became a lecturer (1922), assistant professor (1924) and Professor of Physical Chemistry (1926). He remained at the Institute until 1950, when he became Director of the newly founded Polarographic Institute of the Czechoslovak Academy of Sciences. He revisited London in November 1955 to deliver his presidential address to the Polarographic Society. He died in Prague on 27 March 1967.

Heyrovský began the work that was to lead to the invention of polarography during his student days in London while he was investigating the electrode potential of aluminium. The technique was perfected in 1922, soon after his return to Prague. It depends on detecting the discharge of ions during electrolysis of aqueous solutions. The solution to be analysed is placed in a glass cell containing two electrodes, one above the other. The lower electrode is simply a pool of mercury. The upper electrode, called a dropping mercury electrode, consists of a fine capillary tube through which mercury flows and falls away as a series of droplets. The growing mercury droplet at the tip of the capillary tube constitutes the actual electrode.

With the dropping mercury electrode made, say, the cathode (to analyse for cations in solution), the voltage between the electrodes is slowly increased and the associated current observed on a galvanometer. When a cation is discharged (reduced) at the cathode, the current increases rapidly and then remains at a constant value. At that time, the voltage is characteristic of the cation concerned and the magnitude of the current is a measure of its concentration.

In 1925, together with M. Shikita, Heyrovský developed the polarograph, an instrument that automatically applies the steadily increasing voltage and traces the resulting voltage-current curve on a chart recorder. Such curves are called polarograms.

Polarography can be used to analyse for several substances at once, because the polarogram records a separate limiting current for each. It is also extremely sensitive, being capable of detecting concentrations as little as 1 part per million. Most chemical elements can be determined by the method (as long as they form ionic species) in compounds, mixtures or alloys. The technique has been extended to organic analysis and to the study of chemical equilibria and the rates of reactions in solutions. It can also be used for end-point detection in titrations, a type of volumetric analysis sometimes called voltammetry.

Hinshelwood, Cyril Norman (*1897–1967*), was a British physical chemist who made fundamental studies of the kinetics and mechanisms of chemical reactions. He also investigated bacterial growth. He shared the 1956 Nobel Prize in Chemistry with the Soviet scientist Nikolay Semenov for his work on chain reaction mechanisms.

Hinshelwood was born in London on 19 June 1897, the son of an accountant. His family emigrated to Canada when he was a child, but returned to England after his father's death. He was educated at the Westminster City School, London, from where he won a scholarship to Balliol College, Oxford. The outbreak of World War I in 1914 interrupted his studies and from 1916 to 1918 he worked in the Department of Explosives at the Royal Ordnance Factory at Queensferry, Scotland. He returned to Balliol in 1919 and took the shortened post-war chemistry course, graduating in 1920 and being immediately elected a Fellow of the college. Subsequent academic appointments were as Fellow of Trinity College, Oxford (1921-1937), Dr Lee's Professor of Chemistry in the University of Oxford (1937-1964) and, on his retirement, Senior Research Fellow at Imperial College, London. Hinshelwood was knighted in 1948; he died in London on 9 October 1967.

While he was at the explosive works in Scotland Hinshelwood tried to measure the slow rate of decomposition of solid explosives by monitoring the gases they evolved. His first researches at Balliol pursued this line, and he studied the decomposition of solid substances in the presence and absence of catalysts. He then investigated homogeneous gas reactions. He found initially that the thermal decomposition of the vapours of substances such as acetone (propanone) and aliphatic aldehydes occur by means of first or second order processes. If A and B are the reactants, then the rate of a chemical reaction can be expressed as

$$R = k[A]^x[B]^y,$$

where R is the rate, k is the velocity constant, [A] and [B] are the concentrations of the reactants, and x and y are powers. If $x = 1$ the reaction is said to be first order, if $x = 2$ it is second order, and so on. At that time the activation of chemical reactions was considered only in terms of collision mechanisms - easily applied to bi-molecular reactions but not capable of explaining unimolecular reactions. Hinshelwood showed that even apparently simple decomposition reactions usually occur in stages. Thus for acetone (propanone):

a) $(CH_3)_2CO \rightarrow CH_2 = CO + CH_4$
         acetone
         (propanone)

b) $CH_2 = CO \rightarrow \frac{1}{2}C_2H_4 + CO$

This early work centred on the relationship between temperature, concentration and the influence of second and third components.

Hinshelwood went on to demonstrate that many reactions can be explained in terms of a series - a chain - of interdependent stages. At low temperatures the reaction between hydrogen and oxygen, or hydrogen and chlorine, for example, is comparatively slow because the chain reactions involved terminate at the walls of the vessel. But at high temperatures the chain reactions accelerate the process to explosion point. He provided experimental evidence for the role of activated molecules in initiating the chain reaction.

He also investigated reaction kinetics in aqueous and non-aqueous solutions, together with hydrolytic processes, esterification, and acylation of amines. He published his classic work on reaction kinetics, *Kinetics of Chemical Change*, in 1926.

In 1938 Hinshelwood published with S. Daglay the first of more than 100 papers on bacterial growth. Initially he investigated the effects of various nutrients such as carbohydrates and amino acids on simple non-pathogenic organisms. Later he studied the effects of trace elements and toxic substances such as sulphonamides, proflavine and streptomycin. He considered that all the various chemical reactions that occurred in his bacterial growth experiments were interconnected and mutually dependent, the product of one reaction becoming the reactant for the next - a process he termed "total integration".

Hinshelwood's contributions to both these fields won universal acknowledgement during his lifetime, and he was the recipient of many honours. He was President of the Chemical Society during its Centenary year (1947) and President of the Royal Society at its Tercentenary in 1960. He was a capable linguist and artist, and a year after his death his paintings went on exhibition in Goldsmiths Hall, London.

Hodgkin, Dorothy Mary Crowfoot (*1910-*   ), is a British chemist who has used X-ray crystallographic analysis to determine the structures of numerous complex organic molecules, including penicillin and vitamin B_{12} (cobalamin). She was awarded the 1964 Nobel Prize in Chemistry.

Hodgkin was born on 12 May 1910 in Cairo, where her father, John Crowfoot, was serving with the Egyptian education service. After the family returned to Britain she attended the Sir John Leman School, Beccles, before going to Somerville College, Oxford. In 1928 she indulged her interest in archaeology by accompanying her father on an expedition to Transjordan. After graduation she went to Cambridge University where between 1932 and 1934 she worked on determining the structure of sterols, at a time when X-ray analysis was limited to confirming the correct formula as predicted by organic chemical methods. She developed the technique of X-ray investigation to the point at which it became a very useful analytical method. In 1934 she returned to Oxford to take up a lecturing appointment, and three years later married Thomas Hodgkin, a noted authority on African affairs. She remained at Oxford for a further 33 years until 1970, when she became Chancellor of Bristol University.

While at Cambridge, Hodgkin studied the structures of calciferol (vitamin D_2) and lumisterol and, with C.H. Carlisle, she correctly analysed cholesterol iodide, the first complex organic molecule to be determined completely by X-ray crystallography. On her return to Oxford (1934) she investigated various compounds of physiological importance, especially penicillin, the structure of which she and her co-workers determined before the organic chemists. This work was of national importance at the time, and was to have a lasting effect on the development of

antibiotics. She later elucidated the structure of cephalosporin C, an antibiotic closely related to penicillin.

In about 1948 Hodgkin began her work on vitamin B_{12}, a compound essential to the life of red blood cells in the body; the inability to absorb sufficient vitamin B_{12} from the diet leads to pernicious anaemia. Chemical analysis had suggested that this complex compound has an approximate empirical formula of $C_{61-64}H_{86-92}O_{14}N_{14}PCo$, with a single cobalt atom, a cyanide group and a nucleotide-like group. Hodgkin

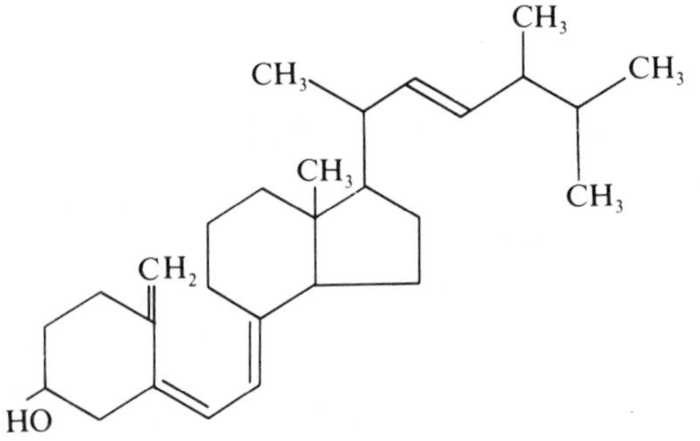

calciferol
(vitamin D_2)

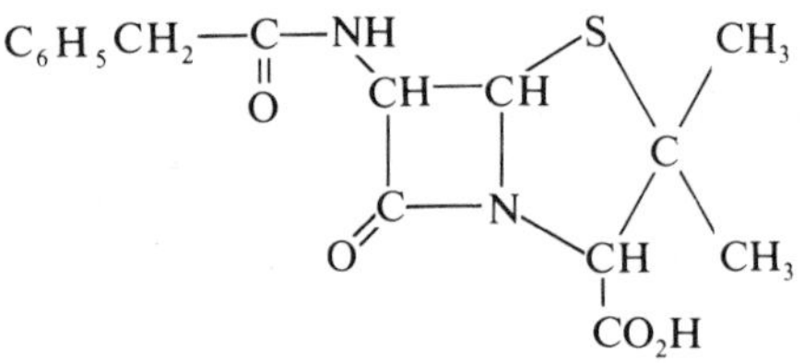

penicillin

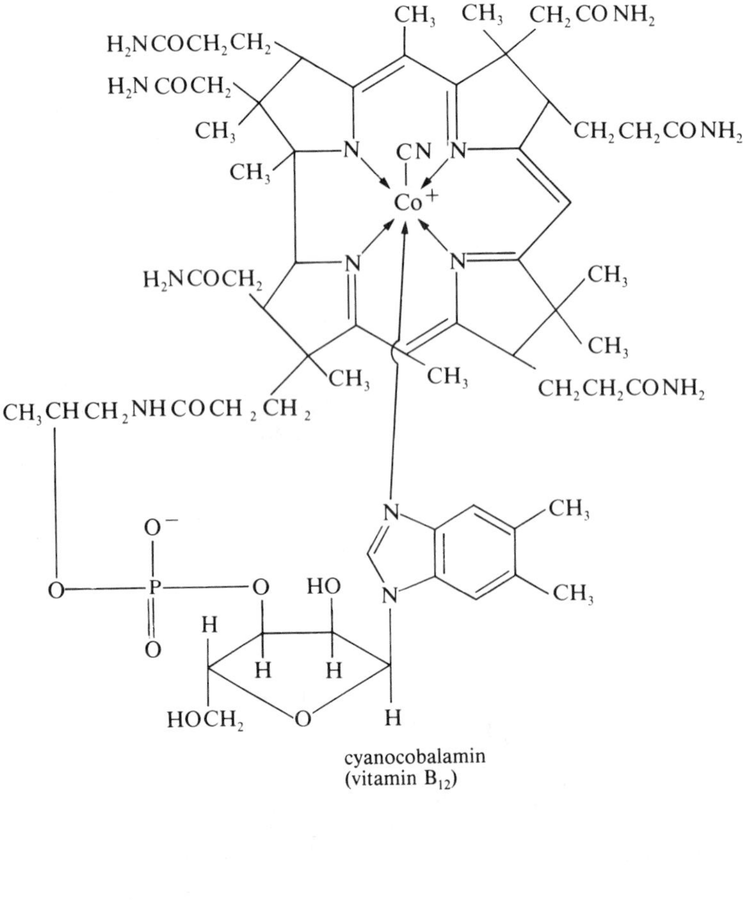

cyanocobalamin
(vitamin B_{12})

and her collaborators collected photographs and data of X-ray diffraction patterns of both wet and dry B_{12}, a hexacarboxylic acid derivative, and a derivative in which a selenium atom had been introduced. Using Fourier series the data were analysed mathematically by one of the first electronic computers, which were just becoming available. After a lengthy and painstaking step-by-step process the structure was finally worked out and announced in 1957 (the empirical formula was found to be $C_{63}H_{88}O_{14}N_{14}PCo$). Work on the biologically active aspect of the molecule continued into the 1960s.

In addition to the 1964 Nobel Prize award, Hodgkin was in 1965 admitted to the Order of Merit, becoming only the second woman to receive this honour (the first was Florence Nightingale).

Hofmann, August Wilhelm (von) (*1818–1892*), a German chemist, was one of the great organic chemists of the nineteenth century and had enormous influence on the development of the subject in both Britain and Germany. Much of his work was connected with coal tar and its constituents, particularly aniline (phenylamine) and phenol. He was the first to explore the chemistry of the aliphatic amines (although not the first to synthesize them) and was the discoverer of the quaternary ammonium salts. His students included those (such as William Perkin) who originated and developed the British synthetic dye industry, and as a chemist he discovered and patented a number of dyes of his own.

Hofmann was born on 8 April 1818 in Giessen, the son of an architect. He entered the local university in 1836 to study law and philosophy, but his interests changed when he attended some of Justus von Liebig's lectures and he continued his studies by specializing in chemistry. In 1841 he obtained his doctorate for a thesis based on investigations into the constitution of coal tar. He then neglected his studies and academic advancement to look after his father, who died in 1843.

In that same year Hofmann became Liebig's assistant and in the spring of 1845 he was appointed briefly to a position in the University of Bonn. Later that year he was requested by Prince Albert, Queen Victoria's consort, to become a professor at the new Royal College of Chemistry in London. He held this position for the next 20 years, during which time the college became amalgamated with the Royal School of Mines. In 1863 he was offered chairs of chemistry in both Bonn and Berlin. He accepted the position vacated by Eilhard Mitscherlich in Berlin, after designing new laboratories for both institutions,

taking up the appointment in 1865 and remaining there until his death. On his seventieth birthday in 1888 he was made a baron, becoming von Hofmann. He died in Berlin on 2 May 1892.

Hofmann's first paper confirmed the presence of aniline in coal tar. He believed that phenol and aniline (phenylamine) were related, and converted the former into the latter by heating phenol with ammonia in a sealed tube for three weeks. Later he prepared nitrobenzene from the light oil distillate of coal tar and made aniline from it by reduction with nascent hydrogen.

From about 1850 Hofmann explored the behaviour and properties of amines, showing that alkyl halides (halogenoalkanes) react with aniline to give secondary and tertiary amines (although Hofmann used different terms for them). He also prepared alkyl amines by the reaction between ammonia and alkyl halides, reporting that he was replacing the hydrogen atoms of ammonia with alkyl groups and thus producing compounds of the "ammonia type". The theory of types held vogue in organic chemistry for a number of years and other organic compounds were classified as the "water", "hydrogen" and "hydrochloric acid" types. Hofmann also set about investigating a "phosphorus" type based on phosphine, PH_3. In 1865 he published *An Introduction to Modern Chemistry* which was a textbook based on the theory of types.

Hofmann produced more complex amines from diamines and alkyl halides. He discovered what is now known as the Hofmann degradation, in which an amide is treated with bromine and alkali (hypobromite) to produce an amine with one fewer carbon atoms:

$$CH_3CONH_2 + Br_2 + 4KOH \rightarrow CH_3NH_2 +$$

acetamide (ethanamide)   methylamine

$$2KBr + K_2CO_3 + 2H_2O$$

2 carbon atoms   1 carbon atom

By the reaction of ethyl iodide (iodoethane) with triethylamine he produced tetraethylammonium iodide, $(C_2H_5)_4N^+I^-$, the first quaternary ammonium salt. He found that the ion $(C_2H_5)_4N^+$ behaved like a sodium or potassium ion, as a "true organic metal". With silver oxide he was able to form from it the strong base $(C_2H_5)_4NOH$, which exists as a solid.

Hofmann was also the first to investigate the structure and properties of formaldehyde (methanal), which he called "methyl aldehyd" and prepared by passing methanol vapour and air over heated platinum. Working with A.A.T. Cahours he also discovered the first unsaturated alcohol, prop-2-en-1-ol, $CH_2=CH.CH_2OH$.

In 1858 Hofmann obtained the dye known as

fuchsine or magenta by the reaction of carbon tetrachloride (tetrachloromethane) with aniline (phenylamine). Later he isolated from it a compound which he called rosaniline and used this as a starting point for other aniline dyes, including aniline blue (triphenyl rosaniline). With alkyl iodides (iodoalkanes) he obtained a series of violet dyes which he patented in 1863. These became known as "Hofmann's violets" and were a considerable commercial and financial success.

On his return to Germany Hofmann founded the Deutsche Chemische Gesellschaft (German Chemical Society). The many reactions and rules that still bear his name are a testimony to his stature as an organic chemist. The term valence is a contraction of his notion of "quantivalence" and he devised much of the terminology of the paraffins (alkanes) and their derivatives which was accepted at the 1892 Geneva Conference on nomenclature. Apart from his ammonia and phosphine types he was not a great theorist but became renowned as an experimental chemist. Yet he is said to have been very clumsy with apparatus, the handling of which he usually left to his more dextrous assistants. He was married four times and had eleven children, eight of whom survived him when he died at the age of 74.

Holley, Robert William (*1922–*), **Nirenberg, Marshall Warren** (*1927–*) and **Khorana, Har Gobind** (*1922–*), are three biochemists who shared the 1968 Nobel Prize in Physiology and Medicine for their work in deciphering the chemistry of the genetic code.

Holley was born on 28 January 1922 in Urbana, Illinois, in the United States. He studied chemistry at the University of Illinois and graduated in 1942. He gained his PhD from Cornell University in 1947, having spent the latter part of World War II engaged on research into penicillin. From 1948 to 1957 he was Assistant Professor and then Associate Professor of Organic Chemistry at the New York State Agricultural Experimental Station at Cornell, when he moved to the Plant Soil and Nutrition Laboratory. In 1962 he became Professor of Biology at Cornell, and in 1966 took up a senior appointment at the Salk Institute for Biological Studies in San Diego, California.

Nirenberg was born in New York City on 10 April 1927. He studied biology at the University of Florida, where he graduated in 1948, gaining his masters degree four years later. He then went to the University of Michigan's Department of Biological Chemistry and gained a PhD in 1957. From 1957 to 1962 he was at the National Institute of Health (Arthritic and Metabolic Diseases), becoming Head of the Laboratory of

Biochemical Genetics there in 1962. He later moved to the Laboratory of Biochemical Genetics at the National Heart, Lung and Blood Institute in Bethesda, near Washington D.C.

Khorana was born in Rajpur, India, on 9 January 1922. He graduated from the University of Punjab in 1943, and gained his masters degree in 1945. He then went to the University of Liverpool, England, and was awarded his PhD in 1948. From 1952 to 1960 he was Head of the Organic Chemistry group of the Research Council of the British Commonwealth in Vancouver, Canada, being Visiting Professor to the Rockefeller Institute in New York City from 1958. He then became Professor of Biology at the Massachusetts Institute of Technology.

Holley's early work in the New York State Agricultural Experimental Station at Cornell concerned plant hormones, the volatile constituents of fruits, the nitrogen metabolism of plants, and peptide synthesis. At the Salk Institute he began to study the factors that influence growth in cultured mammalian cells.

At Cornell he obtained evidence for the existence of transfer RNAs (tRNAs) and for their role as acceptors of activated amino acids. In 1958 he succeeded in isolating the alanine-, tyrosine- and valene-specific tRNAs from baker's yeast and approximately one gram of highly purified ala tRNA was prepared and used in structural studies over the next two-and-a-half years. The technique for elucidating its structure was to break up the molecule into large "pieces", identify the fragments and then reconstruct the original. Eventually Holley and his colleagues succeeded in solving the entire nucleotide sequence of this RNA.

Nirenberg was interested in the way in which the nitrogen bases – adenine (A), cytosine (C), guanine (G) and thymine (T) – specify a particular amino acid. To simplify the task of identifying the RNA triplet responsible for each amino acid, he used a simple synthetic RNA polymer. Using an RNA polymer containing only uracil, for example, he obtained phenylalanine, so he concluded that its code must be UUU. Similarly a cytosine RNA polymer produced only the amino acid proline.

In this way Nirenberg built up a tentative dictionary of the RNA code. He found that certain amino acids could be specified by more than one triplet, and that some triplets did not specify an amino acid at all. These "nonsense" triplets signified the beginning or the end. In this way he assigned values to 50 triplets. He then worked on finding the orders of the letters in the triplets. By labelling one amino acid at a time with carbon-14, and passing the experimental material through a filter that retained only the ribosomes with the tRNA and amino acids attached, he obtained unambiguous results for 60 of the possible codons. Work continued in his laboratory on the role of "synonym" codons, codon recognition by tRNA, and the mechanics of the rate of protein synthesis during viral infection and embryonic differentiation.

Khorana helped to decipher the genetic code by re-creating synthetically each of the 64 possible three-letter words or triplets of DNA nucleotides which work in combination as instructions for the protein-synthesizing mechanism of the cell. He and his co-workers confirmed that the genetic language is linear and consecutive, and that three nucleotides specify an amino acid. They also determined the direction in which the information of messenger RNA is read and showed that code words cannot overlap. Their work gave clear proof that the sequence of nucleotides in DNA specifies the sequence of amino acids in proteins through an RNA that acts as an intermediary.

After 1968 Khorana succeeded in synthesizing an entire functional gene. By 1970 he and his colleagues had constructed a molecule of yeast DNA from chemically synthesized fragments, which were joined in the molecule with enzymes to form a double-stranded helix 77 nucleotides in length. But the gene was not functional. Three years later Khorana synthesized a 126-nucleotide bacterial gene, but this was not functional either. Undeterred, he went on to determine and synthesize additional lengths of nucleotides, known as the "promoter" and "terminator", which make up the start and stop signals for the larger gene. The completed chain was now 207 nucleotides in length. It was inserted into a mutated strain of bacterial virus, which depended for its infectiousness on the proper functioning of the gene. The virus thrived, providing final proof that a synthesized gene can work as well as its naturally created counterpart.

Khorana's achievement made available a technique to change genes and observe the results of those changes. This, in turn, could lead to studies of genetic disorders and the rampant mechanisms of malignant cells. Artificial genes could be used to make bacteria generate valuable proteins (for the human diet), normally obtainable only at great expense from higher organisms.

Hückel, Erich Armand Arthur Joseph (*1896–*),

is a German physical chemist who, with Peter Debye, developed the modern theory that accounts for the electrochemical behaviour of strong electrolytes in solution. In his own right he is known for his discoveries relating to the structures of benzene and similar compounds that exhibit aromaticity.

Hückel was born in Berlin-Charlottenberg on 9 August 1896, the son of a doctor of medicine. When he was three years old the family moved to Göttingen and, after leaving school in 1914, he went to the local university to study physics. He interrupted his studies after two years to take a job concerned with aerodynamics in Göttingen University's Applied Mechanics Institute, under the direction of L. Prandtl. At the end of World War I in 1918 Hückel resumed his studies in mathematics and physics and in 1921 was awarded a doctorate based on a thesis (prepared under the direction of Debye) on the diffraction of X-rays by liquids.

He stayed at Göttingen for the next two years, first as a physics assistant to the mathematician David Hilbert and then in a similar role to Max Born, the Nobel Prizewinning physicist. In 1922 he left to join Debye again, this time at the Zurich Technische Hochschule. He became an unpaid lecturer there, and in 1925 married Annemarie Zsigmondy, the daughter of the colloid chemist Richard Zsigmondy. In 1928 Hückel was awarded a Rockefeller Foundation Fellowship and worked briefly with Frederick Donnan. He also spent some time with Niels Bohr in Copenhagen, before becoming a Fellow of the Notgemeinschaft der Deutschen Wissenschaft at the University of Leipzig. In 1930 he went to the Technische Hochschule at Stuttgart, where he remained until becoming the Professor of Theoretical Physics at the University of Marburg in 1937.

When Hückel started working with Debye in 1922, the prevailing theory of electrolyte solutions was that of Svante Arrhenius, who held that an equilibrium exists in the solution between undissociated solute molecules and the ions from its dissociated molecules. In strong electrolytes, particularly those formed from strong acids and bases, dissociation was considered to be nearly complete. There were, however, many instances which this theory did not adequately explain.

Debye and Hückel suggested that strong electrolytes dissociate completely into ions, explaining the deviations from expected behaviour in terms of attraction and repulsion between the ions. In a series of highly mathematical investigations they found formulae for calculating the electrical and thermodynamic properties of electrolytic solutions, principally dilute solutions of strong electrolytes. But even taking into account the sizes of the ions concerned, they did not find a complete theory for concentrated solutions.

In 1930 Hückel began his work on aromaticity, the basis of the chemical behaviour of benzene, pyridine and similar compounds. The benzene molecule is held together by electrons that are delocalized and contribute to one large hexagonal

(π) bond above and below the plane of the molecule. This accounts for its planar shape and its ability to preserve its structure through chemical reactions. Hückel developed a mathematical approximation for the evaluation of certain integrals in the calculations concerned with the exact nature of the bonding in benzene.

Later in the 1930s he extended his research to other chemical systems that appear to possess the same kind of aromatic nature as benzene (although usually to a lower degree). From this study emerged the Hückel rule for monocyclic systems, which states that for aromaticity to occur the number of electrons contributing to the correct type of bonding (π-bonding) must be $4n+2$, where n is a whole number. When $n=1$, for example, there are six π-electrons, as exemplified by benzene. When $n=2$, the ten π-electrons occur in derivatives of [10]annulene.

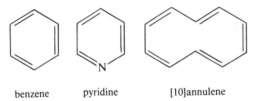

benzene   pyridine   [10]annulene

Examples of aromatic molecules.

There seem to be exceptions to the rule in large ring systems, where the predicted aromaticity does not occur. In general the degree to which a molecule resembles benzene in aromaticity decreases with increasing ring size.

Hückel also carried out research into unsaturated compounds (those with double or triple bonds) and into the chemistry of free radical compounds (those with a free, non-bonding electron).

Hume-Rothery, William *(1899–1968)*, was a British chemist who spent his entire scientific life working on the structures of metals and their alloys. When he began his studies, metallurgy was considered to be a branch of physical chemistry; when he retired, it had come to be regarded as a distinct discipline in its own right.

Hume-Rothery was born on 15 May 1899 at Worcester Park, Surrey. He was educated at Cheltenham College before going to the Royal Military Academy, in anticipation of a career in the army. But his training was brought to a sudden stop by a serious illness that left him totally deaf. He then went to Oxford to study natural sciences, specializing in chemistry and graduating in 1926. He did his post-graduate research and gained his PhD at the Royal School of Mines, where he became interested in metal-

lurgy. He soon returned to Oxford and continued his research into metal alloys, first in the Dyson Perrins Laboratory and later in the old Chemistry Department. For most of this period his research was financed by outside organizations such as the Armourers and Braziers Company, and he did not gain a formal university post until 1938. During World War II he supervised many contracts from the Ministry of Supply and Aircraft Production for work on complex aluminium and magnesium alloys.

In 1955, with the offer to Hume-Rothery of the George Kelley Readership, metallurgy finally became recognized as a discipline within Oxford University. Three years later he received the first professorship in the new Department of Metallurgy. He died in Oxford on 27 September 1968.

While he was working in the Dyson Perrins laboratory Hume-Rothery complained bitterly that vapours from the experiments of neighbouring organic chemists spoiled the finish of the specimens he had prepared for study with a microscope. The accepted method of preparing metals in order to study their structure was to smooth the surface by a series of grinding and polishing operations until it had a mirror finish. The surface was then carefully etched in an acid that attacked certain areas preferentially. The specimen was then viewed under a microscope using indirect reflected light. In the laboratory atmosphere the carefully prepared specimens became corroded, interfering with the study. Hume-Rothery was allowed to move.

Many of Hume-Rothery's early ideas about alloys came from interpreting their microstructures. If metals mix to form an alloy, the melting point, physical strength and microstructure vary with the composition of the alloy. During the later part of the 1920s and the 1930s he and his continuous stream of research students established that the microstructure of an alloy depends on the different sizes of the component atoms, the valency electron concentration, and electrochemical differences. They showed that in a binary (two-metal) alloy, a common crystal lattice is possible if the two types of atoms present have a similar size. And if a common lattice forms, the alloy has a uniform structure. With atoms of widely different sizes, at least two types of lattices may form, one rich in one metal and one rich in the other. The presence of two types of structures can increase the strength of an alloy.

Hume-Rothery and his researchers discovered that the solid solubility of one element in another is extremely restricted if the atomic diameters of the two elements concerned differ by more than 15 per cent. Within the 15 per cent limit, solutions are formed provided that other factors are favourable. In such a solution, the solute (alloying) element replaces some of the atoms of the solvent (primary) metal. Nickel and copper have very similar atomic radii and so form a continuous range of solid solutions – no doubt assisted by the fact that they both have face-centred cubic crystal structures. Zinc crystallizes with a hexagonal structure, so that although zinc and copper alloy over the whole range of compositions, most of the alloys involve two crystal structures – making some brasses much stronger than their component metals. If the two elements differ considerably in electronegativity, a definite chemical compound is formed. Thus steel, an "alloy" of iron and carbon, contains various iron carbides.

All this theory was backed up by experimental work, and Hume-Rothery and his team constructed the equilibrium diagrams for a great number of alloy systems. The experimental procedures became standard practice and work that was noted for its accuracy and a stern appraisal of the source of errors. He went on to make fundamental studies of solid-state transformations and deformation, while continuing his original research, particularly his interest in equilibrium phase diagrams. Today metallurgists can produce "tailor-made" alloys to suit particular and exacting requirements. Without Hume-Rothery's painstaking, systematic studies this would not have become possible.

Hyatt, John Wesley (*1837–1920*), was an American inventor who became famous for his invention of Celluloid, the first man-made plastic.

Hyatt was born in Starkey, New York, on 28 November 1837. As a young man he worked in Illinois as a printer, printing boards and play-pieces for draughts and dominoes at his plant in Albany. Probably with a view to make such play-pieces, he became interested in the material pyroxylin, a partly nitrated cellulose developed in Britain by Alexander Parkes (1813–1890) and D. Spill. Then in the early 1860s the New York company of Phelan and Collender, which manufactured billiard balls, offered a prize of 10,000 dollars for a satisfactory substitute for ivory for making the balls. Hyatt remembered pyroxylin and from it he and his brother Isaac developed, and in 1869 patented, Celluloid (the American trade name: it was called Xylonite in Britain).

Celluloid consisted of a mouldable mixture of nitrated cellulose and camphor. Its chief disadvantages was its inflammability, but nevertheless for several years it was the favoured material for making a wide range of products from shirt collars and combs to toy dolls and babies' rattles. It was used as a flexible substrate for photographic film and, as a substitute for ivory, for making piano keys – and billiard balls. Celluloid was also used as the central "filling" in sandwich-type safety glass for car windscreens. It has gradually been superseded in nearly all uses by other synthetic materials, but in one application it continued to be used: the manufacture of table-tennis balls.

Hyatt was never awarded the Phelan and Collender prize money. He continued to patent his inventions – more than 200 of them, including roller bearings and a multiple-stitch sewing machine. He died in Short Hills, New Jersey, on 10 May 1920.

I

Ingold, Christopher (*1893–1970*), was a British organic chemist who made a fundamental contribution to the theoretical aspects of the subject with his explanation for the mechanisms of organic reactions in terms of the behaviour of electrons in the molecules concerned.

Ingold was born in London on 28 October 1893 but moved to Shanklin, Isle of Wight, when he was a few years old because of his father's ill health. He was educated at Sandown Grammar School and then went to study chemistry at Hartley University College, Southampton (later the University of Southampton), where he graduated in 1913. He began research under J.F. Thorpe at Imperial College, London, investigating spiro-compounds of cyclohexane, but left in 1918 to spend two years as a research chemist with the Cassel Cyanide Company, Glasgow. He returned to Imperial College as a lecturer in 1920, where he met and married Edith Usherwood, who was herself a promising young chemist. From 1924 to 1930 he was Professor of Organic Chemistry at the University of Leeds, when he succeeded Robert Robinson as Professor of Chemistry at University College, London. He remained there for the rest of his career, retiring officially in 1961 (although continuing as an active contributor to the work of the department). Ingold was knighted in 1958. He died in London on 8 December 1970.

Much of Ingold's work at University College was carried out in collaboration with E.D. Hughes. For 30 years he specialized in the concepts, classification and terminology of theoretical organic chemistry. In 1926, for example, he put forward the concept of mesomerism, which allows a molecule to exist as a hybrid of a pair of equally possible structures. This work culminated in his classic reference book *Structure and Mechanisms in Organic Chemistry* (1953), whose second edition (1969) ran to 1,266 pages. His ideas, first published in 1932, are still fundamental to reaction mechanisms taught today. They concerned the role of electrons in elimination and nucleophilic aliphatic substitution reactions, which he interpreted in terms of ionic organic species.

Ingold's work removed much of the "art" from organic chemistry and replaced it with scientific methodology. As he is reputed to have said: "One could no longer just mix things; sophistication in physical chemistry was the base from which all chemists – including the organic – must start."

Ipatieff, Vladimir Nikolayevich (*1867–1952*), was a Russian-born American organic chemist who is best known for his development of catalysis in organic chemistry, particularly in reactions involving hydrocarbons.

Ipatieff was born in Moscow on 21 November 1867, the son of an architect. It was intended that he should have a career in the army so he attended a military school, became an officer in the Imperial Russian Army in 1887, and in 1889 won a scholarship to continue his higher education at the Mikhail Artillery Academy in St Petersburg (now Leningrad). From 1892, the year in which he married, he gave lectures in chemistry at the Academy, and in 1897 he was given permission to go to the University of Munich for a year to study under Johann Baeyer, where one of his fellow students was Richard Willstätter. After a brief period in France studying explosives, he returned to Russia in 1899 as Professor of Chemistry and Explosives at the Mikhail Artillery Academy. In 1908 he gained his PhD from the University of St Petersburg.

Ipatieff's research work was interrupted by World War I and the Russian Revolution, during which he held various administrative and advisory appointments. He was head of the Chemical Committee during World War I, and increased the monthly output of explosives from 60 tonnes to 3,300 tonnes. But he was not a Communist and when, at the age of 64, he went to Berlin in 1930 to attend a chemical conference he accepted the offer of a post in the United States and did not return to the Soviet Union. He was immediately condemned as a traitor by the Soviet authorities and expelled from the Soviet Academy of Sciences. From 1931 to 1935 he was Professor of Chemistry at Northwestern University, Illinois, and acted as a consultant to the Universal Oil Products Company, Chicago. In 1938 this company funded the building of the Ipatieff High Pressure Laboratory at Northwestern. He died in Chicago on 29 November 1952, just after his birthday and ten days before the death of his wife. In 1965 he was posthumously reinstated to the Soviet Academy of Sciences.

While working as a student in Munich in 1897 Ipatieff synthesized the hydrocarbon isoprene, the basis of the rubber molecule. Back in Russia in 1900 he discovered the specific nature of catalysis in high-temperature organic gas reactions, and how using high pressures the method could be extended to liquids. He developed an autoclave called the Ipatieff bomb – for heating liquid compounds to above their boiling points under high pressure. He synthesized methane and iso-octane (2-methylheptane), and produced polyethylene by polymerizing ethylene (ethene).

In Chicago after 1931 Ipatieff began to apply his high-temperature catalysis reactions to petrol with low octane ratings (which produce "knock" or pre-ignition in car engines). The result of the catalytic cracking (or "cat cracking") is petrol with a higher octane rating, and the method became particularly important for the production of aviation fuel during World War II; it is still widely used.

J

Joliot, Jean Frédéric (*1900–1958*), was a French scientist who shared the 1935 Nobel Prize in Chemistry with his wife for their discovery of artificial radioactivity.

Joliot was born in Paris on 19 March 1900, the son of a merchant. He studied engineering and then chemistry at the École de Physique et Chimie in Paris and, after a brief job as a production engineer at a steelworks, joined the staff of the Paris Radium Institute in 1925. There he met Irène Curie, the daughter of Pierre and Marie Curie, and married her in the following year (thereafter she became known as Irène Joliot-Curie; he too is sometimes referred to by the joint name). Joliot gained his doctorate in 1930 for a thesis on the electrochemistry of radioactive elements. He taught at the Sorbonne for two years before becoming Professor of Nuclear Chemistry at the Collège de France. In 1944 he was appointed Director of the atomic synthesis laboratory at the Centre Nationale des Recherches Scientifiques (NRS) in Paris, putting him effectively in charge of the nation's atomic energy programme. In 1946 he was made High Commissioner for Atomic Energy, but was removed from this post in 1950 because of his Communist views. He returned to the Collège de France and then, after his wife's death, took up her professorship at the Sorbonne in 1956. Joliot died in Paris on 14 August 1958.

Joliot and his wife discovered artificial radio-activity early in 1934. They bombarded aluminium with alpha-particles (helium nuclei) from polonium, and observed that positrons continued to be emitted after the alpha-particle source was removed. They had made a short-lived (half-life about 3 minutes) radioactive isotope of phosphorus. Similarly, starting with boron and magnesium they produced new radioisotopes of nitrogen and aluminium. Many other groups of workers, including John Cockroft in Britain and Enrico Fermi in Italy, took up the method and by the end of 1935 about 100 artificial radioactive elements were known.

Joliot continued his experiments, proving (independently of Otto Frisch) that nuclear fission is possible. During World War II he worked on the application of isotopes to the study of biological processes, and was involved in the French Resistance movement. After 1945 he became active in various international peace movements and in the founding of UNESCO.

K

Karrer, Paul (*1889–1971*), was a Swiss organic chemist, famous for his work on vitamins and vegetable dyestuffs. He determined the structural formulae and carried out syntheses of various vitamins, in recognition of which achievement he shared the 1937 Nobel Prize in Chemistry with Walter Haworth.

Karrer was born in Moscow, of Swiss parents, on 21 April 1889, and when he was three years old his family moved to Switzerland. He studied at the University of Zurich under Alfred Werner, gaining his doctorate in 1911. After a year at the Zurich Chemical Institute he went to Frankfurt to work with Paul Ehrlich at the Georg Speyer Haus. In 1918 he returned to Zurich to be Professor of Chemistry and a year later succeeded Werner as Director of the Institute. Karrer remained there until he retired in 1959. He died in Zurich on 18 June 1971.

Karrer's early work concerned vitamin A and its chief precursor carotene. Wackenroder had first isolated carotene (from carrots) in 1831 and in 1907 Richard Willstätter determined its molecular formula to be $C_{40}H_{56}$. Karrer worked out its correct constitutional formula in 1930 (although he was not to achieve a total synthesis until 1950). He showed in 1931 that vitamin A (molecular formula $C_{20}H_{30}O$) is related to the carotenoids, the substances that give the yellow, orange or red colour to foodstuffs such as sweet potatoes, egg yolk, carrots and tomatoes and to non-edible substances such as lobster shells and human skin. There are in fact two A vitamins, compounds known chemically as diterpenoids; vitamin A_1 influences growth in animals and its deficiency leads to night blindness and a hardening of the cornea. Karrer proved that there are several isomers of carotene, and that vitamin A_1 is equivalent to half a molecule of its precursor β-carotene.

β-carotene ($C_{40}H_{56}$)

vitamin A_1
(retinol axerophthol, $C_{20}H_{30}O$)

Karrer later confirmed Albert Szent-Györgyi's constitution of vitamin C (ascorbic acid, so-called by Haworth who synthesized it and shared Karrer's Nobel Prize). In 1935 he solved the structure of vitamin B_2 (riboflavin), the water-soluble thermostable vitamin in the B complex that is necessary for growth and health. It occurs in green vegetables, yeast, meat and milk (from which it was first isolated and hence is also known as lactoflavin). Karrer made extensive studies of the chemistry of the flavins.

vitamin B_2
(riboflavin, $C_{17}H_{20}N_4O_6$)

He also investigated vitamin E (tocopherol), the group of closely related compounds which act as anti-sterility factors. In 1938 he solved the structure of α-tocopherol, the most biologically active component, obtained from wheat-germ oil.

vitamin E
(α-tocopherol, $C_{29}H_{50}O_2$)

For their time, these syntheses were remarkable, being the most advanced so far undertaken. They led to a better understanding of vitamins in metabolism, and acted as a spur to the work of others. In 1930 Karrer published an organic chemistry textbook, *Lehrbuch der organischen Chemie*, which became the standard work for many years, being reprinted in many editions in several languages during the 1940s and 1950s.

Kekulé, Friedrich August (von Stradonitz) (*1829–1896*), was a German organic chemist who founded structural organic chemistry and is best known for his "ring" formula for benzene.

Kekulé was born in Darmstadt on 7 September 1829, a descendant of a Bohemian noble family from Stradonič, near Prague. At first he studied architecture at Giessen, but came under the influence of Justus von Liebig and changed to chemistry. He left Giessen in 1851 and went to Paris, where he gained his doctorate a year later. After working in Switzerland for a while, he went to London in 1854 where he assisted John Stenhouse (1809–1890) and met many leading chemists of the day. When he returned to Germany in the following year he opened a small private laboratory at Heidelberg and became an unpaid lecturer at the university there under Johann von Baeyer. In 1858 he became a professor at Ghent; in 1865 took over the Chair at Bonn vacated by August Hofmann, and remained there until he died. While at Ghent he got married, but his wife died in childbirth. He had three more children by his second marriage of 1876, the same year in which he suffered an attack of measles which left him in poor health for the rest of his life. He was raised to the nobility by William II of Prussia in 1895 and took the name Kekulé von Stradonitz. He died in Bonn on 13 July 1896.

In 1858 Kekulé published a paper in which, after giving reasons why carbon should be regarded as a four-valent element, he set out the essential features of his theory of the linking of atoms. (A similar paper was presented three months later to the French Academy by the Scottish chemist Archibald Couper, but went largely unnoticed.) He postulated that carbon atoms can combine with each other to form chains, and that radicals are not necessarily indestructible, being capable of persisting through one set of reactions only to disintegrate in others. He explained that compounds behave differently under different sets of conditions, although he continued to subscribe to the idea of "types", which he thought were not inflexible but served to emphasize one or more of their properties. He pictured atoms grouping themselves in space and linking with each other to form compounds.

In 1865 Kekulé announced his theory of the structure of benzene, which he envisaged as a hexagonal ring of six interconnected carbon atoms. To make the structure compatible with carbon's valency of four, he postulated alternate single and double bonds in the same ring.

In a dissertation of 1867 outlining his views on molecular diagrams and models, he proposed the tetrahedral carbon atom (that the four valence bonds from a saturated carbon atom are directed towards the corners of a regular tetrahedron), which was to become the cornerstone of modern structural organic chemistry. Kekulé cautiously made it clear that he did not intend all the possible physical implications of his tetrahedral model to be accepted literally. It later became clear, however, that this model fulfilled strictly chemical necessities that he had not foreseen. In 1890 von Baeyer said that Kekulé's molecular models were "even cleverer than their inventor" and modern analytical methods have shown that they are true indicators of how the atoms are arranged in space.

There were two fundamental objections to Kekulé's original ring structure for benzene: it does not behave chemically like a double-bonded substance, and there are not as many di-substituted isomers as the formula would predict. Kekulé acknowledged these shortcomings and in 1872 introduced the idea of oscillation or resonance between two isomeric structures.

His assistant W. Körner (1839–1925) developed in great detail the implications of these structures in the chemistry of benzene and its compounds. The modern view, worked out by Linus Pauling in 1933 by applying quantum theory to Kekulé's resonant structures, postulates a hybrid (mesomeric) state for the benzene molecule with a carbon–carbon bond length in the ring inter-mediate between the normal single- and double-bond values.

Kendrew, John Cowdery (*1917–*), is a British biochemist who shared the 1962 Nobel Prize in Chemistry with Max Perutz for his determination of the structure of the protein myoglobin.

Kendrew was born in Oxford on 24 March 1917. He won a scholarship to Trinity College, Cambridge, in 1936 and graduated from there in 1939, just before the outbreak of World War II. During the war he worked for the Ministry of Aircraft Production, returning to Cambridge in 1945. A year later he was appointed Departmental Chairman of the Medical Council's Laboratory for Molecular Biology, Cambridge, where he remained until 1975. In that year he became Director General of the European Molecular Biology Laboratory at Heidelburg. He was knighted in 1974.

In the late 1940s at Cambridge Kendrew began working with Perutz, whose other molecular biologists at that time included Francis Crick. Their research centred on an investigation of the fine structure of various protein molecules; Kendrew was assigned the task of studying myoglobin, the globular protein resembling haemoglobin which occurs in muscle fibres (where it stores oxygen). He used X-ray diffraction techniques to elucidate the amino-acid sequence in the peptide chains that form the myoglobin molecule (similar to the work of Maurice Wilkins on DNA).

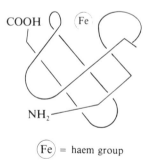

$\overline{Fe}$ = haem group

Hundreds of X-ray diffraction photographs of the crystallized protein were analysed, using electronic computers that were becoming available in the 1950s. By 1960 Kendrew had determined the spatial arrangement of all 1,200 atoms in the molecule, showing it to be a folded helical chain of amino acids with an amino ($-NH_2$) group at one end and a carboxylic ($-COOH$) group at the other. It involves an iron-containing haem group, which allows the molecule to absorb oxygen. In the same year, Perutz determined the structure of haemoglobin.

Kenyon, Joseph (*1885–1961*), was a British organic chemist, best known for his studies of optical activity, particularly of secondary alcohols.

Kenyon was born in Blackburn, Lancashire, the eldest of seven children. He was educated locally and from 1900–1903 worked as a laboratory assistant at Blackburn Technical College. In 1903 he won a scholarship that enabled him to study for a degree, and he graduated two years later. In 1904 he became personal assistant to R.H. Pickard, an industrial chemistry consultant and technical college instructor; in 1906 assistant lecturer and demonstrator at Blackburn Technical College; and in 1907 full lecturer, commencing research under Pickard. He submitted his doctorial thesis to London University in 1914 and in the following year was appointed research chemist to the Medical Research Council. From 1915 to 1916, during World War I, he worked at Leeds University and then until 1920 with William Perkin Jr (1860–1929) at the British Dyestuffs Corporation, Oxford. Finally in 1920 Kenyon became Head of the Chemistry Department at Battersea Polytechnic, London, a year after Pickard had become its Principal; he remained there until he retired in 1950. In 1951 and 1952 he was Visiting Professor at the Universities of Alexandria and Kansas. He died in Petersham on 11 November 1961.

Kenyon published his research on secondary alcohols in 1911 while still working as an undergraduate with Pickard. The problem was to resolve the optically active stereoisomers of secondary octyl alcohol (octan-2-ol). Pickard and Kenyon converted it to secondary octyl hydrogen phthalate by heating it with phthalic anhydride, and showed that the phthalate could easily be resolved using the alkaloids brucine and cinchonidine. They went on to obtain an optically pure series of secondary alcohols and were able to relate rotatory power to chemical constitution. The technique was later used to distinguish between inter- and intramolecular rearrangements.

While at Leeds (1915–1916) Kenyon worked on antidotes for gas gangrene, research that led to the development of chloramine-T for this and other purposes. With Perkin (1916–1920) he studied photographic developers and dyes, although most of their results were published only in confidential reports.

At Battersea Polytechnic Kenyon put forward the "obstacle" theory for the cause of optical activity in certain substituted diphenic acids. He synthesized and attempted to resolve some selenoxides, confirming differences between these and sulphoxides, and investigated the geometric and optical isomerism of the methylcyclohexanols. He pointed out that when the toluene-*para*-sulphonic acids (methylbenzene-4-sulphonic

l-octan-2-ol → *l*-toluene-4-sulphonate (no inversion) → *d*-octan-2-ethanoate (inversion)

l-octan-2-ol → *l*-toluene-4-sulphinate (no inversion) → *d*-octan-2-ol (inversion)

Substituted diphenic esters prove Kenyon's 'obstacle' theory for optical activity.

acids) are prepared by the action of the sulphonic chloride on the corresponding alcohol, the four bonds of the asymmetric carbon atom remain undisturbed – there is no change in configuration. But when the toluene-4-sulphonic esters are converted to the carboxylic esters (by heating them with the alcoholic solutions of the alkali salts of the carboxylic acids), there is an almost 100 per cent inversion of configuration.

He also discovered that the hydroxyl compounds can be converted to the sulphinic esters without inversion (by treatment with toluene-4-sulphinyl chloride) but that treatment of the esters with hypochlorous acid reconverts them into the enantisomers (mirror-images) of the original hydroxyl compounds.

Perhaps Kenyon's most important work in stereochemistry was to prove that in the Beckman, Curtius, Hofmann, Lossen and Schmidt reactions – in which a group migrates from one part of the molecule to another – in no case is the migrating fragment ever kinetically free.

Khorana, Har Gobind. See Holley, Robert William.

Kipping, Frederick Stanley (*1863–1949*), was a British chemist who pioneered the study of the organic compounds of silicon; he invented the term "silicone", which is now applied to the entire class of oxygen-containing polymers.

Kipping was born at Higher Broughton, near Manchester, on 16 August 1863, the son of a bank employee. He was educated at Manchester Grammar School and in 1882 graduated in chemistry from Owens College, Manchester (later Manchester University), with an external degree from the University of London. After four years as a chemist with the Manchester Gas Department, he went to Johann von Baeyer's laboratory in Munich to study under William Perkin Jr, who was to become his close friend and collaborator. Kipping received his doctorate in 1887 and was awarded a DSc degree by the University of London in the same year – the University's first award of this qualification solely for research work.

He then followed Perkin to the Heriot-Watt College, Edinburgh, where he worked as a demonstrator. It was at Edinburgh that the two chemists began work on their classic textbook *Organic Chemistry* (1894), the first to be devoted entirely to this subject and a standard work for the next 50 years. In 1890 Kipping became chief demonstrator at the City and Guilds of London Institute and seven years later he took up the appointment of Professor of Chemistry at Uni-

versity College, Nottingham (later Nottingham University), where he remained until he retired in 1936. He died in Criccieth, Wales, on 1 May 1949.

In his early research Kipping investigated the preparation and properties of optically active camphor derivatives and nitrogen compounds. This interest in stereoisomerism led him in 1899 to look for such isomerism among the organic compounds of silicon, preparing them using the newly available Grignard reagents. He prepared condensation products – the first organosilicon polymers – which he called silicones. He also tried to make silicon analogues of simple carbon compounds, particularly those containing double bonds, although in this he was not successful.

To Kipping the silicon compounds were mere chemical curiosities and as late as 1937 he could not see any practical applications for them. Yet within a very few years, spurred on by the outbreak of World War II, silicones were being used as substitutes for oils and greases. Their chemical inertness and unusual stability at high temperatures make them useful as lubricants, hydraulic fluids, waterlogging compounds, varnishes, greases, synthetic rubbers and various other hydrocarbon substitutes.

siloxane structure

structure of a silicone fluid

Klaproth, Martin Heinrich (*1743–1817*), was a German chemist famous for his discovery of several new elements and for pioneering analytical chemistry.

Klaproth was born in Wernigerode, Saxony (now in East Germany), on 1 December 1743. His home was destroyed by fire when he was eight years old, leaving the family in poverty. He was apprenticed to an apothecary when he was 16, and after moving from employer to employer finally in 1771 he became manager of a pharmacy in Berlin. Nine years later he set up on his own, doing chemical research. He took an appointment as a chemistry lecturer at the Berlin School of Artillery in 1792, and when the University of

Berlin was founded in 1810 it was Klaproth to whom the authorities offered the first Chair in Chemistry, which he held until his death. He died in Berlin in 1 January 1817.

Klaproth's contributions to the discovery and isolation of new elements began in 1789. From the semi-precious gemstone zircon he prepared an oxide ("earth") containing the new metallic element zirconium. In the same year he investigated pitchblende and from this black ore obtained a yellow oxide containing another new metallic element, which he named uranium after the planet Uranus, discovered by William Herschel in 1781. He distinguished strontia (strontium oxide) from baryta (barium oxide) and in 1795 rediscovered and named titanium, acknowledging the prior isolation of the element four years earlier by William Gregor (1761-1817). He isolated chromium in 1797 independently of Louis Vauquelin, but credited Franz Müller (1740-1825) with the priority for the discovery of tellurium, which Klaproth extracted in 1798 and named after *tellus*, the Latin for earth; he refuted, however, the claim to this discovery by the Hungarian chemist P. Kitaibel (1757-1817).

In 1803 Klaproth identified cerium oxide and confirmed the existence of cerium, discovered by Jöns Berzelius in the same year and named after the newly found asteroid Ceres. He also studied the rare earth minerals researched by Johan Gadolin (1760-1852), confirming that they are complex mixtures of very similar substances.

All of Klaproth's work on minerals and new elements hinged on his outstanding ability as a quantitative analytical inorganic chemist, a branch of the science which he can be credited with helping to found. He was a champion of Antoine Lavoisier's antiphlogiston theory of combustion. But he was not reluctant (unlike some of his contemporaries) to publish anomalous results; he did not "modify" his findings to make them suit some preconceived theory. He also applied his analytical skills to various archaeological finds and antiquities, such as metal artefacts, glassware and coins.

Kolbe, Adolf Wilhelm Hermann (*1818-1884*), was a German organic chemist, generally credited as the founder of modern organic chemistry with his synthesis of acetic acid (ethanoic acid) – an organic compound – from inorganic starting materials. (Previously organic chemistry had been considered as the branch of the science devoted to compounds that occur only in living organisms.)

Kolbe was born in Elliehausen, near Göttingen, on 27 September 1818, the eldest of 15 children of a Lutheran pastor; his mother was the daughter of A.F. Hempel, Professor of Anatomy at Göttingen University. He was educated at the Gymnasium at Göttingen, where he was introduced to chemistry by a student who had studied under Robert Bunsen. In 1838 he entered Göttingen University, where he attended lectures by Friedrich Wöhler (who ten years earlier had synthesized urea from ammonium cyanate, arguably the first inorganic-organic transition) and became a great admirer of Jöns Berzelius. He became an assistant to Bunsen at Marburg University in 1842 and three years later accepted an invitation from Lyon Playfair to work with him at the London School of Mines.

During his two-year stay in London Kolbe met many leading chemists of the day, including Edward Frankland who was at that time developing his theory of valency. In 1847 Kolbe moved to Brunswick to join the editorial team on the *Handwortenbuch der Chemie* (founded by von Liebig, Wöhler and Poggendorf), and in 1851 he was appointed Bunsen's successor as Professor of Chemistry at Marburg – a rapid promotion that did not meet with the full approval of the establishment. By 1865 he had moved to Leipzig and had begun to set up the largest and best equipped laboratory of the time, which had its full complement of students within three years. From 1869 he was editor of the *Journal für practische Chemie* and became notorious for his very personal and often violent criticism of the work of his contemporaries. He continued his theoretical and literary work until he died in Leipzig on 25 November 1884.

Kolbe correctly realized that organic compounds can be derived from inorganic materials by simple substitution. He introduced a modified idea of structural radicals, which contributed to the development of the structure theory, and he predicted the existence of secondary and tertiary alcohols. He is best known for his work on the electrolysis of the fatty (alkanoic) acids, for his important preparation of salicylic acid (2-hydroxybenzenecarboxylic acid) from phenol – called the Kolbe reaction, which was to lead to an easy synthesis of the drug aspirin – and for his discovery of nitromethane.

His early work, with Frankland, was on the conversion of nitriles into fatty acids. He then investigated the action of electric currents on organic compounds. But he became an extremely conservative influence on organic chemistry, largely because of his adherence to the ideas of Berzelius. His method of representing molecular structures eventually gave way to the much simpler structural theory based on the work of Friedrich Kekulé, although his unorthodox formulae actually embodied many of the ideas that were developed by Kekulé.

One of the greatest drawbacks of Kolbe's formulae resulted from his refusal to abandon equivalent weights in favour of atomic weights (relative atomic masses). Until 1869, for example, he still followed Berzelius' contention that $C = 6$ and $O = 8$, so that he had to double the number of atoms of these elements in his formulae. He therefore wrote the methyl group as $C_2H_3 -$ and assumed that in acetic (ethanoic) acid the methyl radical was joined to oxalic (ethanedioic) acid and water, which he expressed as $C_2H_3 + C_2O_3 + HO$. He became convinced that methyl groups existed in compounds and could be isolated from them. By electrolysing potassium acetate (ethanoate) he obtained a gas which he thought was "methyl" (really ethane). Frankland had obrained "free ethyl" (really butane) by the action of zinc on ethyl iodide (iodoethane) and both chemists were now certain that they had proved the existence of radicals in organic compounds. Their formulae continued to represent these misapprehensions.

Kolbe explained the relationship between aldehydes and ketones and identified a new group – the carbonyl group. He was able to predict their behaviour on oxidation, and in so doing anticipated the existence of secondary and tertiary alcohols. His later work involved the nitroparaffins (nitroalkanes) and the Kolbe synthesis for salicylic acid. But he never could see the similarity of his formula system and that of Kekulé. In 1858 he bitterly opposed the whole idea of structural formulae and ridiculed the theory of structural isomerism put forward by Jacobus Van't Hoff and Joseph le Bel, which are now regarded as fundamental to structural organic chemistry.

Kornberg, Arthur (*1918–*   ), is an American biochemist who in 1957 made the first synthetic molecules of DNA. For this achievement he shared the 1959 Nobel Prize in Physiology and Medicine with Severo Ochoa. By 1967 he had synthesized a biologically active artificial viral DNA.

Kornberg was born in Brooklyn, New York City, on 3 March 1918. He was educated at local schools and in 1933 graduated from the Abraham Lincoln High School. On a state scholarship he took a pre-medical course at the College of the City of New York, obtaining a BS degree in 1937. A further scholarship enabled him to go on to the University of Rochester School of Medicine from which he gained his medical degree in 1941. Following a year as an intern at the Strong Memorial Hospital in Rochester, he joined the US Coast Guard for a short time. From 1942 to 1945 he worked in the nutritional section of the physiology department of the National Institute of Health in Bethesda, Maryland, becoming Chief of the Enzyme and Metabolic Section from 1947 to 1952. He held senior appointments at the Washington University School of Medicine (1953) and the Stamford University School of Medicine, Palo Alto (1959), before becoming executive head of the Biochemistry Department at Stamford University.

From the beginning of his career, Kornberg was interested in enzymes – not merely what they are but what they do. For many years the fundamental genetic mystery had concerned the ability of a cell to produce one particular enzyme and no other. In 1941 George Beadle and Edward Tatum demonstrated that genes control the processes of life by chemical means and in 1944 Oswald Avery isolated the chemical responsible – the nucleic acid DNA, whose structure was elucidated by Francis Crick and James Watson in 1953. It was known that DNA consists of sugar, phosphate and nucleotides, the "letters" of a genetic alphabet that spell out the "recipe" of a particular genetic trait by controlling the production of the appropriate protein. Another nucleic acid, RNA, translated the DNA code in this complex chemical process.

At Washington University Kornberg set himself the task of producing a giant molecule of artificial DNA. To do this he needed a pre-existing DNA molecule as a template to be copied, the four nucleotides adenine, thymine, guanine and cytosine – known as A, T, G and C – and an enzyme to select and arrange the nucleotides according to the directions from the template and link them together to form the DNA chain. In 1956 he isolated the enzyme DNA polymerase and a year later made an artificial DNA that had all the physical and chemical properties of its natural counterpart, but lacked its genetic activity. One cause of this partial failure was the impurity of the enzyme (which had resulted in errors in the arrangement of nucleotides).

He then took a new and simpler template, the DNA of the virus known as Phi X174, which is single-stranded and in the form of a ring; its activity (infectivity) is lost if the ring is broken. Another enzyme was needed to close the ring and in 1966 it was discovered, and called ligase. Using the natural DNA of Phi X174 as a template, Kornberg and his co-workers mixed the enzyme DNA polymerase, the enzyme ligase, and the four nucleotides. The DNA polymerase ordered the nucleotides into the arrangement dictated by the template and the ligase closed the ring of the artificial DNA so produced.

When the synthetic DNA was added to a culture of bacteria cells (*Escherichia coli*), it infected them and usurped their genetic machinery.

Within minutes the cells had abandoned their normal activity and had started to produce Phi X174 viruses. The synthetic DNA had now become the template for a second generation of synthetic viruses identical to the original: the sequence of 6,000 "building blocks" and the arrangement of the 35 atoms within each was precisely the same in the artificial ones as in the natural ones.

By this achievement, Kornberg has opened the way to future progress in the study of genetics, the possibility of curing hereditary defects and controlling virus infections and cancer.

Kornberg, Hans Leo (*1928–*), is a German-born British biochemist who has made important contributions to the understanding of metabolic pathways and their regulation, especially in micro-organisms.

Kornberg was born in Herford, Germany, on 14 January 1928, and went to Britain in 1939 as a refugee from Nazi persecution. He attended schools in southern England and in Wakefield, Yorkshire, before entering Sheffield University in 1946. He gained his BSc in 1949 and his PhD in 1953, studying under Hans Krebs who in 1937 had determined the tricarboxylic acid cycle (Krebs cycle), the sequence of energy-generating biological reactions in which glucose is converted into carbon dioxide and water. From 1953 to 1955 Kornberg travelled in the United States. studying first the pentose phosphate pathway (an alternative to the Krebs cycle) under E. Racker at Yale and then helping Melvin Calvin at the University of California to resolve a controversy concerning one step of the "dark reaction" of photosynthesis in plants.

On his return to England he joined the Medical Research Council Cell Metabolism Unit headed by Krebs in Oxford. From 1960 to 1975 he was Professor and Head of the Biochemistry Department at the University of Leicester, and then he became the Sir William Dunn Professor of Biochemistry at Cambridge University. He was knighted in 1978.

The tricarboxylic acid (Krebs) cycle has two apparently conflicting roles. One is the complete oxidation (breakdown) of glucose to provide the energy required in all cellular processes – a catabolic role. The other is to provide carbon "skeletons" (backbones of organic molecules) for the various complex compounds essential to cellular function – and anabolic role. Certain simple organisms can survive with only acetate (ethanoate, a two-carbon molecule) as their source of carbon. Kornberg directed his research to seek an answer to the question of how an organism uses acetate to build up larger molecules while at the same time needing to break it down to provide the very energy required for these anabolic functions.

His study led in 1957 to the discovery of the "glyoxylate cycle" in plants, micro-organisms and some worms (glyoxal is ethan-1,2-dial). The cycle's basic function is to convert the two-carbon molecules of acetate into a four-carbon molecule of succinate (buten-1,4-dioate). It is achieved by means of a by-pass reaction in which the decarboxylation reactions of the normal tricarboxylic acid cycle (in which enzymes remove carbon that ultimately is converted to carbon dioxide) are skipped over.

The glyoxylate cycle is localized in subcellular organelles called glyoxysomes in the germinating seeds of higher plants, which use it to convert stored fatty acids into carbohydrates for the production of the energy needed for rapid growth.

Two years later, in 1959, Kornberg discovered the glycerate pathway and in 1960 the dicarboxylic acid cycle, which play important roles in enabling micro-organisms to grow on certain types of nutrients. He investigated the control mechanisms essential to the regulations of these metabolic processes, studying the way in which the cellular economy is balanced to prevent overproduction or waste. He introduced the concept of "anaplerotic reactions", whereby metabolic processes are maintained by special enzymes that replenish materials syphoned off for anabolic purposes.

Kornberg studied the regulation of enzyme activity at the genetic level, where the production of enzymes is largely controlled, and at the cytoplasmic level, where the reaction rates of existing enzymes can be modified. His later research concentrated on the very first step in the processing of food materials, the selective uptake of compounds across cellular membranes. He used mutant bacterial strains which can be grown on specific, defined substrates to rigorously control the nature of the materials entering their cells. This combination of genetic and biochemical approaches provides a unique way of studying both the nature of the transport process and the way in which it is regulated.

Kuhn, Richard (*1900–1967*), was an Austrian-born German organic chemist who worked mainly with carbohydrates and was awarded (but not allowed immediately to accept) the 1938 Nobel Prize in Chemistry for his researches on the synthesis of vitamins.

Kuhn was born into a Jewish family in Vienna on 3 December 1900, the son of a hydraulics engineer. He was first educated at home by his mother, who was a schoolteacher, and at the age of only eight began to attend the Döblinger Gymnasium, where one of his fellow pupils was Wolfgang Pauli (1900–1958) who was later to become a Nobel prizewinning physicist. He was introduced to chemistry by Ernst Ludwig, who was Professor of Medical Chemistry at Vienna University. Kuhn was conscripted into the Austrian army in 1917, and went Vienna University at the end of World War I in 1918. He soon moved to Germany, and completed his university education at the University of Munich where he studied under Richard Willstätter, graduating in 1921 and gaining his PhD a year later with a thesis on enzymes. Kuhn then became Willstätter's assistant, before going in 1926 to teach at the Eidenössische Technische Hochschule in Zurich as Professor of General and Analytical Chemistry. He married one of his students in 1928, and they had six children. In 1929 he became Professor of Organic Chemistry at the University of Heidelberg and Director of the Kaiser Wilhelm (later Max Planck) Institute for Medical Research. He remained there until the late 1930s when he was caught in a Nazi round-up of Jews and imprisoned in a concentration camp. The award to him of a Nobel Prize came after the introduction of Adolf Hitler's policy forbidding any German to accept such an award. But after the end of World War II in 1945 Kuhn received his prize and returned to work in Heidelberg. He became editor of the chemical journal *Annalen der Chemie* in 1948. His health began to fail in 1965 and he died of cancer in Heidelberg on 31 July 1967.

Kuhn's early researches concerned the carotenoids, the fat-soluble yellow pigments found in plants which are precursors of vitamin A. In the early 1930s Kuhn and his co-workers determined the structures of vitamin A and vitamin B_2 (riboflavin) and isolated them from cow's milk, at about the same time as Paul Karrer was doing similar work. Then in 1938 they took about 70,000 litres of skimmed milk and after a painstaking series of extractions isolated from it 1 gram of vitamin B_6 (pyridoxine).

In the 1940s Kuhn continued to carry out research on carbohydrates, studying alkaloid glycosides such as those that occur in tomatoes, potatoes and other plants of the genus *Solanum*. In 1952 he returned to experiments with milk, extracting carbohydrates from thousands of litres of milk using chromatography. This work led in the 1960s to the investigation of similar sugar-type substances in the human brain; many of these chemicals were synthesized for the first time by Kuhn and his co-workers.

L

Langmuir, Irving (*1881–1957*), was an American physical chemist who is best remembered for his studies of adsorption at surfaces and for his investigations of thermionic emission. For his work on surface chemistry he was awarded the 1932 Nobel Prize in Chemistry. Unlike most scientists of world renown he did most of his research in commercial environment, not in an academic institution.

Langmuir was born in Brooklyn, New York City, on 31 January 1881. He attended local elementary schools before his family moved to Paris for three years, where he was a boarder at a school in the suburbs. His interests in the practical aspects of science were fostered by his brother Arthur. In 1895 the family returned to the United States to Philadelphia, and Langmuir went to the Chapel Hill Academy and later to the Pratt Institute in Brooklyn. After High School he entered the School of Mines at Columbia University and graduated in 1903 with a degree in metallurgical engineering. His postgraduate studies were undertaken at the University of Göttingen under the guidance of Hermann Nernst; he gained his PhD for a thesis on the recombination of dissociated gases. After a brief period as a teacher in New Jersey, he joined the General Electric Company in 1909 at their research laboratories at Schenectady and remained there until he retired in 1950; he was its Assistant Director from 1932 until 1950. He died in Falmouth, Massachusetts, on 16 August 1957.

Langmuir's work at Columbia concerned the dissociation of water vapour and carbon dioxide around red-hot platinum wires. His first studies at General Electric involved the thermal conduction and convection of gases around tungsten filaments. Langmuir showed that the blackening on the inside of "vacuum-filled" electric lamps was caused by evaporation of tungsten from the filament. The introduction of nitrogen into the glass bulb prevented evaporation and blackening, but increased heat losses which were overcome by making the tungsten filament in the form of a coiled coil.

At the same time, Langmuir was carrying out research on electric discharges in gases at very low pressures, which led to the discovery of the Child–Langmuir space-charge effect: the electron current between electrodes of any shape in vacuum is proportional to the 3/2 power of the potential difference between the electrodes. He also studied the mechanical and electrical properties of tungsten lamp filaments to which thorium oxide had been added. He showed that high thermal emissions were caused by diffusion of thorium to form a monolayer on the surface. One consequence was the development of an improved vacuum pump based on the condensation of mercury vapour. This work also initiated his 1934 patent for an atomic welding torch, in which the recombination of hydrogen atoms produced by an electric arc between tungsten electrodes generated heat at temperatures in the order of 6,000°C.

For three years Langmuir considered the problems of atomic structure. Building on Gilbert Lewis' atomic theory and valency proposals, Langmuir suggested that chemical reactions occur as a consequence of a desire by an atom to achieve a full shell of eight outer electrons. He was the first to use the terms electrovalency (for ionic bonds between metals and non-metals) and covalency (for shared-electron bonds between non-metals).

During the 1920s Langmuir became particularly interested in the properties of liquid surfaces. He went on to propose his general adsorption theory for the effect of a solid surface during a chemical reaction. He made the following assumptions:

(a) The surface has a fixed number of adsorption sites; at equilibrium at any temperature and gas pressure, a fraction θ of the sites are occupied by adsorbed particles and a fraction $1 - \theta$ are unoccupied;

(b) The heat of adsorption is the same for all sites and is independent of the number of sites occupied;

(c) There is no interaction between molecules on different sites, and each site can hold only one adsorbed molecule.

From this model he formulated Langmuir's adsorption isotherm, which can be expressed as

$$1/\theta = 1 + 1/bP,$$

where θ = fraction of sites occupied, b is a constant based on rate constants of evaporation and condensation, and P = pressure.

During World War II Langmuir was responsible for work that led to the generation of improved smoke screens using smoke particles of an optimum size. He later applied this knowledge to particles of solid carbon dioxide and silver iodide which were scattered from aircraft to seed water droplets for cloud formation, in an attempt to make rain.

Lapworth, Arthur (*1872–1941*), was a British organic chemist whose most important work was the enunciation of the electronic theory of organic reactions (independently of Robert Robinson).

Lapworth was born in Galashiels, Scotland, on 10 October 1872, the son of the geologist Charles Lapworth who was teaching there at the time. The family moved to Birmingham on his father's appointment as Professor of Geology at Mason College, which Lapworth also attended to study chemistry. He graduated in 1893 and went to the London City and Guilds College to do research, first under H. E. Armstrong on the chemistry of naphthalene and then with Frederick Kipping in studies of camphor. Lapworth, Kipping and their contemporary William Perkin Jr became related by marrying three sisters – Lapworth already with the coincidence of having the same birthday as Henry Cavendish. From 1895 to 1900 Lapworth was a demonstrator at the School of Pharmacy then Head of the Chemistry Department at Goldsmiths College, London. In 1909 he moved to Manchester, where he spent the rest of his life, first as Senior Lecturer in Organic and Physical Chemistry at the University and finally in 1922 holding the senior professorship in the department. In his latter years he developed a painful illness. He died in Manchester on 5 April 1941.

In Lapworth's early work on camphor he recognized an intramolecular change, related to the pinacol-pinacolone rearrangement, which made possible the acceptance of Bredt's structure for camphor.

A little later he began a study of reaction mechanisms, notably of cyanohydrin formation from carbonyl compounds and the benzoin condensation reaction of benzaldehyde. The results of this

pinacol
(2, 3-dimethylbutan-2, 3-diol)

↓ H +

pinacolone
(2, 2-dimethylbutan-3-one)

camphor

work entitle Lapworth to be regarded as one of the founders of modern physical-organic chemistry. He was one of the first to emphasize that organic compounds can ionize, and that different parts of an organic molecule behave as though they bear electrical charges, either permanently or at the moment of reaction.

With the development of theories of valency based on the electronic structure of the atom, Lapworth was able to refine some speculations about "alternative polarities" in organic compounds into a classification of reaction centres as either anionoid or cationoid, the changes being determined by the influence of a key atom such as oxygen. In the mid-1920s, when he collaborated on these concepts with Robert Robinson, a controversy arose with Christopher Ingold and his school who were developing a similar approach to the problem but using a different terminology (nucleophilic for anionoid and electrophilic for cationoid). Ingold's terminology eventually gained general acceptance and the controversy, although occasionally sharp, was fruitful and Lapworth's last paper in 1931 bore Ingold's name as co-author.

Lavoisier, Antoine Laurent (*1743–1794*), was a French chemist, universally regarded as the founder of modern chemistry. His contributions to the science were wide ranging, but perhaps his most significant achievement was his discrediting and disproof of the phlogiston theory of combustion, which for so long had been a stumbling block to a true understanding of chemistry.

Lavoisier was born in Paris on 26 August 1743 into a well-off family. His mother died when he was young and he was brought up by an aunt. He received a good education at the Collège Mazarin, where he studied astronomy, botany, chemistry and mathematics. In 1768 he was elected an associate chemist to the Academy of Sciences; he eventually became its Director in 1785 and Treasurer in 1791.

Also in 1768 Lavoisier became an assistant to Baudon, one of the farmers-general of the revenue, and later he became a full member of the *ferme générale*, employed by the government as tax collectors. He married 14-year-old Marie Paulze, daughter of a tax farmer, in 1771 and the following year his father bought him a noble title. In 1775 he was made *régisseur des poudres* and improved the method of preparing saltpetre (potassium nitrate) for the manufacture of gunpowder. A model farm he set up at Frénchines in 1778 applied scientific principles to agriculture, and he drew up various agricultural schemes as secretary to the committee on agriculture, to which he was appointed in 1785. Two years later he became a member of the provincial assembly of Orléans, in which position he initiated many improvements for the community, such as workhouses, savings banks and canals. He was also a member of various other committees and commissions, including that formed in 1790 to rationalize the system of weights and measures throughout France, which ultimately led to the founding of the metric system.

During the French Revolution, Lavoisier came under suspicion because of his membership of the *ferme générale* (from which he derived a considerable income) and because of his marriage to one of its senior executives, although his wife acted as his scientific assistant, taking notes and even illustrating some of his books. Jean-Paul Marat, an extremist revolutionary whose membership of the Academy of Sciences had been blocked by Lavoisier, accused him of imprisoning Paris and preventing air circulation because of the wall he had built round the city in 1787. He fled from his home and laboratory in August 1792 but was arrested in the following November and sent for trial by the revolutionary tribunal in May 1794. At a cursory trial Lavoisier was one of 28 unfortunates sentenced to death. He was guillotined on 8 May 1794 and buried in a common grave. His widow later (1805) married the American physicist Benjamin Thompson (count Rumford).

Among Lavoisier's early scientific work were papers on the analysis of the mineral gypsum (hydrated calcium sulphate), on thunder, and a refutation that water changes into "earth" if it is distilled repeatedly. He helped the geologist J.E. Guettard to compile a mineralogical atlas of France.

But his most significant experiments concerned combustion. He found that sulphur and phosphorus increased in weight when they burned because they absorbed "air", and reported these results in a note he left with the Academy of Sciences in 1772. He also discovered that when litharge (lead(II) oxide) was reduced to metallic lead by heating with charcoal it lost weight because it had lost "air". Then in 1774 Joseph Priestley produced "dephlogisticated air" and Lavoisier grasped the true explanation of combustion, inventing the name oxygen (acid-maker) for the substance that combined with caloric and formed "oxygen gas". He coined the word azote for the "non-vital air" (nitrogen) that remained after the oxygen in normal air had been used up in combustion. In June 1783 he published his finding that the combustion of hydrogen in oxygen produces water, although unknown to him this fact had already been announced by the British chemist Henry Cavendish. Lavoisier burned various organic compounds in oxygen and determined their composition by weighing the carbon dioxide and water produced – the first experiments in quantitative organic analysis. Lavoisier's finding were universally accepted after the publication of his clear and logical *Traité élémentaire de chemie* in 1789, in which he listed all the chemical elements then known (although some of these were in fact oxides).

After establishing that organic compounds contain carbon, hydrogen and oxygen, Lavoisier showed by weighing that matter is conserved during fermentation as with more conventional chemical reactions. From quantitative measurements of the changes during breathing, he discovered the composition of respired air and showed that carbon dioxide and water are both normal products of respiration.

Lavoisier also made many studies outside the field of chemistry. With Pierre Laplace he experimented with calorimetry and other aspects of heat. He began to use solar energy for scientific purposes as early as 1772 and observed that "the fire of ordinary furnaces seems less pure than that of the sun". He anticipated later theories about the interdependence of sequential processes in plant and animal life forms, as described in one of his papers discovered only many years after his death. His great contribution to science was summed up by Joseph Lagrange who said, on the day after Lavoisier was guillotined at the Place de la Revolution, "It required only a moment to sever that head, and perhaps a century will not be sufficient to produce another like it."

Leblanc, Nicolas (*1742-1806*), was a French industrial chemist who devised the first commercial process for the manufacture of soda (sodium carbonate), which became the general method of making the chemical for a hundred years.

Leblanc was probably born in Ivoy-le-Pré, Indre, on 6 December 1742, although there is some doubt as to the exact place and date. His father was an ironmaster and paid for his son's education as an apothecary's apprentice; he went on to study medicine, qualifying as a doctor. In 1780 he became physician and assistant to the future duc d'Orléans (Philippe Égalité). Leblanc invented his famous process in the 1780s and in 1791, using capital supplied by the duke, he built a factory for making soda at St Denis, near Paris. But the duc d'Orléans was guillotined in 1793 during the French Revolution and Leblanc was forced to run the factory at no profit, giving all the output to the state. He had no money left to re-establish the process when the factory was handed back to him by Napoleon in 1802. He became a pauper and committed suicide at St Denis on 16 January or February 1806.

Soda was an important industrial chemical in the second half of the eighteenth century for making glass, soap and paper. It was made by calcining wood, seaweed and other vegetable matter, hence its common name soda ash. Common salt (sodium chloride) was, however, plentiful and in 1775 the French Academy of Sciences offered a cash prize for the first person to devise a commercially practical way of making soda from salt. Leblanc invented his process in 1783 (although he never received the prize money).

In the Leblanc process, salt (sodium chloride) was dissolved in sulphuric acid to form sodium sulphate:

$$2NaCl + H_2SO_4 \rightarrow Na_2SO_4 + 2HCl$$

The large amounts of hydrogen chloride generated in this reaction were released into the atmosphere. The sodium sulphate (called salt cake) was then roasted with powdered coal and crushed chalk or limestone (calcium carbonate) to yield a dark residue ("black ash") which was made up mainly of sodium carbonate and calcium sulphide:

$$2Na_2SO_4 + 2CaCO_3 + 4C \rightarrow 2Na_2CO_3 + 2CaS + 4CO_2$$

The sodium carbonate was dissolved out of the residue with water and recrystallized by heating the solution. The waste calcium sulphide that remained was known as "galligu".

Leblanc patented the process in 1791, and at his first factory produced 350 tonnes of soda a year. But the patent was rendered useless by the activities of the Revolutionary government, which confiscated the factory. The process was adopted and used throughout Europe, particularly in England, and earned large amounts of money for the soda manufacturers (who by the 1860s were making 180,000 tonnes of soda a year using the Leblanc process) and for the makers of sulphuric acid, one of the starting materials.

After the development of the ammonia-soda

process by Ernest Solvay in the 1860s, the Leblanc process gradually fell into disuse, although from time to time it was given a new lease of life by modifications. In the 1850s the British industrial chemists Henry Deacon (1822–1876) and Ferdinand Hurter (1844–1898) introduced the improvement of catalytically oxidizing the waste hydrogen chloride to chlorine, which was absorbed by lime to make bleaching powder, then much in demand by the Lancashire textile industry. In the late 1880s Alexander Chance (1844–1917), of the Birmingham glassmaking family, turned his attention to calcium sulphide, the other main waste product of the Leblanc process. He used carbon doxide to react with an aqueous slurry of the obnoxious waste to produce hydrogen sulphide gas (and leave calcium carbonate), which he then oxidized to sulphur in a Claus kiln. By the 1890s in Britain alone the Chance process, as it came to be known, was producing 35,000 tonnes of sulphur each year. Eighty years after Leblanc's death, his process and its adaptations were still providing chemical industry with some of its most important basic raw materials. The last Leblanc plant (in Bolton, Lancashire) did not close until 1938.

Le Châtelier, Henri Louis (*1850–1936*), was a French physical chemist who is best known for the principle named after him which states that if any constraint is applied to a system in chemical equilibrium, the system tends to adjust itself to counteract or oppose the constraint.

Le Châtelier was born in Paris on 8 October 1850, the son of France's Inspector-General of Mines. He was educated at the Collège Rollin in Paris and went to study science and engineering at the École Polytechnique, although his studies were interrupted by the Franco-Prussian War (1870–1871). He graduated in 1875 then, after working for two years as a mining engineer, he took up an appointment as Professor of Chemistry at the École des Mines in 1877. In 1898 he moved to the Collège de France as Professor of Mineral Chemistry, before finally settling at the Sorbonne in 1908 as Professor of Chemistry in succession to Henri Moissan (1852–1907). He worked for the Ministry of Armaments during World War I and retired in 1919. He died at Miribel-les-Échelles, Isère, on 17 September 1936.

Le Châtelier's first major contribution was to temperature measurement, a subject that followed naturally from his high-temperature studies of metals, alloys, glass, cement and ceramics. In 1887 he devised a platinum/rhodium thermocouple for measuring high temperatures by making use of the Seebeck effect (the generation of a current in a circuit made up of two dissimilar metals with the junctions at different temperatures; the magnitude of the current is proportional to the difference in temperature). Le Châtelier also made an optical pyrometer which measures temperature by comparing the light emitted by a high-temperature object with a standard light source.

This work involving flames and thermometry led him to thermodynamics, and in 1884 Le Châtelier put forward the first version of his principle, in which he stated that a change in pressure on an equilibrium system results in a movement of the equilibrium in the direction that opposes the pressure change. By 1888 he had generalized the principle as the *Loi de stabilité de l'equilibre chimique* and applied it to any change that affects chemical equilibrium. In its general form Le Châtelier's principle is all-embracing, and includes the law of mass action, as formulated by Cato Guldberg (1836–1902) and Peter Waage (1833–1900) in 1864. It is particularly relevant in predicting the effects of changes in temperature and pressure on chemical reactions: for example, it predicts that a rise in temperature or an increase in pressure should facilitate or accelerate a reaction that is reluctant to take place at normal temperatures and pressures. Industrial chemists, such as Fritz Haber and his process for synthesizing ammonia, were soon to make good use of the principle. It also agreed with the new thermodynamics being worked out in the United States by Josiah Willard Gibbs. Le Châtelier was largely responsible for making Gibbs' researches known in Europe, translating his papers into French and performing experiments to test the phase rule. He also wrote extensively about labour relations and efficiency in industry. In 1895 he put forward the idea of the oxyacetylene torch for cutting and welding steel.

Lewis, Gilbert Newton (*1875–1946*), was an American theoretical chemist who made important contributions to thermodynamics and the electronic theory of valency. He is best known for his explanation of the behaviour of acids and bases.

Lewis was born in Weymouth, Massachusetts, on 23 October 1875. He was educated at the preparatory school of the University of Nebraska and Harvard, from which he graduated in 1896, gaining his MA in 1898 and his PhD a year later for a thesis on the electrochemical and thermochemical relations of zinc and cadmium amalgams. He remained at Harvard for a year as an instructor, before going to Europe on a travelling scholarship to study under Friedrich Ostwald at Leipzig and Hermann Nernst at Göttingen. He then went to the Philippines for a year as Superintendent of Weights and Measures and Chemist at the Bureau of Science in Manila. He returned to the United States in 1905 to join the research team of A.A. Noyes at the Massachusetts Institute of Technology. In 1912 he became Chairman of the Chemistry Department at the University of California, where he remained until his death. He died in his laboratory at Berkeley on 23 March 1946.

During his seven years at MIT Lewis published more than 30 papers, including fundamental work on chemical thermodynamics and free energies. At Berkeley he set about reorganizing and rejuvenating the department, appointing staff with a wide-based chemical knowledge rather than specialists.

In 1916 Lewis began his pioneering work on valency. He postulated that the atoms of elements whose atomic mass is higher then helium's have inner shells of electrons with the structure of the preceding inert gas. The valency electrons lie outside these shells and may be lost or added to comparatively easily to form ionic bonds. He went on to state that bonding electrons prefer to pair up – the idea of the covalent bond. Much of this work involved the building of bridges between inorganic and organic chemists, who had often considered that polar (predominantly ionic) and non-polar (predominantly covalent) substances bore little relation to each other. Lewis also drew attention to the unusual properties of molecules that have an odd number of electrons, such as nitric oxide (nitrogen monoxide, NO).

A molecule of chlorine with a covalent bond involving the sharing of a pair of electrons by the two atoms, and two hybrid forms of a molecule of nitric oxide (nitrogen monoxide), each with an odd (unpaired) electron.

In 1923 Lewis and M. Randall published *Thermodynamics and the Free Energy of Chemical Substances*, which was the culmination of 20 years' research in compiling data on free energies (ΔG). Until the early years of this century it was considered that the heat of reaction (ΔH) could be taken as a measure of chemical affinity and that changes in enthalpy could be used to predict the direction of the reaction. It was later realized that free energy is the correct basis for such predictions. Lewis' treatise listed the free energies of 143 important substances, which could be used to evaluate the outcome of several hundred reactions. This work was linked to the determina-

tion of the electrode potentials of more than a dozen elements.

Also in 1923 Lewis published his highly influential book *Valence and the Structure of Atoms and Molecules*. In it he put forward a new definition of a base as a substance that has a lone pair of electrons which may be used to complete the stable group of another atom, and defined an acid as a substance that can use a lone pair from another molecule in completing the stable group of one of its own atoms. In other words, a base supplies a pair of electrons for a chemical bond, and an acid accepts such a pair. This definition, which has stood the test of time, was remarkable because it was the first to suggest that bases include substances which do not produce hydroxyl ions.

Previously, according to the Brönsted-Lowry theory, it was thought that an acid is a substance capable of donating a proton (hydrogen ion) to an acceptor substance, a base. Lewis proved his theory by carrying out acid-base reactions, detected by colour changes to indicators, in non-aqueous, hydrogen-free solvents such as tetrachloromethane (carbon tetrachloride) in which proton transfer was not possible.

For several years during the mid-1930s Lewis' research team carried out investigations on heavy water and deuterium (which had been discovered in 1932 by Harold Urey, one of Lewis' former students). In his later years he carried out studies on the excited electron states of organic molecules, contributing to the understanding of the colour of organic substances and the complex phenomena of phosphorescence and fluorescence. Lewis died in his laboratory while performing experiments on fluorescence.

Libby, Willard Frank (*1908–1980*), was an American chemist best known for developing the technique of radiocarbon dating, for which he was awarded the 1960 Nobel Prize in Chemistry.

Libby was born in Grand Valley, Colorado, on 17 December 1908, the son of a farmer. He received his university education at the University of California, Berkeley, from which he graduated in 1931 and gained his PhD in 1933. He then took a teaching appointment at Berkeley and in 1941, soon after the outbreak of World War II, moved to Columbia University, New York, to work on the development of the atomic bomb (the Manhattan Project). After the war, in 1945, he became Professor of Chemistry at the University of Chicago's Institute for Nuclear Studies. From 1954 to 1959 he was a member of the United States Atomic Energy Commission, then in 1959 he returned to the University of California to become Director of the Institute of Geophysics. He died in Los Angeles on 8 September 1980.

During the early 1940s at Columbia Libby worked on the separation of uranium isotopes for producing fissionable uranium-238 for the atomic bomb. Back in Chicago after the war he turned his attention to carbon-14, a radioactive isotope of carbon that had been discovered in 1940 by Serge Korff. It occurs as a small constant percentage of the carbon in the carbon dioxide in the atmosphere – resulting from cosmic ray bombardment – and in the carbon in the tissues of all living plants and animals. Carbon-14 has an extremely long half-life (5,730 years) but when the plant or animal dies, it accumulates no more of the radioactive isotope, which steadily decays and changes into nitrogen. Libby reasoned that a determination of the carbon-14 content of anything derived from plant or animal tissue – such as wood, bones, cotton or woollen cloth, hair or leather – gives a measure of its age (or the time that has elapsed since the plant or animal died). He and his co-workers accurately dated ancient Egyptian relics by measuring the amount of radiocarbon they contained using a sensitive Geiger counter. By 1947 they had developed the technique so that it can date objects up to 50,000 years old. It has proved to be extremely useful in geology, anthropology and archaeology. In 1946 Libby showed that tritium (a radioactive isotope of hydrogen of mass 3) is formed by the action of cosmic rays and devised a method of dating based on the amount of tritium in the water in an archaeological specimen. Later workers extended the method using other isotopes, such as potassium-40.

Liebig, Justus von (*1803–1873*), was a German organic chemist, one of the greatest influences on nineteenth-century chemistry. Through his researches and those of his ex-students, he had a profound influence on the science for nearly 100 years. To the schoolchild of today he is best known for the piece of chemical apparatus that he made popular and which still bears his name (the Liebig condenser). A better measure of his status is the fact that his students, assistants and co-workers included such famous chemists as Edward Frankland, Joseph Gay-Lussac, August von Hofmann, Friedrich Kekulé, Friedrich Wöhler and Charles Wurtz.

Liebig was born in Darmstadt, Hesse, on 12 May 1803. His father sold drugs, dyes, pigments and other chemicals and carried out his own chemical experiments, to which Liebig was introduced as a boy. When he was 15 years old he was apprenticed to an apothecary and first went to university to study under Karl Kastner at Bonn (where Liebig was arrested for his liberalist political activity) and then he accompanied Kastner to Erlangen University, where he gained his PhD in 1822 when he was still only 19 years old. Financed by the Grand Duke of Hesse, Liebig went to Paris for two years where Alexander von Humboldt (1769–1859) obtained a position for him in Joseph Gay-Lussac's laboratory at the Arsenal. He also made the acquaintance of Louis Thénard (1777–1857), who with von Humboldt recommended the 21-year-old Liebig for the Chair of Chemistry at the small University of Giessen. He stayed there for 27 years (1825–1852), building up a prestigious teaching laboratory. In 1840 he founded the journal *Annalen der Chemie* and was made a baron in 1845. Then in 1852 he moved to the University of Munich but, because of failing health, did less active research himself and concentrated on lecturing and writing. He remained there for the rest of his life and died in Munich on 18 April 1873.

In the early 1820s Liebig investigated fulminates, at the same time that Wöhler was independently working with cyanates. In 1826 Liebig prepared silver fulminate (modern formula AgCNO) and Wöhler made silver cyanate (AgNCO). When they reported their results they assigned the same formula to the two different compounds, which stimulated Jöns Berzelius' work that led to the concept of isomers.

Liebig and Wöhler became friends and continued their researches together. In 1832, from a study of oil of bitter almonds (benzaldehyde; phenylmethanal), they discovered the benzoyl radical (C_6H_5CO-). They showed that benzaldehyde can be converted to benzoic acid and made a number of other related compounds, such as benzyl alcohol and benzoyl chloride. The benzene ring had, in fact, conferred unusual stability to the benzoyl grouping, allowing it to persist in the various reactions. Liebig and Wöhler introduced the idea of compound radicals in organic chemistry, although they found no other radicals that as convincingly supported their theory and found themselves in an acrimonius dispute over the matter with Berzelius and Jean Baptiste Dumas. They had, however, tried to introduce a degree of systematization into the confused field of organic chemistry. To facilitate this work, many new methods of organic analysis were introduced by Liebig, and he devised ways of determining hydrogen, carbon and halogens in organic compounds.

From 1838 Liebig's work centred on what we would now call biochemistry. He studied fermentation (but would not acknowledge that yeast is a living substance, a view also subscribed to by Berzelius that brought them both into contention with Louis Pasteur) and analysed various body fluids and urine. He calculated the calorific values of foods, emphasizing the role of fats as a source of dietary energy and even developed a beef extract - long marketed as Liebig extract. Liebig also applied his chemical knowledge to agriculture. He demonstrated that plants absorb minerals (and water) from the soil and postulated that the carbon used by plants comes from carbon dioxide in the air rather than from humus in the soil. He also thought, incorrectly, that ammonia in rainwater passed into the soil and provided plants with their sole source of nitrogen. He thus advocated the use of artificial fertilizers in agriculture instead of animal manure, although his original formulation omitted essential nitrogen compounds.

In later life his rather rigid views made Liebig even more dogmatic in his statements - often labelled as arrogance by both his friends and his antagonists - but by then he was an established authority and his opinions were seldom questioned. It is said that he could be grossly unfair, stimulating controversy and admitting an error only when it no longer mattered; only his life-long friend Wöhler seems to have continued to have survived Liebig's irascibility.

Linnett, John Wilfred (*1913-1975*), was a British chemist of wide ranging interests, from spectroscopy to reaction kinetics and molecular structure.

Linnett was born in Coventry on 3 August 1913. He was educated at the local King Henry VIII School and in 1931 won a scholarship to read chemistry at St John's College, Oxford, from which he graduated in 1934. He was awarded his doctorate three years later for a thesis on the spectroscopy and photochemistry of the metal alkyls; he continued this work in 1938 during a visit to Harvard. From 1938 to 1965 Linnett was at Oxford, becoming a Reader in 1962. In 1965 he was appointed Professor of Physical Chemistry at Emmanuel College, Cambridge, where he remained for the rest of his research life. He became Master of Sidney Sussex College, Cambridge, in 1970, Deputy Vice-Chancellor of Cambridge University in 1971 and Vice-Chancellor from 1973 to 1975. He died on 7 November 1975.

The beginning of Linnett's career coincided with the outbreak of World War II in 1939. During that period he participated in a broad project aimed at providing methods of protection from gas attacks, such as developing catalysts that would oxidize carbon monoxide. After the war he studied molecular force fields, the measurement of burning velocities in gases, the recombination of atoms at surfaces, and theories of chemical bonding.

His work on explosion limits concentrated on the reaction between carbon monoxide, hydrogen and oxygen, which led to the study of atomic reactions on surfaces, such as the efficiency of the surface recombination of hydrogen atoms on palladium/gold, palladium/silver and copper/nickel alloys. In the early 1960s he was using mass spectroscopy for the direct sampling of reacting systems. In 1967, using this technique, he discovered that the HCO radical attracts the hydrogen from the methyl group of acetaldehyde (ethanal):

$$\cdot HCO + CH_3CHO \rightarrow CO + H_2 + \cdot CH_2CHO$$

The following year he extended the method to study the pyrolysis of mixtures of methyl iodide (iodomethane, CH_3I) and nitric oxide (nitrogen monoxide, NO) and attempted to account for the formation of N-N bonds in the reaction of methyl radicals with excess nitric oxide.

In 1960, while visiting Berkeley on a Cherwell Memorial Fellowship, Linnett originated his important modification to the Lewis-Langmuir octet rule concerning valency electrons. He proposed that the octet should be considered as a double quartet of electrons rather than as four pairs, and in this way he was able to explain the stability of "odd electron" molecules such as nitric oxide.

nitric oxide
(nitrogen monoxide)

combination
NO

dimer
N_2O_2

Nitrogen has five valence electrons and oxygen has six; there are $2\frac{1}{2}$ bonds (or electron pairs) linking the two atoms. In the dimer N_2O_2, however, there are five bonds with two sets of coincident electrons, whereas in the five bonds of 2NO the quartets of each spin do not have the same orientation. The 2NO version should therefore have the lower electron-electron repulsion energy. Linnett and his co-worker Hirst described this analysis as the non-pairing method to distinguish it from the valence-bond and molecular-orbital methods.

Linnett published more than 250 scientific papers and two textbooks, in one of which (*Wave Mechanics and Valency*) he explains to the experimental chemist the processes and techniques involved in the application of wave mechanics to the electronic structures of atoms and molecules.

Lipscomb, William Nunn (*1919–*), is an American chemist whose main interest is in the relationships between the geometric and electronic structures of molecules and their chemical and physical behaviour. Much of his work has been carried out with the boron hydrides.

Lipscomb was born in Cleveland, Ohio, on 9 December 1919, so sharing a birthday with Claude Berthollet, Fritz Haber and Karl Scheele. He graduated from the University of Kentucky in 1941 and gained his PhD from the California Institute of Technology in 1946. During World War II he was associated with the Office of Scientific Research and Development Projects. He taught at the University of Minnesota from 1946 to 1959, and at the University of Harvard after 1959.

Lipscomb studied the boron hydrides and their derivatives to elucidate problems about electron deficient compounds in general. He developed low-temperature X-ray diffraction methods to study simple crystals and established the structures of these compounds, which are not readily described using the usual electron pair-bonding method. He and other research workers related them to the polyhedral structures of borides. Using the simpler members of the series, they developed bonding theories that account for filled electron shells in terms of three-centre two-electron bonds. They also proposed molecular orbital descriptions in which the bonding electrons are delocalized over the whole molecule. Much of this work was summarized in Lipscomb's book *Boron Hydrides*, published in 1963.

Lipscomb went on to investigate the carboranes, $C_2B_{10}H_{12}$, and the sites of electrophilic attack on these compounds using nuclear magnetic resonance spectroscopy (NMR). This work led to the theory of chemical shifts. The calculations provided the first accurate values for the constants that describe the behaviour of several types of molecules in magnetic or electric fields. They also gave a theoretical basis for applying quantum mechanics to complex molecules, with wide potential for both inorganic and organic chemical problems. Lipscomb and his co-workers developed the idea of transferability of atomic properties, by which approximate theories for complex molecules are developed from more

exact calculations for simpler but chemically related molecules, using high-speed computers. With Pitzer, Lipscomb made the first accurate calculation of the barrier to internal rotation about the carbon-carbon bond in ethane.

Lipscomb's team developed X-ray diffraction techniques for studying simple crystals of nitrogen, oxygen, fluorine and other substances that are solid only below liquid nitrogen temperatures. They also determined the molecular structure of cyclo-octatetraene iron and the tricarbonyl complexes of natural products. One of these, leurocristine, is used in leukaemia therapy. Lipscomb also elucidated the three-dimensional structure of carboxypeptidase A, one of the largest globular proteins with a molecular weight of 34,400.

Longuet-Higgins, Hugh Christopher (*1923–*), is a versatile British theoretical chemist whose main contributions have involved the application of precise mathematical analyses, particularly statistical mechanics, to chemical problems.

Longuet-Higgins was born at Lenham, Kent, on 11 April 1923. He was educated at Winchester College and won a scholarship to Balliol College, Oxford, where he worked under Charles Coulson and obtained his doctorate in 1947. He continued at Oxford as a Research Fellow, before spending a year studying molecular spectroscopy with Robert Mulliken (*1896–*) in Chicago. On his return to Britain in 1949 Longuet-Higgins was appointed a Lecturer and Reader in Theoretical Chemistry at the University of Manchester, and it was there that he turned his attention to statistical mechanics, work which he pursued further while he was Professor of Theoretical Physics at King's College, London, from 1952 to 1954. In that year he became Professor of Theoretical Chemistry at Cambridge, where he stayed for 13 years. In 1967 he took a Royal Society Research Fellowship at Edinburgh University to study artificial intelligence and information-processing systems, which he thought had a closer bearing on true biology than purely physio-chemical studies. Then in 1974 he moved to Sussex University, where he expanded this field into studies of the mechanisms of language and the perception of music.

Longuet-Higgins made his first contribution to theoretical chemistry when he was only 20 years old and still an undergraduate. He overthrew the previously held views about the structures of the boron hydrides, the simplest of which, diborane (B_2H_6), was thought structurally to resemble ethane. Longuet-Higgins pointed out that spectroscopic evidence suggested a bridged structure.

ethane   diborane

cyclobutadiene
(hypothetical)

or

transition metal ion
(actual)

This hypothesis later proved to be correct, but not before he had also predicted the structures of other borohydrides and the then unknown beryllium hydride. He returned to this work after 23 years and predicted the existence of the ion $(B_{12}H_{12})^{2-}$, whose stability was strikingly verified several years later.

For his doctorate in 1947 Longuet-Higgins developed, with Coulson, the orbital theory of conjugated organic molecules, deriving theoretically results that had been known experimentally for decades. He continued this work in Chicago, showing how the properties of conjugated systems can be derived by combining into molecular orbital theory a study of "non-bonding" orbitals. This work led directly to Michael Dewar's famous linear combination of molecular orbital theory. A later collaboration between Dewar and Longuet-Higgins resulted in the discovery of a system (biphenylene) in which the molecular orbital theory and the then more fashionable resonance theory gave contrary predictions. They published their findings in 1957 and several years later experimental results confirmed the molecular orbital predictions.

The work in statistical mechanics which Longuet-Higgins began at Manchester in 1949 made important contributions to many fields. He formulated a theory to describe the thermodynamic properties of mixtures, which he later extended to polymer solutions. He also investigated the optical properties of helical molecules and continued his work on electronic spectra.

At Cambridge, from 1954, he used mathematical techniques to make theoretical chemical predictions. He predicted, for example, that cyclobutadiene (which had defeated all attempts to prepare it) should exist as a ligand attached to an atom of a transition metal; such a compound was successfully prepared three years later.

In a larger piece of work, he applied group theory to define the elements of symmetry of non-rigid molecules, such as hydrazine (N_2H_4), and thus was able to classify the individual quantum levels of the molecule. This, in turn, allowed analysis of the spectra of such molecules and the evaluation of their molecular characteristics.

Other work of this nature involved the study of a group of important organic reactions known as electrocyclic rearrangements, of which the best known is the Diels-Alder reaction. With W. Abrahamson, Longuet-Higgins discovered symmetry principles in combination with molecular orbital theory which permit clear predictions to be made about the outcomes of such reactions, some of which seem to be quite contrary to others. In this and his other contributions Longuet-Higgins demonstrated the large part he has played in advancing chemistry from a science of largely practical experiment to one of predictive theory.

Lonsdale, Kathleen (*1903-1971*), was an X-ray crystallographer who rose from the most humble background to become one of the best known workers in her field, being among the first to determine the structures of organic molecules. She also paved the way in a male dominated world for the many women who followed in her footsteps.

Lonsdale was born, as Kathleen Yardley, in Newbridge, Ireland, on 28 January 1903, the youngest of the ten children of the local postmaster. The family was desperately poor – her father drank heavily – and four of her brothers died in infancy. An elder brother, unable to take up a scholarship to secondary school because he had to work to help to support the family, later became one of the first wireless operators and founded a school of wireless telegraphy in the north of England.

The family moved to England in 1908 and settled in Seven Kings, Essex. Kathleen went to the local elementary school until 1914, when she won a scholarship to the County High School for Girls in nearby Ilford. For her last two years there she had to attend classes at the boys' school as the only girl to study chemistry, physics and higher mathematics. At the age of 16 she went to Bedford College for Women in London, switching from mathematics to physics after one year. She graduated as top student in the University in 1922 and W.H. Bragg immediately offered her a place in his research team at University College, London, and then later at the Royal Institution.

In 1927 she married Thomas Lonsdale and moved to Leeds. There she had three children and worked in the Physics Department of Leeds University. She moved back to London in 1931 and carried out research for 15 years at the Royal Institution, first under Bragg and then with Henry Dale. In May 1945 she and Marjory Stephenson became the first women to be elected to the Royal Society. In 1946, after World War II, Lonsdale became Professor of Chemistry and Head of the Department of Crystallography at University College, London, and only then (at the age of 43) did she start university teaching and developing her own research school. She was made a Dame in 1956 and in 1968 became the first woman President of the British Association for the Advancement of Science. She died in Bexhill-on-Sea, Sussex, on 1 April 1971.

In her first post under Bragg she worked with W.T. Astbury trying to relate space group theory to the phenomenon of X-ray diffraction by crystals. She assembled her own apparatus and the first organic crystal she measured was succinic acid (butanedioic acid). At Leeds she used a grant from the Royal Society to buy an ionization spectrometer and electroscope and correctly solved the structure of crystals of hexamethylbenzene provided by Christopher Ingold, who was then Professor of Chemistry at Leeds. Her solution for hexachlorobenzene was less complete but important as the first investigation using Fourier analysis. Lonsdale was a competent mathematician and did all her own calculations, aided only by logarithm tables. When she returned to work with Bragg in London she derived the structure factor formulae for all space groups.

At the Royal Institution she researched many subjects. She was interested in X-ray work at various temperatures and thermal motion in crystals. She also used divergent beam X-ray photography to investigate the textures of crystals. Lonsdale continued this work at University College, while also studying solid-state reactions, the pharmacological properties and crystal structures of methonium compounds, and the composition of bladder and kidney stones.

Lonsdale's attitudes were influenced by the Society of Friends (Quakers) and at the outbreak of World War II in 1939 she did not register for employment, regarding all war as evil. On being fined £2 she refused to pay and was sent to prison at Holloway for one month. One result of this experience was a commitment to pacifism and a lifelong interest in prison visiting.

Lynen, Feodor (*1911–*   ), is a German biochemist known for his research into the synthesis of cholesterol in the human body and into the metabolism of fatty acids. For this work he shared the 1964 Nobel Prize in Physiology and Medicine with the American biochemist Konrad Bloch.

Lynen was born in Munich, Bavaria, on 6 April 1911. He studied at the University of Munich, gaining his doctorate in 1937. In the same year he married the daughter of his professor, Heinrich Wieland. He remained on the academic staff at Munich as a lecturer (1942–1946), Associate Professor (1947–1953) and Professor of Biochemistry (from 1953). Between 1954 and 1972 he was Director of the Max Planck Institute for Cell Chemistry in Munich, and from 1972 Director of the Max Planck Institute for Biochemistry.

Cholesterol is a key substance in the body, the starting material for adrenal cortical hormones, sex hormones and other steroids. Lynen in Munich and Bloch in the United States studied the complicated mechanism by which cholesterol is formed. Bloch found that the basic unit for cholesterol synthesis is the simple acetate (ethanoate) ion, a chemical fragment containing only two carbon atoms. Fritz Lipmann postulated that the substance known as co-enzyme A, which he isolated in 1947, might be the carrier of the fragment. In 1951 Lynen isolated "active acetate" from yeast and found it to be identical to acetyl co-enzyme A, a combination of co-enzyme A and a two-carbon fragment, thus confirming Lipmann's hypothesis. Bloch then found an intermediate compound, squalene – a long hydrocarbon containing 30 carbon atoms. Lynen and Bloch corresponded and worked out the 36 steps involved in the synthesis of cholesterol. The final stage was found to be the transformation of the carbon chain of squalene ($C_{30}H_{50}$) into the four-ring molecule of cholesterol.

cholesterol

Lynen also worked on the biosynthesis of fatty acids, isolating from yeast an enzyme complex which acts as a catalyst in the synthesis of long-chain fatty acids from acetyl co-enzyme A and malonyl co-enzyme A. His study of fatty acids also elucidated a series of energy-generating reactions that occur when fatty acids from food are respired to form carbon dioxide and water. From this research has resulted the more general conclusion that repeated condensation of two-carbon fragments originating from acetate is the basis of the synthesis of many natural substances.

M

Mcbain, James William (*1882–1953*), was a Canadian physical chemist whose main researches were concerned with colloidal solutions, particularly soap solutions.

McBain was born in Chatham, New Brunswick, and entered the University of Toronto at the age of 17, graduating in chemistry and mineralogy. He spent the winter of 1904–1905 at the University of Leipzig, which at that time was at the height of its academic activity in physical chemistry. His first academic appointment was as a lecturer at the University of Bristol in 1906, a post he held until he became the first Leverhulme Professor of Chemistry there in 1919. In 1926 he went to the United States to become Professor of Chemistry at the University of Stanford, California; he became Emeritus Professor in 1947, six years before he died.

McBain's first research concerned the rate of oxidation of ferrous (iron (II)) salts on exposure to air. But he was soon attracted to colloid chemistry and a study of simple soaps. As early as 1910 he showed that aqueous solutions of soaps such as sodium palmitate are good electrolytic conductors. He discovered the interesting anomaly that there are maxima and minima in the conductivity versus concentration curves. In his next investigation he examined the degrees of hydrolysis for various concentrations of soap. He postulated the existence of highly mobile carriers of negative electricity with mobilities similar to that of the citrate ion. This led to the concept of the "association ion" or "ionic micelle", which has since proved invaluable in elucidating the properties of a large class of colloidal systems, including soaps, detergents and dyes.

McBain and his co-workers also developed new apparatus for their studies. They improved on the method of Northrop and Anson for determining the diffusion constants of substances in solution by passing them through discs of sintered glass. They developed a simple and elegant transparent air-driven ultra-centrifuge. McBain pointed out that in sedimentation of an equilibrium system

such as that which exists in soap solutions above the micelle point, the rapidly moving micelles dissociate as they leave their normal environment of the equilibrium concentration of monomer, but as the material collects at the periphery of the centrifuge rotor, micelles naturally reform. To determine the thermodynamic properties of soap solutions he examined the possibility of using various methods: osmotic pressures, lowering of vapour pressure, and lowering of freezing point. Ultimately he developed his own method based on the lowering of the dew point.

In aqueous solution the micelle (association particle) encloses the non-polar or chain portions of the molecules, with the carboxyl or hydrophilic portions on the outside of the sphere. McBain pointed out that invert micelles should exist, with the polar heads clustered together at the centre, and these should be capable of dissolving substances that are usually insoluble. Such micelles in aqueous solutions should be able, for example, to dissolve hydrocarbons. He gave the name "solubilization" to this phenomenon and spent much time and energy to experiments in this field. He also introduced the term cosolvency to describe the process of effecting solution by means of a mixture of liquid solvents.

McBain also questioned the idea that the surface phase in simple solutions was only one monolayer thick (as implied by the experimental work of Frederick Donnan and the theoretical proposals of Irving Langmuir). Above the micelle point there are several distinct species of potentially active materials (anions, undissociated molecules and micelles), all of which could accumulate at the surface. McBain proved that orientated underlayers do exist beneath the monolayers of soap, and he devised an ingenious apparatus for determining their actual composition. William Hardy came to a similar conclusion that molecular orientation is not confined to a monolayer of liquid in contact with a solid surface but that long-range forces give rise to cybotactic layers of considerable thickness (cybotactics are regions of "order" of molecules within the structure of a liquid).

Another phenomenon studied by McBain was the adsorption of gases and vapours by solids. Various processes can take place simultaneously: physical sorption, chemisorption, and - by "activating" the solid or forming it into a skeletonized structure - permeation of the solid by the gas or vapour. McBain introduced the generalized term sorption to include all such cases. He devised the McBain–Bakr spring balance, which provides a continuous record of the quantities and rate of sorption by direct weighing.

Martin, Archer John Porter (*1910-*   ), is a British biochemist who shared the 1952 Nobel Prize in Chemistry with his co-worker Richard Synge for their development of paper chromatography.

Martin was born in London on 1 March 1910, the son of a doctor of medicine. He was educated at Bedford School and then went to Cambridge University, where he graduated in 1932 and gained his PhD three years later, having been influenced by J.B.S. Haldane. He worked at the Dunn Nutritional Laboratories for two years, leaving in 1938 to join the Wool Industries Research Association at Leeds. In 1946 he became head of the biochemistry division in the research department of the Boots Pure Drug Company in Nottingham, and he held this position until 1948 when he was appointed to the staff of the Medical Research Council. He worked first at the Lister Institute of Preventive Medicine and then at the National Institute for Medical Research, where he was head of the division of physical chemistry from 1952 to 1956 and Chemical Consultant from 1956 to 1959. He became Director of the Abbotsbury Laboratory from 1959 to 1970, Consultant to Wellcome Research Laboratories (1970-1973), at the University of Sussex (1973-1978) and since 1980 has been Invited Professor of Chemistry at the École Polytechnique at Lausanne, Switzerland.

In his first researches, at the Dunn Nutritional Laboratory, Martin investigated problems relating to vitamin E. After 1938, at Leeds, he was involved in a study of the felting of wool. The work for which he was to become famous began in 1941, when he and Synge began the development of partition chromatography for separating the components of complex mixtures (of amino acids). In their method a drop of the solution to be analysed is placed at one end of a strip of filter paper and allowed to dry. That end of the strip is then immersed in a solvent which as it moves along the strip carries with it, at different rates, the various components of the mixture, which thus become separated and spread out along the strip of paper. Their positions are revealed by spraying the dried strip with a reagent that produces a colour change with the components; Martin and Synge used ninhydrin to record the positions of amino acids. The "developed" strip is called a chromatogram.

The technique combines two different principles, adsorption chromatography (devised by the Russian botanist Mikhail Tswett in 1903 and later revived by Richard Willstätter) and countercurrent solvent extraction for partitioning components between solvents - hence the name partition chromatography. It also has the advantage of requiring only a small sample of material and

has proved to be a powerful tool in analytical chemistry, particularly for complex biochemicals.

In 1953 Martin and A.T. James began working on gas chromatography, which separates chemical vapours by differential adsorption on a porous solid. The versatility of both techniques has been extended by using radioactive tracers in the mixture to be analysed, when the positions of components in the resulting chromatogram can be found by using a counter.

Mendeleyev, Dmitri Ivanovich (*1834-1907*), was a Russian chemist whose name will always be linked with his outstanding achievement, the development of the Periodic Table. He was the first chemist really to understand that all elements are related members of a single ordered system. He converted what had hitherto been a highly fragmented and speculative branch of chemistry into a true, logical science. The spelling of his name has been a source of confusion to students and frustration to editors for more than a century, and the forms Mendeléeff, Mendeléev and even Mendelejeff can all also be found in print.

Mendeleyev was born in Tobol'sk, Siberia, on 7 February 1834, the youngest of the 17 children of the head of the local high school. His father went blind when Mendeleyev was still a child, and the family had to rely increasingly on their mother for support. He was educated locally but could not gain admission to any Russian university (despite his mother's attempts on his behalf with the authorities at Moscow) because of the supposedly backward attainments of those educated in the provinces. In 1855 he finally qualified as a teacher at the Pedagogical Institute in St Petersburg (now Leningrad). He took an advanced degree course in chemistry, and in 1857 obtained his first university appointment.

In 1859 he was sent by the government for further study at the University of Heidelberg where he made valuable contact with the Italian chemist Stanislao Cannizzaro, whose insistence on a proper distinction between atomic and molecular weights influenced Mendeleyev greatly. In 1861 he returned to St Petersburg and became Professor of General Chemistry at the Technical Institute there in 1864. He could find no textbook adequate for his students' needs and so he decided to produce his own. The resulting *Principles of Chemistry* (1868-1870) won him international renown; it was translated into English in 1891 and 1897.

Mendeleyev began work on his periodic law in the late 1860s, and he went on to conduct research in various other fields. Then in 1890 he chose to be a spokesman for students who were protesting against unjust conditions. For these allegedly

			Ti=50	Zr=90	?=180
			V=51	Nb=94	Ta=182
			Cr=52	Mo=96	W=186
			Mn=55	Rh=104.4	Pt=197.4
			Fe=56	Ru=104.4	Ir=198
			Ni=Co=59	Pd=106.6	Os=198
H=1			Cu=63.4	Ag=108	Hg=200
	Be=9.4	Mg=24	Zn=65.2	Cd=112	
	B=11	Al=27.4	?=68	Ur=116	Au=197?
	C=12	Si=28	?=70	Sn=118	
	N=14	P=31	As=75	Sb=122	Bi=210?
	O=16	S=32	Se=79.4	Te=128?	
	F=19	Cl=35.5	Br=80	I=127	
Li=7	Na=23	K=39	Rb=85.4	Cs=133	Te=204
		Ca=40	Sr=87.6	Ba=137	Pb=207
		?=45	Ce=92		
		?Er=56	La=94		
		?Yt=60	Di=95		
		?In=75.6	Th=118?		

Mendeleyev's original (1869) Periodic Table, with similar elements on the same horizontal line.

improper activities he was retired from the university and became controller of the Bureau for Weights and Measures, although from 1893 he received no other professorial appointment. He died in St Petersburg on 2 February 1907, five days before his seventy-third birthday. His nomination for the 1906 Nobel Prize in Chemistry failed by one vote (the award went to Henri Moissan) but his name became recorded in perpetuity 50 years later when element number 101 was called mendelevium.

Before Mendeleyev produced his periodic law, understanding of the chemical elements had long been an elusive and frustrating task. The attempts by various chemists to put the whole field into some intelligible reference system had acted rather like the progressively stronger lenses of a microscope in bringing a sensed but unseen object into clear vision. According to Mendeleyev the properties of the elements, as well as those of their compounds, are periodic functions of their atomic weights (relative atomic masses). In 1869 he stated that "the elements arranged according to the magnitude of atomic weights show a periodic change of properties". Other chemists, notably Lothar Meyer in Germany, had meanwhile come to similar conclusions, Meyer publishing his findings independently.

Mendeleyev compiled the first true Periodic Table, listing all the 63 elements then known. Not

H	O	I a	b	II a	b	III a	b	IV a	b	V a	b	VI a	b	VII a	b	VIII
	He	Li		Be		B		C		N		O		F		
	Ne	Na		Mg		Al		Si		P		S		Cl		
	A	K		Ca		Sc		Ti		V		Cr		Mn		Fe Co Ni
			Cu		Zn		Ga		Ge		As		Se		Br	
	Kr	Rb		Sr		Y		Zr		Nb		Mo		Tc		Ru Rh Pd
			Ag		Cd		In		Sn		Sb		Te		I	
	Xe	Cs		Ba		La*		Hf		Ta		W		Re		Os Ir Pt
			Au		Hg		Tl		Pb		Bi		Po		At	
	Rn	Fr		Ra		Ac		Th		Pa		U†				

* = Lanthanons (Rare Earths)

† = Actinons

Modern Periodic Table based on Mendeleyev's ideas, with similar elements in vertical columns.

all elements would "fit" properly using the atomic weights of the time, so he altered indium from 76 to 114 (modern value 114.8) and beryllium from 13.8 to 9.2 (modern value 9.013). In 1871 he produced a revisionary paper showing the correct repositioning of 17 elements.

Also in order to make the table work Mendeleyev had to leave gaps, and he predicted that further elements would eventually be discovered to fill them. These predictions provided the strongest endorsement of the periodic law. Three were discovered in Mendeleyev's lifetime: gallium (1871), scandium (1879) and germanium (1886), all with properties that tallied closely with those he had assigned to them.

Farsighted though Mendeleyev was, he had no notion that the periodic recurrences of similar properties in the list of elements reflect anything in the structures of their atoms. It was not until the 1920s it was realized that the key parameter in the periodic system is not the atomic weight but the atomic number of the elements – a measure of the number of nuclear protons or electrons in the stable atom. Since then great progress has been made in explaining the periodic law in terms of the electronic structures of atoms and molecules.

Among Mendeleyev's other investigations were the specific volumes of gases and the conditions that are necessary for their liquefaction. Following visits to the oilfields of the Caucasus and in the United States he examined the origins of petroleum. He was convinced that the future held great possibilities for manned flight, and in 1887 he made an ascent in a balloon to observe an eclipse of the Sun. He farmed a small estate and applied his scientific knowledge to improve the yield and quality of crops, an endeavour invaluable for Russia's predominantly agricultural economy.

Meyer, Julius Lothar (*1830–1895*), was a German chemist who, independently of Dmitri Mendeleyev, produced a periodic law describing the properties of the chemical elements.

Meyer was born in Varel, Oldenburg, on 19 August 1830, the son of a doctor of medicine. He began his university career by studying medicine at Zurich. He then took courses in chemistry at Heidelberg (under Robert Bunsen), in physics at

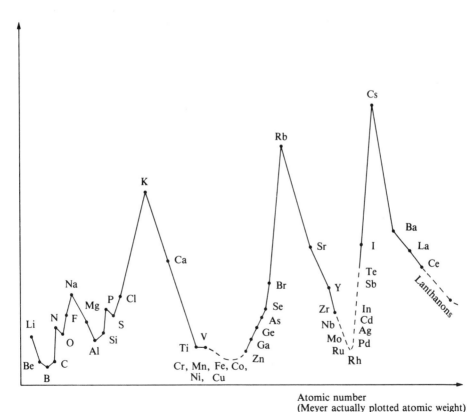

Part of the Lothar Meyer curve (with modern additions).

Königsberg and in pathology at Würzburg, where he qualified as a physician in 1854. Four years later he gained his PhD from the University of Breslau. On the basis of this wide combination of interests he began his career as a science educator in 1859, holding various appointments until he became Professor of Chemistry at Karlsruhe Polytechnic in 1868. In 1876 he was appointed the first Professor of Chemistry at Tübingen University, where he remained for the rest of his life. He died in Tübingen on 11 April 1895.

In his book *Modern Chemical Theory* (1864), a lucid exposition of the contemporary principles of the science of chemistry, Meyer drew up a table which presented all the elements according to their atomic weights (relative atomic masses), relating the weights to chemical properties. In 1870 he published the results of his further researches in the form of a graph of atomic volume (atomic weight divided by density) against atomic weight, which demonstrated the periodicity in the variation of the elements' properties. He showed that each element will not combine with the same numbers of hydrogen or chlorine atoms, establishing the concept of valency. He coined the terms univalent, bivalent, trivalent and so on, according to the number involved. Consequently it became customary to divide the elements into groups defined by the number of hydrogen atoms with which a given element can combine (or displace).

Despite the fact that Meyer had reached his conclusions quite independently of Mendeleyev, he never claimed priority for his findings. And unlike Mendeleyev, he made no predictions about the composition and properties of any elements still to be discovered.

Meyer, Viktor (*1848–1897*), was a German organic chemist who is best known for the method of determining vapour densities (and hence molecular weights) named after him. He was also the discoverer of the heterocyclic compound thiophene.

Meyer was born in Berlin on 8 September 1848. His undergraduate studies were carried out partly at Heidelberg (under Robert Bunsen), at Berlin (under Johann von Baeyer) and at Würtemberg. He gained his PhD at Heidelberg in 1867 while only 19 years old and three years later was appointed Professor of Chemistry at Stuttgart Polytechnic. In 1872 he progressed to the Technische Hochschule at Zurich and in 1885 he became a professor at Göttingen. When Bunsen died in 1889, Meyer succeeded to his professorship at Heidelberg. A long period of working with iodine and bromine at high temperatures undermined his health and, in a fit of depression, he committed suicide by taking cyanide on 8 August 1897.

Meyer's discovery about the nature of vapour densities was based largely on previous work in this field, notably that of the Italian physical chemist Amadeo Avogadro who as early as 1811 had indicated the difference between atoms and molecules. Later, in his celebrated law, Avogadro maintained that equal volumes of two gases contain the same numbers of molecules (when the temperatures and pressures are also equal). When the two volumes of gas combine chemically, the individual atoms join to form molecules, whose volume depends on the proportion in which the atoms combine.

This welcomingly straightforward definition of one of the key processes in experimental chemistry met with little acceptance from the leading chemists of the day until, in 1871, Meyer gave an incontestable demonstration of its validity. He determined the molecular weights of volatile substances formed in this way by measuring their vapour densities (molecular weight, or relative molecular mass, is twice the vapour density).

He went on to a series of pyrotechnical studies in which he determined the vapour densities of inorganic substances at high temperatures. The results of this work, undertaken with his brother Karl, were published in 1885 in their book *Pyrotechnical Research*. At about the same time, Meyer described his organic vapour density studies in his *Textbook of Organic Chemistry* (2 vols, 1883–1896).

In 1883, in the course of a lecture demonstration on the nature of benzene, Meyer was surprised to discover that the substance did not react in the way he had predicted. Benzene obtained from petroleum reacted as expected, whereas a purer sample synthesized from benzoic acid did not. From the impure benzene Meyer isolated thiophene, a heterocyclic compound containing sulphur, which much later was to become an important component of various synthetic drugs.

In the Viktor Meyer method for determination of vapour density (and hence relative molecular mass or molecular weight, which is twice the vapour density), the apparatus shown is used. A known mass of a volatile liquid is rapidly vaporized by raising its temperature well above the boiling point and the volume occupied by the resulting vapour is determined by measuring the volume of air it displaces. The inner tube (Viktor Meyer tube) contains a little sand to break the fall of the small bottle of liquid introduced at the top (after removing the stopper) and the heating jacket causes the liquid to boil, pushing off the ground-glass stopper of the small bottle. The heavy vapour remains at the bottom of the V-M tube and an equal volume of air is displaced and collected "over water". This volume is converted to standard temperature and pressure and, by using the fact that the relative molecular mass in grams occupies 22.4 litres at stp (or the vapour density in grams occupies 11.2 litres), these values can be found.

The Viktor Meyer method is simple to carry out and adaptable, only small amounts of the volatile liquid being needed and the method can be used over a wide temperature range.

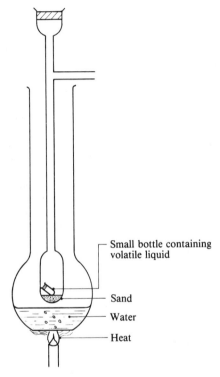

- Small bottle containing volatile liquid

- Sand

- Water

- Heat

Viktor Meyer's apparatus for measuring vapour density.

Meyerhof, Otto Fritz *(1884-1951)*, was a German-born American biochemist who shared (with Archibald Hill) the 1922 Nobel Prize in Physiology and Medicine for his research into the metabolic processes involved in the action of muscles.

Meyerhof was born on 12 April 1884 in Hanover, the son of a merchant. He attended school in Berlin but was often absent because of a kidney disorder, as a result of which he received much of his early education at home. Later he became a medical student at the universities of Freiburg, Berlin, Strasbourg and Heidelberg. In 1909 he graduated from Heidelberg and worked in a medical laboratory there until 1912, when he

moved to the University of Kiel as an assistant in the department of physiology, becoming a professor at the university in 1918. Shortly after receiving his Nobel Prize, he was offered a Chair in Biochemistry in the United States. To retain him in Germany, Meyerhof was appointed the head of a new department specially created for him at the Kaiser Wilhelm Institute for Biology in Berlin-Dahlem; he held this position from 1924 to 1929, when he became Head of the Department of Physiology in a new institute for medical research at the University of Heidelberg. As a result of Adolf Hitler's rise to power in the 1930s, Meyerhof left Germany in 1938 and went to Paris, where he became Director of Research at the Institut de Biologie Physiochimique. In 1940, when France fell to Germany in the early part of World War II, he fled to the United States, where he was appointed Research Professor of Physiological Chemistry at the University of Pennsylvania, Philadelphia, a position he held for the rest of his life. Meyerhof became an American citizen in 1948, and he died three years later on 6 October 1951.

Meyerhof's early work concerned energy exchanges in nitrifying bacteria, about which he published three papers between 1916 and 1917. He then became interested in the mechanism by which energy from food is released and utilized by living cells. In 1920 he showed that, in anaerobic conditions, the amounts of glycogen metabolized and of lactic acid produced in a contracting muscle are proportional to the tension in the muscle. He also demonstrated that between 20 and 25 per cent of the lactic acid is oxidized during the muscle's recovery period and that energy produced by this oxidation is used to convert the remainder of the lactic acid back to glycogen. Meyerhof introduced the term glycolysis to describe the anaerobic degradation of glycogen to lactic acid, and showed the cyclic nature of energy transformations in living cells. The complete metabolic pathway of glycolysis - known as the Embden-Meyerhof pathway (after Meyerhof and a co-worker) - was later worked out by Carl and Gerty Cori. Despite these and later revisions, Meyerhof's work remains the basic contribution to our knowledge of the very complex processes involved in muscular action.

Continuing his research on intracellular energy metabolism, between 1926 and 1927 Meyerhof demonstrated that glycolysis is not the result of bacterial activity, and in 1928, working with Lohmann, discovered that 50,000 joules per gram molecule of phosphate are liberated during the hydrolysis of creatine phosphate. In the following year Lohmann discovered adenosine triphosphate (ATP) in muscle and, with Meyerhof, began to study the new concept of oxidative phosphorylation. In the 1940s Meyerhof found in the microsomes in muscle cells a new ATPase enzyme that is magnesium activated.

Midgley, Thomas (*1889-1944*), was an American industrial chemist and engineer who discovered that tetraethyl lead is an efficient anti-knock additive to petrol (preventing pre-ignition in car engines) and introduced Freons as the working gases in domestic refrigerators. Today the most commonly used is Freon 12, which is difluorodichloromethane, CF_2Cl_2.

Midgley was born in Beaver Falls, Pennsylvania, on 18 May 1889, the son of an engineer and inventor. He studied mechanical engineering at Cornell University, graduating in 1911. During early World War I he worked on torpedo control systems. In 1916 he went to Ohio to work in the research department of an engineering firm, the Dayton Engineering Laboratories Company. He became a vice-president of the Ethyl Corporation in 1923 and ten years later was a director of the Ethyl–Dow Chemical Company. In 1940 he contracted poliomyelitis and became paralysed. He died in Worthington, Ohio, on 2 November 1944.

While working for the Dayton Engineering Company, Midgley discovered empirically that ethyl iodide (iodoethane) prevents pre-ignition in car engines using low-octane fuel. He spent several years teaching himself the relevant chemistry and looking for a less expensive additive. In 1921 he experimented with tetraethyl lead, showing it to be an efficient anti-knock agent. It is still widely employed, although many people question its use because of the possible environmental health hazard of lead in the atmosphere. Midgley used ethyl bromide (bromoethane) in his research, which led him to investigate the bromine in sea water and demonstrate a method for its extraction. Dayton Engineering was taken over by General Motors and he continued to work in their research laboratories.

In 1930 Midgley introduced Freon (CF_2Cl_2) as a non-inflammable, non-toxic refrigerant, which rapidly replaced ammonia, methyl chloride (chloromethane) and sulphur dioxide as the volatile but liquefiable gas in the mechanisms of domestic refrigerators. This gas and closely related compounds are still used universally for this purpose in freezers, fridges and air-conditioning units. For many years after World War II, Freons were also extensively used as propellants in aerosol containers. A hypothesis that continued release of these compounds into the atmosphere could damage the Earth's ozone layer (which acts as a filter to prevent excessive ultraviolet radiation reaching the surface of the Earth) led to restrictions or bans on the use of Freon propellants in the 1970s.

Miller, Stanley Lloyd (*1930-*), is an American chemist who carried out a key experiment that demonstrated how amino acids, the building blocks of life, might have arisen in the primeval oceans of the primitive Earth.

Miller was born in Oakland, California, on 7 March 1930. He graduated from the University of California in 1951 and three years later gained his PhD from the University of Chicago. From 1954 to 1955 he was a post-doctorial Jewett Fellow at the California Institute of Technology and then he worked for five years in the Department of Biochemistry at the Columbia College of Physicians and Surgeons, first as an Instructor in Biochemistry and then as Assistant Professor. From 1960 he held appointments at the University of California in San Diego as Assistant Professor, Associate Professor and finally Professor of Chemistry.

While working for his PhD under Harold Urey, Miller set himself the task of trying to account for the origin of life on Earth. He chose as the experimental substances the components that had been proposed for the Earth's primitive atmosphere by Urey and Alexandr Oparin. He used sterilized and purified water under an "atmosphere" of methane, ammonia and hydrogen, which he circulated for a week past an electric discharge (to simulate the likely type of energy source). He then analysed the mixture and surprisingly, after such a relatively short experimental period, found organic compounds such as simple amino acids. These were of great significance because of their ability to combine together to form proteins.

It is important when assessing the significance of the results (which have been duplicated by various other workers since) to bear in mind the time scale of the experiment in comparison with that for the origination of life on Earth. If the conditions of Miller's experiment had been continued for millions of years (instead of just seven days) and other plausible prebiotic syntheses added in, the oceans of the primordial Earth – analogous to the water used in the experiment – would have become rich with a whole range of different types of organic molecules: the so-called prebiotic soup.

There are many other steps that are needed to develop a system that is capable of self-replication. Some of these have also been worked out in the laboratory, such as the prebiotic syntheses of purines, pyrimidines and sugars needed to make up RNA or DNA. And we still do not know how the nucleic acids first began to self-replicate.

Mills, William Hobson (*1873–1959*), was a British organic chemist famous for his work on stereochemistry and on the synthesis of cyanine dyes.

Mills was born in London on 6 July 1873, although his family came from Lincolnshire and he was educated at Spalding Grammar School. He then went to Uppingham School and Jesus College, Cambridge, where he began research under Thomas Easterfield and became a Fellow of the college in 1899. Also in 1899 he went for two years to Tübingen in Germany to work under Hans von Pechmann; while there he met the British inorganic chemist Nevil Sidgewick, who was to become his lifelong friend. He returned to England in 1902 as head of chemistry at the Northern Polytechnic Institute, London, and ten years later he was appointed Professor of Natural Philosophy at Jesus College. In 1919 he became a university lecturer and in 1931 the university created for him a Readership in Stereochemistry, a post he held until he retired in 1938. He died in Cambridge on 22 February 1959.

Mills' early research concerned stereochemistry, particularly optical isomerism – the phenomenon in which pairs of (usually organic) compounds differ only in the arrangements of their atoms in space. Certain oximes (derivatives of aldehydes and ketones) were known to exist in two or more isomeric forms. In 1931, with B.C. Saunders, Mills prepared the *ortho*-carboxyphenylhydrazone of β-methyl-trimethylenedithiolcarbonate and resolved it into two optically active forms. This work confirmed the theory of Arthur Hantzsch and Alfred Werner that optical isomerism of oximes is caused by the non-planar orientation of the nitrogen atom valencies.

It had also been recognized that a spirocyclic compound consisting of two carbon rings linked together by a common carbon atom should show optical activity if the rings possessed appropriate substituents to ensure molecular dissymmetry. In 1921 Mills and C.R. Nodder synthesized and resolved the first compound of this kind, the keto-dilactone of benzophenone-2,4,2',4'-tetracarboxylic acid.

Chemists had realized that a suitably substituted compound of allene (propadiene) would also be dissymmetric, but had been unable to synthesize any such compound with acidic or

basic groups for resolution. After six years of patient research Mills and Maitland synthesized an allene derivative with two phenyl and two naphthyl substitutents.

$$H_2C = C = CH_2$$
allene

pair of isomers with "large" substituents A and B

αγ-biphenyl-αγ-di-α-naphthyl allene

By extending these general methods, they went on to show that the nitrogen atom of a quaternary ammonium salt has a tetrahedral configuration (like a carbon atom), and is not situated at the centre of a square-based pyramid. On the other hand, in 1935 Mills and his co-workers produced stereochemical evidence that a four co-ordinated platinum atom has a planar as opposed to a tetrahedral configuration.

Other workers were puzzled by the fact that a biphenyl molecule shows optical activity if there are suitable substituents in the 2, 2', 6 and 6' positions. In 1926 Mills was the first to point out that the size of the substituents can prevent the free rotation of the two phenyl groups about their common axis. He then became interested in the general problem of restricted rotation and investigated substituted derivatives of naphthalene, quinolene and benzene.

Mills' other field of research was into the synthesis of cyanine dyes. In 1905 German chemists had synthesized pinacyanol, which when added to photographic emulsions extended their sensitivity into the red region of the spectrum, as well as into the blue, violet and ultraviolet regions. Mills and his co-workers investigated similar dyestuffs for preparing photographic emulsions, mainly for use by the military in World War I.

After his retirement Mills had more time to devote to his interest in natural history, especially to the British bramble plant, *Rubus fructiosus*. His collection of 2,200 specimens of 320 of the 389 "microspecies" of this plant is arranged in systemmatic order and now housed in the Botany Department of Cambridge University.

Mitscherlich, Eilhard (*1794-1863*), was a German chemist, famous for his discovery of isomorphism (the phenomenon in which substances of analogous chemical composition crystallize in the same crystal form). He also synthesized many organic compounds for the first time.

Mitscherlich was born in Neuende, Jever (now part of Wilhelmshaven, West Germany), on 17 January 1794, the son of a minister. He was educated at Jever and in 1811 entered Heidelberg University to study Oriental languages, later continuing this study at Paris, with the intention of becoming a diplomat. The fall of Napoleon ended that prospect and he returned to Germany, enrolling at Göttingen to read science and medicine. He thought that he might reach the Orient as a ship's doctor (since he could not do so as a diplomat) but became increasingly interested in chemistry and in 1818 went to Berlin to work in the laboratory of the botanist Heinrich Link. There he began his study of crystallography.

In 1819 Mitscherlich met Jöns Berzelius while he was visiting Berlin, and when the Prussian Minister of Education offered Berzelius the professorship of chemistry at Berlin University following the death of Martin Klaproth, he declined but recommended Mitscherlich for the appointment. But at only 25 years old Mitscherlich was thought to be too young and as a compromise he was sent to Stockholm to work with Berzelius for two years, to widen his knowledge of chemistry. He returned to Berlin in 1822 as Assistant Professor of Chemistry, becoming Professor three years later (finally succeeding Klaproth) and retaining the appointment until his death. He died in Berlin on 28 August 1863.

Mitscherlich began studying crystals in Link's laboratory in 1818. He observed that crystals of potassium phosphate and potassium arsenate appear to be nearly identical in form. He asked the mineralogist Gustav Rose (1798-1873) to instruct him in exact crystallographic methods so that he could make precise measurements, and then applied spherical trigonometry to the data he obtained. In his first publication he announced that the sulphates of various metals, as well as the double sulphates of potassium and ammonium, crystallize in like forms provided that they have the same amounts of water of crystallization. He further stated his hope that "through crystallographic examination the composition of bodies will be determined with the same certainty and exactness as through chemical analysis".

Berzelius immediately recognized the importance of Mitscherlich's work and applied it to his determinations of atomic weights; he was later able to correct the atomic weights (relative atomic masses) of 27 elements. While he was in Stockholm, Mitscherlich extended his researches to phosphates, arsenates and carbonates, publishing the results in 1822 and introducing the term isomorphism. He continued the work after his return to Berlin, refining his isomorphism law and establishing more and more classes of compounds to which it applies. In 1827, during the course of this work, he discovered selenic acid.

In 1834 Mitscherlich synthesized benzene (introducing the name, which he termed *Benzin*) by heating calcium benzoate (the calcium salt of benzene carboxylic acid). Two years earlier he had synthesized nitrobenzene, and he went on to prepare azobenzene, benzophenone and benzene sulphonic acid. He recognized that the part played by the oxides of nitrogen in the chamber process for making sulphuric acid is that of a catalyst, and showed that yeast (which in 1842 he identified as a micro-organism) can invert sugar in solution. He maintained his early interest in geology and mineralogy, and was particularly concerned with the production of artificial minerals, achieving valuable experimental results in this area.

In 1829 Mitscherlich published his influential *Lehrbuch der Chemie*, which in less than 20 years had run to four further new editions in German as well as two in French and one in English. This work continued Mitscherlich's lectures on all aspects of pure and applied chemistry (and included a considerable amount of physics), characterized by their exemplary clarity and ingenious experiments.

Mitscherlich's youngest son also became a chemist and, with help from his father, developed the Mitscherlich process for extracting cellulose from wood pulp by boiling it with calcium bisulphite (calcium hydrogen sulphite), which became the basis of the German cellulose industry.

Mond, Ludwig (*1839–1909*), was a German-born chemist who established many industrial chemical processes in Britain. He gave his name to a method of extracting nickel from nickel carbonyl, one of its volatile organic compounds.

Mond was born at Kassel on 7 March 1839, the son of a well-to-do Jewish merchant. He studied chemistry at Marburg (under Adolf Wilhelm Hermann Kolbe) and Heidelberg (under Robert Bunsen) but did not proceed to a doctorate, instead embarking in 1858 on a career of short-term employment in chemical industry. In 1859 he was working in a small soda works at Ringkuhl, near Kassel, where he initiated a new process for the recovery of sulphur. This attitude, that of making good commercial use of hitherto wasted by-products, was to help to shape his career as an industrial chemist. In 1862 he accepted an invitation from a Lancashire industrial chemist to apply his idea for the recovery of sulphur from the alkali waste from the Leblanc process for making soda. For several years, Mond travelled regularly between John Hutchinson's works in Widnes and Utrecht in Holland, where another Leblanc soda works was being constructed. He died in London of heart disease on 11 December 1909.

From 1867 Mond made his home in Britain and increased his involvement in the alkali industry, to meet the ever-growing needs of textile manufacturers. Then in 1872 he met Ernest Solvay, the Belgian industrial chemist who had devised the ammonia-soda (Solvay) process for making sodium carbonate from ammonia and salt. Using the royalties from his sulphur-recovery process Mond, and his partner John Brunner, became the sole British licensees of the Solvay process. His works at Winnington near Northwich in Cheshire eventually superseded those still using the now out-dated Leblanc process, although it was several years before it came into full production. The Brunner, Mond Company became the most successful in its field, employing more than 4,000 people by the end of the century, with the world's largest output of alkali.

In 1879 Mond became interested in the production of ammonia, an intermediate in the Solvay process which was increasingly being used as an artificial fertilizer. One outcome was the development of the Mond producer gas process, in which carbon monoxide and hydrogen are produced by alternately passing air and steam over heated coal or coke (and the hydrogen used to convert nitrogen into ammonia). By the early 1900s, Mond's Dudley Port Plant in Staffordshire was using 3 million tonnes of coal each year to make producer gas (Mond gas). An interesting extension of this work was the attempt, with the assistance of K. Langer, to turn the energy of the fuel directly into electrical energy. This early fuel cell, which used porous plates moistened with sulphuric acid, was not developed further at that time. Mond also hoped to recover the chlorine from the waste calcium chloride from the Solvay process, but this endeavour was also largely unsuccessful.

One unexpected result of the producer gas process came from Mond's observation that nickel is corroded by gases containing carbon monoxide. This led in 1889 to the discovery of nickel carbonyl, $Ni(CO)_4$, one of the first organometallic compounds. After two years work, with Langer and Quincke, he had developed a new extraction process for nickel. The Mond Nickel Company was founded at Clydach, Swansea, to produce nickel from Canadian ores by the thermal decomposition of nickel carbonyl; it later became the British manufacturing plant of Imperial Nickel Limited.

Mond became a rich man. He was generous with his wealth during his lifetime, and among various trusts founded that for the building of the Davy Faraday Laboratory at the Royal Institution, London. He lived in Italy towards the end of his life, and bequeathed a valuable collection of paintings to the British National Gallery. His son Robert (1867–1938) became a scientist and egyptologist and was knighted, and his other son Alfred (later Lord Melchett) (1868–1930) was a successful politician and the first Chairman of Imperial Chemical Industries when it was founded in the 1920s. Mond's great-grandson Julian Mond, the third Lord Melchett, became the first Chairman of the British Steel Corporation in 1967.

Müller, Paul Hermann (*1899–1965*), was a Swiss chemist, known for his development of DDT as an insecticide, for which he was awarded the 1948 Nobel Prize in Medicine.

Müller was born in Olten, Solothurn, on 12 January 1899. He received his early education in Basle and worked in the electrical and chemical laboratories of several industrial firms before continuing his academic studies. He gained his doctorate in chemistry at Basle in 1925 and then went to work for J.R. Geigy, researching principally into dyestuffs and tanning agents; he subsequently joined the staff of Basle University. He died in Basle on 12 October 1965.

In 1935 Müller started work on a research project designed to discover a substance that would kill insects quickly but have little or no poisonous effect on plants and animals, unlike the arsenical compounds then in use. He concentrated his search on chlorine compounds and in 1939 synthesized dichlorodiphenyl trichloroethane (DDT) – which had first been prepared 65 years earlier by the German chemist Othmar Zeidler, who had not been aware of its insecticidal properties.

The Swiss government successfully tested DDT against the Colorado potato beetle in 1939 and by 1942 it was in commercial production. Its first important use was in Naples, where a typhus epidemic broke out soon after the city had been captured by American forces in 1943; in January of the following year the population of Naples was sprayed with DDT to kill the body lice that are the carriers of typhus. A similar potential epidemic was arrested in Japan in late 1945 after the American occupation of the country.

For the following 20 years the use of DDT was to have a profound effect on the health of the world, both by killing insect vectors such as the mosquitoes that spread malaria and yellow fever and by combating insect pests that feed on food crops. Gradually the uses of DDT in public hygiene and in agriculture became limited by increasing DDT-resistance in insect species, and it has been supplanted by new synthetic insecticides. Also DDT is a very stable chemical compound; it does not break down and tends to accumulate in the environment, disrupting food chains and presenting a hazard to animal life. By the 1970s its use had been banned in several countries.

N

Natta, Giulio (*1903–*), is an Italian chemist who shared the 1963 Nobel Prize in Chemistry with Karl Ziegler for his work on the production of polymers.

Natta was born in Imperia, near Genoa, on 26 February 1903, the son of a judge. He obtained his doctorate in chemical engineering from the Polytechnic Institute in Milan in 1924 and then held professorships in general chemistry at the University of Pavia, in physical chemistry at Rome, and in industrial chemistry at Turin. In 1938 he returned to Milan Polytechnic as Professor of Chemistry and Director of the Industrial Chemistry Research Institute. There he was charged by the government to investigate the problems of producing artificial rubber, because the supply of natural rubber had ceased with the approaching imminence of World War II.

In 1953 Natta began intensive studies of macro-molecular chemistry. These investigations were initiated by knowledge obtained through a licence arrangement between Ziegler and the Italian company of Montecatini, of which Natta was a consultant. Ziegler had discovered how to synthesize linear polythene of high molecular weight at low pressures using as a catalyst a resin containing ions of titanium or aluminium. Because the polymer was made up of unbranched chains it was tougher and had a higher melting point than previous types of polythene.

Natta used these catalysts to polymerize propylene (propene, $CH_3CH = CH_2$). Early in 1954 he found that part of the polymer is highly crystalline and realized that it must have an ordered structure. He confirmed this using X-ray crystallography and coined the term "isotactic" to describe the polymer's symmetrical structure. He also postulated that the surface of the catalyst must be highly regular to give rise to isotactic polymers.

After 1954 he continued to study the mechanism of the reaction and its stereo-specific aspects. He made other similar catalysts and produced new polymers, such as those *cis*-buta-1,4-diene and co-polymers of ethylene (ethene) and propylene (propene), both potentially important synthetic rubbers.

Natta's early work on heterogeneous catalysts formed the basis for modern industrial syntheses of methyl alcohol (methanol), of formaldehyde (methanal) from methyl alcohol, of propionaldehyde (butanal) from propylene (propene) and carbon monoxide, and of succinic acid (butandioic acid) from acetylene (ethyne), carbon monoxide and synthetic gas.

The isotactic polymers he discovered after 1954 showed remarkable and unexpected properties of commercial importance, such as high melting point, high strength, and an ability to form films and fibres. It was realized that a new type of polymerization, called co-ordination polymerization, was involved. The growth of the polymer chain occurs by insertion of monomer between the existing chain and the solid surface of the catalyst, which controls the geometry of the reaction. (In other types of polymerization the catalyst remains remote from the growing end of the chain and therefore has no effect on the reaction geometry.)

Nernst, Hermann Walther (*1864–1941*), was a German physical chemist who made basic contributions to electrochemistry and is probably best known as the discoverer of the Third Law of Thermodynamics. He was awarded the 1920 Nobel Prize in Chemistry.

Nernst was born in Briessen, East Prussia

(now Wabreźno, Poland), on 25 June 1864, the son of a civil servant and judge. He was educated at Grandenz Gymnasium, and went on to read natural sciences at university. He continued his studies with Albert von Ettinghausen at Graz, took a PhD degree under Freidrich Kohlrausch at Würzburg in 1886, and became an assistant to Friedrich Wilhelm Ostwald at Leipzig in the following year. Under their influence his interests narrowed into aspects of physical chemistry. In 1891 he became a Reader in Physics at Göttingen University and three years later, after a new laboratory had been built, the first Professor of Physical Chemistry. In 1905 he moved to a similar position in Berlin as successor to Hans Landolt (1831–1910), and remained there until 1922. Nernst then became President of the Physikalisch-Technische Reichsanstalt for two years, but relinquished this post to return to Berlin University as Professor of Physics and Director of the Physical Laboratory, where he stayed until he retired in 1934. No subscriber to the politics of Nazi Germany (two of his daughters married Jews), he spent his latter years in farming and agriculture on his country estate at Zibelle near the Polish border. He had a heart attack on 18 November 1941 and died at Muskan, near Berlin; his body was later re-interred in Göttingen, where his academic career began.

Nernst's first publication (1886) described his work with von Ettinghausen at Graz. What became known as the Ettinghausen-Nernst effect concerns the establishment of a potential difference across a metal plate along which there is a temperature gradient and a magnetic field. These experiments were significant in the development of the electronic theory of metals, according to which both thermal and electrical conduction are caused by the motion of electrons.

Working with Kohlrausch, an expert in electro-chemistry, Nernst studied solution chemistry. Theories presented in the late 1880s are still in use today; every pH measurement depends on them, as does the use and theory of indicators and buffer solutions.

Nernst's theory concerning solids in contact with a liquid developed from the supposition that metals go into solution only as positive ions, the driving force being a "solution pressure" which is opposed by the osmotic pressure of its ions in solution. The solution acquires a positive charge and the metal a negative one, if the metal is high in the electrochemical series. (A metal low in the electro-chemical series has a low solution pressure and collects metal ions to become positively charged.) The Nernst equation relates ionic concentration, c, electrode potential, E:

$$E = E_0 \pm \frac{RT}{zF} \log_e c$$

where R is the gas constant, T the temperature, z the valency of the ion, F Faraday's constant, and E_0 the standard electrode potential. Nernst was also the first to advocate that the electrochemical standard be based on the hydrogen electrode. This work led to the theory of solubility product (1890), which had been initiated by Ostwald who had shown that it could be used as the basis for a system of qualitative and quantitative analysis.

The work on thermodynamics was carried out in Berlin in 1905-1906. Developing the theories of Hermann von Helmholtz, Nernst formulated the Third Law of Thermodynamics. It may be stated in various ways, one expression being:

If the entropy of each element in a crystalline state be taken as zero at the absolute zero of temperature, then every substance has a finite positive entropy but at absolute zero the entropy may become zero and does so in the case of a perfect crystalline substance.

Nernst and his students collected accurate thermodynamic data to substantiate the law. In 1911, with Frederick Lindemann (later Lord Cherwell), Nernst constructed a special calorimeter for measuring specific heats at low temperatures.

Two other significant contributions to physical chemistry concerned chemical equilibria and photochemistry. With Fritz Haber he studied equilibria in commercially important gas reactions, such as the reversible reaction between hydrogen and carbon dioxide to form water and carbon monoxide. He also examined the hydrogen/nitrogen reaction at high pressures (the basis of the Haber process). In 1918 Nernst investigated reactions that are initiated by light. He proposed that the fast reaction between chlorine and hydrogen begins when light causes chlorine molecules to dissociate into atoms:

$$Cl_2 + h\nu \rightarrow 2Cl \cdot$$

A chlorine atom then reacts with a hydrogen molecule to form hydrogen chloride and a hydrogen atom:

$$Cl \cdot + H_2 \rightarrow HCl + H \cdot$$

The hydrogen atom reacts with a chlorine molecule to produce another chlorine atom, and the process continues as a chain reaction:

$$H \cdot + Cl_2 \rightarrow HCl + Cl \cdot$$

Like many great scientists of the time, Nernst did not restrict himself to one narrow field. In

1897 he invented an electric lamp which, instead of a carbon filament, had a "glower" made from zirconium oxide and some rare earth oxides. It was a good source of infra-red and highly successful until superseded ten years later by the tungsten filament lamp. Even so, Nernst sold his patent for a million marks, and used the money to become a pioneer motorist. Many early automobiles had difficulty climbing hills, but Nernst devised a method of injecting nitrous oxide (dinitrogen monoxide) into the cylinders when the engine got into difficulties. In the 1920s he invented a "Neo-Bechstein" piano which amplified sounds produced at low amplitudes. Although acoustically correct, it did not find favour with musicians or concert audiences.

During an academic career of about 50 years, Nernst published 157 papers and 14 books, one of which, *Theoretische Chemie* (1895), became the recommended text for a generation of physical chemists throughout the world.

Newlands, John Alexander Reina (1837–1898), was a British chemist who preceded Dmitri Mendeleyev in formulating the concept of periodicity in the properties of chemical elements, although his ideas were not accepted at the time.

Newlands was born in Southwark, London, on 26 November 1837, the second son of a Presbyterian minister; his mother, née Mary Reina, was of Italian descent. He was educated by his father and in 1856 entered the Royal College of Chemistry, London, where he studied for a year under August Hofmann. He then became assistant to J.T. Way, the Royal Agricultural Society's chemist. He stayed with Way until 1864, except for a short time in 1860 when he served as a volunteer with Giuseppe Garibaldi in Italy. In 1864 Newlands set up in practice as an analytical chemist, supplementing his income by teaching chemistry. He seems to have made a special study of sugar chemistry, and in 1868 became chief chemist in a sugar refinery belonging to James Duncan, with whom he developed a new system for cleaning sugar and introduced a number of improvements in processing. The business declined as a result of foreign competition, so he left the refinery and again set up as an analyst, this time in partnership with his brother

B.E.R. Newlands. The brothers revised an established treatise on sugar growing and refining, in collaboration with C.G.W. Lock, one of the original authors. Newlands died in London on 29 July 1898.

Newlands' early papers on organic compounds (the first suggesting a new nomenclature and the second proposing the compilation of tables to show the relationships between compounds) were hampered by the absence of any clear ideas about structure and valency. But they did show his inclination towards systematization. His first communication to *Chemical News* in February 1863 on the numerical relationships between atomic weights (relative atomic masses) of similar elements was a summary, with some of his own observations, of what had been pointed out by others, of whom he credited only Jean Baptiste Dumas. Two main phenomena had been observed: that there existed groups of three elements (the "triads" of Johann Döbereiner) of similar properties, the atomic weight of the middle one being the mean of those of the other two; and that the difference between the atomic weights of analogous elements seemed often to be multiples of eight.

Like many of his contemporaries, Newlands first used the terms equivalent weight and atomic weight without any distinction in meaning, and in this first paper he used the values accepted by his predecessors. Then in 1864 he employed Alexander Williamson's values (based on the system of Stanislao Cannizzaro) in a table of the 61 then known elements in order of their "new" atomic weights. In a second table he grouped 37 elements into 10 classes, most of which contained one or more triads. He attributed the incompleteness of the table to uncertainty regarding the properties of some of the more recently discovered elements, and to the possible existence of additional, undiscovered elements. For example he considered that silicon (atomic weight 28) and tin (atomic weight 118) were the extremities of a triad, the middle member of which was unknown. Thus his later claim to have predicted the existence of germanium (atomic weight 73, the mean of 28 and 118) before Mendeleyev is valid.

He went on to number the elements in the order of their atomic weights, giving the same number

Group	No.		No.		No.		No.		No.	
a	N	6	P	13	As	26	Sb	40	Bi	54
b	O	7	S	14	Se	27	Te	42	Os	50
c	F	8	Cl	15	Br	28	I	41	—	—
d	Na	9	K	16	Rb	29	Cs	43	Tl	52
e	Mg	10	Ca	17	Sr	30	Ba	44	Pb	53

to any two having the same weight, and observed that elements with consecutive numbers frequently either belonged to the same group or occupied similar positions in other groups. He set out the list as a table, as shown on p. 102.

The difference in number between the first and second members of a group was seven. In Newlands' words: "The eighth element starting from a given one is a kind of repetition of the first, like the eighth note in an octave of music." One or two transpositions were made to give acceptable groupings; the omitted element (number 51) would have been mercury, which he clearly could not group with the halogens.

A year later, in 1865, he again drew attention to the difference of seven (or a multiple thereof) between the ordinal numbers of the elements in the same group, and termed the relationship the law of octaves. This time he put all 62 elements (including the newly discovered indium) in a table:

H	1	F	8	Co,Ni	22	Br	29	Pd	36	I	42	Pt,Ir	50	Cl	15
Li	2	Na	9	Cu	23	Rb	30	Ad	37	Cs	44	Tl	53	K	16
Be	3	Mg	10	Zn	25	Sr	31	Cd	38	Ba,V	45	Pb	54	Ca	17
B	4	Al	11	Y	24	Ce,La	33	U	40	Ta	46	Th	56	Cr	19
C	5	Si	12	In	26	Zr	32	Sn	39	W	47	Hg	52	Ti	18
N	6	P	13	As	27	Di,Mo	34	Sb	41	Nb	48	Bi	55	Mn	20
O	7	S	14	Se	28	Rh,Ru	35	Te	43	Au	49	Os	51	Fe	21

This forcing of the elements into too rigid a framework weakened his case, precluding the possibility of gaps in the sequence which, when filled, would lead to a more acceptable grouping. When he read his paper to the Chemical Society in 1866 he was severely criticized and even ridiculed – G.C. Foster, Professor of Physics at University College, London, is reputed to have asked Newlands if he had ever examined the elements when listed in alphabetical order. More seriously, he pointed out the unacceptability of any system that separated chromium from manganese, and iron from cobalt and nickel.

Discouraged, Newlands did no more work on his theories until after the publication of Mendeleyev's Periodic Table in 1869. Newlands claimed priority, particularly after the award of the Davy Medal of the Royal Society to Mendeleyev and Lothar Meyer in 1882. His persistence was eventually rewarded in 1887, when the medal was awarded to him nearly 25 years after he had first published his work.

Nirenberg, Marshall Warren. *See* Holley, Robert William.

Nobel, Alfred Bernhard (*1833-1896*), was a Swed-ish industrial chemist and philanthropist who invented dynamite and endowed the Nobel Foundation, which after 1901 awarded the annual Nobel Prizes.

Nobel was born in Stockholm, Sweden, on 21 October 1833, the son of a builder and industrialist. His father, Immanuel Nobel, was also something of an inventor, and his grandfather had been one of the most important Swedish scientists of the seventeenth century. Alfred Nobel attended St Jakob's Higher Apologist School in Stockholm before the family moved to St Petersburg (now Leningrad), Russia, where he and his brothers were taught privately by Russian and Swedish tutors, always being encouraged to be inventive by their father. From 1850 to 1852 Nobel made a study trip to Germany, France, Italy and North America, improving his knowledge of chemistry and mastering all the necessary languages. During the Crimean War (1853-1856), Nobel worked in St Petersburg in his father's company, which produced large quantities of munitions. After the war his father went bankrupt, and in 1859 the family returned to Sweden. During the next few years Nobel developed several new explosives and factories for making them, and became a rich man. He spent the latter years of his life in San Remo, and died there on 10 December 1896.

Gun-cotton, a more powerful explosive than gunpowder, had been discovered in 1846 by the German chemist Christian Schönbein. It was made by nitrating cotton fibre with a mixture of concentrated nitric and sulphuric acids. A year later the Italian Ascanio Sobrero discovered nitroglycerin, made by nitrating glycerin (glycerol). This extremely powerful explosive gives off 1,200 times its own volume of gas when it explodes, but for many years it was too dangerous to use because it can be set off much too easily by rough handling or shaking. Alfred and his father worked independently on both explosives when they returned to Sweden, and in 1862 Immanuel Nobel devised a comparatively simple way of manufacturing nitroglycerin on a factory scale. In 1863 Alfred Nobel invented a mercury fulminate detonator for use with nitroglycerin in blasting.

In 1864 the nitroglycerin factory blew up, killing Nobel's younger brother and four other people. Nobel turned his attention to devising a safer method of handling the sensitive liquid nitroglycerin. After many experiments he patented dynamite (in Sweden, Britain and the United States) in 1867. It is an easily handled, solid, ductile explosive consisting of nitroglycerin absorbed by keiselguhr, a porous diatomite mineral.

Guhr dynamite, as it was known, had certain technical weaknesses. Continuing his research, Nobel in 1875 created blasting gelatin or gelignite, a colloidal solution of nitrocellulose (gun cotton) in nitroglycerin, which in many ways proved to be an ideal explosive. Its power was somewhat greater than that of pure nitroglycerin, it was less sensitive to shock, and it was strongly resistant to moisture.

The Nobels had long been trying to improve blasting powder. In 1887 Alfred Nobel produced a nearly smokeless blasting powder called ballistite, a mixture of nitroglycerin and nitrocellulose with camphor and other additives. Upon ignition it burned with almost mathematical precision in concentric layers. Nobel's last development was progressive smokeless powder, a further product of ballistite devised in his San Remo laboratory.

Nobel's interests as an inventor were not confined to explosives. He worked in electrochemistry, optics, biology and physiology and helped to solve many problems in the manufacture of artificial silk, leather and rubber, and of artificial semi-precious stones from fused alumina. In his will, made in 1895, he left almost all his fortune to a foundation that would award annual prizes to "those who, during the preceding year, shall have conferred the greatest benefit on mankind". In 1958 the new element number 102 was named nobelium in his honour.

Norrish, Ronald George Wreyford (*1897–1978*), was a British physical chemist who studied fast chemical reactions, particularly those initiated by light. For his achievements in this area, he shared the 1967 Nobel Prize in Chemistry with his coworker George Porter and the German chemist Manfred Eigen.

Norrish was born in Cambridge on 9 November 1897. He was educated at Perse School, Cambridge, and won a scholarship to the University. His studies where interrupted by World War I, during which he was an officer in the artillery. He graduated from Cambridge two years after returning in 1919, gaining his PhD in 1924. He was made a Fellow of Emmanuel College, Cambridge, in 1925 and became Professor of Physical Chemistry in 1937. He retired in 1965 and died, in Cambridge, on 7 June 1978.

Norrish began working in photochemistry in 1923 with E.K. Rideal, studying the reactions of potassium permanganate solution. For the next few years he investigated the photochemistry of nitrogen dioxide. Then in 1928 his paper on the photochemistry of glyoxal (ethan-1,2-dial, $(CHO)_2$) announced his studies of various aldehydes and ketones. This led to the recognition of what became known as the Norrish type I and type II reactions, which may be generalized as:

$$\text{Type I} \quad \begin{cases} R^1COR^2 + h\nu \rightarrow \dot{R}^1 + \dot{C}OR^2 \\ \qquad\qquad \rightarrow \dot{R}^1 + \dot{R}^2 + CO \end{cases}$$

Type II $\quad R^1COCH_2CH_2R^2 + h\nu \rightarrow R^1COCH_3 + CH_2{:}CHR^2$, in which the alkyl radicals R^1 and R^2 contribute one or two carbon atoms.

Up to the mid-1930s, Norrish studied the correlation between photodecomposition and physical phenomena such as spectral character and phosphorescence. Then his studies were again interrupted, this time by World War II. During this period his department contributed to the war effort, investigating methods of suppressing the flash from guns and developing incendiary materials.

Norrish's interest in using intense flashes of light to initiate photochemical reactions seems to have been stimulated by his work during the war with his student George Porter. Flash photolysis makes use of a powerful "photoflash" to bring about the rapid dissociation of a compound into radicals or ions. A second spectroscopic flash triggered at a precise time interval after the first allows the transient species to be observed. By varying the time delay between the two flashes, Norrish was able to study the kinetics of the formation and decay of such short-lived entities, even if they existed for only microseconds.

Norrish went on to apply these techniques to the study of chain reactions. He established, for example, that the retarding effect of hydrogen chloride in a pure system and one containing oxygen can be attributed to the process:

$$\dot{H} + HCl \rightarrow H_2 + \dot{C}l$$

In his investigation of the combustion of hydrocarbons, he studied the transition between slow reactions and ignition, demonstrating the existence of degenerate or delayed branching. He also made pioneering studies of the kinetics of polymerization. He and his co-workers discovered the gel-effect, which occurs in the later stages of free-radical polymerization and results from the steadily decreasing rate of chain termination that sets in when the viscosity becomes high. He also correlated the photolysis of certain polymers with his type I and II reactions.

Norrish was largely responsible for the advance of reaction kinetics to a distinct discipline within physical chemistry. He was one of the first to realize the power of absorption spectroscopy for identifying intermediates and products of thermal and photochemical gas reactions and to introduce high vacuum techniques for handling gases.

Nyholm, Ronald Sydney (*1917–1971*), was an Australian inorganic chemist famous for his work on the co-ordination compounds (complexes) of the transition metals. He was also interested in science education, and was responsible for many of the changes in chemistry teaching methods in British schools.

Nyholm was born in Broken Hill, New South Wales, on 29 January 1917, the fourth of the six children of a railway employee whose father had emigrated to Australia from Finland. He was educated at local schools and in 1934 won a scholarship to go to study natural sciences at Sydney University. He worked for a short time as a research chemist with the Ever Ready Battery Company near Sydney and in 1940 became a member of the staff of Sydney Technical College, where he worked on the co-ordination compound of rhodium. In 1947, after World War II, he was awarded an ICI Fellowship to University College, London, where he studied under Christopher Ingold and became a lecturer. He returned to Austrialia in 1951 as Associate Professor of Inorganic Chemistry at the University of New South Wales, Sydney. Four years later he again went to Britain to take up a professorship at University College, and in 1963 he was made Head of the Chemistry Department. He was granted a knighthood in 1967 for his services to science. He was killed in a car accident on the outskirts of Cambridge on 4 December 1971.

Nyholm was introduced to co-ordination chemistry during his final undergraduate year at Sydney by George Burrows, with whom he worked on the reactions between ferric (iron(III)) chloride and the simple arsines. Then Nyholm and F.P.J. Dwyer studied the co-ordination compounds of rhodium, again using arsines as ligands.

Diarsine had been synthesized in 1937 by Chatt and Mann, and Nyholm met Chatt in London in 1948 and realized that the arsenic compound might help with his own work. He prepared the complex formed between diarsine and palladium chloride, and went on to use the same ligand to prepare stable compounds of transition metals in valence states that previously had been thought to be unstable. For example, he prepared an octahedral complex of nickel(III), in which the nickel has a co-ordination number of six.

diarsine

diarsine complex
of palladium chloride

diarsine complex ion
containing nickel (III)

He also made the diarsine complexes of the tetrachloride and tetrabromide of titanium(IV), the first example of an 8-co-ordination compound of a first-row transition metal.

Nyholm also systematically exploited physical methods to study the structures and properties of co-ordination compounds. He used potentiometric titrations to determine oxidation states, and electrical conductivity measurements to discover the nature of the charged species in which the co-ordinated transition metal was contained. He also employed X-ray crystallography and nuclear magnetic resonance spectroscopy (NMR), and found that magnetic moment seemed to give the closest connection between electronic structure, chemical structure and stereochemistry. He always insisted that the three main branches of chemistry – physical, inorganic and organic – are closely interwoven and that methods from one could often be used to solve problems in another.

Nyholm maintained his interest in the teaching side of chemistry, and was a member of the Science Research Council from 1967 to 1971. It was partly as a result of his influence that the Nuffield Foundation set up the Science Teaching Project. As Chairman of the Chemistry Consultative Committee he was largely responsible for the Nuffield O Level chemistry course in British schools and for changes to the O and A level syllabuses. He was a strong advocate of an integrated approach to the teaching of chemistry, particularly at the introductory levels.

Ochoa, Severo (*1905–*), is a Spanish-born American biochemist who reproduced in the laboratory the way in which cells synthesize nucleic acids by their use of enzymes. For this achievement, he shared the 1959 Nobel Prize in Physiology and Medicine with Arthur Kornberg.

Ochoa was born in Luarca on 24 September 1905, the youngest son of a lawyer. He graduated from the University of Málaga in 1921 and obtained a degree in medicine from the University of Madrid eight years later. He lectured at Madrid from 1931 to 1936. He spent a year in Germany at the University of Heidelberg in 1936 before going to Britain for three years at Oxford University. He then went to the United States in 1940 and was an Instructor and Research Associate at Washington University from 1941 to 1942. Ochao moved to New York University, first as a Research Associate in the College of Medicine and then from 1954 to 1975 as a professor in the Department of Biochemistry. He joined the Roche Institute of Molecular Biology in 1975. Ochoa became an American citizen in 1956.

Ochoa's early work concerned biochemical pathways in the human body, especially those involving carbon dioxide. But his main research has been into nucleic acids and the way in which their nucleotide units are linked together, either singly (as in RNA) or to form two helically wound strands (as in DNA).

In 1955 Ochoa obtained an enzyme from bacteria that was capable of joining together similar nucleotide units to form a nucleic acid, a type of artificial RNA. (Nucleic acids containing exactly similar nucleotide units do not occur naturally, but the method of synthesis used by Ochoa was the same as that employed by a living cell.) He also found that strands of similar nucleotides form random small fibres, but when mixed with a similar preparation made from a different nucleotide, two-stranded helixes form, one strand from each preparation.

Ochoa's synthesis of an RNA was the result of outstanding experimental work. Research by other workers soon yielded further important results. For example Arthur Kornberg, working independently, isolated an enzyme that will link different nucleotides to form nucleic acids that closely resemble natural ones.

Onsager, Lars (*1903–1976*), was a Norwegian-born American theoretical chemist who was awarded the 1968 Nobel Prize in Chemistry for his work on reversible processes.

Onsager was born in Oslo on 27 November 1903. He was educated at the local High School and then at the Norges Tekniske Høgskole in Trondheim, where he studied chemical engineering. During the five years at Trondheim he acquired the mathematical skills he was to use later on, and developed an interest in electrolytes. After qualifying in 1925 he went to Zurich to work as a research assistant to Peter Debye. He emigrated to the United States in 1928 and was appointed an Associate in Chemistry at Johns Hopkins University, Baltimore. He was not, however, a success as a lecturer (because his course did not attract a sufficient number of students) and he soon moved to Brown University, where he was a research instructor from 1928 to 1933.

In 1933 he went to Europe to visit the Austrian electrochemist Falkenhagen, and while there met and married Falkenhagen's sister. His lectures at Brown University were no more comprehensible to the students, who christened his course "Sadistical Mechanics". Also in 1933 he took up an appointment at Yale, becoming Assistant Professor in Chemistry a year later. The university authorities were disconcerted to have a plain "Mr" as a professor, and urged Onsager to submit one of his published papers as a PhD thesis. Onsager chose "Solutions to the Mathieu equation of period 4π and certain related functions". The chemistry department were unable to make anything of it so they passed it to the physics department, which in turn passed it to the mathematics department. The final outcome was an award of a PhD by the bemused chemists. It is little wonder that the students at Yale were no kinder than those at Brown and described Onsager's lectures as "Advanced Norwegian I and II". His almost total failure as a lecturer probably came from the fact that he could not appreciate that others were unable to understand the topics that interested him. He did, however, remain at Yale for the rest of his career.

Onsager was not required to do military service during World War II because he had not yet become an American citizen and his wife was Austrian; he adopted American nationality in 1945. After retirement he bought a farm at Tilton, New Hampshire, and grew his own crops. He died in Coral Gables, Florida, on 5 October 1976.

In 1925 Peter Debye and Erich Hückel had put forward a new theory of electrolytes based on the idea that the electrostatic field of a dissolved ion is effectively screened by surrounding ions of opposite charge. They were able to calculate the activity coefficient for any ion in dilute solution although the calculated values for conductivity differed considerably from experimental values, particularly for strong electrolytes. When Onsager went to Zurich in 1925 he told Debye that he thought the electrolyte theory was incorrect – and was offered a research assistantship. Debye had assumed that one particular ion should be thought of as moving uniformly in a straight line, while all other ions undergo Brownian motion. Onsager showed that this constraint should be lifted and the result, known as the Onsager limiting law, gave better agreement between calculated and actual conductivities. He went on to investigate dielectric constants of polar liquids and solutions of polar molecules.

At Brown University Onsager submitted a PhD thesis on what is now a classic work on reversible processes, but the authorities turned it down. It was published in 1931 but ignored until the late 1940s; in 1968 it earned Onsager a Nobel Prize. He then turned his attention to the equilibrium states in the muta-rotation (change in optical rotation) of sugars. Riiber had shown in 1922 that galactose exists in at least three tautomeric forms (interconvertible stereoisomers). Onsager proposed that the equilibrium states between these forms must conform to the principle of "detailed balancing", as conceived by Gilbert Lewis, and showed that this idea is thermodynamically equivalent to the principle of "least dissipation" used by Hermann von Helmholtz in his theory of galvanic diffusion cells and by Lord Kelvin in his theories about thermoelectric phenomena.

Onsager also looked at the connection between microscopic reversibility and transport processes. He found that the key to the problem is the distribution of molecules and energy caused by random thermal motion. Ludwig Boltzmann had shown that the nature of thermal equilibrium is statistical and that the statistics of the spontaneous deviation is determined by the entropy. Using this principle Onsager derived a set of equations known as Onsager's law of reciprocal relations, sometimes called the Fourth Law of Thermodynamics. It has many applications to cross-coefficients for the diffusion of pairs of solutes in the same solution, and for the various interactions that can occur between thermal conduction, diffusion and electrical conduction. He announced these ideas in the late 1930s, but not until 1960 did the theory received experimental confirmation.

During and after World War II Onsager made calculations concerning the two-dimensional Ising lattice (an assembly of particles or "spin" located at the vertices of an infinite space lattice; the simplest case is a two-dimensional planar square lattice). It can be used as a model to describe ferromagnetism and anti-ferromagnetism of gaseous condensations, phase separations in fluid mixtures and metallic alloys. Onsager's treatment showed that the specific heat approaches infinity at the transition point. In 1949 he published a paper which established a firm statistical basis for the theory of liquid crystals, and at Cambridge in 1951–1952 he put forward a theory concerned with diamagnetism in metals.

Ostwald, Friedrich Wilhelm (*1853–1932*), was a Russian-born German physical chemist famous for his contributions to solution chemistry and to colour science. He was awarded the 1909 Nobel Prize in Chemistry for his work on catalysis, chemical equilibria and reaction velocities.

Ostwald was born of German parents in Riga, Latvia, on 2 September 1853; his father was a master cooper. He was good at handicrafts when he was a boy, a skill that was later to stand him in good stead when he had to make his own chemical apparatus. He was educated at the Realgymnasium in Riga and in 1872 went to the University of Dorpat (Tartu) in Estonia to study chemistry under Carl Schmidt and Johann Lemberg. He also studied physics under Arthur von Oettingen, and was awarded his PhD in 1878. While working for his doctorate, he lectured at Dorpat on the theory of chemical affinity and was Oettingen's assistant. He married in 1880; his son Wolfgang (1883–1943) was also to become a notable chemist, and his daughter Grete wrote her father's biography in 1953.

In 1881 Ostwald was appointed Professor of Chemistry at Riga. Six years later he accepted what was then the only Chair in Physical Chemistry in Germany, at the University of Leipzig, and in 1898 celebrated the official dedication of the new Physico-chemical Institute there, of which he was made Director. He retired in 1906, having been appointed the first German exchange professor to Harvard (1905–1906). In 1901 he had moved his family and his huge library to "Landhaus Energie", a house in Grossbothen, and after 1909 devoted an increasing amount of his time to philosophy. He died in Leipzig on 4 April 1932.

As a student Ostwald worked out that the magnitude of a chemical change could be calculated from any measurable change in a physical property that accompanies it. In 1887 he determined the volume changes that take place during the neutralization of acids by bases in dilute solutions, and in 1879 proposed that the rate at which compounds such as zinc sulphide and calcium oxalate are dissolved by various acids be used as a measure of the acids' relative affinities. He read the memoir by Svante Arrhenius on the "galvanic conductibility of electrolytes" in 1884 and became an enthusiastic supporter of the new theory of ionic dissociation. He was then able to redetermine the affinities of the acids using Arrhenius' electrolytic conductivity method.

In 1885 and 1887 Ostwald published the two volumes of his ambitious textbook *Lehrbuch der allgemeinen Chemie*. Also in 1887, together with Jacobus Van't Hoff and Arrhenius, he founded the journal *Zeitschrift für physikalische Chemie*.

In 1888 he proposed the Ostwald dilution law, which relates the degree of dissociation of an electrolyte, α, to its total concentration c expressed in moles per litre (dm^3). It states that

$$k = \alpha^2 c / (1 - \alpha)$$

The constant, k, neglects the activity coefficient and is therefore not a true thermodynamic constant K. The equation is important historically because it was the form in which the law of mass action was first applied to solutions of weak organic acids and bases. Ostwald then worked on the theory of acid-base indicators.

Ostwald turned his attention to catalysis in 1900. He discovered a method of oxidizing ammonia to convert it to oxides of nitrogen (for making nitric acid) by passing a mixture of air and ammonia over a platinum catalyst. By means of this technique (using ammonia from the Haber process), and by later developments connected with it, Germany became independent of supplies of Chilean nitrates and was able to continue the manufacture of explosives during World War I after the Allies had blockaded its ports. Ostwald patented the Ostwald-Bauer process for the manufacture of nitric acid from ammonia.

From 1909 Ostwald became interested in science methodology and the organizational aspects of science, in a world language, in internationalism and in pacifism. He enlarged the premises at "Landhaus Energie" and built a laboratory for colour research. He devised a "colour wheel" for relating the various colours to their shades and tints. His studies of colour theory and the techniques of painting are noteworthy, and his book *Grosse Männer* on the lives of famous scientists shows great insight into the factors that make for great men.

P

Paneth, Friedrich Adolf (*1887-1958*), was an Austrian chemist known for his contribution to the development of radiotracer techniques and to inorganic chemistry.

Paneth was born in Vienna on 31 August 1887, the second of the three sons of the well known physiologist Joseph Paneth. He was educated in Vienna and attended the universities of Munich and Glasgow before obtaining his PhD from Vienna in 1910. From 1912 to 1918 he worked as assistant to Stefan Meyer at the Vienna Institute for Radium Research – in 1913 he spent a short time with Frederick Soddy in Glasgow and visited Ernest Rutherford's laboratory in Manchester. He spent two years (1917-1919) at the Prague Institute of Technology and three (1919-1922) at the University of Hamburg, before going to the University of Berlin. From 1929 until 1933 he was Professor and Director of the Chemical Laboratories at the University of Königsberg.

Because of the growth of Nazi movement, Paneth left Germany in 1933 and went to Imperial College, London, as a reader and guest lecturer. Six years later he moved to Durham University as Professor of Chemistry, where he stayed until 1953. During World War II he was head of the chemical division of the Joint British and Canadian Atomic Energy Team in Montreal, and from 1949 to 1955 served as President of the Joint Commission on Radioactivity, an organization of the International Council of Scientific Unions. In 1953 Paneth returned to Germany to become Director of the Max Planck Institute for Chemistry in Mainz. He died in Vienna on 17 September 1958.

One of Paneth's first chemical papers was concerned with the acid-catalysed rearrangement of the two organic compounds quinidine and cinchonidine. But he soon became much more involved with radioactive substances. He unsuccessfully tried to chemically separate radium D and thorium B from lead, and eventually realized that they must both be isotopes of lead. In collaboration with the Hungarian chemist Georg von Hevesy he extended this work into research on using radium D and thorium B as indicators – radioactive tracers – to determine the solubility of the slightly soluble compounds lead sulphide and lead chromate.

A similar attempt to separate the radioactive products of thorium decay led to the preparation and isolation of bismuth hydride, BiH_3, and to the realization that radium E and thorium C are isotopes of bismuth. It was only by the use of radioactive isotopes that the minute quantities of bismuth hydride formed could be detected. In order to decompose the hydride and concentrate the metal from the unstable hydrides he studied, such as those of bismuth, lead, tin and polonium, he used a method known as the mirror deposition technique. The metal formed a metallic mirror on the inside of a heated tube through which the hydride was passed. He then developed a better method involving the electrolysis of the metal sulphate. He prepared several grams of a new tin hydride, SnH_4, and made intensive investigations of its properties.

The work on metal hydrides led, in turn, to that on free radicals. In 1929, while at the University of Berlin, Paneth and Wilhelm Hofeditz announced the preparation and identification of the free methyl radical from lead tetramethyl.

Also in the period up to 1929 he developed sensitive methods for determining trace amounts of helium. Using spectroscopy and, later, mass spectroscopy, he determined the helium content of natural gas from various sources, measured its rate of diffusion through glass, measured the amount of helium in rocks and meteorites, and unsuccessfully tried to measure the helium produced by attempted transmutations from light elements into helium. From 1929 to the end of his life, meteorites dominated his interests. He estimated the ages of iron meteorites to be in the range 10^8 to 10^9 years, and speculated that they were formed within the solar system.

In the late 1930s Paneth succeeded in obtaining measurable amounts of helium by the neutron bombardment of boron; he had induced an artificial transmutation. He then began to investigate the trace elements in the stratosphere. He determined the helium, ozone and nitrogen dioxide content of the atmosphere and investigated the extent of gravitational separation of the components of the atmosphere. He found none below 60 km, but discovered a measurable change in relative concentration above this altitude. He then went back to studying free radicals and explored the use of radioactive isotopes to combine with them in a mirror removal technique.

Pauling, Linus Carl (*1901-*), is an American theoretical chemist and biologist whose achievements rank among the most important of any in twentieth-century science. His main contribution has been to molecular structure and chemical bonding. He is one of the very few people to have been awarded two Nobel Prizes: he received the 1954 Nobel Prize in Chemistry (for his work on intermolecular forces) and the 1962 Peace Prize. Throughout his career his work has been noted for the application of intuition and inspiration, assisted by his phenomenal memory; he has often carried over principles from one field of science and applied them to another.

Pauling was born in Portland, Oregon, on 28 February 1901, the son of a pharmacist. He began his scientific studies at Oregon State Agricultural College, from which he graduated in chemical engineering in 1922. He then began his research at the California Institute of Technology, Pasadena, gaining his PhD in 1925. From 1925 to 1927 he was a post-doctoral fellow in Europe, where he met the chief scientists of the day who were working on atomic and molecular structure: Arnold Sommerfield in Munich, Niels Bohr in Copenhagen, Erwin Schrödinger in Zurich, and William Henry Bragg in London. He became a full professor at Pasadena in 1931 and left there in 1936 to take up the post of Director of the Gates and Crellin Laboratories, which he held for the next 22 years. He also held university appointments at the University of California, San Diego, and Stanford University, and during the 1960s spent several years on a study of the problems of war and peace at the Center for the Study of Democratic Institutions at Santa Barbara, California. His last appointment was as Director of the Linus Pauling Institute of Science and Medicine at Menlo Park, California.

Pauling's early work reflects his European experiences. In 1931 he published a classic paper, "The Nature of the Chemical Bond", in which he used quantum mechanics to explain that an electron-pair bond is formed by the interaction of two unpaired electrons, one from each of two atoms, and that once paired these electrons cannot take part in the formation of other bonds. It was followed by the book *Introduction to Quantum Mechanics* (1935), of which he was co-author. He was a pioneer in the application of quantum mechanical principles to the structures of molecules, relating them to interatomic distances and bond angles by X-ray and electron diffraction, magnetic effects and thermochemical techniques.

It was Pauling who introduced the concept of hybrid orbitals in molecules to explain the symmetry exhibited by carbon atoms in most of its compounds. The electrons in the ground state and in the excited state of the carbon atom can be represented as follows:

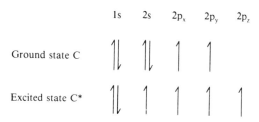

Distribution of electrons in a carbon atom.

One of the $2p$ electrons can then form sp hybrid orbitals with the $2s$ electron; two $2p$ atomic orbitals remain:

Two linear sp hybrid orbitals.

In acetylene (ethyne), for example, overlap of two *sp* hybrid orbitals between two carbon atoms results in a linear molecule. A hydrogen atom is bonded to each end by overlap between the carbons' *sp* orbitals and the *s* orbitals of the hydrogens. (The remaining carbon *p* orbitals also overlap to form two π bonds which, together with the σ bond just described, account for the traditional triple bond in this molecule.)

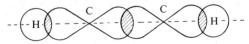

σ bonds in acetylene (ethyne).

The structures of many other organic molecules can be explained in a similar way.

Pauling also investigated electronegativity of atoms and polarization (movement of electrons) in chemical bonds. He assigned electronegativities on a scale up to 4.0. A pair of electrons in a bond are pulled preferentially towards an atom with a high electronegativity. In hydrogen chloride, HCl, for example, hydrogen has an electronegativity of 2.1 and chlorine of 3.5. The bonding electrons are pulled towards the chlorine atom, giving it a small excess negative charge (and leaving the hydrogen atom with a small excess positive charge), polarizing the hydrogen – chlorine bond.

$$H - Cl \qquad H \overset{..}{\underset{..}{:}} Cl : \qquad H \rightarrow Cl \qquad \overset{\delta+ \quad \delta-}{H - Cl}$$

electron pair pulled towards chlorine atom   *polarized molecule*

Electronegativity values can be used to show why certain substances, such as hydrochloric acid, are acid, whereas others, such as sodium hydroxide, are alkaline.

H 2.1			
C 2.5	N 3.0	O 3.5	F 4.0
Si 1.8	P 2.1	S 2.5	Cl 3.0
Ge 1.8	As 2.0	Se 2.4	Br 2.8

Electronegativities of some elements.

For compounds whose molecules cannot be represented unambiguously by a single structure, Pauling introduced the idea of resonance hybridization. An example is carbon dioxide, CO_2.

$$O = C = O \qquad O \leftarrow C \Rrightarrow O \qquad O \Lleftarrow C \rightarrow O$$

Resonance hybrids (canonical forms) of carbon dioxide.

The true structure is regarded as an intermediate between two or more theoretically possible structures, which are termed canonical forms.

These and Pauling's other ideas on chemical bonding are fundamental to modern theories of molecular structure. Much of this work was consolidated in his book *The Nature of the Chemical Bond, The Structure of Molecules and Crystals* (1939).

In the 1940s Pauling turned his attention to the chemistry of living tissues and systems. He applied his knowledge of molecular structure to the complexity of life, principally to proteins in blood. With Robert Corey, he worked on the structures of amino acids and polypeptides. They proposed that many proteins have structures held together with hydrogen bonds, giving them helical shapes. This concept assisted Francis Crick and James Watson in their search for the structure of DNA, which they eventually resolved as a double helix.

In his researches on blood, Pauling investigated immunology and sickle-cell anaemia. Later work confirmed his hunch that the disease is genetic and that normal haemoglobin and the haemoglobin in abnormal "sickle" cells differ in electrical charge. Throughout the 1940s he studied living materials; he also carried out research on anaesthesia. At the end of this period he published two textbooks, *General Chemistry* (1948) and *College Chemistry* (1950), which are still best sellers.

Like many of his contemporaries, Pauling became concerned about the proliferation of nuclear weapons and their atmospheric testing during the 1950s. He presented to the United Nations a petition signed by 11,021 scientists from throughout the world urging an end to nuclear weapons testing, a view reinforced in his book *No More War* (1958). For these efforts he was awarded the Nobel Peace Prize in 1962, the year in which the International Nuclear Test Ban Treaty was signed.

Pelletier, Pierre-Joseph (*1788–1842*), was a French chemist whose extractions of a whole range of biologically active compounds from plants founded the chemistry of the alkaloids, the most important of which discovered by him was quinine.

Pelletier was born in Paris on 22 March 1788, the son of a distinguished chemist and pharmacist. He studied at the École de Pharmacie, qualifying in 1810. He was awarded his doctorate in 1812 and three years later was appointed Assistant Professor of Natural History and Drugs at the École. He was promoted to full Professor in 1825 and in 1832 made Assistant Director of the school itself. He was elected to the French Academy in 1840, the same year in which illness forced him to retire from the École. He died in Paris on 19 July 1842.

In his early career, Pelletier was concerned with the analysis of gum resins and the colouring matter in plants. In 1813, working with the physiologist François Magendie (1783-1855), he produced reports on opopanax, sagapenum, asafoetida, myrrh, galbanum and caranna gum. His first major success came in 1817 when he discovered the emetic substance in ipecacuanha root; he called it emetine.

The following four years were particularly productive. Together with Joseph Caventou he investigated the action of nitric acid on the nacreous material of human gall-stones and the green pigment in leaves, which they named chlorophyll. In 1818 Pelletier obtained crotonic acid from croton oil and analysed carmine from cochineal. Pelletier and Caventou then isolated ambrein from ambergris, but it was their discovery of plant alkaloids that brought international fame: strychnine in 1818, brucine and veratrine in 1819, and - most important of all - quinine in 1820. Quinine is the chief alkaloid in cinchona bark and for the next hundred years was the only effective treatment for malaria, representing the first successful use of a chemical compound in combating an infectious disease.

During the following 20 years Pelletier continued his alkaloid and phytochemical research. In 1823, with Jean Baptiste Dumas, he obtained firm evidence for the presence of nitrogen in alkaloids, something he had failed to confirm in earlier work with Caventou. He later carried out researches on strychnine and developed procedures for its extraction from nux vomica. He also made chemical examinations of upas, improved the method of manufacturing quinine sulphate, and isolated cahinca acid, the bitter crystalline substance from cahinca root.

In 1832 Pelletier reported his discovery of a new opium alkaloid, narceine; he also claimed to have been the first to isolate thebaine (which he called paramorphine). In partnership with Walter, he went on to study the oily hydrocarbons obtained by the destructive distillation of amber and bitumen. In a similar study (1837-1838) of an oily by-product of pine resin - used in the manufacture of illuminating gas - he discovered a substance he called retinaphte, later known as toluene (now methylbenzene).

Few people have discovered as many pharmaceutically important natural products as Pelletier did. Their powerful effects and their use in medical practice introduced specific chemical compounds into pharmacology instead of the imprecise plant extracts and mixtures used previously.

Perkin, William Henry (*1838-1907*), was a British chemist who achieved international fame for his accidental discovery of mauve, the first aniline dye and the first commercially significant synthetic dyestuff.

Perkin was born in Shadwell, South London, on 12 March 1838, the son of a builder. His father wanted him to become an architect and he was educated at the City of London School, where he became interested in chemistry; encouraged by Thomas Hall, one of his teachers, he carried out experiments at home. At the early age of 15 he persuaded his father to let him enter the Royal College of Chemistry, London, and two years later became an assistant to August Hofmann, who was Professor of Chemistry there. Perkin's discovery of mauve occurred during the Easter vacation of 1856 when he was still only 18. With the help of his father he set up a factory to manufacture the dye, and so founded the whole of the British synthetic dyestuffs industry. He was knighted in 1906 on the fiftieth anniversary of his famous discovery. He died in Sudbury, Middlesex, on 14 July 1907.

In one of his early home experiments Perkin looked at the reduction products of dinitrobenzene and dinitronaphthalene and obtained a coloured substance initially named nitrosonaphthyline. It was the first example of the group of azo dyes produced from naphthalene.

In 1856 Perkin set himself the ambitious task of trying to synthesize quinine. He used chromic acid to oxidize toluidine (4-methylphenylamine) and obtained only a dirty dark precipitate. He then repeated the experiment using aniline (phenyl amine) and again produced a dark precipitate. But extracted with alcohol it gave an intensely purple solution, which contained the new dye which Perkin called aniline purple - later named mauve by French textile manufacturers. He sent a sample to the dyestuff company of Pullars in Perth, Scotland, which reported favourably once they had found a satisfactory mordant.

Despite advice to the contrary by Hofmann, Perkin decided to develop the dye himself commercially. His father put up the money and his brother, T.D. Perkin (1831–1891), helped with the laboratory work. Without any connections in the textile industry and with only a small experimental quantity of the dye, they built a new factory at Greenford Green (now Perivale), to the west of London in Middlesex, which was opened in 1859. Initially they had difficulty getting supplies of benzene (to make aniline, which was at that time a rare substance, found only in a few research laboratories) and nitric acid (to prepare nitrobenzene). Perkin patented the process, after establishing that someone under the age of 21 could do so; it was soon copied but involving more expensive oxidizing agents than the simple acidified potassium dichromate he used.

4-aminoazobenzene
(aniline yellow, a basic azo dye)

mauve
(aniline purple)

alizarin yellow
(a mordant dye)

In the following years Hofmann also patented several commercial dyes based on the methylation and ethylation of magenta (discovered by Verguin in 1859), producing violets and rosanilines. At the company of Roberts and Dale in Manchester, H. Caro (1834–1911) discovered a new way of making mauve and with Martins introduced Manchester brown and Martins yellow. Other new dyes included crysaniline, rosolic acid, aniline green, aniline black and diphenylamine blue. Perkin's chance discovery had resulted in a new dyestuffs industry based on coal tar (the source of benzene and aniline). Commercial demand for mauve died within ten years and it was superseded. Perkin's factory introduced new dyes based on the alkylation of magenta, and in 1868 he established a new route for the synthesis of alizarin (independently of Caro and Karl Graebe, who in the same year patented a process for making alizarin). The natural dye was derived from the madder plant, and within a few years the growing of the crop was no longer a commercial proposition in Europe.

The starting point for alizarin was anthracene, another coal-tar derivative. Eventually one tonne of alizarin was prepared during 1869, and by 1871 Perkin's company was producing one tonne every day. Perkin's business acumen was considerable and he became a wealthy man. He sold the factory and retired from industry in 1874 at the age of 36 to continue his academic research.

Even before this time Perkin had investigated various other organic compounds. In 1860, with B.F. Duppa (1828–1873), he established that glycine (aminoethanoic acid) can be obtained by heating bromoacetic acid (bromoethanoic acid) with ammonia. They also showed that tartaric acid (2,3-dihydroxybutanoic acid), fumaric acid and maleic acid (*trans*- and *cis*-ethene-1,2-dicarboxylic acids) are related and they synthesized racemic acid from dibromosuccinic acid (2,3-dibromobutan-1,4-dioic acid).

In the late 1860s Perkin prepared unsaturated acids by the action of acetic anhydride on aromatic aldehydes, a method known as the Perkin synthesis. In 1868 he synthesized coumarin, the first preparation of a synthetic perfume. He also investigated the effects of magnetic fields on the chemical structures of substances.

In 1906 on the fiftieth anniversary of the discovery of mauve a Jubilee celebration was held at the Royal Institution in London, attended by major chemists from throughout Europe. Pride of place at the dinner which followed was a specimen of benzene first isolated by Michael Faraday in 1825, the parent substance upon which the dyestuffs industry was founded.

The Perkin synthesis of coumarin.

coumarin

Perkin married twice and had three sons and four daughters. The eldest son, also named William Henry (1860-1929), became a Professor of Chemistry at the University of Manchester, where he established a research team devoted to organic chemistry; he later moved to Oxford University. Another son, Arthur George (1861-1937), was also a skilled organic chemist; between 1916 and 1937 he was Professor of Colour Chemistry and Dyeing at the University of Leeds.

Perutz, Max Ferdinand (*1914-*), is an Austrian-born British molecular biologist who shared the 1962 Nobel Prize in Chemistry for his solution of the structure of the haemoglobin molecule; his co-worker John Kendrew, who had determined the structure of myoglobin, was the other winner of the Prize.

Perutz was born in Vienna on 19 May 1914. Both his parents came from families of textile manufacturers and expected their son to study law before entering the family business. But at school at the Theresianum in Vienna he became interested in chemistry and in 1932 entered the University of Vienna to study the subject. A course in organic biochemistry, given by F. von Wessely, fired his imagination and after graduation he tried (but failed) to get a place at Cambridge University to study under Frederick Gowland Hopkins.

In 1936 Perutz became a research student at the Cavendish Laboratory, Cambridge, where he worked on X-ray crystallography under John Bernal (1901-1971); he has remained at Cambridge for the rest of his academic career. In 1939 he received a grant from the Rockefeller Foundation and was appointed research assistant to William Lawrence Bragg; he gained his PhD a year later. Perutz continued his researches and in 1947 was appointed head of the newly constituted

Molecular Biology Unit of the Medical Research Council. In 1957 he formally proposed to the Council the idea of a new laboratory, backed by N.F. Mott, Bragg's successor as Cavendish Professor. Five years later Perutz became Chairman of the new Laboratory of Molecular Biology and held this post until his retirement in 1979.

Perutz first applied the methods of X-ray diffraction to proteins at the Cavendish Laboratory. Following a conversation with F. Haurowitz in Prague in 1937, he began work on determining the structure of haemoglobin. There were enormous difficulties and it was not until 16 years later, in 1953, that he discovered a suitable method. He found that if he added a single atom of a heavy metal such as gold or mercury to each molecule of protein the diffraction pattern was altered slightly. Kendrew, who had joined Perutz in 1945, used a similar technique for the smaller molecule of myoglobin.

Using high-speed computers, which were just becoming available, they analysed hundreds of X-ray pictures and in 1958 Perutz published his first findings on the structure of haemoglobin. By 1960 they had worked out the precise structures of both proteins. Haemoglobin turned out to have 574 amino-acid units in four folded chains, each similar to the single chain of myoglobin. Their basic helical structure confirmed the prediction made ten years earlier by Linus Pauling that protein strands are twisted.

In his later work on haemoglobin Perutz tried to interpret the mechanism by which the molecule transports oxygen in the blood in terms of its molecular structure. He became especially interested in the effect of the protein globulin on the iron-containing haem group, which is related to the effect of protein on the catalytic properties of metals and co-enzymes.

The sequences of the 20 different amino-acid

residues along the α and β globin chains are determined genetically; occasionally mutations lead to an alteration in one of the sequences. People who carry some of these mutations may suffer from a lack of red blood cells (anaemia) or have too many red cells, because the stability of the oxygen-carrying mechanism of the haemoglobin molecule is impaired. This was the first time that the symptoms of an inherited disorder had been interpreted in terms of the molecular structure of a biochemical. It holds the hope that a treatment may be found for the most common inherited haemoglobin disorder, sickle-cell anaemia.

Petit, Alexis-Thérèse (*1791–1820*), was a French scientist who worked mainly in physics but whose collaboration with Pierre Dulong resulted in a discovery that was to play an important part in chemistry in the determination of atomic weights (relative atomic masses).

Petit was born in Vesoul, Haute-Saône, on 2 October 1791. He went to school at Besançon and at the age of only 16 entered the École Polytechnique in Paris. He graduated in 1809 – after only two years – and a year later was appointed Professor of Physics at the Lycée Bonaparte. He was awarded his doctorate in 1811 for a thesis on capillary action. In 1814 he became an assistant professor at the École, succeeding to a full professorship a year later. The last years of his life were darkened by the death in 1817 of his wife (sister of the physicist Dominique Arago) and by illness. He contracted tuberculosis and died, in Paris, on 21 June 1820 in only his twenty-ninth year. He was succeeded at the École Polytechnique by his friend and colleague Dulong.

Petit's early research was conducted in collaboration with his brother-in-law Dominique Arago (1786–1853). They examined the effect of temperature on the refractive index of gases. Their results led Petit to doubt the validity of the then accepted corpuscular theory of light and to become an early supporter of the wave theory.

In 1815 the offer of a prize in a scientific competition on the measurement of temperature and cooling laws stimulated Petit and Dulong to begin their fruitful, albeit short, collaboration. Their results established the importance of the gas thermometer (they won the competition and were awarded the prize in 1818). They continued working in this area, examining the specific heats (specific heat capacities) of various solids and in 1819 announced the famous Dulong–Petit law of atomic heats. This stated that, for most solid elements, the product of the specific heat and atomic weight (termed the atomic heat) is a constant, equal to 5.97. The modern expression of the law is that the product of the specific heat

capacity and relative atomic mass is approximately constant and equal to three times the universal gas constant (**R**), or 25.07 kJ/mol/K.

The law applies at room temperature only, and not to lighter solid elements such as boron and carbon; the constant tends to zero as temperature falls towards absolute zero. Chemists who at that time were having difficulty determining atomic weights (and distinguishing them from equivalent weights) now had a method of estimating the approximate weight merely by measuring the specific heat of a sample of the element concerned.

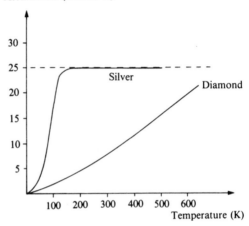

Atomic heat plotted against temperature.

Polanyi, Michael *(1891–1976)*, was a Hungarian-born British physical chemist, particularly noted for his contributions to reaction kinetics. In later life he diverted his attention to social philosophy, in which he became equally renowned. Throughout his career he voiced his firm belief in the right of the scientist to seek the truth unhampered by external constraints.

Polanyi was born in Budapest on 12 March 1891, so sharing a birthday with Charles Friedel and William Perkin. He entered the University of Budapest in 1909 to study medicine, but after graduation went to the Technische Hochschule at Karlsruhe as a student of chemistry under Georg Bredig. After service as a medical officer during World War I, he returned briefly to Karlsruhe before joining the Kaiser Wilhelm Institute of Fibre Chemistry in Berlin. In 1923, at the invitation of Fritz Haber, Polanyi moved to the Institute for Physical and Electro-Chemistry. But he became increasingly disturbed by the influence of the Nazi Party, especially its dismissal of Jewish scientists, and in 1933 he accepted the Chair of Physical Chemistry at Manchester, England.

During the 1940s, Polanyi made the decision to concentrate on philosophy and in 1948 he transferred to the newly created Chair of Social Studies at Manchester. On retiring from this position in 1958 he moved to Merton College, Oxford, as Senior Research Fellow. He died at Northampton on 22 February 1976.

Polyani's early researches in chemical physics resulted in several papers on the adsorption of gases by solids. He introduced the idea of the existence of an attractive force between a solid surface and the atoms or molecules of a gas; he also suggested that the adsorbed surface is a multilayer and not subject to simple valency interactions. His other work of about that time extended the theory of Hermann Nernst (which stated that the entropy of a system approaches zero as the temperature decreases towards absolute zero). Polanyi showed that an increase in pressure must have the same effect, although in practice the highest attainable laboratory pressure is less effective than a very modest temperature increase.

At Berlin Polanyi's interest turned to X-ray analysis, using the newly developed rotating crystal method. He and his co-workers improved the technique and applied it to the determination of the structure of cellulose fibres. He also investigated the physical and mechanical properties of various materials; he grew crystals of metals and devised a special apparatus to measure their shear and rupture strengths.

Even as early as 1920 Polanyi recognized that the current theories of chemical reaction rates were simplifications of the truth. The collision theory postulated that only molecules with a certain critical energy would react. Working first under Haber and then at Manchester Polanyi extended this idea and produced theories of rates of association and dissociation based on the angular momenta of the colliding particles. Then quantum mechanics presented the kineticist with a powerful new tool. Reactions were considered in terms of the variation in potential energy of a system, which could be plotted as a function of the distance between reacting nuclei to produce a diagram somewhat resembling a contour map. The configuration of the components at the "mountain pass" was defined as the activated complex, and the "height" of the pass represented the activation energy.

Polanyi and Eyring investigated the reaction between a hydrogen atom and a hydrogen molecule

$$H + H_{2(para)} \rightarrow H + H_{2(ortho)}$$

and made the first reasonable accurate determination of its energy surface (ortho- and para-hydrogen are isomers that differ only in the direction of spin of their nuclei).

Polanyi also played a part in solving a problem that had long been puzzling kineticists. It was known that in the hydrogen-iodine equilibrium

$$H_2 + I_2 \rightleftharpoons 2HI$$

the rate of reaction is given by the equation

$$\frac{d[HI]}{dt} = K[H_2][I_2],$$

where K is a constant. But in the apparently analogous reaction between hydrogen and bromine, experiment showed the reaction rate to be given by

$$\frac{d[HBr]}{dt} = \frac{k[H_2][Br_2]^{\frac{1}{2}}}{m + [HBr]/[Br_2]},$$

where k and m are constants. This expression implies that the velocity of the reaction is inhibited by the presence of the product HBr. Polanyi and others proposed a chain mechanism for the reaction:

initiation $\qquad Br_2 \rightarrow 2Br$
propagation $\quad Br + H_2 \rightarrow HBr + H$
$\qquad\qquad\qquad H + Br_2 \rightarrow HBr + Br$
inhibition $\qquad H + HBr \rightarrow H_2 + Br_2$
termination $\qquad 2Br \rightarrow Br_2$

In his new philosophical role at Manchester Polanyi was active in the Society for Freedom in Science. He advocated that scientific research need not necessarily have a pre-stated function and expressed the belief that a commitment to the discovery of truth is the prime reason for being a scientist. His principal work was an investigation of the processes by which high-level skills such as craftsmanship and connoisseurship are acquired and the means by which such skills are shared and extended. His move to Oxford in 1958 coincided with the publication of his book *Personal Knowledge*, of which he said "The principal purpose of this book is to achieve a frame of mind in which I may firmly hold what I believe to be true, even though I know it may conceivably be false".

Porter, George (*1920-*), is a British physical chemist who developed the technique of flash photolysis for the direct study of extremely fast chemical reactions, for which achievement he shared the 1967 Nobel Prize in Chemistry with Ronald Norrish and Manfred Eigen. He has also inspired others – particularly young people – by his television appearances and lectures at the Royal Institution.

Porter was born in Stainforth, Yorkshire, on 6 December 1920, sharing a birthday with his eminent predecessors in chemistry Joseph Gay-Lussac and Nicolas Leblanc. He graduated from Leeds University in 1941, during World War II, and spent the next four years as a Radar Officer in the Royal Navy. He then went to Cambridge University where he carried out research from 1945 to 1949 under Ronald Norrish. From 1952 to 1954 he was Assistant Director of Research at Cambridge and Assistant Director of the British Rayon Research Association for a year in 1955. He then became Professor of Physical Chemistry at Sheffield University and was made Head of the Chemistry Department in 1963. Since 1966 Porter has been Director and Fullerian Professor of Chemistry at the Royal Institution, as well as Director of the Davy Faraday Research Laboratory. He was knighted in 1972.

In 1947, while working with Norrish, Porter began using quick flashes of light to study transient species in chemical reactions, particularly free radicals and excited states of molecules. He studied very fast reactions having short-lived intermediates. In 1950 he could detect entities that exist for less than a microsecond; by 1967 he had reduced the time limit to a nanosecond, and by 1975 he could detect species that lasted for as little as a picosecond (10^{-12} sec.). His early work dealt with reactions involving gases (mainly chain reactions and combustion reactions), but he later extended the technique to solutions. He developed a method of stabilizing free radicals by trapping them in the structure of a supercooled liquid (a glass), a technique called matrix isolation. He enabled flash photolysis to be applied to organic chemistry, biochemistry and photobiology. Using laser beams, he extended the technique to study reactions beyond the microsecond range. Today photochemical methods are used to synthesis hydrocarbons for fuels and chemical feedstocks.

One of Porter's main interests since the early 1960s has been the mechanism of photosynthesis in plants, which proceeds via "light" and "dark" stages. He studied the light-harvesting mechanisms of chloroplasts and the primary processes that occur in the first nanosecond of photosynthesis.

Few modern scientists of Porter's calibre have devoted so much time to the education of young people and non-specialists about the importance and excitement of scientific studies. Part of this involvement has been spent maintaining the great tradition of the Royal Institution. He has contributed to many television programmes, particularly BBC Television's *Young Scientist of the Year* series.

Prelog, Vladimir (*1906-*   ), is a Jugoslav-born Swiss organic chemist famous for his studies of alkaloids and antibiotics, and for his work on stereochemistry. He shared the 1975 Nobel Prize in Chemistry with John Cornforth.

Prelog was born in Sarajevo on 23 July 1906. He spent his early years in Zagreb and went to Hungary to study chemistry at the Institute of Technology in Prague, where he also did postgraduate research. From 1929 to 1934 he worked in Prague as a chemist in a laboratory for the preparation of fine chemicals. Then in 1935 he went back to Jugoslavia to become a lecturer and later Associate Professor of Organic Chemistry in the University of Zagreb's Technical Faculty. But in 1941, after the German occupation at the beginning of World War II, Prelog moved to Zurich to be a lecturer at the Swiss Federal Institute of Technology. He became an Associate Professor in 1947, and ten years later he was made a full Professor, succeeding the 1939 Nobel Prize-winner Leopold Ružiča. Prelog retired in 1976.

Alkaloids were the subject of Prelog's early research, and one of his first achievements was the determination of the structure of the antimalarial quinine alkaloids. In 1945 he showed that Robert Robinson's formulae for strychnine alkaloids were incorrect (they were later rectified), and he derived the structures of steroid alkaloids from plants of the genera *Solanum* and *Veratrum* (the latter with Derek Barton). He also investigated many other alkaloids using classical organic chemistry, confirming the findings by X-ray crystallography.

In the 1940s, after his move to Zurich, Prelog studied many lipoid extracts from animal organs – the work with Ružička that resulted in the discovery of various steroids and the elucidation of their structures. Then, with W. Keller-Shlierlein, he investigated metabolic products of micro-organisms and with a number of other researchers isolated various new complex natural products that have interesting biological properties. These include antibiotics and bacterial growth factors.

Many of these classes of metabolites have molecules that contain large rings. Prelog became interested in their stereochemistry, and looked at the relationships between the spatial structure and chemistry of many large-membered rings. He researched the steric course of asymmetric syntheses and succeeded in determining the then unknown absolute configurations of the steroids and terpenes. He used asymmetric synthesis as a sensitive tool for studying the details of reaction mechanisms, such as the synthesis of cyanhydrin.

Prelog demonstrated experimentally that some micro-organisms have the ability to reduce the carbonyl group of certain alicyclic substrates in a highly stereospecific way. Together with Cahn and Christopher Ingold, he developed a widely used system for defining chirality (or handedness) in organic compounds and of stereoisomerism in general. The comprehensive molecular topology that evolved from this work is gradually replacing classical stereochemistry.

Priestley, Joseph (*1733-1804*), was an English chemist and theologian. He entered chemistry when it was making the transition from alchemy to a theoretical science. An outstanding practical scientist, he combined experimental flair with quantitative accuracy, skills which led him to discover several new gases, including oxygen. He was less dynamic as a theorist; his conservatism made him a life-long supporter of Georg Stahl's phlogiston theory of combustion despite mounting evidence - much of it provided by Priestley himself - refuting the principle. Outside his scientific work his life was far from harmonious. He was an outspoken man of radical views which brought him notoriety, and eventually drove him to leave his native country.

Priestley was born in Fieldhead, near Leeds, on 13 March 1733, the son of a cloth-dresser. His mother died when he was only seven years old and he was brought up by an aunt, who introduced him to Calvinism. In 1752 he attended the Dissenting Academy at Daventry, and three years later he entered the ministry as Presbyterian Minister at Needham Market, Suffolk. He moved to Nantwich, Cheshire, in 1758 and in 1761 became tutor in languages at Warrington Academy. A year later he married May Wilkinson, sister of the iron-master John Wilkinson. On a trip to London in 1766 he met the American scientist Benjamin Franklin (1706-1790) who aroused in Priestley an interest in science; thereafter he combined scientific research with his clerical and social duties.

In 1767 Priestley returned to Leeds as minister of a chapel at Mill Hill. He did his most productive work between 1773 and 1780, when he was librarian and literary companion to Lord Shelburne, whom he accompanied on a journey to France in 1774. While in Paris he met Antoine Lavoisier and told him of his experiments with "dephlogisticated air" (soon to be named oxygen by Lavoisier).

By 1780 Priestley's outspoken criticisms as a Dissenter had become an embarrassment to Lord Shelburne, who retired his companion on a small pension. Priestley moved to Birmingham to become minister of a chapel called the New Meeting. He also joined the Lunar Society, in company with the inventors James Watt and Matthew Boulton, Josiah Wedgwood, Erasmus Darwin (grandfather of Charles Darwin) and a number of less notable inventors and scientists. In Birmingham Priestley continued to voice loudly his opposition to the Established Church and his support of the French Revolutionaries. In 1791, on the second anniversary of the storming of the Bastille, the people of Birmingham rioted and vented some of their wrath on Priestley and other Dissenters, whose homes were ransacked. Priestley escaped to London and settled for a while in Hackney, but his unpopularity mounted, exacerbated by an offer of citizenship from France (by the very people who executed Lavoisier in 1794). In that same year Priestley emigrated to America, to Northumberland in Pennsylvania. He rejected the offer of a professorship at the University of Pennsylvania, preferring to live a life of comparative solitude in Northumberland, where he died on 6 February 1804.

Influenced by Franklin, Priestley's early work of 1767 onwards was in physics, particularly electricity and optics. He established that electrostatic charge is concentrated on the outer surface of a charged body and that there is no internal force. From this observation he proposed an inverse square law for charges, by analogy with gravitation. Priestley's house in Leeds was near a brewery, and it was his interest in the process of fermentation that turned him to chemistry, particularly gases. He experimented with the gas produced during fermentation - the layer of "fixed air" (carbon dioxide) over a brewing vat - and showed it to be the same as that reported by Joseph Black in 1756. He dissolved the gas under pressure in water, beginning a European craze for soda water.

At Lord Shelburne's estate at Calne, Wiltshire, he continued experimenting with gases. He used a large magnifying glass to focus the Sun's rays to produce high temperatures. He invented the pneumatic trough for collecting gases over water, and overcame the problem of handling water-soluble gases by collecting them over mercury.

An early discovery, in 1772, was "nitrous air" (nitric oxide, or nitrogen monoxide, NO). Priestley found that a sample of the gas left in contact with iron filings and sulphur decreased in volume and that the new gas produced supported combustion. He had reduced nitric oxide to nitrous oxide (dinitrogen monoxide, N_2O), Humphry Davy's "laughing gas". In the same year he became the first person to isolate gaseous ammonia by collecting it over mercury (previously ammonia was known only in aqueous solution).

It had long been known that burning sulphur gives off a choking gas. In 1774 Priestley made the same gas by heating oil of vitriol (concentrated sulphuric acid) with mercury. He also produced it by heating the acid with copper turnings, a method still used today to make sulphur dioxide (SO_2).

Priestley's most famous discovery was that of oxygen. In 1772 he had shown that a gas necessary to animal life is liberated by plants. Two years later he prepared the same gas by heating red calyx of mercury (mercury(II) oxide, HgO) or minium (red lead, Pb_3O_4). His investigation of the properties of the new gas showed it to be superior to common air. A mouse trapped in a container of it stayed conscious twice as long as in ordinary air, and breathing it had no adverse effects (apart from leaving a peculiar light feeling in the chest). When he mixed the new gas with nitrous air (NO) there was a diminution in volume and yet another, red gas (nitrogen dioxide, NO_2) was formed. From all of these observations Priestley concluded that he had prepared dephlogisticated air - i.e. air from which the fiery principle of phlogiston had been removed. The Swedish chemist Karl Scheele independently prepared oxygen in 1772, but his tardiness in publication resulted in Priestley being credited with the discovery.

Prigogine, Ilya (*1917-*), is a Russian-born Belgian theoretical chemist who was awarded the 1977 Nobel Prize in Chemistry for widening the scope of thermodynamics from the purely physical sciences to ecological and sociological studies.

Prigogine was born in Moscow on 22 January 1917. When he was four years old his parents emigrated to Western Europe, and settled in Belgium in 1929. He studied at the University of Brussels, gaining his doctorate in 1941. In 1951 he became Professor of the Université Libre de Bruxelles and in 1959 was appointed Director of the Instituts Internationaux de Physique et de Chemie. From 1961 to 1966 he was Professor of the Department of Chemistry at the Enrico Fermi Institute for Nuclear Studies and the Institute for the Study of Metals at the University of Chicago. From 1967 he held the position of Director of the Center for Statistical Mechanics and Thermodynamics at the University of Texas in Austin, concurrently with his professorship in Brussels.

Prigogine's work has been concerned with applying thermodynamic principles to new disciplines. Observation of many physical systems has shown that there is a general tendency to assume the state in which they are most disordered. This occurs by means of processes that dissipate energy and which can in principle produce work. But it was not understood how it is possible for a more orderly system, such as a living creature, to arise spontaneously from a less orderly system and yet maintain itself despite the tendency towards disorder. It is now known that order can be created and preserved only by processes that flow "uphill" in the thermodynamic sense. They are compensated by "downhill" events. These interrelated occurrences owe their existence to the absorption of energy from the surroundings and are consistent with thermodynamic laws.

During the late 1940s Prigogine developed mathematical models of what he called dissipative systems of this kind, to show how they might have come about. His models demonstrated how matter and energy can interact creatively, forming organisms that can sustain themselves and grow in opposition to the general drift towards universal chaos. Dissipative systems can exist only in harmony with their surroundings.

Prigogine showed that dissipative systems exhibit two types of behaviour: close to equilibrium, their order tends to be destroyed; far from equilibrium, order can be maintained and new structures formed. The probability of order arising out of disorder, by pure chance, is infinitesimal; but the formation of an ordered dissipative system makes it possible to create order out of chaos. These ideas have been applied to examine how life originated on Earth, to the dynamic equilibria in ecosystems, to the preservation of world resources, and even to the prevention of traffic jams.

Proust, Joseph Louis (*1754-1826*), was a French chemist who discovered the law of constant composition, sometimes also called Proust's law, which states that every true chemical compound has exactly the same composition no matter how it is prepared.

Proust was born in Angers on 26 September 1754, the son of an apothecary. He was brought up to follow his father's profession, studying chemistry under Guillaume Rouelle at the Jardin du Roi and working as an apothecary-chemist in La Salpêtrière Hospital in Paris and lecturing at the Palais Royal. In the 1780s, before the beginning of the French Revolution, he went to Spain and spent the next 20 years in Madrid. He taught at various academies and carried out his own research in a well-equipped laboratory (The Royal Laboratory) provided by his patron, King Charles IV of Spain. In 1808 Napoleon invaded Spain and French soldiers wrecked Proust's laboratory. He returned to France a poor man, was elected to the Academy of Sciences in 1816, and eked out his retirement on a small pension provided to him as an Academician by Louis XVIII. He died in Angers on 5 July 1826.

Proust's reputation as a chemist rests on his extraordinary ability as an analyst. He identified grape sugar (glucose) and distinguished between it and sugar from other sources. Before his work on chemical compounds in the early 1800s in

Madrid, the prevailing view in chemistry was that of Claude Berthollet who had stated (and in 1803 published in his *Statique Chemique*) that the composition of compounds could vary over a wide range, depending on the proportions of reactants used to produce them. In 1799 Proust prepared and analysed copper carbonate produced in various ways and compared the results with those obtained by analysing mineral deposits of the same substance; he found them all to have the same composition. Similar results with other compounds led Proust to propose the law of constant composition (he ascribed the errors in Berthollet's experiments to impurities and inaccurate analyses). Proust's law influenced John Dalton's thinking about atomic theory – in 1808 Dalton proposed the law of definite proportions. The proportions of the elements in a compound result from the linking of definite (usually small) numbers of atoms to form molecules, giving the compound a constant composition. After a long controversy Berthollet finally conceded that Proust was right. Both chemists did agree, however, that the rate of a chemical reaction does depend on the masses of the reactants.

Prout, William (*1785–1850*), was a British chemist who pioneered physiological chemistry, but who is best known for formulating Prout's hypothesis, which states that the atomic weights of all elements are exact multiples of the atomic weight of hydrogen. And since at that time (1815) the atomic weight of hydrogen was taken to be 1.0, the hypothesis implied that all atomic weights are whole numbers. Prout has often been confused with his contemporary the French chemist Joseph Proust (and Prout's hypothesis has been mistaken – in name – for Proust's law of constant composition).

Prout was born in Horton, Gloucestershire, on 15 January 1785 into a prosperous and well-established West Country family. He began by studying medicine at Edinburgh University, qualifying in 1811. He then set up a medical practice in London and established a private chemical laboratory. From 1813 he wrote about and gave lectures in "animal chemistry" and began his own researches into the chemistry of physiological processes. He published his atomic weight hypothesis anonymously in 1815. He continued to experiment, widening his interests to include some physics. He died in London on 9 April 1850.

In his early researches Prout studied various natural secretions and products, including blood, urine, gastric juices, kidney and bladder stones, and even cuttle-fish ink. He became convinced that the products of secretion derive from the chemical breakdown of body tissues. In 1818 he isolated urea and uric acid for the first time, and six years later he found hydrochloric acid in digestive juices from the stomach. In 1827 he became the first scientist to classify the components of food into the three major divisions of carbohydrates, fats and proteins.

His anonymous paper of 1815 was comprehensively entitled "On the Relation between the Specific Gravities of Bodies in their Gaseous State and the Weight of Their Atoms". From the determinations of atomic weights (relative atomic masses) that had been made Prout observed that many were whole-number multiples of that of hydrogen. The hypothesis implied that all other elements were in some way multiples or compounds of hydrogen, which was therefore the basic building block of matter.

Prout's hypothesis gave even more stimulus to the making of accurate determinations of atomic weights – work that inevitably proved the hypothesis to be wrong (for example chlorine has an atomic weight of 35.5). The idea was therefore largely abandoned until the work on isotopes by Frederick Soddy and others more than a century later finally accounted correctly for non-integral atomic weights (resulting from a natural mixture of isotopes).

Prout also studied the gases of the atmosphere and in 1832 made accurate measurements of the density of air. He devised a barometer for making precise atmospheric pressure measurements, and the Royal Society adopted its design for a national standard barometer.

Pyman, Frank Lee (*1882–1944*), was a British organic chemist, famous for his contributions to pharmaceutics and chemotherapy.

Pyman was born in Malvern on 9 April 1882. He was educated at Dover College, where his interest in chemistry began, and in 1899 entered Owens College of Victoria University, Manchester, at a time when it was the centre of organic chemistry research in Britain. He graduated in 1902 and went to Zurich Polytechnic for two years, but because Zurich University did not at that time recognize Polytechnic students he submitted his PhD thesis to Basle University, which granted him the degree in 1904.

On his return to Britain Pyman took a job in the Experimental Department of the Wellcome Chemical Works at Dartford, Kent, in 1906. During World War I he worked on the preparation of drugs needed to treat British troops overseas. In 1919 he was appointed Professor of Technological Chemistry in Manchester University and Head of the Department of Applied Chemistry at the College of Technology. He stayed at Manchester for eight years then in 1927 took up the appointment of Director of Research at the Boots Pure Drug Company's laboratories at Nottingham, where he remained until he died, in Nottingham, on 1 January 1944.

Pyman began research at the Wellcome Chemical Works under Jowett and worked with him for nine years, resulting in his life-long interest in the glyoxalines (glyoxal is ethanedial), cyclic amidines with therapeutic properties. He was particularly interested in the relationship between their chemical constitution and their physiological action. He later tried to relate chemical constitution with the local anaesthetic action of the substituted amino alkyl esters. After 1915 Jowett moved to the Imperial Institute, but he continued to send Pyman samples for examination. From one such (bark of *Calmatambin glabrifolium*) Pyman isolated a glycoside, which led him to study the constitution of the anhydro-bases made from it by the Hofmann degradation – which converts an amide into a amine with one fewer carbon atoms. This work placed him in the forefront of British organic chemistry and revealed the existence of a substance whose molecules contained a ten-membered heterocyclic ring. He also examined alkaloids, and became the first person to isolate a natural substance containing an asymmetric nitrogen atom.

Pyman undertook the preliminary processing work in connection with the preparation of the drugs Salvarsan (arsphenamine) and Neosalvarsan, which were needed at the outbreak of World War I to deal with syphilis. He also synthesized an alkaloidal compound used in the treatment of amoebic dysentery among troops during the war. Another alkaloid was used as a uterine haemostat under the name "Lodal".

Among compounds synthesized by Pyman were histidine and other simple bases of biological importance, such as guanidine. He continued to work with glyoxalines, synthesizing them and testing their effectiveness as antiseptics, pressor drugs, antimalarials and hypoglycaemic substances. He also investigated arsenicals, acridines (used as powerful antiseptics) and the organic salts of bismuth. He studied the relationship between chemical constitution and the pungency of amides, and examined the preservative properties of hops.

R

Ramsay, William (*1852-1919*), was a British chemist famous for his discovery of the rare gases,

for which achievement he was awarded the 1904 Nobel Prize in Chemistry.

Ramsay was born in Glasgow on 2 October 1852, the son of an engineer (whose father, Ramsay's grandfather, founded the Glasgow Chemical Society). Despite this technical and scientific background, Ramsay received a classical education and entered the University of Glasgow in 1866, when he was only 14 years old, to take an Arts course. Two years later he went to work in the laboratory of the Glasgow City Analyst, where he soon made up the deficiencies in his science education, and in 1870 he left for Germany to carry out research in organic chemistry under Rudolf Fittig (1835-1910) at Tübingen, gaining his PhD in 1873.

Ramsay then returned to Glasgow as an assistant at Anderson's College (later the Royal Technical College), followed by a post at the University. In 1880 he was appointed Professor of Chemistry at the newly created University College of Bristol (later Bristol University) and a year later became Principal of the College. Then in 1887 he moved to become Professor of Chemistry at University College, London, as successor to Alexander Williamson, where he remained until he retired in 1912. He was knighted in 1902. After retirement he moved to a house near High Wycombe, Buckinghamshire, where he continued some research in converted stables. At the outbreak of World War I in 1914 he became busy as a member of various committees. But his health deteriorated and he died at High Wycombe on 23 July 1916.

In the early 1870s, at Glasgow, Ramsay initially continued research in organic chemistry, investigating alkaloids and pyridine. During 1876 he met J.B. Henney, a young chemist who was interested in the chemistry of minerals. Together they studied water loss in salts and later the solubility of gases in solids.

At Bristol (1880-1887) Ramsay worked principally on liquid-vapour systems, relying heavily on able assistants such as Sydney Young because much of his time as Principal was taken up obtaining financial support for the new college.

At University College, London, his first action was to reorganize the out-of-date laboratory. He and his students investigated diketones, the metallic compounds of ethylene (ethene), and the atomic weight (relative atomic mass) of boron. Ramsay became interested in an article in *Nature* (September 1892) by Lord Rayleigh in which he reported finding a difference in the densities of samples of nitrogen extracted from air and from chemical sources. After corresponding with Rayleigh, Ramsay undertook to study the problem. With the help of his assistant Percy Williams, he passed nitrogen from air over heated magnesium (to form magnesium nitride). After this treatment, about 6 per cent of the gas still remained; further treatments reduced the volume of the residual gas even further, until they were left with an unknown gas of density 20 (oxygen = 16). Despite losing the sample in a laboratory accident, they finally established that it was the new element argon (which had contaminated the nitrogen derived from air).

Early in 1895 Ramsay became interested in helium, a gas known from spectrographic evidence to be present on the Sun but yet to be found on Earth. W.F. Hillebrand had reported that certain uranium minerals produced an inert gas on heating, and Ramsay repeated these experiments and obtained sufficient of the gas to send a sample to William Crookes for spectrographic analysis. Crookes confirmed that it was helium. Ramsay and his co-workers soon made the connection between helium and argon and in his book *The Gases of the Atmosphere* (1896) he repeated his earlier suspicion that there was an eighth group of new elements at the end of the Periodic Table. He drew up a table with gaps for the unknown elements:

Hydrogen	1.01	Helium	4.2	Lithium	7.0
Fluorine	19.0	?		Sodium	23.0
Chlorine	35.5	Argon	39.2	Potassium	39.1
Bromine	79.0	?		Rubidium	85.5
Iodine	126.9	?		Caesium	132.0
?	169.0	?		?	170.0

During the next decade Ramsay and Morris Travers sought the remaining rare gases by the fractional distillation of liquid air. Ramsay often used demonstrations and public lectures to show the existence of these gases, and he announced the discovery of neon in 1894 at a meeting in Toronto. Krypton and xenon took until 1898 to isolate. The last member of the series, radon, is a product of radioactive decay. It was identified in 1901 from a minute sample prepared by Ramsay and Robert Whytlaw-Gray (1877–1958).

Regnault, Henri Victor (*1810–1878*), was a German-born French physical chemist who is best known for his work on the physical properties of gases. In particular he showed that Boyle's law applies only to ideal gases. He also invented an air thermometer and a hygrometer, and he discovered carbon tetrachloride (tetrachloromethane).

Regnault was born in Aachen, Germany (Aix-la-Chapelle) on 21 July 1810. His father, an officer in Napoleon's army, was killed in the Russian campaign of 1812 and his mother died a few months later. His education was supervised by a

friend of his father, who found him a job in a draper's shop in Paris. Although he was very poor, Regnault managed to take lessons and in 1830 was admitted to the École Polytechnique in Paris, from which he graduated two years later. He spent two more years at the École des Mines before leaving France to study mining techniques and metallurgical processes in various parts of Europe. After short periods of research under Justus Liebig at Giessen and Jean-Baptiste Boussingault at Lyons, he returned to the École Polytechnique in 1836 as an assistant to Joseph Gay-Lussac and in 1840 succeeded him to the Chair in Chemistry. In the same year he was elected to the chemical section of the Académie des Sciences but his interests were already turning to physics and he became Professor of Physics at the Collège de France in 1841, where over the next 13 years he performed his most important experimental work.

From 1854 Regnault lived and worked at Sèvres as Director of the famous porcelain factory and was still engaged on research there when, in 1870, all his instruments and books were destroyed by Prussian soldiers. This blow and the death of his son late in the Franco-Prussian War left him a broken man and his last years were clouded by grief and personal disability. He died in Auteuil, near Paris, on 19 January 1878.

In his chemical work, nearly all of which dates from between 1835 and 1839, Regnault followed no unified programme of research. His major contributions were to organic chemistry. He studied the action of chlorine on ethers, leading to the discovery of vinyl chloride (monochloroethene), dichloroethylene (dichloroethene), trichloroethylene (trichloroethene) and carbon tetrachloride (tetrachloromethane).

Regnault was encouraged by Jean Baptiste Dumas, who had long advocated the measurement of specific heats as a means of investigating atomic composition. He began by measuring the specific heats of a wide range of substances, during which work (1839 to 1842) he conclusively demonstrated the approximate nature of Dulong and Petit's law and confirmed the validity of F.E. Neumann's extension of the law from elements to compounds.

In 1842 he was commissioned by the Minister of Public Works to redetermine all the physical constants involved in the design and operation of steam engines. This led Regnault to begin the research on the thermal properties of gases, for which he is now best known. He found that nearly all ordinary gases behave in much the same way and that the nature of this behaviour could generally be described by the perfect gas laws, which can define the volume of a gas in terms of its pressure, temperature and number of molecules (Boyle's law), Charles' or Gay-Lussac's law, and Avogadro's law). He painstakingly measured the coefficients of expansion of various gases and by 1852 had shown how real gases depart from the "ideal" or "perfect" behaviour required by Boyle's law – it was left to Johannes van der Waals to formulate a mathematical statement of the variation ten years later. Regnault also calculated that absolute zero is at $-273°C$. He redetermined the composition of air, and performed experiments on respiration in animals.

Richards, Theodore William (*1868-1928*), was an American chemist who gained worldwide fame for his extremely accurate determinations of atomic weights (relative atomic masses). For this work he was awarded the 1914 Nobel Prize in Chemistry.

Richards was born in Germantown, Pennsylvania, on 31 January 1868, the son of a painter father and author mother. He received his early education at home, and then in 1882 he went to Haverford College, initially to study astronomy but changing to chemistry because of his poor eyesight. He graduated three years later and went to Harvard, where he gained his chemistry degree in 1886. He remained at Harvard to do research under Josiah Cooke (1827-1894), who set him the task of testing Prout's hypothesis (that all atomic weights are whole numbers) by determining the ratio by weight of hydrogen to oxygen in water. He was awarded his PhD for this work in 1888. Richards was then granted a travelling fellowship and he visited several European universities, where he came into contact with such influential chemists as Viktor Meyer and Lord Rayleigh. He became an Instructor in Chemistry at Harvard in 1894; he also met Friedrich Wilhelm Ostwald and Hermann Walther Nernst on a second trip to Europe in 1895. He declined the offer of a professorship at Göttingen University in 1901 in favour of the position of Professor of Chemistry at Harvard, which he retained for the rest of his career. He died in Cambridge, Massachusetts, on 2 April 1928.

Richards' determinations of atomic weights were based on painstakingly precise quantitative measurements, for which he introduced various new analytical techniques. He devised a method of keeping samples sealed and dry so that they could not absorb moisture before or during weighing. For accurately determining the endpoint in silver nitrate titrations (which usually depend on the first appearance or last disappearance of a precipitate) he invented the nephelometer, a means of comparing the turbidity of two solutions. He made accurate atomic weight measurements for 25 elements; his co-workers determined 40 more, improving on the "standard" values obtained by Jean Stas in the 1860s. In 1913 he detected differences in the atomic weights of ordinary lead and samples extracted from uranium minerals (which had arisen by radioactive decay) – one of the first convincing demonstrations of the uranium decay series and confirming Frederick Soddy's prediction of the existence of isotopes. It also revealed a germ of truth in Prout's defunct hypothesis. Richards also investigated the physical properties of the elements, such as atomic volumes and the compressibilities of non-metallic solid elements.

Robertson, Robert (*1869-1949*), was a British chemist whose main work was concerned with improvements to explosives for military use.

Robertson was born in Cupar, Fife, on 17 April 1869. He was educated at the Madras Academy and St Andrews University, where he took extra lessons in chemistry in order to gain a BSc degree as well as his MA. After a short period as assistant to the Glasgow City Analyst he obtained a post at the Royal Gunpowder Factory at Waltham Abbey, Essex (at the time when the military were changing from black powder to smokeless nitro compounds as propellant explosives for cartridges). The results of his work on nitrocellulose were incorporated into his doctorial thesis of 1897. He was put in charge of the main laboratory in 1900 and seven years later was appointed Superintending Chemist in the Research Department at Woolwich Arsenal. The work of the Department was increased tremendously during World War I, and in 1918 Robertson was knighted for his services. On the retirement of James Dobbie in 1921 Robertson became the Government Chemist, a position he held until he left government service in 1936 and went to work at the Davy Faraday Laboratory at the Royal Institution. At the outbreak of World War II in 1939 his offer to return to the Explosives Research Department at Woolwich was gladly accepted; he went back to the Royal Institution in 1945. He died in London on 28 April 1949.

From 1900, at Waltham Abbey, Robertson studied the Will test for measuring the rate of decomposition of gun-cotton (nitrocellulose) and in 1906 introduced an improved method of purifying nitrocellulose. As a result of his work the propellant in British ammunition was changed from Mark I Cordite to the more stable MD Cordite. His appointment to Woolwich in 1907 coincided with the analysis of defects in British ammunition that had been revealed during the South African War. The new explosive tetryl (trinitrophenylmethylnitramine) was developed, as were detonators for Lyddite (picric aid, 2,4,6-trinitrophenol); work began on the use of TNT (trinitrotoluene, 2,4,6-trinitromethylbenzene) as a high explosive for military purposes. Robertson continued his investigations into the stability of Cordite, showing that the presence of impurities can be a critical factor (and leading to improved methods of manufacture and storage).

At the beginning of World War I the British government became concerned about supplies of TNT, which was limited by the availability of toluene (methylbenzene), manufactured from coal tar or extracted from Borneo petroleum, which is rich in aromatic hydrocarbons. Robertson's researchers solved the considerable problems of "diluting" TNT with ammonium nitrate to produce a new high explosive, Amatol.

After Robertson became the Government Chemist in 1921 he welcomed the opportunity to carry out research unfettered by the secrecy that had inevitable surrounded his previous work. Many of his investigations were carried out to assist the Department of State. These included the carriage of dangerous goods by sea, the determination of sulphur dioxide and nitrous gases in the atmosphere, the elimination of sulphur dioxide from the gaseous products of combustion at power stations, the possible effects on health of tetraethyl lead additives to petrol, the determination of iodine in biological substances, and the preservation of photographic reproductions of valuable documents. He was also concerned with the determination of carbon monoxide and nitrous oxide (dinitrogen monoxide) and in an investigation of the extraction of minerals (such as potassium chloride and bromine) from the waters of the Dead Sea.

Later work on infra-red absorption spectroscopy in collaboration with J.J. Fox and E.S. Hiscocks greatly stimulated research in this field. Robertson's improvements in spectrographic equipment also permitted his study of diamonds from various natural sources.

Robinson, Robert (*1886-1975*), was a British organic chemist who, during a long and distinguished career, made many contributions to the science. Among the many and wide-ranging topics he researched were alkaloids, steroids and aromatic compounds in general. For his work on alkaloids and other biologically significant sub-

stances derived from plants he was awarded the 1947 Nobel Prize in Chemistry.

Robinson was born in Bufford, near Chesterfield, on 13 September 1886, the son of a local manufacturer. It was intended that he should enter his father's business but after graduating in chemistry from Manchester University in 1905, he embarked on an academic career. He obtained his doctorate in 1912 and then held the Chair in Organic Chemistry successively at Sydney University (1912-1915), Liverpool (1915-1920), St Andrews (1920-1922), Manchester (1922-1929) and Oxford (1929-1955). He was knighted in 1939. In 1957 he founded the influential journal *Tetrahedron*. He died in Great Missenden on 8 February 1975.

Robinson's life-long interest in plant materials began with his study of the colourless material brazilin and its red oxidation product brazilein, which occur in brazilwood. This work led on to an investigation of anthocyanins (red and blue plant pigments) and anthoxanthins (yellow and brown pigments). He studied their composition and synthesis, and related their structure to their colour. His first synthesis in this area, that of callistephin chloride, was carried out in 1928.

In his research on alkaloids he worked out the structure of morphine in 1925 and by 1946 he had devised methods of synthesizing strychnine and brucine - using only "classical" techniques of organic chemistry - and so influenced all structural studies of natural compounds that contain nitrogen. He also suggested biosynthetic pathways for the production of such substances in nature. While not always correct, these proposals confirmed his relentless and convincing assertion that, since nature involves chemical substances, it must obey laws recognized by chemists.

He began research on steroids at Oxford and his studies of the sex hormones, bile acids and sterols were fundamental to the general methods now used to investigate compounds of this type. His discovery that certain synthetic steroids could produce the same biological effects as do the natural oestrogenic sex hormones led to the preparation of stilboestrol, hexoestrol and dienoestrol, paving the way for pharmaceutical applications such as the contraceptive "pill" and treatments for infertility in women.

In 1942, spurred on by the needs of World War II, Robinson investigated the properties of the antibiotic penicillin and elucidated its structure. His methods were later applied to structural investigations of other antibiotics.

Throughout his career Robinson was also concerned with the theoretical aspects of organic chemistry. He began by studying the polarization (electron displacement) in the carbon-chlorine

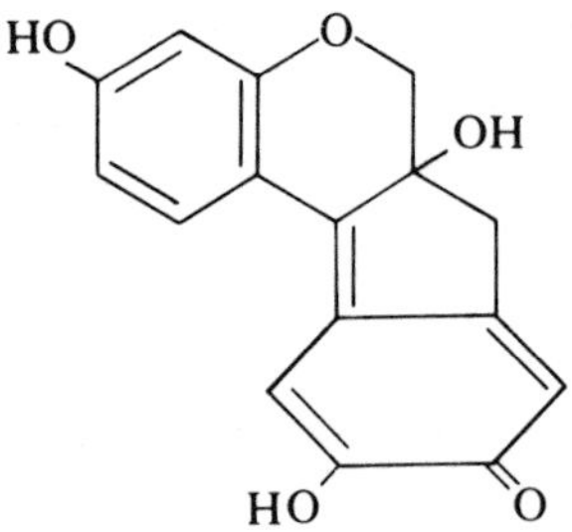

brazilein
(red plant pigment)

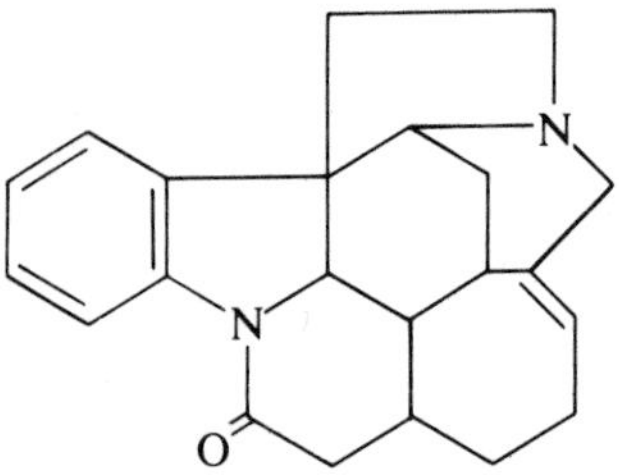

strychnine
(alkaloid)

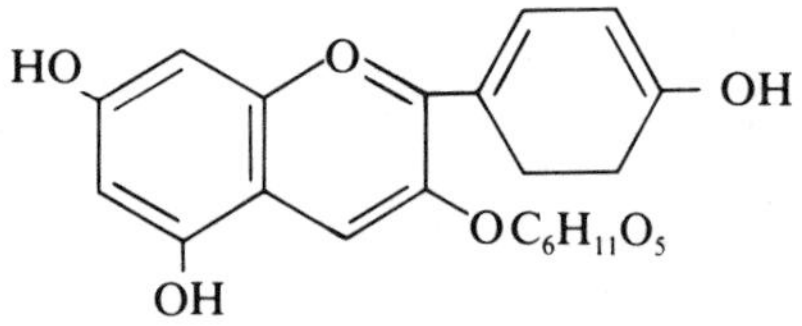

callistephin
(anthocyanin-type flower pigment)

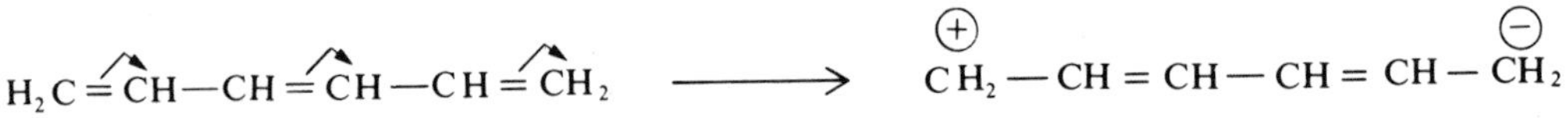

$$H_2C = CH-CH = CH-CH = CH_2 \longrightarrow \overset{\oplus}{C}H_2 - CH = CH - CH = CH - \overset{\ominus}{C}H_2$$

Polarization in a conjugate system.

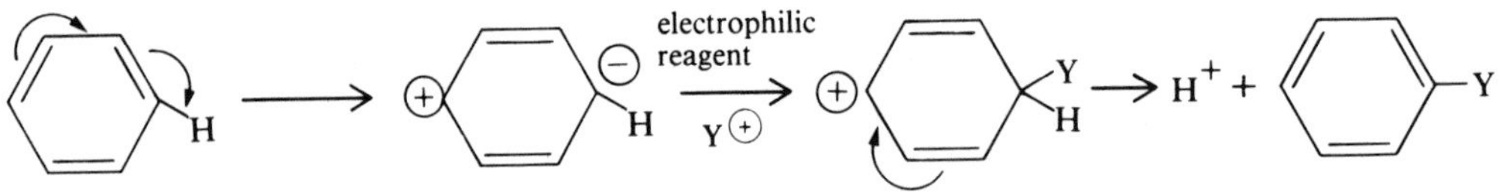

electrophilic
reagent

$$\longrightarrow \quad \overset{\ominus}{\bigcirc} \quad \overset{Y\oplus}{\longrightarrow} \quad \bigcirc \overset{Y}{\underset{H}{}} \longrightarrow H^+ + \bigcirc Y$$

Reaction in an aromatic compound.

covalent bond and progressed to investigating conjugate systems, which involve alternate single and double carbon–carbon bonds. He showed that if the original double bonds are sufficiently weak, pairs of electrons can transfer from them to intervening single bonds along the chain. He introduced the method of representing such electron transfer by means of "curly arrows" on a structural formula. This theory is particularly relevant to aromatic compounds, in which the presence of a substituent in the benzene ring influences further substitution and how fast such substitution takes place. Robinson worked out the theory that governs this important type of reaction and how it is affected by the nature of the reagent concerned: electrophilic reagents attack preferentially positions in which there are an excess of electrons, nucleophilic reagents attack electron-deficient positions.

In his later years Robinson became interested in the composition of petroleum and how it originated on Earth, and he suggested routes by which petroleum products may have originated from amino acids and other chemicals present before life as we know it began.

He was Professor of Organic Chemistry at St Andrews in the early 1920s at the same time as his predecessor, Walter Norman Haworth, was at Durham University. Between them they led contemporary work on an extremely wide range of natural products (Haworth's main area of study was carbohydrates) and many of today's structural and synthetic methods are based on their pioneering work.

S

Sabatier, Paul (*1854–1941*), was a French organic chemist who investigated the actions of catalysts in gaseous reactions. He is particularly remembered for his work, with his assistant Abbé Jean-Baptiste Senderens (1856–1936), on catalytic

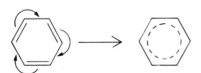

Robinson formula for benzene.

hydrogenation of gaseous hydrocarbons. For this research he shared the 1912 Nobel Prize in Chemistry with François Grignard.

Sabatier was born in Carcassone, Aude, on 5 November 1854, and was educated locally and at Toulouse. In 1887 he entered the École Normale Supérieure in Paris, graduating three years later. He spent the next year as a teacher at the Lycée in Nîmes and then became assistant to Pierre Berthelot at the Collège de France. He was awarded his doctorate in 1880 for a thesis on metallic sulphides. After a year of further research in Bordeaux he went in 1882 to Toulouse, where he was appointed Assistant Professor of Physics, later transferring to a similar position in chemistry. When in 1884 he reached the age of 30, the minimum for a full professorial appointment, he was duly installed as Professor of Chemistry. He retained the position for the rest of his long life, declining the offers of the Chairs at the Sorbonne and the Collège de France in 1907. He died in Toulouse on 14 August 1941.

Sabatier's early researches were concerned with physical and inorganic chemistry. Among many investigations he correlated the colours of chromates and dichromates with their acidity, and was the first chemist to prepare pure hydrogen sulphide. In 1895 he became interested in the role of metal catalysts through the work on nickel carbonyl by Ludwig Mond. In the following year he produced somewhat similar compounds by the action of the oxides of nitrogen on finely divided metals.

In his next series of experiments, begun in 1897, he studied the reaction of ethylene (ethene) and hydrogen on a heated oxide of nickel. He found that the reduced nickel formed catalysed the hydrogenated acetylene (ethyne) in a similar way, and converted benzene vapour into cyclohexane. With his assistant Sanderens he extended the method to the hydrogenation of other unsaturated and aromatic compounds. He also synthesized methane by the hydrogenation of carbon monoxide using a catalyst of finely divided nickel. He later showed that at higher temperatures the same catalysts can be used for dehydrogenation, enabling him to prepare aldehydes from primary alcohols and ketones from secondary alcohols.

Sabatier later explored the use of oxide catalysts, such as manganese oxide, silica and alumina. Different catalysts often gave different products from the same starting material. Alumina, for example, produced olefins (alkenes) with primary alcohols, which yielded aldehydes with a copper catalyst.

He explained the action of catalysts in terms of "chemisorption", the formation of unstable compounds on the surface of a catalyst. He cited an improvement in catalytic action with decreasing particle size and the poisoning effect of impurities as evidence for this theory. He also postulated that the suitability of a catalyst for a particular reaction depends on its chemical nature as well as its physical properties (because different catalysts give different products from the same reaction).

Later catalytic hydrogenation was applied to liquid hydrocarbons by Vladimir Ipatieff, leading to applications such as the hardening of natural oils by hydrogenation and the development of the margarine and modified fats industry.

Saint-Claire Deville, Henri Étienne (1818–1881),

was a French inorganic chemist who worked on high-temperature reactions and is best known for being the first to extract metallic aluminium in any quantity.

Saint-Claire Deville was born on 11 March 1818 in the West Indies on the island of St Thomas, Virgin Islands (then Danish territory), the son of the French Consul there. He was educated in France and studied science and medicine, learning chemistry under Louis Thénard (1777–1857). He gained his medical degree in 1844 and a year later he became Dean and Professor of Chemistry at the newly established University of Besançon. In 1851 he followed Antoine Balard (an ex-assistant of Thénard) as Professor of Chemistry at the École Normale in Paris and took over from Jean Baptiste Dumas at the Sorbonne in 1859. He died in Boulogne-sur-Seine on 1 July 1881.

In 1827 Friedrich Wöhler had isolated small quantities of impure aluminium from its compounds by the drastic method of heating them with metallic potassium. Saint-Claire Deville substituted the safer sodium. He first had to prepare sufficient sodium metal but by 1855 he had obtained enough aluminium to cast a block weighing 7 kg. The process was put into commercial production and within four years the price of aluminium had fallen to one-hundredth of its former level. (It was to decrease even further 27 years later when Charles Hall in the United States and Paul Héroult in France independently discovered the method for electrolytically extracting aluminium.)

Saint-Claire Deville also investigated the chemistry and metallurgy of magnesium and platinum, made the first preparation of a monobasic acid "anhydride" when he made nitrogen pentoxide (dinitrogen pentoxide, N_2O_5), and studied the high-temperature decomposition of gases into atomic species. In organic chemistry he made one of the first extractions of toluene (methylbenzene; phenylmethane), in 1841, while experimenting with tolu balsam and turpentine oil.

Sanger, Frederick (*1918–*), is a British biochemist who worked out the sequence of amino acids in various protein molecules. For his work on insulin he was awarded the 1958 Nobel Prize in Chemistry. For determining the sequence in the DNA molecule, he became one of the very few scientists to receive two Nobel Prizes when in 1980 he shared the Chemistry Prize with the American molecular biologists Paul Berg (1926–) and Walter Gilbert (1932–).

Sanger was born in Rendcomb, Gloucestershire, on 13 August 1918, the son of a doctor. He was educated at Bryanston School and at St John's College, Cambridge, from which he graduated in 1939. He then began research in biochemistry, gaining his PhD in 1943 and working as a Research Fellow until 1951. In that year he joined the staff of the Medical Research Council and since 1961 has been Head of the Protein Chemistry Division of the Council's Molecular Biology Laboratory at Cambridge.

Beginning in 1943 Sanger and his co-workers determined the sequence of 51 amino acids in the insulin molecule, using samples of the hormone obtained from cattle pancreases. By 1945 he had discovered a compound, Sanger's reagent (2,4-dinitrofluorobenzene), which attaches itself to amino acids and so he was able to break the protein chain into smaller pieces and analyse them using paper chromatography. By 1953 he had determined the sequence for insulin, and even shown that there are small but precise differences between the structures of insulins from different animals. He also worked out the structures of other proteins, including various enzymes.

In the late 1950s Sanger turned his attention to the sequence of the nucleotides that link to form the protein strands in the nucleic acids RNA and DNA. The double-helix structure of DNA had been determined by Francis Crick and James Watson in 1953, and within the next few years other workers had identified enzymes that can join nucleotides to form chains and others that can cut existing chains into shorter pieces. Sanger used the chain-cutting type of enzyme to identify nucleotides and their order along the chain, and in 1977 he and his co-workers announced that they had established the sequence of the more than 5,000 nucleotides along a strand of RNA from the bacterial virus called R17. They later worked out the order for mitochondrial DNA, which has approximately 17,000 nucleotides.

Scheele, Karl William (*1742–1786*), was a Swedish chemist, arguably the greatest of the eighteenth century. He anticipated or independently duplicated much of the pioneering research that was taking place at that time in France and England, and isolated many elements and compounds for the first time. Among his many discoveries were the elements oxygen and chlorine, although delays in publishing his findings often resulted in other chemists being credited with priority. He never took a university appointment, doing all his research privately while practising as an apothecary.

Scheele was born on 9 December 1742 in Stralsund, Pomerania, at a time when it belonged to Sweden (it was more often German territory and is now in East Germany), the seventh of eleven children of a poor family. He received little education until 1756 when at the age of 14 he became an apothecary's apprentice at Göteborg (Gothenburg) and learned basic chemistry through reading, observation and experiment. He progressed from position to position, moving to Malmö in 1765, Stockholm in 1768 and finally Uppsala in 1770, still practising as an apothecary. In Uppsala he met Johann Gahn (1745–1818) who introduced him to the famous Swedish chemist Torbern Bergman (1735–1784), who in turn recognized Scheele's talents and publicized his work. In 1775 Scheele moved to run a pharmacy in the small town of Köping on Lake Mälaren in Västmanland, where he remained for the rest of his life despite opportunities to take academic posts in Germany and England, and an offer from the Prussian Frederick II to serve as court chemist. Also in 1775 he was elected to the Swedish Royal Academy of Sciences, a unique honour for a mere apothecary's assistant. As Scheele approached middle age his health – never good – began to fail and he suffered from rheumatic pain and possibly the toxic effects of some of the chemicals he experimented with; long hours of intense work also took their toll. He married on his deathbed and died, at Köping, aged only 43 on 21 May 1786.

Scheele's research did not appear to follow a particular plan, and he seems to have experimented in an indiscriminate way with the various substances he came across in his work. But even if his approach lacked system, he nevertheless made a huge contribution to chemistry. His original discoveries alone make a formidable list, and the major ones are worth itemizing; ignoring chronology and combining inorganic discoveries with those in organic chemistry, they include the following:

arsenic acid	chlorine
arsine	copper arsenite
barium oxide (baryta)	(Scheele's green)
benzoic acid	gallic acid
calcium tungstate	glycerol
(scheelite)	hydrogen cyanide and
citric acid	hydrocyanic acid

hydrogen fluoride
hydrogen sulphide
lactic acid
malic acid
manganese and
   manganates
molybdic acid
nitrogen

oxalic acid
oxygen
permanganates
silicon tetrafluoride
tartaric acid
tungstic acid
uric acid

Undoubtedly the most significant of these are chlorine and oxygen. Scheele also discovered that the action of light modifies certain silver salts (50 years before they were first used in photographic emulsions). He isolated phosphorus from calcined bones and obtained uric acid from bladder stones. He studied molybdenum disulphide (molybdenite, MoS_2) and showed how it differs from graphite (molybdena) – both substances have similar physical properties and both are still used as solid lubricants. He demonstrated the different oxidation states of copper, iron and mercury.

Scheele's discovery of oxygen began – as did Antoine Lavoisier's – with a study of air. He first showed that air consists of two main gases, one of which ("fire air") supports combustion and one of which ("vitiated air" or "foul air") does not. In various experiments on air he consumed the "fire air" component to leave the "vitiated air" – Scheele was a staunch believer in the phlogiston theory of combustion. Then in a series of preparations during 1771 and 1772 he produced "fire air" (oxygen) in various ways chemically: by the action of heat on saltpetre (potassium nitrate) or manganese dioxide; by heating heavy metal nitrates (and absorbing the nitrogen dioxide also formed in lime water), and by heating mercuric (mercury(II)) oxide (Joseph Priestley's method of 1774). He showed that oxygen is involved in the respiration of plants and fish. Scheele described these experiments in his only major publication, *A Chemical Treatise on Air and Fire*, written in about 1773 in German, the language that Scheele normally used in speech and writing. The introduction to the book was written by Bergman, who took so long to provide his text that publication did not actually take place until 1777. This was three years after Priestley had prepared oxygen and published his findings, and credit is now usually given to him. (The name oxygen – meaning "acid producer" – was coined by Lavoisier, who mistakenly thought that all acids contain oxygen.)

Following on from this work Scheele isolated chlorine in 1774 by heating manganese dioxide with hydrochloric acid, but he thought that it was a compound of oxygen – "dephlogisticated muriatic (hydrochloric) acid" – and did not recognize it as an element. This distinction was made a generation later by Humphry Davy who through his work on hydrochloric acid also discredited Lavoisier's theory that all acids contain oxygen.

Schoenheimer, Rudolf (*1898–1941*), was a German-born American biochemist who first used isotopes as tracers to study biochemical processes.

Schoenheimer was born in Berlin on 10 May 1898. After graduating in medicine from the University of Berlin in 1923, he spent the next ten years in various teaching posts in Germany. Then in 1933 he emigrated to the United States, where he became a member of the College of Physicians and Surgeons at the University of Columbia. He committed suicide in New York City on 11 September 1941, while still at the peak of his career.

Schoenheimer introduced the use of isotopic tracers into biochemical research in 1935. Deuterium (heavy hydrogen) had become fairly easily available for the first time, thanks mainly to the work of Harold Urey, who was also at Columbia. Schoenheimer used deuterium to replace some of the hydrogen atoms in molecules of fat which he fed to laboratory animals. It had previously been thought that fat stored in body tissues remained immobile, just lying there until starvation demanded its use. On analysing the body fat of rats four days after feeding them deuterated fat, he found that about half of the labelled fat was being stored – i.e., ingested fat was being stored by the animal and stored fat was being used. There was a rapid turnover and the body constituents, far from being static, were changing constantly and dynamically.

Urey prepared the isotope nitrogen-15 at about this time, and Schoenheimer soon used it to label amino acids, the basic building blocks of proteins. In a series of experiments, in which he fed a single labelled amino acid to an animal, he traced the fate of that acid in the animal's proteins. He again found that there is constant action, even though the overall movement may be small, with the protein molecules constantly changing and shifting. He had thus established that many component molecules of the body are continually being broken down and built up. He summarized his findings in his book *The Dynamical State of Bodily Constituents*.

After World War II researchers such as Melvin Calvin went on to use radioactive isotopes, such as those of carbon and phosphorus, to investigate biochemical pathways in living animals. These techniques were developed from the pioneering work of Rudolf Schoenheimer.

Seaborg, Glenn Theodore (*1912–*), is an American physical chemist who is best known for his researches on the synthetic transuranium elements. For this work he shared the 1951 Nobel Prize in Chemistry with his co-worker Edwin McMillan (1907–).

Seaborg was born in Ishpeming, Michigan, on 19 April 1912 into a Swedish immigrant family; his father was a machinist. When he was ten years old the family moved to Los Angeles, where he graduated from High School in 1929. He went to study literature at the University of California but changed to science and graduated in 1934. He then went to study at Berkeley under Gilbert Lewis, gaining his PhD in 1937 and spending a further two years as one of Lewis' research associates; he became an instructor in 1939. During part of World War II Seaborg was a section chief at the metallurgical laboratory at Chicago University, where much of the early work on the atomic bomb was carried out. After the war, in 1945, he was appointed Professor of Chemistry and Associate Director of the Radiation Laboratory at Berkeley, becoming Chancellor of the campus from 1958 until 1961. In that year he was made Chairman of the US Atomic Energy Commission and held the appointment for ten years. He returned to the Lawrence Berkeley Laboratory in 1971.

The transuranium elements are all those that lie beyond uranium in the Periodic Table, i.e. all elements of atomic number higher than 92. They constitute the majority of the Actinides (elements 89 to 103), so-called by analogy with the Lanthanides or Rare Earths. They are all radioactive and none occurs to any appreciable extent in nature; they are synthesized by transmutation reactions. Of the 13 synthetic transuranium elements known in the early 1970s, Seaborg was involved in the identification of nine: plutonium (atomic number 94), americium (95), curium (96), berkelium (97), californium (98), einsteinium (99), fermium (100), mendelevium (101) and nobelium (102).

Seaborg and his collaborators discovered plutonium in 1940 by bombarding uranium with deuterons in the Berkeley 60-inch cyclotron. The first isotope found had a mass of 238, and the more important (because it is fissionable) plutonium-239 was discovered in 1941 (by neutron bombardment of U-238). In 1944 helium bombardment of Pu-239 yielded Cm-242, the first isotope of curium. Americium, as Am-241, was identified by Seaborg and others at the Metallurgical Laboratory in 1944–1945. Helium bombardment of Am-241 at Berkeley produced berkelium (as Bk-249) at the end of 1949, and three months later the minute amount of Cm-242 available was also bombarded with helium to form californium-245. Einsteinium was identified in the debris from the "Mike" nuclear explosion staged by the Los Alamos Scientific Laboratory in November 1952, where it arose from the radioactive decay of heavy uranium isotopes. Another decay product, fermium-255, was discovered in January 1953. Helium bombardment was again used in early 1955 to create mendelevium-256 out of Es-253. Nobelium, element 102, was discovered in spring 1957 at the Nobel Institute of Physics in Stockholm.

As Chairman of the Atomic Energy Commission Seaborg encouraged the rapid growth of the American nuclear power industry. Many of the isotopes he discovered have also found other uses in industry and in medicine.

Semenov, Nikolay Nikolayevich (*1896–*), is a Soviet physical chemist who studied chemical chain reactions, particularly branched-chain reactions which can accelerate with explosive velocity. For his work in this area he shared the 1956 Nobel Prize in Chemistry (the first Soviet Nobel prizewinner) with the British physical chemist Cyril Hinshelwood.

Semanov was born on 3 April 1896 in Saratov, Russia (now in the Russian SFSR). In 1913 he went to the University of Petrograd (now Leningrad) and despite the turmoil of World War I and the Russian Revolution he graduated in 1917. During the next 25 years he held appointments at various research establishments in Leningrad (as Petrograd had become). From 1920 to 1931 he worked at the A.F. Ioff Physical-Technical Institute, becoming a professor in 1928. From 1931 he directed the Institute of Chemical Physics at the Soviet Academy of Sciences before moving to the Moscow State University in 1944, where he became Head of the Department of Chemical Kinetics.

In 1913 Max Bodenstein introduced the idea of a chain reaction to account for various gas reactions. Semenov developed this theory in the 1920s and showed how certain violently explosive reactions – particularly those involving combustion – can be explained in terms of branching chains: each branch in the reaction pathway starts more than one new reaction, thus rapidly accelerating the overall effect. He summarized his results in 1934 in his influential book *Chemical Kinetics and Chain Reactions* (English translation, 1935).

Semenov also played an important part in resisting narrow interpretations of Marxist-Leninism in its application to chemistry. In this way he helped to keep Soviet chemistry progressing and avoiding unprofitable detours such as that caused by Lysenkoism in biology.

Sidgewick, Nevil Vincent (*1873–1952*), was a British theoretical chemist best known for his contributions to the theory of valency and chemical bonding.

Sidgewick was born in Oxford on 8 May 1873 into a talented family. His father and two of his uncles were faculty members at the universities of Oxford and Cambridge, and another uncle was Archbishop of Canterbury. He was educated at home until he was 12 years old, when he went to Rugby School to study both classics and science. His application for a classical scholarship to Oxford in 1891 was unsuccessful, but the following year he was offered a scholarship in natural sciences to Christ Church College. His tutor, the physical chemist Vernon Harcourt, was one of the first people to study reaction kinetics in physical chemistry. Sidgewick graduated in natural sciences in 1895 and went on to perform the extraordinary feat of graduating also in classics two years later. After a year as a laboratory demonstrator, he went to Germany in 1899 to study under Georg Bredig in Wilhelm Ostwald's department at Leipzig. He returned to Britain for a while to recover from an illness, then went back to Germany for two years to work under von Pechmann in Tübingen. He was awarded his doctorate in 1901 and became a Fellow at Lincoln College, Oxford. He remained at Oxford for the rest of his life, becoming a Reader in 1924 and a supernumerary Professor of Chemistry in 1935, although he did travel abroad frequently in the 1920s and 1930s. He died in Oxford on 15 March 1952.

Sidgewick did little significant work before 1920, spending much of his time teaching and writing his successful and readable book *The Organic Chemistry of Nitrogen* (1910). On a sea voyage to attend a meeting of the British Association in Australia in 1914 he travelled with Ernest Rutherford, and the two scientists forged a lifelong friendship. Sidgewick became absorbed by the study of atomic structure and its importance in chemical bonding, although this work was interrupted by World War I, during which he acted as an unpaid consultant to the Department of Explosive Supplies.

After the war Sidgewick's productivity increased. He extended Gilbert Lewis' ideas on electron sharing to explain the bonding in coordination compounds (complexes) then being studied by Alfred Werner, with a convincing account of the significance of the dative bond. Together with his students he demonstrated the existence of and wide-ranging importance of the hydrogen bond. He summarized this stage of his work in *The Electronic Theory of Valency* (1927).

In 1931 Sidgewick made his first visit to the United States as Baker non-resident lecturer in chemistry at Cornell University. He assimilated the new advances in theoretical chemistry such as Erwin Schrödinger's wave mechanics and Werner Heisenberg's uncertainty principle. He also took notice of the new techniques for the determination of physical forces between atoms and the structures of molecules. These advances were surveyed in his 1933 book called *Some Physical Properties of the Covalent Link in Chemistry*.

World War II sharply reduced the extent of Sidgewick's overseas travel and the amount of academic research being carried out throughout the world. This permitted him to catch up on the vast amount of literature that had been published in the 1930s and to produce another monumental, definitive two-volume work, *The Chemical Elements and their Compounds*, which was published in 1950. Once more he demonstrated his ability to consider and systematize the diverse work of other people and to provide an insight into a broad subject area for the benefit of scholars and students.

Soddy, Frederick (*1877–1956*), was a British chemist who was responsible for major advances in the early developments of radiochemistry, being mainly concerned with radioactive decay and the study of isotopes. For this work he was awarded the 1921 Nobel Prize in Chemistry. He was also a controversial character, holding firm views – with which very few people agreed – about the relationship between science and society.

Soddy was born in Eastbourne, Sussex, on 2 September 1877, the youngest of seven children. He attended Eastbourne College and became much influenced by his chemistry teacher R.E. Hughes, with whom he published his first scientific paper in 1894 (at the age of only 17). He went to the University College of Wales at Aberystwyth for a year after leaving school, winning an open scholarship to Merton College, Oxford, in 1895. He graduated with top honours three years later; William Ramsay was his external examiner. He spent two years doing research at Oxford, but achieved little of note.

Then in 1900, at the age of 23, he applied for but was refused the Professorship of Chemistry at the University of Toronto in Canada. He followed this up with a personal visit, which did little to promote his case, and visited Montreal on his way back to Britain. There he was offered a junior demonstrator's post at McGill University, in Ernest Rutherford's department. Soddy accepted and formed a fruitful partnership with Rutherford.

Soddy returned to London in 1902 and worked with Ramsay at University College. In 1904 he went on a brief tour of Australia as an extension lecturer for London University and on his return took up an appointment as a lecturer in physical chemistry at the University of Aberdeen, where he developed the theory of isotopes. In 1914 he was promoted to the Chair in Chemistry, finally achieving the professorship he had striven for since 1900. During World War I he was involved in research aimed at contributing to the war effort.

Then in 1919 he was appointed Dr Lees Professor of Chemistry at Oxford, in the hope that he would build up an active research group in the field of radiochemistry. Soddy was instrumental in modernizing the laboratories and active in teaching, but he did little further original research. His interests turned increasingly to political and economic theory and, although he wrote prolifically on these subjects, he was unable to raise the interest or enthusiasm of others, particularly the university authorities. He retired early, in 1936, soon after the death of his wife, which affected him deeply. He travelled in Asia for a while, visiting thorium mines. During and after World War II he became increasingly concerned with how atomic energy was being put to use (as early as 1906 he had realized the tremendous potential in the energy locked up in uranium), and tried to arouse a more active sense of social responsibility among his fellow scientists to halt what he saw as a dangerous trend in the development of human society. He died in Brighton on 22 September 1956.

Soddy's first major scientific contribution, the disintegration law, was the result of his work with Rutherford in Montreal. They postulated that radioactive decay is an atomic or sub-atomic process, a theory that was immediately accepted. They proposed that there are two radioactive decay series beginning with uranium and thorium and both ending in lead, in which a parent radioactive element breaks down into a daughter element by emitting either an alpha-particle or a beta-particle. Soon a third series, beginning with actinium, was also demonstrated; it too ends in lead. (A fourth series beginning with neptunium and ending with bismuth was not discovered until after World War II.)

Soddy and Rutherford also predicted that helium should be a decay product of radium, a fact that Soddy and Ramsay proved spectrographically in 1903. In 1911 Soddy published his alpha-ray rule, which states that the emission of an alpha-particle from an element results in a reduction of two in the atomic number (Russel's beta-ray rule holds that the emission of a beta-particle causes an increase of one in atomic number). The displacement law, introduced by Soddy in 1913, combines these rules and explains the changes in atomic mass and atomic number for all the radioactive intermediates in the decay processes.

Also in 1913 Soddy and Theodore Richards independently demonstrated the occurrence of different forms of lead in minerals from different sources. These could be added to the plethora of chemically inseparable "elements" which displayed different radioactive properties – there were far more new elements than there were available places in the Periodic Table. Then Soddy brought order to chaos by proposing that the inseparable elements are in fact identical substances (in the chemical sense), differing only in atomic weight (relative atomic mass) but having the same atomic number. He named the multiple forms isotopes, meaning *same place* because they occupied the same place in the Periodic Table. It is now known that all the elements above bismuth (atomic number 83) have at least one radioactive isotope, as do many lighter elements (such as phosphorus). The existence of isotopes also explained anomalies in atomic weight determinations, which were often found to be caused by the existence of isotopes in elements that were neither radioactive nor formed by radioactive decay.

Soddy was a scientist of great foresight; he predicted the use of isotopes in geological dating and the possibility of harnessing the energy of radioactive nuclei. He was capable of thorough experimentation and dramatic interpretation of the results, having the courage to propose unifying hypotheses. The change in interest that overtook him in middle life was a consequence of what he regarded as the disturbing events that were taking place in the world around him.

Solvay, Ernest (*1838–1922*), was a Belgian industrial chemist who invented the ammonia-soda process, also known as the Solvay process, for making the alkali sodium carbonate.

Solvay was born in Rebecq-Rognon, near Brussels, on 16 April 1838, the son of a salt refiner. He was not a healthy child and had little formal education; by his late teens he was working as a bookkeeper for his father. In his spare time he carried out chemical experiments in a small home laboratory. In 1860 he went to Schaarbeek to work for an uncle who directed a gasworks, and there learned about the industrial handling of ammonia both as a gas and as an aqueous solution. Within a year he had discovered and patented the reactions that are the basis of the Solvay process. Trial production at a small plant in Schaarbeek failed; for two years Solvay knew he had the chemistry right, but could not solve the considerable problems of chemical engineering (problems that had nearly bankrupted several other industrial chemists earlier in the century). With the help of his brother Alfred he raised the necessary capital to build a full-scale works at Couillet, which was opened in 1863. By the summer of 1866 the process was well established, and a second factory was opened at Dombasle in 1873.

Solvay was as much a businessman as a chemist and he soon realized that there was more money to be made from granting licences to other manufacturers than there was in making soda. (One of the licensees was the Brunner Mond Company in Cheshire, England, whose alkali division was later to become part of Imperial Chemical Industries.) Throughout the world, the Solvay process replaced the old Leblanc process, which required more energy (heat) and produced more obnoxious waste materials, releasing huge quantities of hydrogen chloride into the atmosphere. Towards the end of the nineteenth century the price of soda fell dramatically. Solvay became a very rich man and entered politics, becoming a member of the Belgian Senate and a Minister of State. He endowed many educational institutions throughout Belgium. During World War I he helped to organize food distribution. He lived to be 84 years old and died in Brussels on 26 May 1922.

The Solvay process uses as raw materials sodium chloride (common salt), calcium carbonate (limestone) and heat energy; ammonia is also used as a carrier of carbon dioxide, but is theoretically not consumed by the process. First the limestone is heated to yield calcium oxide (lime) and carbon dioxide:

$$CaCO_3 \rightarrow CaO + CO_2$$

The ammonia is dissolved in a solution of sodium chloride (brine), and the ammoniacal brine allowed to trickle down a tower against an upflow of carbon dioxide. The products of the resulting reaction are ammonium chloride (which stays in solution) and sodium bicarbonate (sodium hydrogen carbonate), which forms a precipitate:

$$NH_3(aq) + CO_2(g) + NaCl(aq) + H_2O$$
$$\rightarrow NaHCO_3(s) + NH_4Cl(aq)$$

Finally the sodium bicarbonate is filtered off and heated to yield sodium carbonate:

$$2NaHCO_3 \rightarrow Na_2CO_3 + CO_2 + H_2O$$

Ammonia is recovered from the filtrate by reacting it with the calcium oxide from the heated limestone, producing calcium chloride as the only waste product. The key technical development is the use of countercurrent carbonating towers, which are usually employed in series to get maximum yield.

Stahl, Georg Ernst (*1660–1734*), was an early German chemist and physician who founded the phlogiston theory of combustion. This theory was one of the great dead-ends of chemistry which was to dominate - and mislead - the science for nearly a century. Nevertheless it was instrumental in stimulating much thought and experiment, and helped to bring about the change from alchemy to chemistry.

Stahl was born in Ansbach, Franconia, on 21 October 1660, the son of a Protestant clergyman. He studied medicine under Georg Wedel (1645–1721) at the University of Jena, where a fellow student was Friedrich Hoffmann (1660–1742); Stahl occupied a teaching post at Jena a year before he gained his medical degree in 1684. He became a physician to the Duke of Sachsen-Weimar in 1687 and seven years later, on the recommendation of Hoffmann, he moved to the new University of Halle as its first Professor of Medicine, where his course included lectures in chemistry. In 1716 he moved again to Berlin to become personal physician to King Frederick I of Prussia, a position he retained until his death. He died in Berlin on 14 May 1734.

The phlogiston theory had its beginnings in 1667 in the ideas of Jochim Becher (1635–1681), who thought that combustible substances contain an active principle which he termed *terra pinguis* (fatty earth). Jan van Helmont called the combustible element phlogiston, but Stahl formulated the theory. The phlogiston theory is simple: when a substance is burned or heated it loses phlogiston; reduction of the products of combustion (with, say, charcoal) reverses the process and phlogiston is restored. For example, when metallic lead is heated it forms a powdery calx (so the metal must have been a combination of calx and phlogiston). Then when the calx is heated with charcoal, it absorbs phlogiston from the charcoal and becomes metallic lead again. When charcoal is heated on its own, it leaves hardly any ash (calx) and so must be particularly rich in phlogiston.

The theory was the first attempt at a rational explanation for combustion (and what we would term oxidation), and had obvious appeal to the chemists of the time who were familiar with the reduction processes - often using charcoal - associated with the smelting of metals. The first doubts about the phlogiston theory came when chemists began weighing the reactants and products of such reactions. When metals are calcined (oxidized by heating in air) they get heavier - and yet they should *lose* phlogiston and become lighter. Also a calx demonstrably becomes lighter when it is reduced back to metal, instead of getting heavier as it once more takes up phlogiston.

Stahl himself made such quantitative determinations, but accounted for the observations by stating that phlogiston is weightless or can even have negative weight; it might be as insubstantial as "caloric" (heat) and flow from one substance to another. The falsity of these assumptions and of the whole phlogiston theory was finally proved by Antoine Lavoisier in the 1770s with his experiments on combustion (and by the discovery of oxygen by Karl Scheele and Joseph Priestley).

Stas, Jean Servais (*1813–1891*), was a Belgian analytical chemist who is remembered for making the first accurate determinations of atomic weights (relative atomic masses).

Stas was born in Louvain on 21 August 1813. He initially studied medicine, and although he qualified as a doctor he never practised. After graduation he went to Paris as an assistant to Jean Baptiste Dumas, working mainly in organic chemistry. In 1840 he was appointed Professor of Chemistry at the École Royale Militaire in Brussels, and he advised the Belgian government on military topics related to chemistry. In middle age he developed a disorder of the throat, which made it difficult for him to give lectures. He left the Military School in 1869 and three years later he became Commissioner of the Mint, but his liberalist views did not coincide with the monetary policy of the government and he left the post in 1872. He spent the rest of his life in retirement, although he still voiced his anti-clerical opinions and was openly critical of the part played by the Church in education. He died in Brussels in 13 December 1891.

While he was working with Dumas in Paris, Stas helped to re-determine the atomic weights of oxygen and carbon, showing them both to be almost exactly whole numbers (and that of carbon to be 12, not 6 as had previously been assumed). These results gave new support to William Prout's hypothesis of 1815 (that all atomic weights are whole numbers). Beginning in the mid-1850s, Stas spent more than ten years measuring accurately the atomic weights of many elements, using oxygen = 16 as a standard. He gradually found more and more elements with non-integral atomic weights, and finally he discredited completely Prout's hypothesis. His results provided the foundation for the work of Dmitri Mendeleyev and others on the periodic system, and remained the standards of accuracy until they were superseded 50 years later by the determinations of the American chemist Theodore Richards.

Staudinger, Hermann (*1881–1965*), was a German organic chemist who pioneered polymer chem-

istry. His contribution was finally recognized when he was 72 years old with the award of the 1953 Nobel Prize in Chemistry.

Staudinger was born in Worms, Hesse, on 23 March 1881, the son of a physician. His university education included studies at Halle (where he obtained his PhD in 1903), Munich and Darmstadt. He taught in Strasbourg, at the Technische Hochschule in Karlsruhe from 1908 to 1912 as Professor of Organic Chemistry in association with Fritz Haber, and as Professor of General Chemistry at Zurich from 1912 to 1926, where he succeeded Richard Willstätter. In 1926 he was appointed Professor of Chemistry at the University of Freiburg-im-Breisgau, where he remained until he retired in 1951. In 1940 he was made Director of the Chemical Laboratory and Research Institute for Macromolecular Chemistry. After 1951 his department at Freiburg became the State Research Institute for Macromolecular Chemistry and he was made an emeritus professor. He died in Freiburg on 8 September 1965.

Staudinger's first research, under D. Vorländer at Halle, concerned the malonic esters of unsaturated compounds. Then in 1907 under Johannes Thiele (1865-1918) at Strasbourg he made the unexpected discovery of the highly reactive ketenes, the substances that give the aroma to coffee.

It was in Karlsruhe that Staudinger began the work for which he was to become famous, the study of the nature of polymers. He devised a new and simple synthesis of isoprene (the monomer for the production of the synthetic rubber polyisoprene) and with C.L. Lautenschläger prepared polyoxymethylenes. All this work was done at a time when most chemists thought that polymers were disorderly conglomerates of small molecules. From 1926 Staudinger put forward the view – not immediately accepted – that polymers are giant molecules held together with ordinary chemical bonds. To give credence to the theory he made chemical changes to polymers that left their molecular weights almost unchanged; for example he hydrogenated rubber to produce a saturated hydrocarbon polymer.

To measure the high molecular weights of polymers he devised a relationship, now known as Staudinger's law, between the viscosity of polymer solutions and their molecular weight. Viscometry is still widely used for this purpose in the plastics industry and in polymer research. Eventually X-ray crystallography was to confirm some of his predictions about the structures of polymers, particularly the long-chain molecular strands common to many of them.

Although Straudinger had no conception of how information is stored in nucleic acids or how such information is transferred to proteins, in 1936 he made a remarkably accurate prediction: "Every gene macromolecule possesses a quite different structural plan which determines its function in life." In his book *Macromolekulare Chemie und Biologie* (1947) he anticipated the molecular biology of the future.

Stock, Alfred (*1876-1946*), was a German inorganic chemist best known for his preparations of the hydrides of boron (called boranes) and for his campaign for better safety measures in the use of mercury in chemistry and industry.

Stock was born in Danzig (now Gdańsk, Poland) on 16 July 1876. He studied chemistry at the University of Berlin under Emil Fischer, and after receiving his doctorate became Fischer's assistant. In 1909 he moved to Breslau, to join the staff of the Inorganic Chemistry Institute. After a period at the Kaiser Wilhelm (later Max Planck) Institute in Berlin, he became Director of the Chemistry Department at the Technische Hochschule in Karlsruhe in 1926, where he remained until he retired ten years later. He died in Karlsruhe on 12 August 1946.

Stock began studying the boron hydrides – general formula B_xH_y – in 1909 at Breslau. By treating magnesium boride (Mg_3B_2) with an acid he produced B_4H_{10}. He went on to prepare several other hydrides and in 1912 devised a high-vacuum method for separating mixtures of them. Many contain more hydrogen atoms in their molecules than ordinary valency rules will allow, at least if normal covalent bonds are involved. Their structures were finally worked out by Linus Pauling, Hugh Christopher Longuet-Higgins, William Lipscomb and others. In the 1960s boron hydrides found their first practical use as additives to rocket fuels.

In 1921 Stock prepared beryllium (scarcely known before in the metallic state) by electrolysing a fused mixture of sodium and beryllium fluorides. This successful extraction method made beryllium available for industrial use, as in special alloys and glasses and for making windows in X-ray tubes. By 1923 Stock was suffering from chronic mercury poisoning caused by prolonged exposure to the liquid metal and its vapour – a fate previously shared by many other chemists. He introduced sensitive tests for mercury and devised improved laboratory techniques for dealing with the metal to minimize the risk of accidental poisoning.

Svedberg, Theodor (*1884-1971*), was a Swedish physical chemist who invented the ultracentrifuge to facilitate his work on colloids. For his contributions to colloid chemistry he was awarded the 1926 Nobel Prize in Chemistry.

Svedberg was born in Fleräng, near Gävle, on 30 August 1884. As a secondary school student he became interested in natural sciences (particularly botany), and resolved to study chemistry in the belief that many of the unsolved problems in biology could be explained as chemical phenomena. He entered Uppsala University in 1904 and remained associated with it for the rest of his life. He obtained a BSc in 1905 and his PhD two years later, with a thesis on his studies of colloidal solutions. In 1912 he was appointed to the first Chair in Physical Chemistry in Sweden. When he retired from this post in 1949, he became Head of the new Gustav Werner Institute of Nuclear Chemistry. He resigned in 1967 and died in Örebro on 25 February 1971.

Colloid chemistry was Svedberg's interest for 20 years. By 1903 he was already influenced by the work of Hermann Nernst, Richard Zsigmondy and, particularly, Georg Bredig. Bredig had devised a method of preparing metal sols by passing an electric arc between metal electrodes submerged in a liquid. Svedberg used alternating current with an induction coil having its spark gap in a liquid. In this way he prepared a number of new organosols from more than 30 metals, which were more finely dispersed and much less contaminated than Bredig's. Also the method was reproducible, so that such sols could be used for quantitative analyses in physico-chemical studies. Using an ultramicroscope, he studied the Brownian motion of particles in these sols and correlated the observations with the effects of temperature, viscosity and the nature of the original solvent. These experiments confirmed the theories of Albert Einstein about Brownian motion.

Svedberg also had a continuing interest in radioactive processes and, with D. Stronholm, experimented with isomorphic co-precipitation of various radioactive substances. He discovered that thorium-X crystallizes with lead and barium salts (but not with others), anticipating Frederick Soddy's demonstration of the existence of isotopes. By about 1923 Svedberg had also investigated a totally different subject, the chemistry involved in the formation of latent images in photographic emulsions.

In 1924 Svedberg constructed the first ultracentrifuge, a development which made a timely and significant contribution to the study of large molecules. Its ability to sort particles by weight can reveal the presence of contaminants in a sample of a new protein, or distinguish between various long-chain polymers in substances such as cellulose and other natural polymers. His other researches in the 1930s confirmed his view that these substances consist of well defined uniform molecules.

During World War II the Swedish government asked Svedberg to investigate methods of producing synthetic rubber (at that time, polychloroprene). This research led to the establishment of a small manufacturing plant in the north of Sweden. He also studied other synthetic polymers, introducing electron microscopy to study natural and regenerated cellulose, X-ray diffraction techniques to investigate cellulose fibres, and electron diffraction to analyse colloidal micelles and crystallites.

In the late 1930s Svedberg's interest in radiochemistry prompted a need to increase the capacity for making radioactive isotopes. Finance from the Swedish industrialist Gustaf Werner was used to build a large cyclotron, founding the Gustaf Werner Institute of Nuclear Chemistry.

After his official retirement in 1949, Svedberg became the head of the institute and recruited the staff. One group worked on the biological and medical applications of the cyclotron, while another group investigated the effects of radiation on macromolecules, together with problems in radiochemistry and radiation physics.

Synge, Richard Lawrence Millington (*1914–*), is a British biochemist who has carried out research into methods of isolating and analysing proteins and related substances. He is best known for the work on paper chromatography he did with Archer Martin, for which they shared the 1952 Nobel Prize in Chemistry.

Synge was born in Liverpool on 28 October 1914, the son of a stockbroker. He attended Winchester School from 1928 to 1933 and then went to Trinity College, Cambridge, graduating in 1936; he gained his PhD five years later. He went to work as a biochemist at the Wool Industries Research Association in Leeds, and then in 1943 moved to the Lister Institute of Preventive Medicine in London. In 1948 he was put in charge of protein chemistry at the Rowett Research Institute in Aberdeen. He spent the year 1958–1959 with the New Zealand Department of Agriculture at its Ruakura Animal Research Station. Since 1967 he had been employed as a biochemist at the Food Research Institute of the Agricultural Research Council in Norwich.

In the early 1940s there were crude chromatographic techniques for separating proteins in a reasonably large sample, but no sufficiently refined method existed for the separation of individual amino acids. Martin and Synge, who worked together both at Cambridge and in Leeds, evolved the technique of using porous filter paper worked together both at Cambridge and in Leeds, evolved the technique of using porous filter paper

in chromatography. A spot of mixed amino-acid solution is placed at the end of a strip of filter paper and allowed to dry. The paper is then dipped in a solvent which either creeps up it by capillary action (ascending chromatography) or down the paper if it hung below the level of the solvent. As the solvent passes the mixture the various amino acids move with it, but at different rates. The filter paper is then dried, and sprayed with a "developer" such as ninhydrin solution. On heating the paper the positions of the amino acids are revealed as dark spots and can be identified by comparing them with the spots produced by known amino acids. Several mixtures can be analysed at once by applying several spots to a wide piece of paper.

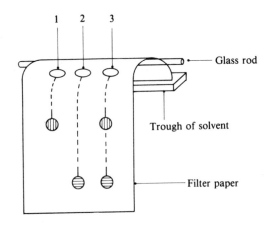

Spot 1 contains substance A

Spot 2 contains substance B

Spot 3 contains a mixture of substances A and B

Descending chromatography.

The technique described is one-dimensional paper (or partition) chromatography, because the solvent spreads the amino acids in only one direction. If the chromatogram is dried, but before being treated with ninhydrin is rotated through 90° and dipped in solvent again (either the same or a different one), the amino acids can be resolved even more clearly. This version is known as two-dimensional chromatography.

Martin and Synge announced their method in 1944 and it became an immediate success, being applied widely and adapted to many experimental problems. It was soon demonstrated that not only the type but the concentration of each amino acid can be determined. Synge was able to work out the exact structure of Gramicidin-S, a simple antibiotic peptide, which led in 1953 to Frederick

Sanger's elucidation of the complete sequence of insulin. Other chromatographic techniques since developed include gas, thin-layer, ion exchange; gel filtration and, most recently, high-pressure liquid chromatography.

Szent-Györgyi, Albert, von Nagyrapolt (*1893-*), is a Hungarian-born American biochemist who studied the physiology of muscle contraction and has carried research into cancer. He is best known, however, for his work on vitamin C, for which he was awarded the 1937 Nobel Prize in Physiology and Medicine.

Szent-Györgyi was born in Budapest on 16 September 1893, into a family of scientists. He completed his early education in Budapest and entered the Medical School at the university there in 1911. During his first year he began research in his uncle's laboratory, and three years later he had published a series of papers on the structure of the vitreous body in the eye. During World War I he served in the Austro-Hungarian army on the Russian and Italian fronts, and was decorated for bravery. But he soon left the army with a (self-inflicted) wound and returned to his studies in Budapest, gaining his medical degree in 1917. During the 1920s he studied at various universities in Germany, the Netherlands, Belgium, the United States and Britain. He obtained his PhD from Cambridge University in 1927 and returned to Hungary in 1937 to the University of Szeged. Szent-Györgyi was active in the anti-Nazi underground movement during World War II and after the war he became Professor of Biochemistry at the University of Budapest. Unhappy with the Soviet regime, in 1947 he emigrated to the United States where he joined the staff of the Marine Biological Laboratories at Woods Hole, Massachusetts. He became an American citizen in 1955. For 32 years he was Director of the National Institute of Muscle Research and since 1975 has been Scientific Director of the National Foundation for Cancer Research.

Szent-Györgyi published his first significant piece of research in 1928 while he was at Cambridge working under Frederick Hopkins. He isolated a substance from the adrenal glands and called it hexuronic acid, because the molecule appeared to contain six carbon atoms. He isolated the same substance from cabbages and oranges, both rich sources of vitamin C. Back in Hungary in the early 1930s he discovered that paprika - a major crop in the locality around Szeged - is an extremely rich source of the acid, which he prepared as pure white crystals and in 1932 proved to be the same as the substance (first discovered in 1907) that prevents scurvy in human beings; his announcement was anticipated

by only two weeks by Charles King. Szent-Györgyi suggested that the acid be called antiscorbutic acid, although it finally became known as ascorbic acid. His work made it possible for Walter Haworth and Paul Karrer to synthesize ascorbic acid (vitamin C), for which they were awarded the 1937 Nobel Prize in Chemistry, the same year in which Szent-Györgyi received the Physiology Prize.

Szent-Györgyi also studied the uptake of oxygen by minced muscle tissue. Left undisturbed, the tissue gradually absorbed less and less oxygen as some substance in it was used up. In 1935 he found that activity was restored by adding any one of four closely related four-carbon compounds: fumaric acid, malic acid, succinic acid, or oxaloacetic acid. This discovery was later used by Hans Krebs in working out the Krebs' (tricarboxylic acid) cycle.

In 1940 Szent-Györgyi isolated two kinds of muscle protein from myosin which, until then, had been thought to be the single basic component of muscle tissue. One was composed of rod-shaped particles and the other was in the form of minute globular beads. The former retained the name myoscin and the latter was called actin; he re-named the combined compound actomyosin. When adenosine triphosphate (ATP) is added to it, a change takes place in the relationship of the two components which results in the contraction of the muscle itself.

During the late 1940s Szent-Györgyi made further investigations into the chemistry of the citrus fruits and extracted the so-called vitamin P from lemon peel. It is a complex compound of three flavonoids whose function is to reduce the fragility of capillary blood vessels. The breakdown of capillaries is a common result of prolonged radiation therapy in cancer patients, and can be countered by administering "vitamin P".

In the 1960s Szent-Györgyi began studying the thymus gland, which had been shown to play a part in the setting up of the body's immunological system. He isolated several compounds from the thymus that seem to be involved in the control of growth. At the National Foundation for Cancer Research he has been carrying out research on the processes of cell division. In 1976, in his eighty-fourth year he published a book entitled *Electronic Biology and Cancer*.

T

Tiselius, Arne Wilhelm Kaurin (*1902–1971*), was a Swedish physical biochemist who discovered the complex nature of proteins in blood serum and developed electrophoresis as a technique for studying proteins. For this work he was awarded the 1948 Nobel Prize in Chemistry.

Tiselius was born in Stockholm on 10 August 1902 into an academic family. His father died when he was only four years old, and the remaining family moved to Göteborg. At school he became interested in chemistry and biology and in 1921 he went to Uppsala University to study under Theodor Svedberg, the leading Swedish physical chemist at that time. In 1924 he gained an MA in chemistry, physics and mathematics and later the same year submitted his doctorial thesis on electrophoresis (the migration of charged colloidal particles in an electric field). He became an assistant to Svedberg and remained associated with the university for the rest of his career. He joined the faculty in 1930 and eight years later he was made Director of the new Institute of Biochemistry. In the year 1934–1935 he worked in the United States at the Frick Chemical Laboratory at Princeton University. He retired in 1968 and died in Stockholm on 29 October 1971.

Tiselius began his research in Svedberg's laboratory in 1925. At that time Svedberg was developing the ultracentrifuge and Tiselius used the new machine to study the sizes and shapes of protein molecules. He observed that many substances that appeared to be homogeneous in the ultracentrifuge could be separated by electrophoresis. This was particularly true of serum proteins, but he changed the direction of his research and did not return to this problem for a number of years.

He then investigated zeolite minerals, which have a unique capacity to exchange their water of crystallization for other substances, the crystal structure remaining intact even after the water has been removed under vacuum. Tiselius studied the optical changes that occur when the dried crystals are re-hydrated. He did this work at Princeton, and while there discussions with such scientists as Karl Landsteiner (1868–1943) and Leonor Michaelis (1875–1949) made him reopen his research into more effective separation methods for biochemistry.

On his return to Uppsala he reconstructed his electrophoresis apparatus and used it to separate the proteins in horse serum. He obtained four protein bands with different mobilities. The fastest moving band corresponded to the serum albumin boundary and the next three revealed for the first time the existence of three electrophoretically different components which he named α-, β- and γ-globulin. He observed the bands optically by measuring changes in their refractive indices.

He also became interested in adsorption methods of separation and devised a new quantitative optical technique for observing the eluate from a chromatography column. In 1943 he showed that "tailing" during elution can be prevented by adding to the eluting solution a substance of higher adsorption affinity than any of the components in the mixture. He called this method displacement analysis. In 1954 he used calcium phosphate in the hydroxyl-apatite form as an adsorbent for proteins with phosphate buffers as eluting agents.

Tiselius made a decisive contribution to chromatography. His characteristic method of working was to take well recognized, qualitative experimental phenomena and establish their theoretical basis. As a result he was able to introduce improvements to existing techniques and to devise new ones. During the last ten years of his life he became very concerned about the possible threat to mankind by the advance of science. He believed that the Nobel Foundation was in a unique position to be able to bring pressure to bear on the most pertinent problems of mankind, and he founded the Nobel Symposia which take place every year in each of the five Prize fields to discuss the social, ethical and other implications of the award-winning work.

Todd, Alexander Robertus, Lord (*1907–   *), is one of the leading chemists of this century and has made outstanding contributions to the study of natural substances. For his work on nucleotides and co-enzymes he was awarded the 1957 Nobel Prize in Chemistry.

Todd was born in Glasgow on 2 October 1907. He was educated at Allan Glen School and at Glasgow University, graduating in 1929. He went to the University of Frankfurt for two years, gaining his doctorate in 1931. From 1931 to 1934 he studied at Oxford University under Robert Robinson. After leaving Oxford he spent two years at the University of Edinburgh as Assistant in Medical Chemistry, and from there he went to the Lister Institute of Preventive Medicine in London. In 1937 he became Reader in Biochemistry at the University of London and a year later was appointed the Sir Samuel Hall Professor of Chemistry and Director of the Chemical Laboratories at Manchester University. He took up the

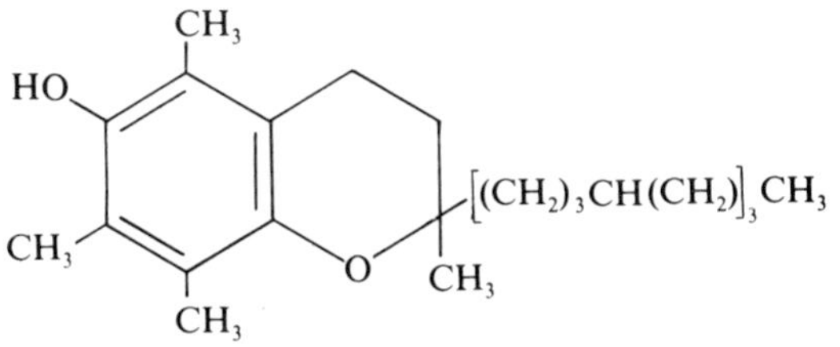

vitamin E
(tocopherol)

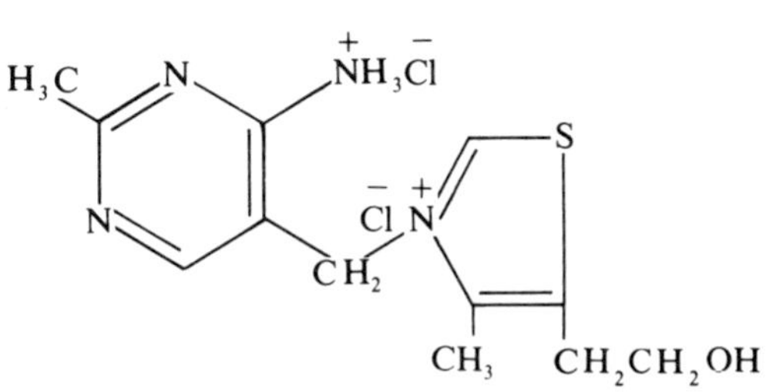

vitamin B$_1$
(thiamin)

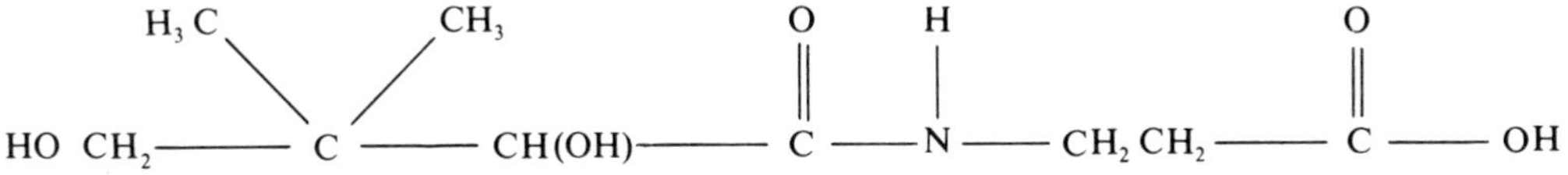

pantothenic acid

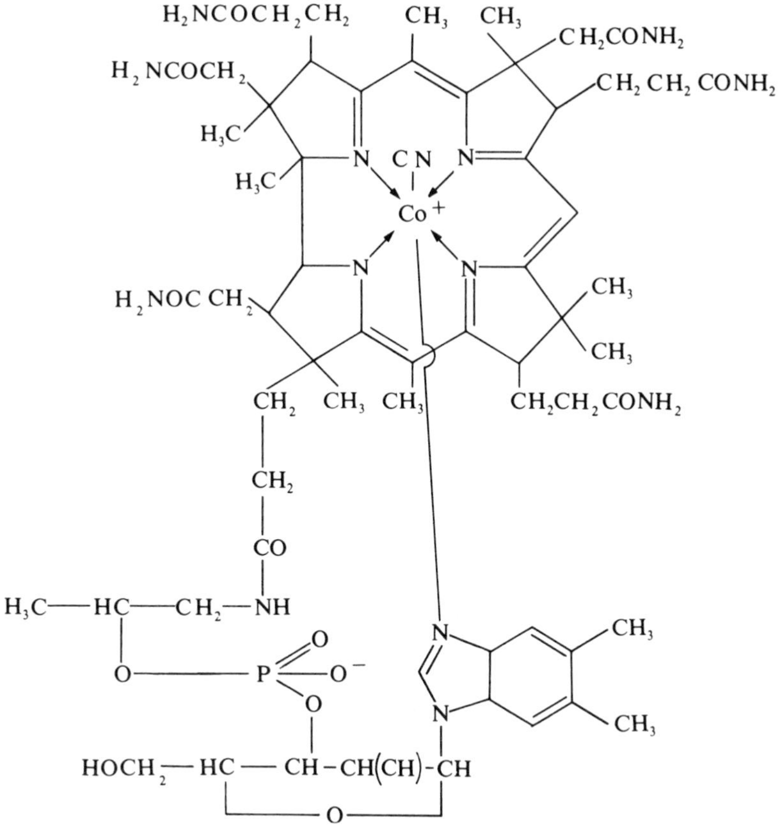

vitamin B$_{12}$
(cyanocobalamin)

Professorship of Organic Chemistry at Cambridge University in 1944, where he remained until he retired in 1971. He was knighted in 1954 and in 1962 was created Baron Todd of Trumpington; he became Master of Christ's College, Cambridge, in 1963.

Todd began his research in 1931 with Robinson, investigating the synthesis of the water-soluble plant pigments called anthocyanins. In 1936 he began his work on vitamins with the synthesis of the water-soluble vitamin B_1 (aneurin or thiamin), deficiency of which causes the disease beriberi. It is essential for the correct metabolism of carbohydrates; its diphosphate forms the co-enzyme of carboxylase. He went on to study pantothenic acid, the so-called "filtrate factor" of B vitamins which has been of therapeutic value in treating certain anaemias. Todd later worked on the structure of the fat-soluble vitamin E (tocopherol), deficiency of which affects fertility or muscular activity. In 1955 Todd and his co-workers, with Dorothy Hodgkin, established the structure of vitamin B_{12} (cyanocobalamin), deficiency of which causes pernicious anaemia.

In the late 1940s and early 1950s Todd also worked on nucleotides – compounds of a base (such as purine), a pentose sugar and phosphoric (V) acid. The term is applied to certain co-enzymes, such as nicotinamide adenine dinucleotide (NAD); to compounds formed by partial hydrolysis of nucleic acids; and to nucleic acids themselves, which can be regarded as polynucleotides. He synthesized adenosine triphosphate (ATP) and adenosine diphosphate (ADP), the key substances in the energy-generating biochemical process in the body. He developed new methods for the synthesis of all the major nucleotides and their related co-enzymes, and established in detail the chemical structures of the nucleic acids, such as DNA (deoxyribonucleic acid), the hereditary material of cell nuclei. During the course of this work, which provided the essential basis for further developments in the fields of genetics and of protein synthesis in living cells, Todd also devised an approach to the synthesis of the nucleic acids themselves.

Travers, Morris William (*1872-1961*), was a British chemist famous for his association with William Ramsay on the discovery of the rare gases.

Travers was born in Kensington, London, on 24 January 1872, the second of four sons of a London physician. He was educated at Ramsgate (1879-1822) and Woking (1882-1885), before going to Blundell's School in Tiverton, Devon, because it had a good chemistry laboratory. He went to University College, London, in 1889 and graduated in chemistry in 1893. He was then advised to study organic chemistry, and in 1894 began research at Nancy University with Alban Haller. But after a few months he returned to London to University College and became a demonstrator under William Ramsay. In 1898 he gained his DSc and became an assistant professor, being promoted to Professor of Chemistry in 1903 as successor to S. Young. He went to Bangalore in 1906 as Director of the new Indian Institute of Scientists.

He returned to Britain at the outbreak of World War I in 1914 and directed the manufacture of glass at Duroglass Limited, Walthamstow, becoming President of the Society of Glass Technology. In 1920 he became involved with high-temperature furnaces and fuel technology, including the gasification of coal. He was made Honorary Professor of Chemistry at Bristol University in 1927, and retired in 1937. During World War II he served as an adviser and consultant to the Explosives Section of the Ministry of Supply. He died at his home in Stroud, Gloucestershire, on 25 August 1961.

Travers returned to London to assist Ramsay in 1894, at the time of the discovery of argon, the first of the rare gases to be found. Then after the discovery of helium a year later, he helped Ramsay to determine the properties of both new gases. They also heated minerals and meteorites in the search for further gases, but found none. Then in 1898 they obtained a large quantity of liquid air and subjected it to fractional distillation. Spectral analysis of the least volatile fraction revealed the presence of krypton. They examined the argon fraction for a constituent of lower boiling point, and discovered neon. Finally xenon, occurring as an even less volatile companion to krypton, was found and identified spectroscopically.

The physicist James Dewar (1842-1923) had succeeded in liquefying hydrogen in 1898, but Travers independently constructed the necessary apparatus. Using liquid hydrogen, Ramsay and Travers were able to condense the neon fraction from air while the helium fraction remained gaseous. In this way they obtained enough neon by mid-1900 to complete their study of the rare gases. Travers continued his researches in cryogenics and made the first accurate temperature measurements of liquid gases. He also helped to build several experimental liquid air plants in Europe.

In his later work at Bristol, Travers studied the thermal decomposition of organic vapours and investigated gas and heterogeneous reactions. In 1956, when he was over 80 years old, he published *Life of Sir William Ramsay*, a biography of his partner of 50 years earlier.

Tswett, Mikhail (*1872-1919*), was an Italian-born Russian scientist who made an extensive study of plant pigments and developed the technique of chromatography to separate them. His name is sometimes also spelled Tsvett.

Tswett was born in Asti, Italy, on 14 May 1872 of a Russian father and an Italian mother. His father was a civil servant in Russia, where his mother had grown up; they had stopped in Asti en route to Switzerland when he was born. His mother died soon afterwards and his father had to leave the baby with a nurse in Lausanne when he returned to Russia. Tswett spent his childhood and youth in Lausanne and Geneva and in 1891 he entered the Department of Mathematics and Physics at Geneva University. He graduated in physical and natural sciences in 1893 and obtained his doctorate three years later. His first scientific publication, of 1894, was on plant anatomy. In 1897 he went to Russia to do research at the Academy of Sciences and the St Petersburg (now Leningrad) Biological Laboratory. His foreign degrees were not acceptable in Russia so he took an MSc degree at Kazan University in 1901. For the next six years he worked at Warsaw University before being offered a teaching appointment at the Warsaw Veterinary Institute. In 1908 he moved to the Warsaw Technical University and obtained a doctorate in botany in 1910. During World War I he organized the work of the Botany Department of the Warsaw Polytechnic Institute, which was evacuated to Moscow and Gorky. In 1917 he was appointed Professor of Botany and Director of the Botanical Gardens at Yuriev University (Estonia), but under threat of German invasion had to move once again to Voronezh. He died there on 26 June 1919.

Tswett opposed the view that green leaves contain only two plant pigments, chlorophyll and xanthophyll. In 1900 he showed that there are two types of chlorophyll, termed chlorophyll a and chlorophyll b, which differ in colour and absorption spectra. He obtained a pure sample of chlorophyll a, but isolating the b type proved to be troublesome. By 1906 he had devised an adsorption method of separating the pigments. He ground up leaves in petroleum ether and let the liquid trickle down a glass tube filled with powdered chalk or alumina. As the mixture seeped downwards, each pigment showed a different degree of readiness to attach itself to the absorbent, and in this way the pigments became separated as different coloured layers in the tube. To get samples of single pigments, he pushed the absorbent out of the tube, cut off the coloured pieces of the column with a knife, and extracted the pigment from each piece separately using a solvent. Tswett called the new technique chromatography from the fact that the result of the analysis was "written in colour" along the length of the adsorbent column. Eventually he found six different pigments. The new method attracted little attention until it was rediscovered by scientists such as Richard Willstätter and Richard Kuhn (1900-1967). By the late 1940s it had become one of the most versatile methods of chemical analysis, particularly in biochemistry, especially after Archer Martin and Richard Synge had developed paper chromatography.

U

Urey, Harold Clayton (*1893-1981*), was an American chemist who in 1931 discovered heavy water and deuterium, the isotope of hydrogen of mass 2. For this extremely significant discovery, which was to have a profound effect on future research in chemistry, physics, biology and medicine, he was awarded the 1934 Nobel Prize in Chemistry.

Urey was born in Walkerton, Indiana, on 29 April 1893 and educated at schools in De Kelb County, Kendallville and Walkerton. He graduated from High School in 1911 and worked as a schoolteacher for three years in Indiana and Montana. He went to Montana State University, Missoula, in 1917, gaining his BS degree three years later. During 1918 and 1919 he worked as a research chemist at the Barrett Chemical Company in Philadelphia, where he helped to produce war materials. From 1919 to 1921 he was an Instructor in Chemistry at Montana State University, and went to the University of California in Berkeley, where he developed his interest in physical and mathematical chemistry. He received his PhD in 1923 and during the following year was a Fellow of the American Scandinavian Foundation and attended the Institute of Theoretical Physics at the University of Copenhagen. He studied there under Niels Bohr, who was engaged on his pioneering work on the theory of atomic structure.

After Urey returned to the United States he worked for five years as an Associate in Chemistry at Johns Hopkins University in Baltimore, Maryland. Then from 1929 to 1934 he was Associate Professor of Chemistry at Columbia University, New York City, and was Ernest Kempton Adams Fellow there from 1933 to 1936. He was appointed full Professor of Chemistry in 1934, and from 1939 to 1942 was the Executive Officer of the Chemistry Department. During

World War II he was Director of Research of the Substitute Alloy Materials Laboratories at Columbia, which became part of the Manhattan Project for the development of the atomic bomb. In 1945 Urey became Professor of Chemistry at the Institute of Nuclear Studies at the University of Chicago, and from 1952 to 1958 was Martin A. Ryerson Professor of Chemistry there. In 1958 he was named Professor-at-Large of Chemistry at the University of California in La Jolla; he was also a member of the Space Science Board of the Academy of Sciences. He died in La Jolla on 5 January 1981.

Urey discovered deuterium (heavy hydrogen, symbol D) in 1931 with F.G. Brickwedde and G.M. Murphy. He predicted that it would be possible to separate hydrogen from HD (whose molecules contain one hydrogen atom and one deuterium atom) by the distillation of liquid hydrogen, taking advantage of the difference in their vapour pressures. In heavy water, D_2O, both hydrogen atoms of normal water (H_2O) are replaced by deuterium atoms. Two years after its discovery by Urey, the American chemist Gilbert Newton obtained nearly pure heavy water by fractional electrolysis of water. Today it is manufactured by a process that involves isotopic chemical exchange between hydrogen sulphide and water. Its chief use is as a moderator to slow down fast neutrons in a nuclear reactor.

Urey was one of the first to calculate thermodynamic properties from spectroscopic data, particularly the equilibrium constants for exchange reactions between isotopes. He went on to isolate heavy isotopes of carbon, nitrogen, oxygen and sulphur. Urey's group provided the basic information for the separation of the fissionable isotope uranium-235 from the much more common uranium-238 by gaseous diffusion of their fluorides. After World War II he worked on tritium for use in the hydrogen bomb.

The evolution of the Earth is another topic that has exercised Urey's mind. It was traditionally believed a molten Earth had formed by processes similar to those that occur in oil-smelting furnaces. Today there is evidence to suggest that the Earth and other planets were formed by condensation and accumulation from a dust cloud at low temperatures. Urey theorized that the final accumulation of the Earth had occurred at 0°C from small planetary particles containing metallic iron, carbon, iron carbide, titanium nitride and some ferrous (iron(II)) sulphide. He considered that most gases had been lost during the previous high-temperature phase, leaving a primitive atmosphere consisting of hydrogen, ammonia, methane, water vapour, nitrogen and hydrogen sulphide. In 1952 he suggested that some of these

molecules could have united spontaneously to form the basic "building blocks" of life. The iron core of the Earth would have accumulated slowly through geological history from a mixture of metallic iron and silicates, meaning that the Earth was not molten at the time when its materials had accumulated. Urey also contributed to theories about the origin of the Moon, subscribing to the view that it had not formed from the Earth but had a separate origin.

Van der Waals, Johannes Diderik (*1837–1923*), was a Dutch scientist whose theoretical work on gases made an important contribution to chemistry and physics, a fact recognized by the award to him of the 1910 Nobel Prize in Physics. His theories about interatomic forces also added to knowledge about molecular structure and chemical bonding.

Van der Waals was born in Leyden (Leiden), the Netherlands, on 23 November 1837, the son of a carpenter. He began his career as a teacher in primary schools, then entered Leyden University in 1862 to study physics, while at the same time working as secondary school physics teacher, becoming Headmaster of the school at The Hague in 1866. Following on from the work of Rudolf Clausius and other molecular theorists, Van der Waals laid the foundation for most of his future studies in his doctorial thesis of 1873, *"Over de continuiteit van den gasen vloeistoftoestand"* ("On the continuity of the gaseous and liquid states"). It received immediate recognition and was soon translated into other European languages. In 1887 he became Professor of Physics at the new University of Amsterdam (formerly the Amsterdam Athenaeum), and remained there until he retired in 1907; he was succeeded by his son. He died in Amsterdam, after a long illness, on 8 March 1923.

Using fairly simple mathematics, Van der Waals' 1873 thesis explained in molecular terms various phenomena of vapours and liquids that had been observed experimentally by Thomas Andrews and others, especially the existence of critical temperature (above which a gas or vapour cannot be liquefied by pressure alone, no matter how great). The law of corresponding states which Van der Waals developed some years later gave a somewhat better "fit" between the theory and the experimental data and became a useful guide in work on the liquefaction of the so-called permanent gases.

The Van der Waals equation of state attempts to explain the behaviour of real gases, as opposed to the "ideal" or "perfect" gas laws of Robert Boyle and Jacques Charles (or Joseph Gay-Lussac), which combined to give the equation $PV = RT$. It still links pressure (P), volume (V) and absolute temperature (T), but introduces two other constants a and b (R remains the universal gas constant):

$$\left(P + \frac{a}{V^2}\right)(V - b) = RT$$

The term a/V^2 accounts for intermolecular attraction, determined by integrating over an "attraction sphere" that extends round each molecule. The constant b accounts for the non-overlapping of molecules and their finite size. Both constants, a and b, are different for different gases. Van der Waals was also able to work out equations for isotherms (how the volume of a gas or liquid changes with pressure at a particular temperature) and calculate the parameters of the critical point.

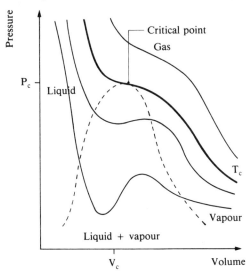

Van der Waals isotherms.

T_c, P_c and V_c are the critical temperature, pressure and volume. In terms of the constants a, b and R from the Van der Waals equation of state, they are given by:

$$T_c = 8a/27bR \qquad P_c = a/27b^2 \qquad V_c = 3b$$

By extension, Van der Waals' results were also applied to other thermodynamic quantities and phenomena, such as the Joule–Thomson effect, saturated vapour pressures, supercooling, and so on.

The cohesive attraction between molecules in a liquid became known as Van der Waals' forces. The same forces are postulated for molecular crystals such as those of graphite and naphthalene. In graphite, for example, normal covalent bonds hold together hexagonal arrays of carbon atoms in planes, which are themselves bonded in parallel "layers" by Van der Waals' forces. A shearing force can fairly readily overcome these weak forces, allowing the planes to slip or slide over each other, which accounts for the existence of well defined cleavage planes in solid graphite and its effectiveness as a lubricant.

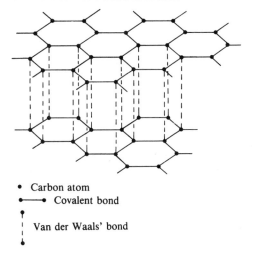

- Carbon atom
- Covalent bond

Van der Waals' bond

Van der Waals' forces in graphite.

Van't Hoff, Jacobus Henricus (*1852–1911*), was a Dutch theoretical chemist who made major contributions to stereochemistry, reaction kinetics, thermodynamics and the theory of solutions. In 1901 he was awarded the first Nobel Prize in Chemistry.

Van't Hoff was born in Rotterdam on 30 August 1852, the son of a doctor. At school he showed great ability at mathematics, but decided to study chemistry at the Polytechnic at Delft. In 1871 he attended the University of Leyden (Leiden), and a year later went to Bonn to study under Friedrich Kekulé, who was unimpressed by his Dutch student so Van't Hoff moved to Paris and worked with Charles Adolphe Wurtz at the École de Médecine. He returned to the Netherlands and obtained his doctorate at Utrecht in 1874, taking up a lectureship in physics at the Veterinary College there two years later. In 1878 he became Professor of Chemistry, Mineralogy and Geology at the University of Amsterdam and stayed there until 1896. In that year he moved to Berlin to become a Professor to the Prussian Academy of

Sciences, with an honorary professorship at Berlin University as well. He remained there until he died, in Berlin, on 1 March 1911.

Van't Hoff had made his first major contribution to chemistry even before he was awarded his doctorate. In 1874 he announced the results of his research into conformational analysis of organic compounds, which hinged on what we would now call the stereochemistry of the carbon atom. He postulated that the four valencies of a carbon atom are directed towards the corners of a regular tetrahedron. This allows it to be asymmetric (connected to four different atoms or groups) in certain compounds, and it is these compounds that exhibit optical activity. Van't Hoff ascribed the ability to rotate the plane of polarized light to the asymmetric carbon atom in the molecule, and showed that optical isomers are left- and right-handed forms (mirror images) of the same molecule. A similar idea was put forward independently in Paris two months later by Joseph le Bel, who had studied under Wurtz at the same time as had Van't Hoff.

Van't Hoff's first ideas about chemical thermodynamics and affinity were published in 1877, and consolidated in his *Études de dynamique chemique* (1884), translated into English in 1886. He applied thermodynamics to chemical equilibria,

is in equilibrium, the system will adjust itself so as to annul, as far as possible, the effect of that change.

In the field of reaction kinetics, Van't Hoff announced his findings at the same time as, but independently of, Cato Guldberg and Peter Waage in 1867. They all developed the fundamental law of reaction kinetics which assumes that, at constant temperature, the rate of any simple chemical reaction is proportional to the product of the concentrations of the various reacting substances – a statement of the law of mass action.

Van't Hoff also introduced the modern concept of chemical affinity as the maximum work obtainable as the result of a reaction, and he showed how it can be calculated from measurements of osmotic pressure, gas pressure, and the electromotive force of reversible galvanic cells. In 1886 he published the results of his study of dilute solutions and showed the analogy between them and gases, because they both obey equations of the type $PV = RT$.

In the 1880s he became friends with Svante Arrhenius. The theories of Van't Hoff on osmotic pressure and those of Friedrich Ostwald on the affinity of acids accorded well with Arrhenius' views on electrolytes and the three scientists worked together to get their new theories

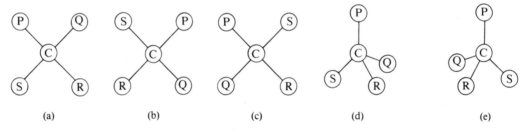

(a) (b) (c) (d) (e)

Van't Hoff introduced the idea of a tetrahedral carbon atom. The three square structures a, b and c are all equivalent (rotating b 90° anti-clockwise gives a, rotating c 180° along the axis P–R also gives a). The tetrahedral structures d and e are mirror images of each other, but one cannot be rotated in any way to make it the same as the other; they represent a pair of (optical) stereoisomers.

developing the principles of chemical kinetics and describing a new method of determining the order of a reaction. He deduced the connection between the equilibrium constant and temperature in the form of an equation known as the Van't Hoff isochor. He generalized it in the form of what he called the principle of mobile equilibrium, which is a special case of Le Châtelier's principle, which he had independently formulated in the same year. It may be stated thus:

If a change occurs in one of the factors (such as temperature or pressure) under which a system

accepted. In 1887 they started the important journal *Zeitschrift für physikalische Chemie*, whose first volume contained the famous paper by Arrhenius on electrolytic dissociation and the fundamental paper of Van't Hoff. He was the first to apply thermodynamics systematically to solutions, although the treatment could have been more generally applicable had he used the thermodynamic system derived by Josiah Gibbs between 1875 and 1879.

After he moved to Berlin in 1896 Van't Hoff studied the behaviour of the various salts from the deposits at Stassfurt.

Vauquelin, Louis Nicolas (*1763-1829*), was a French chemist who worked mainly in the inorganic field analysing minerals and is best known for his discoveries of chromium and bery-llium. He rose from humble birth to be one of the influential scientists of his time.

Vauquelin was born in Saint-André d'Héberôt, Calvados, on 16 May 1763, the son of a Normandy peasant farm labourer. He too worked on the land as a boy until 1777 when he became apprenticed to an apothecary in Rouen. Two years later he moved to Paris and eventually became a laboratory assistant at the Jardin du Roi under Antoine Fourcroy (1755-1809), who recognized Vauquelin's ability, befriended him and began a nine-year collaboration. In 1791 he was made a member of the Academy of Sciences and from that time he helped to edit the journal *Annales de Chemie*, although two years later he left the country for a while during the height of the French Revolution. On his return in 1794 he became Professor of Chemistry at the École des Mines in Paris. He described various analytical techniques in his *Manuel de l'essayeur* (1799), which led in 1802 to his being appointed to the position of Assayer to the Mint. On Fourcroy's death in 1809 he succeeded him as Professor of Chemistry at the University of Paris (and gave a home to Fourcroy's two elderly sisters). He was elected to the Chamber of Deputies in 1828 and died a year later, in his birthplace, on 14 November 1829.

Vauquelin did most of his important work in inorganic chemistry in the late 1790s while he was at the École des Mines. He analysed various minerals, often using specimens supplied by the mineralogist René Haüy (1743-1822). In a Siberian lead mineral called crocolite he discovered chromium in 1797, naming the element from *chromos* because so many of its compounds are brightly coloured. (Martin Klaproth made the same discovery a few months later.) Vauquelin also examined emeralds and the mineral beryl and recognized that they contained another new element which was eventually called beryllium, although at first he called it glucinium because of the sweet taste of some of its salts. The element itself was not isolated until 1828 by Friedrich Wöhler.

In organic chemistry, Vauquelin also made some significant discoveries. In 1806, working with asparagus, he isolated the amino acid aspargine, the first one to be discovered. He also discovered pectin and malic acid in apples, and isolated camphoric acid and quinic acid.

Volhard, Jacob (*1834-1910*), was a German chemist who is best remembered for various significant methods of organic synthesis. He also made contributions to inorganic and analytical chemistry.

Volhard was born at Darmstadt on 4 June 1834. He completed his undergraduate studies and worked under Justus von Liebig at the University of Giessen. He then held professorial appointments at three German universities: Munich (1864-1879), Erlangen (1879-1882)

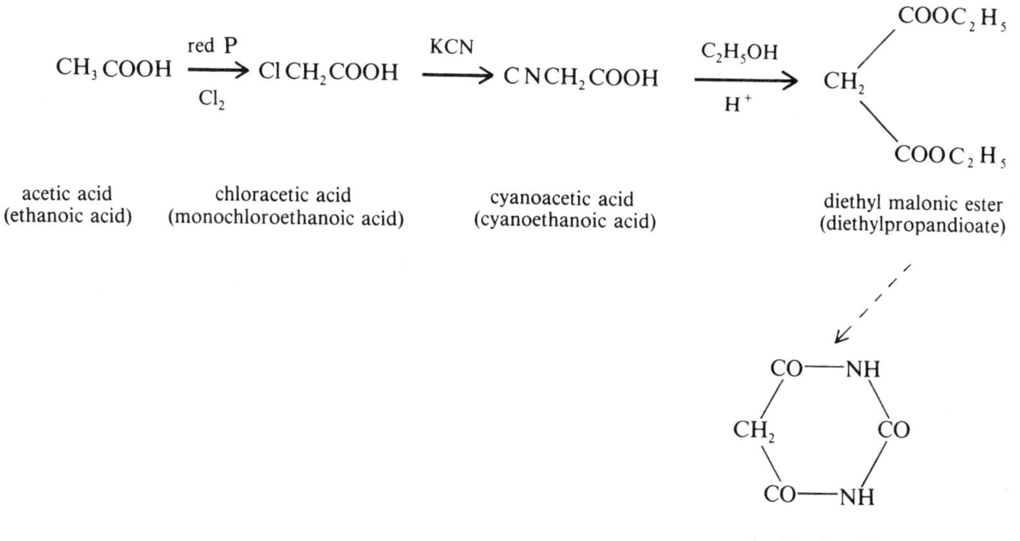

$$CH_3COOH \xrightarrow[Cl_2]{red\ P} ClCH_2COOH \xrightarrow{KCN} CNCH_2COOH \xrightarrow[H^+]{C_2H_5OH} CH_2 \begin{matrix} COOC_2H_5 \\ \\ COOC_2H_5 \end{matrix}$$

| acetic acid (ethanoic acid) | chloracetic acid (monochloroethanoic acid) | cyanoacetic acid (cyanoethanoic acid) | diethyl malonic ester (diethylpropandioate) |

barbituric acid
(5, 5'-diethylbarbituric acid = Veronal)
(5, 5'-dipropylbarbituric acid = Proponal)

and Halle (1882-1910). He remained at Halle until his death on 16 June 1910.

Volhard is best known for his development of a method of quantitatively analysing for an element via silver chloride.

A chloride solution of the element to be determined is titrated with an excess of standard silver nitrate solution, and the residual silver nitrate analysed against standard ammonium (or potassium) thiocyanate solution. Bromides can also be determined using this technique. The end-point is usually detected by using a ferric (iron(III)) indicator, such as iron alum.

During the 1860s Volhard developed methods for the syntheses of the amino acids sarcosine (N-methylaminoethanoic acid) and creatine, and the heterocyclic compound thiophen; he also did research on guanidine and cyanimide. His method of preparing halogenated organic acids has become known as the Hell–Volhard–Zelinsky reaction, in which the acid is treated with chlorine or bromine in the presence of phosphorus (iodine is not sufficiently reactive to take part in the reaction). It is specific for α-hydrogen atoms (generating the α-chloro- or α-bromo-acid) and can therefore be used to detect their presence. The α-hydrogens are replaced selectively, and the reaction can be stopped at the mono- or di-halogen stage by using the correct amount of halogen; with excess halogen, all the α-hydrogens are substituted. The reaction is also useful for syntheses because the substituted halogen atom(s) can easily be replaced by a cyanide group (by treatment with potassium cyanide), which in the presence of an aqueous acid and ethyl alcohol (ethanol) yields the corresponding malonic ester (diethylpropandioate), from which barbiturate drugs can be synthesized.

Von Baeyer, Johann Friedrich Wilhelm Adolf. *See* Baeyer.

Von Liebig, Justus. *See* Liebig.

Von Stradonitz, Friedrich August Kekulé. *See* Kekulé.

Wald, George (*1906–*), is an American biochemist who has investigated the biochemical processes of vision that take place in the retina of the eye. For this work he shared the 1967 Nobel Prize in Physiology and Medicine with the Swedish

physiologist Ragnar Granit (1900–   ) and his fellow-American Haldan Hartline (1903–   ).

Wald was born in New York City on 18 November 1906 and educated at the university there, graduating in 1927. He gained his PhD from Columbia University five years later. From 1932 to 1934 he studied in Europe as a National Research Council fellow, first under Otto Warburg in Berlin and then with Paul Karrer in Zurich, who did the pioneering work on vitamin A. When Wald returned to the United States he joined the staff at Harvard University and remained there for the rest of his career; he was appointed Professor of Biology in 1948. In the 1970s Wald rose to fame outside the area of science for his outspoken comments against United States involvement in the Vietnam War.

Wald began his work on the chemistry of vision in the early 1930s. The key to the process is the pigment called visual purple, or rhodopsin, which occurs in the rods (dim-light receptors) of the retina. In 1933 he discovered that this substance consists of the colourless protein opsin in combination with retinal, a yellow carotenoid compound that is the aldehyde of vitamin A. Rhodopsin molecules are split into these two compounds when they are struck by light, and the enzyme alcohol dehydrogenase then further reduces the retinal to form vitamin A. In the dark the process is reversed and the compounds recombine to restore the rhodopsin to the retinal rods. The process does not work with 100 per cent efficiency and over a period of time some of the retinal is lost. This deficiency has to be made up from the body's stores of vitamin A (which is supplied through the diet), but if the stores are inadequate the visual process in dim light is affected and night blindness results.

Wald and his co-workers went on to investigate how these biochemical changes trigger the electrical activity in the retina's nerves and the optic nerve. In the 1950s they found the retinal pigments that detect red and yellow-green light, and a few years later identified the pigment for blue light. All of these – the three primary colour pigments – are related to vitamin A, and in the 1960s Wald demonstrated that the absence of one or more of them results in colour blindness.

Werner, Alfred (*1866–1919*), was a French-born Swiss chemist who founded the modern theory of co-ordination bonding in molecules (formerly inorganic co-ordination compounds were known by the generic term "complexes"). For this achievement he was awarded the 1913 Nobel Prize in Chemistry.

Werner was born on 12 December 1866 in Mulhouse, Alsace, when it was part of France (four years later at the end of the Franco-Prussian War it became German territory). He was the son of a foundry worker and, despite his parents' French sympathies, received a German education. He began studying chemistry and experimenting on his own when he was 18 years old, and in 1885, while doing military service with the German army, attended lectures at the Karlsruhe Technische Hochschule. A year later he entered the Zurich Polytechnic, graduating with a diploma in chemistry in 1889. He spent 1890 with Pierre Berthelot in Paris, but returned to Zurich the following year, becoming a full professor in 1895. He had to cease work in 1915 because of severe arteriosclerosis, and he died in Zurich on 15 November 1919.

Although Werner is recognized mainly for his discoveries in inorganic chemistry, his first major success was in 1890 in organic chemistry. With his teacher Arthur Hantzsch (1857-1935) he described the structure and stereochemistry of oximes (organic compounds containing the $=N-$OH group, prepared by adding hydroxylamine, NH_2OH, to aldehydes or ketones). He showed that these compounds could exhibit geometrical isomerism in the same way as a compound containing a carbon–carbon double bond, and explained their structures by suggesting that the nitrogen bonds are directed in space tetrahedrally (extending the theories of Jacobus Van't Hoff and Joseph le Bel about the carbon atom).

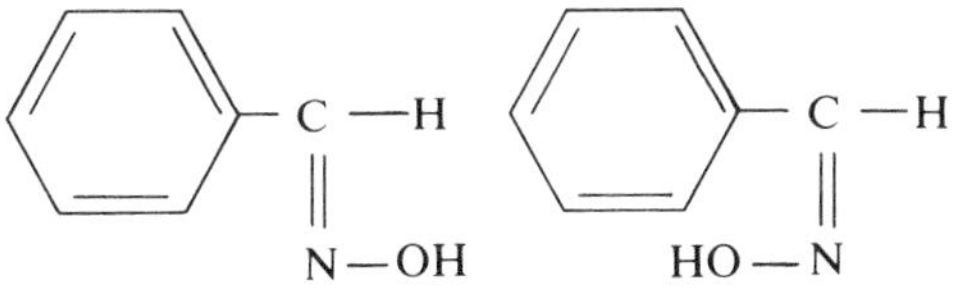

syn

anti

amphi

The two stereoisomers of benzaldoxime.

syn (*trans*)   anti (*cis*)

Werner developed his theory about bonding in co-ordination compounds as part of his Habilitation thesis for obtaining a university teaching position. In addition to ionic and covalent bonds, Werner proposed the existence of a set of co-ordination bonds resulting from an attractive force from the centre of an atom acting uniformly in all directions. The number of groups or "ligands" that can thus be bonded to the central atom depends on its co-ordination number and determines the structure (geometry) of the resulting molecules. Common co-ordination numbers are 4, 6 and 8. Neutral ligands (such as ammonia and water) leave the central atom's ionic charge unchanged; ionic ligands (such as chloride or cyanide ion) alter the central charge accordingly.

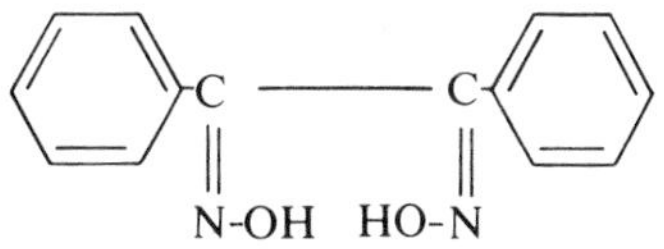

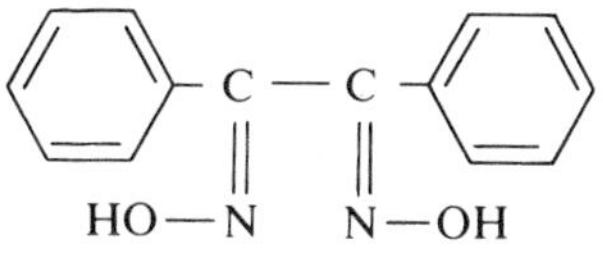

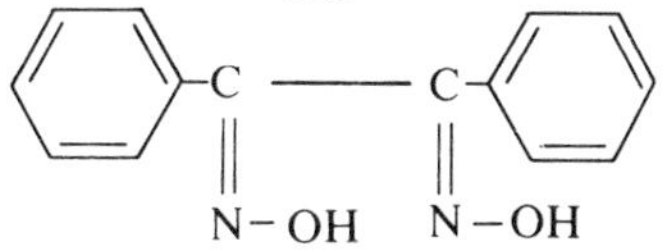

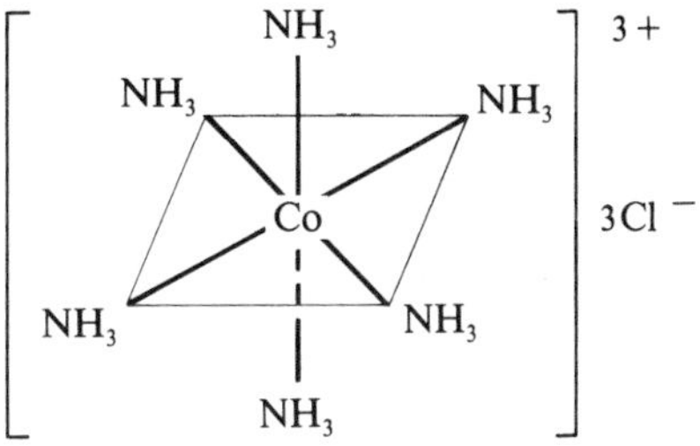

Structure of $Co(NH_3)_6Cl_3$
Co-ordination number 6

A typical Werner-type co-ordination compound is hexamminocobalt(III) chloride, $[Co(NH_3)_6]Cl_3$, in which the cobalt has a co-ordination number of 6 – there are six co-ordinate bonds from it to the six ammonia molecules. The cobalt's valence (oxidation state) of $+3$ is balanced by the three negatively-charged chloride ions. The six ammonias are located at the corners of a regular octahedron. Werner was able to demonstrate the theory experimentally by preparing geometrical isomers of compounds of the type diamminoplatinum chloride, which is square planar in shape:

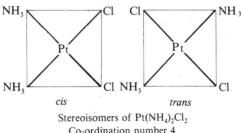

cis   *trans*

Stereoisomers of $Pt(NH_4)_2Cl_2$
Co-ordination number 4

More complicated molecules, particularly those having as a ligand ethylene diamine (1,2-diaminoethene, abbreviated to "en"), exhibit optical isomerism through a pair of mirror-imaged stereoisomers.

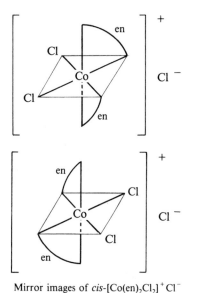

Mirror images of *cis*-[Co(en)₂Cl₂]⁺ Cl⁻
Co-ordination number 6

*A pair of optically isomeric co-ordination
compounds.*

Ethylene diamine is bi-functional and acts as a bridge between a pair of co-ordinate bonds. Some ligands of this type, such as ethylene diamine tetra-acetic acid (EDTA) and its salts, are used to "mop up" metal ions – for example, as antidotes for poisoning by heavy metals such as copper and lead.

Wieland, Heinrich Otto (*1877–1957*), was a German organic chemist, particularly noted for his work on determining the structures of steroids and related compounds. He also studied other natural compounds, such as alkaloids and pterins, and contributed to the investigation of biological oxidation. For his work on steroids, he was awarded the 1927 Nobel Prize in Chemistry.

Wieland was born in Pforzheim on 4 June 1877, the son of a chemist, and educated at the local grammar school. Beginning in 1896 he attended several universities: Munich, Berlin, Stuttgart and finally Munich again under Friedrich Thiele. He obtained his PhD in 1901 and spent most of his career in the chemistry faculty of the University of Munich. He became a lecturer there in 1904, and Senior Lecturer in Organic Chemistry in 1913. During World War I, in 1917, he moved

to the Technische Hochschule (also in Munich) and almost immediately took a year's leave of absence to work on chemical warfare research under Fritz Haber at the Kaiser Wilhelm Institute of Chemistry at Berlin-Dahlem. After the war Wieland returned to his post as professor at the Technische Hochschule, moving to the University of Freiburg in 1921. He finally returned to Munich in 1925 as Professor of Chemistry and Director of the Baeyer Laboratory as successor to Richard Willstätter. He remained there until he retired in 1950, when he was made Emeritus Professor. He died in Munich on 5 August 1957.

Most of Wieland's early work was concerned with organic nitrogen compounds. He investigated the addition of nitrogen oxides to double bonds in compounds such as terpenes (proposing the existence of nitrogen–nitrogen bonds in dimeric nitrogen oxides). In 1909 he published a method for, and described the mechanism whereby, fulminic acid could be prepared from ethyl alcohol (ethanol), nitric acid and mercury. Two years later he gave the first demonstration of the existence of nitrogen free radicals by oxidizing diphenylamine to form tetraarylhydrazine, and decomposing it by heating it in toluene.

After World War I Wieland's interest turned to the chemistry of biologically important compounds. He had begun studying the bile acids as early as 1912, showing that the three newly discovered acids have similar structures related to that of cholesterol (at that time being investigated by Adolf Windaus at Göttingen). The importance of steroids became even more apparent with the realization that vitamin D and the gonadotrophic hormones also belong to this class of compound. Using classical chemical methods Wieland later worked out what he thought was the basic skeleton of a steroid molecule (for which he was awarded the Nobel Prize), but it was found to be incorrect. In 1932 he collaborated with O. Rosenheim (who used X-ray analysis) and H. King to produce the somewhat modified structure which is still accepted today.

Wieland did other work with the bile acids, demonstrating their role in converting fats into water soluble cholic acids (a key process in digestion). He was the first to prepare the carcinogen methylcholanthrene, and went on to study the poisons produced in the skins of some species of toads, which are chemically similar to the bile salts. He also determined the structures of and synthesized many toadstool poisons, such as phalloidine from the deadly *Amanita* fungus. This led him to an investigation of alkaloids from both plant and animal sources. He isolated and determined the structures of the *Lobelia* alkaloids, and made incomplete studies of the structures of

146

strychnine and curare. At the suggestion of one of his students he began research into the composition and synthesis of pterins, the pigments that give the colour to butterflies' wings (and one of which is the precursor of the essential human dietary factor folic acid).

Also after World War I Wieland began work on biological oxidation – the process within living tissues by which food substances such as glucose are converted to carbon dioxide and water with the liberation of energy for metabolism. He held the view that the oxidation was in fact a catalytic dehydrogenation. Using palladium as a catalyst in the absence of oxygen he was able to prove experimentally that this was the case; he also experimented with anaerobic microbial systems. This proposal was in direct opposition to the findings of Otto Warburg (1873-1970), who had shown that biological oxidation was an addition of oxygen moderated by iron-containing enzymes. The controversy sparked a long and lively debate, and stimulated a great deal of research. In the end both workers were shown to be correct; both catalytic dehydrogenation and oxidation steps do occur in the complex biochemical pathway of energy production in tissues.

Wilkinson, Geoffrey. *See* Fischer, Ernst Otto.

Williamson, Alexander William (*1824-1904*), was a British organic chemist who made significant discoveries concerning alcohols and ethers, catalysis, and reversible reactions.

Williamson was born in London on 1 May 1824, of Scottish parents; his father was a clerk in the East India company. A boyhood accident cost him an arm and the sight in one eye; when he was 16 years old his father retired and the family moved to the Continent. Williamson went to Heidelberg University to study medicine, but was persuaded by Leopold Gmelin (1788-1853) to change to chemistry. He then studied under Thomas Graham at University College, London, and Justus von Liebig at Giessen University, from which he gained his PhD in 1846. After a period in Paris studying methematics, he became Professor of Chemistry at University College, London, in 1849, where he remained until he retired in 1887. He died in Haslemere, Surrey, on 6 May 1904.

Beginning in 1850 Williamson studied alcohols and ethers and showed that they are both of the same type – the theory of types was fast gaining ground in organic chemistry. For example, amines are regarded as belonging to the "ammonia type" (NH_3), with one or more of ammonia's hydrogen atoms replaced by organic (alkyl) radicals. Williamson ascribed alcohols and ethers to the "water type". In an alcohol, one

of the hydrogen atoms of water (H_2O or HOH) is replaced by an alkyl radical (R) to give a compound R.OH, such as ethyl alcohol (ethanol) C_2H_5OH. In an ether, both of water's hydrogens are replaced, either by the same alkyl radical (R) or by two different ones (R and R') to give compounds of the form R.O.R, such as diethyl ether (ethoxyethane), $(C_2H_5)_2O$, or of the form R.O.R', such as methyl ethyl ether (methoxyethane), $CH_3OC_2H_5$. Williamson was the first to make "mixed" ethers, with two different alkyl groups, and his method is still known as the Williamson synthesis. It involves treating an alkoxide with an alkyl halide (haloalkane). For example:

$$CH_3I \quad + C_2H_5ONa$$

methyl iodide (iodomethane)   sodium ethoxide

$$\rightarrow CH_3OC_2H_5 + \quad NaI$$

methyl ethyl ether   sodium iodide

The original way of making diethyl ether is by treating ethyl alcohol (ethanol) with sulphuric acid. In 1854 Williamson suggested that the reation takes place in two stages. First the substances react to form ethyl sulphate:

$$2C_2H_5OH + H_2SO_4 \rightarrow (C_2H_5)_2SO_4 + 2H_2O$$

Then the ethyl sulphate reacts with further alcohol to form diethyl ether and liberate sulphuric acid:

$$(C_2H_5)_2SO_4 + 2C_2H_5OH \rightarrow 2(C_2H_5)_2O + H_2SO_4$$

The sulphuric acid turns up unchanged at the end of the reactions but has been essential to them: it has acted as a catalyst. This as the first time that anyone had explained the action of a catalyst in terms of the the formation of an intermediate compound.

The theory of types has now outlived its usefulness. But it was important in the mid-nineteenth century because through the work of Williamson and others it established some sort of order among the confusion that then prevailed in organic chemistry.

Some of the reactions of alcohols and ethers are reversible (i.e., the products of a reaction may recombine to form the reactants), a phenomenon first noted and described by Williamson in the early 1850s. Using modern notation, if P and Q are the reactants and R and S are the products, the reversible reaction is written:

$$P + Q \rightleftharpoons R + S$$

An example is the esterification reaction between ethyl alcohol (ethanol) and acetic acid (ethanoic acid) to form ethyl acetate (ethanoate):

$$C_2H_5OH + CH_3COOH \rightleftharpoons CH_3COOC_2H_5 + H_2O$$

If the rate of the forward reaction is the same as that of the reverse reaction, all four compounds (P, Q, R and S) coexist and the system is said to be in dynamic equilibrium (a term also introduced by Williamson).

Willstätter, Richard (*1872–1942*), was a German organic chemist, best known for his investigations of alkaloids and plant pigments, such as chlorophyll, for which he was awarded the 1915 Nobel Prize in Chemistry.

Willstätter was born in Karlsruhe on 13 August 1872, the son of a textile merchant. He studied chemistry at the Munich Technische Hochschule under Johann von Baeyer, and after graduation worked under A. Einhorn (1857–1917) and was awarded his doctorate in 1894 for a thesis on the structure of cocaine. He worked as Baeyer's assistant for several years, and then in 1905 became a professor at the Technische Hochschule in Zurich. From 1912 to 1916 he was Director of the chemistry section of the Kaiser Wilhelm Institute at Berlin-Dahlem, but his work was interrupted by World War I and at the request of Fritz Haber he turned his attention to the design of an effective gas mask. In 1916 he succeeded Baeyer as a full professor at Munich, but resigned in 1925 because of mounting anti-Semitism. He continued working privately – supervising over the telephone some research at the university. At the start of World War II in 1939 he finally left Germany and went to live in exile in Switzerland. He died in Locarno on 3 August 1942.

Willstätter's first research work was on alkaloids. Following his doctorial study of cocaine in 1894, he went on to investigate tropine and atropine, and by 1898 had determined their structures and syntheses. From the pomegranate alkaloid pseudo pelletierine he prepared cyclo-octatetraene, an eight-carbon ring compound with alternate single and double bonds, analagous to benzene.

pseudopelletierene   cyclo-octatetraene

He also worked on quinones, and by following William Perkin's method of oxidizing aniline (phenylamine) with chromic acid determined the structure of the dyestuff aniline black.

Willstätter then began his research into blood pigments and plant pigments. He showed that chlorophyll is not a single homogeneous substance but is made up of four components: two green ones, chlorophyll a ($C_{55}H_{72}O_5N_4Mg$) and chlorophyll b ($C_{55}H_{70}O_6N_4Mg$), and two yellow ones, carotene ($C_{40}H_{56}$) and xanthophyll ($C_{40}H_{56}O_2$). He found that the blue-green chlorophyll a and yellow-green chlorophyll b exist in the ratio of 3:1, and that the ratio of xanthophyll to carotene is 2:1. In order to separate the complex substances he re-developed the technique of chromatography, first used in studies of chlorophyll by Mikhail Tswett in Russia in 1906, at about the same time as Willstätter was doing his work in Switzerland. It came as a surprise that the chlorophylls contain magnesium, later shown to be linked to four pyrrole rings like the iron atom in the haem group of the red blood pigment haemoglobin.

Soon after his return to Germany Willstätter had to abandon his research into plant pigments because during World War I the large quantities of solvents needed for chromatography became unobtainable. After the war he took up the study of enzymes and of catalytic hydrogenation, particularly in the presence of oxygen. He worked on the degradation of cellulose, investigated fermentation and pioneered the use of hydrogels for absorption. He tried to prove, incorrectly, that enzymes are not proteins.

Wittig, Georg (*1897–   *), is a German chemist, best known for his method of synthesizing olefins (alkenes) from carbonyl compounds, a reaction often termed the Wittig synthesis. For this achievement he shared the 1979 Nobel Prize in Chemistry with the British-born American chemist Herbert Brown.

Wittig was born in Berlin on 16 June 1897. He was educated at the Wilhelms-Gymnasium and then at Kassel and Marburg Universities. He was a lecturer at Marburg from 1926 to 1932, and then Head of Department at the Technische Hochschule in Brunswick from 1932 to 1937. He became a Special Professor at the University of Freiburg in 1937, and then from 1944 until 1956 was Professor and Institute Director at Tübingen. He became a professor at Heidelberg in 1956, and remained there until 1967, when he became Emeritus Professor.

In the Wittig reaction, which he first demonstrated in 1954, a carbonyl compound (aldehyde or ketone) reacts with an organic phosphorus compound, an alkylidenetriphenylphosphorane, $(C_6H_5)_3P=CR_2$, where R is a hydrogen atom or an organic radical. The alkylidene group ($=CR_2$) of the reagent reacts with the oxygen atom of the carbonyl group to form a hydrocarbon with a double bond, an olefin (alkene). In general,

$$(C_6H_5)_3P = CR_2 + R'_2CO$$
$$\text{reagent} \qquad\qquad \text{ketone}$$

$$\rightarrow (C_6H_5)_3PO + R'_2C = CR_2$$
$$\qquad\qquad\qquad\qquad \text{alkene}$$

The reaction is widely used in organic synthesis, for example to make squalene (the synthetic precursor of cholesterol) and vitamin D_3.

Wöhler, Friedrich (*1800-1882*), was a German chemist who is generally credited with having carried out the first laboratory synthesis of an organic compound, although his main interest was inorganic chemistry.

Wöhler was born at Eschershein, near Frankfurt-am-Main, on 31 July 1800, the son of a veterinary surgeon in the service of the Crown Prince of Hesse-Kassel. He entered Marburg University in 1820 to study medicine, and after a year transferred to Heidelberg, where he studied in the laboratory of Leopold Gmelin (1788-1853). He gained his medical degree in 1823, but Gmelin had persuaded Wöhler to study chemistry and so he spent the following year in Stockholm with Jöns Berzelius, beginning a life-long association between the two chemists. From 1825 to 1831 he occupied a teaching position in a technical school in Berlin, and from 1831 to 1836 he held a similar post at Kassel. In 1836 he became Professor of Chemistry in the Medical Faculty of Göttingen University, as successor to Friedrich Strohmeyer (1776-1835), and remained there for the rest of his career, making it one of the most prestigious teaching laboratories in Europe. He died in Göttingen on 23 September 1882.

In Wöhler's first research in 1827 he isolated metallic aluminium by heating its chloride with potassium; he then prepared many different aluminium salts. In 1828 he used the same procedure to isolate beryllium. Also in 1828 he carried out the reaction for which he is best known. He heated ammonium thiocyanate - a crystalline, inorganic substance - and converted it to urea (carbamide), an organic substance previously obtained only from natural sources. Until that time there had been a basic misconception in scientific thinking that the chemical changes undergone by substances in living organisms were not governed by the same laws as were inanimate substances; it was thought that these "vital" phenomena could not be described in ordinary chemical or physical terms. This theory gave rise to the original division between inorganic (non-vital) and organic (vital) chemistry, and its supporters were known as vitalists, who maintained that natural products formed by living organisms could never be synthesized by ordinary chemical means. Wöhler's synthesis of urea was a bitter blow to the vitalists and did much to overthrow their doctrine. It involved an isomerization reaction:

$$NH_4OCN \xrightarrow{\text{heat}} O = C \begin{cases} NH_2 \\ NH_2 \end{cases}$$
$$\text{ammonium} \qquad\qquad\qquad \text{urea}$$
$$\text{cyanate} \qquad\qquad\qquad\quad \text{(carbamide)}$$

Wöhler worked with Justus von Liebig in a number of important investigations. In 1830 they proved the polymerism of cyanates and fulminates, and two years later announced a series of studies of benzaldehyde (benzenecarbaldehyde) and the benzoyl (benzenecarboxyl) radical. In 1837 they investigated uric acid and its derivatives. Wöhler also discovered quinone (cyclohexadiene-1,4-dione), hydroquinone or quinol (benzene-1,4-diol) and quinhydrone (a molecular complex composed of equimolar amounts of quinone and hydroquinone).

In the inorganic field Wöhler isolated boron and silicon and prepared silicon nitride and hydride. He prepared phosphorus by the modern method, and discovered calcium carbide and showed that it can be reacted with water to produce acetylene (ethyne):

$$CaC_2 + 2H_2O \rightarrow Ca(OH)_2 + C_2H_2$$
$$\text{Calcium} \qquad\qquad\qquad\qquad\quad \text{acetylene}$$
$$\text{carbide} \qquad\qquad\qquad\qquad\qquad \text{(ethyne)}$$

He demonstrated the analogy between the compounds of carbon and silicon, and just missed being the first to discover vanadium and niobium. He also obtained pure titanium and showed the similarity between this element and carbon and silicon. He published little work after 1845, but concentrated on teaching.

Wollaston, Hyde William (*1766-1828*), was a British chemist and physicist who developed the technique of powder metallurgy and discovered rhodium and palladium, two elements similar to platinum.

Wollaston was born in East Dereham, Norfolk, on 6 August 1766, one of 17 children of an academic family. His father Rev. Francis Wollaston was an amateur astronomer, and his elder brother Francis John Hyde Wollaston became a Professor of Chemistry at Cambridge University. Wollaston was educated at Charterhouse School and at Caius College, Cambridge, from which he graduated in medicine in 1793. He practised as a doctor for seven years and then in 1800 moved to London and devoted the rest of his life to scientific research. He died of a brain tumour on 22 December 1828.

Wollaston initiated the technique of powder metallurgy when working with platinum and trying to get it into a workable, malleable form. Using aqua regia (a mixture of concentrated nitric and hydrochloric acids) he dissolved the platinum from crude platina, a mixed platinum-iridium ore. He then prepared ammonium platinichloride, which he decomposed by heating to yield fine grains of platinum metal. The grains were worked using heat, pressure and hammering to form sheets, which he sold to industrial chemists for making corrosion-resistant vessels; manufacturers of sulphuric acid were willing to pay high prices for such a useful metal. Wollaston kept his method secret, and made £30,000 from selling platinum, much of which he donated to various scientific societies to help to finance their researches.

In 1803, while investigating platinum ores, Wollaston discovered palladium. Within a year he also found rhodium, again a metal with similar properties to platinum.

He was a great supporter of John Dalton's atomic theory and published several papers based on the law of multiple proportions. In 1808 he suggested that a knowledge of the arrangements of atoms in three dimensions would be a great leap forward (although a century was to pass before this became possible). He advocated the use of "equivalents" in quantitative chemical calculations, from which the concept of normality (now superseded by molarity) was developed.

Wollaston also worked in various areas of physics. In optics he suggested the total reflection method for measuring refractivity (later developed by Pulfrich and Abbe) and drew attention to the dark lines (later called Fraunhofer lines) in the solar spectrum. In 1807 he developed the camera lucida, which was to inspire William Fox Talbot to his discoveries in photography. He also invented a reflecting goniometer for accurately measuring the angles of crystals in minerals.

In 1801 Wollaston established the important physical principle that "galvanic" and "frictional" electricity are the same. He also stated that the action in the common voltaic cell is due to the oxidation of the zinc electrode. In early 1821 he reported that there is "a power ... acting circumferentially round the axis of a wire carrying a current" and tried in Humphry Davy's laboratory at the Royal Institution to make a current-carrying wire revolve on its axis. These experiments were unsuccessful and the final demonstration of the effect is now attributed to Michael Faraday. In 1824 the British Weights and Measures Act incorporated the Imperial gallon, equivalent to 10 pounds weight of water as suggested by Wollaston in 1814. (But as a member of a Royal Commission in 1819 Wollaston was instrumental in the rejection of the decimal system of weights and measures.)

Woodward, Robert Burns (*1917-*), is an American organic chemist famous for his syntheses of complex biochemicals. For his outstanding contribution to this area of science he was awarded the 1965 Nobel Prize in Chemistry.

Woodward was born in Boston on 10 April 1917. He went to the Massachusetts Institute of Technology in 1933, while he was still only 16 years old, gaining his BS degree three years later and his PhD a year after that. He went to Harvard in 1938, at the age of 21, and has remained there for the rest of his academic career. He has held various appointments, including Assistant Professor (1944–1946), Associate Professor (1946–1950), full Professor (1950–1953), Morris Loeb Professor (1953–1960) and Donner Professor of Science (1960 onwards). From 1973–1974 he was also Todd Professor of Chemistry and Fellow of Christ's College, Cambridge.

Woodward's first important research was in collaboration with William Doering when in 1944 they achieved a total synthesis of quinine (from simple starting materials). In 1947 he worked out the structure of penicillin and two years later that of strychnine. In the early 1950s he began to synthesize steroids, such as cholesterol and cortisone (1951) and lanosterol (1954). In that same year he synthesized the poisonous alkaloid strychnine and lysergic acid, the basis of the hallucinogenic drug LSD. In 1956 he made reserpine, the first of the tranquillizing drugs, and four years later he prepared chlorophyll. Turning his attention again to antibiotics, he and his co-workers produced a tetracycline in 1962 and cephalosporin C in 1965. In 1971 came the culmination of ten years' work, involving collaboration with Swiss chemists – the synthesis of vitamin B_{12} (cyanocobalamin). Many of these syntheses were among the most complicated ever attempted in organic chemistry, involving many stages that had to be carefully selected for stereospecificity and maximum yield. Yet so well worked out were they that many have become the basis of commercial manufacture of drugs and other useful biochemicals.

Wurtz, Charles Adolphe (*1817–1884*), was a prominent French organic chemist, best known for his synthetic reactions and for discovering ethylamine and ethylene glycol (1,2-ethanediol). His major contribution, however, was the elevation of the standard of organic chemistry research in mid-nineteenth century France to a level that challenged the excellence of the German universities.

Wurtz was born in Wolfisheim, near Strasbourg, on 26 November 1817, the son of a clergyman. Given the choice of studying theology or medicine, he chose the latter as being nearer his real interest, chemistry. He attended the University of Strasbourg and graduated with a medical degree in 1843. He spent a year at Giessen, where he met and studied with Justus von Liebig and August Hofmann. In 1844 he moved to Paris and became an assistant to Jean Baptiste Dumas at the Faculty of Medicine. He later succeeded him as Lecturer in Organic Chemistry (1849), Professor of Organic Chemistry (1853) and Dean of the Faculty of Medicine. In 1874 he accepted the Professorship of Organic Chemistry at the Sorbonne and was able to relinquish the heavy administrative duties of Dean and concentrate on teaching and writing. He also held public office as Mayor of the 7th Arrondissement of Paris and as a Senator. He died in Paris on 12 May 1884.

Wurtz initially worked on the oxides and oxyacids of phosphorus; in 1846 he discovered phosphorus oxychloride ($POCl_3$). He later turned to organic chemistry, at first studying aliphatic amines. In 1849 he made his famous discovery of ethylamine, the first organic derivative of ammonia (whose existence had been predicted by Liebig), and went on to prepare various amines and diamines.

In 1855 Wurtz discovered a method of producing paraffin hydrocarbons (alkanes) using alkyl halides (halogenoalkanes) and sodium in ether. The method was named the Wurtz reaction (sometimes also known as the Wurtz–Fittig reaction) and has subsequently been used to synthesize hydrocarbons as high up the homologous series as $C_{60}H_{122}$. It was adapted by Edward Frankland, who substituted zinc for sodium.

Wurtz discovered ethylene glycol (1,2-ethanediol) in 1856, which led to methods of preparing glycolic acid (hydroxyethanoic acid), choline and other substances. He discovered aldol (3-hydroxybutanal) while investigating the polymerization of acetaldehyde (ethanal), devised a method of making esters from alkyl halides, and in 1867, with Friedrich Kekulé, synthesized phenol from benzene.

Throughout his work in organic chemistry, Wurtz enthusiastically applied the theory of types as propounded by Charles Gerhardt (1816–1856). He was active at a time when chemistry was undergoing great upheavals, and took clear stands on the many issues under debate.

Z

Ziegler, Karl (*1898–1973*), was a German organic chemist famous for his studies of polymers, for which he shared the 1963 Nobel Prize in Chemistry with Giulio Natta.

Ziegler was born at Helsa, near Kassel, on 26 November 1898, the son of a clergyman. He gained his doctorate from Marburg University in 1923 and then held teaching appointments at Frankfurt-am-Main, Heidelberg and Halle. In 1943 he became Director of the Kaiser Wilhelm (later Max Planck) Institute for Coal Research at Mülheim, where he remained for the rest of his career. He died in Mülheim on 12 August 1973.

In 1933 Ziegler discovered a method of making compounds that contain large rings of carbon atoms, later used to synthesize musks for making perfumes, and in 1942 he developed the use of N-bromosuccinimide for brominating olefins (alkenes). In 1945, after World War II, he began research on the organic compounds of aluminium. He found a method of synthesizing aluminium tri-alkyls from aluminium metal, hydrogen and olefins and demonstrated that it is possible to add ethylene (ethene) stepwise to the aluminium–carbon bond of aluminium tri-alkyls to make higher aluminium tri-alkyls. These higher compounds can be converted into alcohols for use in the manufacture of detergents. He also discovered that nickel will catalyse the exchange of groups attached to aluminium by ethylene and liberate higher olefins. Using electrochemical techniques, he prepared various other metal alkyls from the aluminium ones, the most important of which is tetraethyl lead, which is used as an anti-knock additive to petrol.

His most important discovery came in 1953 when he and a student (E. Holzkamp) were repeating a preparation of higher aluminium tri-alkyls by heating ethylene with aluminium tri-alkyl. To their surprise the ethylene (ethene) monomer ($CH_2 = CH_2$) was completely converted to the dimer butylene (but-1,2-ene, $CH_3CH_2CH = CH_2$). They found the explanation to be that the autoclave used for the experiment contained traces of colloidal nickel left from a previous catalytic hydrogenation experiment. This led them to the discovery that organometallic compounds mixed with certain heavy metals polymerize ethylene at atmospheric pressure to produce a linear polymer of high molecular weight (relative molecular mass) and with valuable properties, such as high melting point. All previous processes have the disadvantage of needing high pressures and produced low-melting, partly branched polymers.

Also in 1953 Ziegler and Natta discovered a family of stereo-specific catalysts which are capable of introducing an exact and regular structure to various polymers. They found that they could use the Ziegler-type catalyst triethyl aluminium conbined with titanium tetrachloride (titanium(IV) chloride) to polymerize isoprene so that each molecule in the long-chain polymer formed is in a regular position and almost identical to the structure of natural rubber. This discovery formed the basis of nearly all later developments in man-made plastics, fibres, rubbers and films derived from such olefins as ethylene (ethene) and butadiene (but-1,2:3,4-diene).

Zsigmondy, Richard Adolf (*1865-1929*), was an Austrian-born German colloid chemist who invented the ultramicroscope. For this achievement, and his other work with colloids, he was awarded the 1925 Nobel Prize in Chemistry.

Zsigmondy was born in Vienna on 1 April 1865, the son of a dentist. His early education and first year at University were at Vienna, then he went to Munich and obtained his PhD in organic chemistry in 1889. He became a research assistant in Berlin and then a lecturer in chemical technology at the Technische Hochschule in Graz. In 1897 he joined the Glass Manufacturing Company in Jena, but left in 1900 to carry out his own private research. From 1908 he was Professor of Inorganic Chemistry at Göttingen University. He retired a few months before his death, in Göttingen, on about 23 September 1929.

In Berlin, Zsigmondy worked with the physicist August Kundt (1839-1894) on inorganic inclusions in glass. At Jena he became concerned with coloured and turbid glasses and he invented the famous Jena milk glass. This was the work that aroused his interest in colloids, because it is colloidal inclusions that give glass its colour or opacity. He recognized that the red fluids first prepared by Michael Faraday by the reduction of gold salts are largely colloidal analogues of ruby glass and worked out a technique for preparing them reproducibly. His belief that the suspended particles in such gold sols are kept apart by electric charges was generally accepted, and the sols became model systems for much of his later work on colloids.

In 1903, working with H.F.W. Siedentopf, he constructed the first ultramicroscope, with which it is possible to view individual particles in a colloidal solution. Unlike a conventional microscope, in which the illumination is parallel with the instrument's axis, the ultramicroscope uses perpendicular illumination. With such dark-field illumination, individual particles become visible by scattering light (the Tyndall effect), much as moving dust particles are illuminated by a sunbeam. Furthermore the technique makes it possible to detect particles much smaller than the resolving power of the microscope. Ernst Abba, Director of the Jena Glass Company, put all the company's facilities at Zsigmondy's disposal to develop the apparatus, even though at that time he had no formal links with the firm and no professional attachments at all. It was for this work that Zsigmondy was made a professor at Göttingen.

Using the ultramicroscope Zsigmondy was able to count the number of particles in a given volume and indirectly estimate their sizes; he could detect particles down to a diameter of 3 millimicrons. Much of his research continued to centre on gold sols ("purple of Cassius"). Several noted chemists had already studied such sols, but it was not known whether they contain a mixture or a compound. In 1898 he showed that it is a mixture of very small gold and stannic acid particles. He also showed that colour changes in sols reflect changes in particle size caused by coagulation when salts are added, and that the addition of agents such as gelatin stabilizes the colloid by inhibiting coagulation. At Göttingen he investigated ultrafiltration and its use for colloids; he also studied such systems as silica gels and soap gels.

Zsigmondy's work began a study of importance to the understanding of all sols, smokes, fogs, foams and films. His conclusions clarified problems in biochemistry, bacteriology and soil physics. The ultramicroscope has remained of great importance in colloid research, although somewhat superseded by the electron microscope.

Glossary

Words which appear in italic type are explained in the glossary.

acetylene The former name of the unsaturated hydrocarbon ethyne (C_2H_2) and generic name of the members of a *homologous series* of organic compounds of general formula C_nH_n, *where n = 2* or more. See *alkyne*.

acid A substance that has a tendency to lose *protons* and forms *hydrogen ions* in solution. The hydrogen atom(s) of an acid may be replaced by a metal atom (or atoms) or an ammonium ion to form a *salt*. An acid with two replaceable hydrogens (such as sulphuric acid, H_2SO_4) is termed dibasic; an acid with more than two replaceable hydrogens (such as orthophosphoric acid, H_3PO_4) is termed polybasic. Solutions of acids have a *pH* of less than 7; their presence may be detected by using an *indicator*, such as litmus (which turns red in the presence of an acid). An acid may be neutralized by reacting it with a *base*.

actinide (or actinon) Any of the group of elements that follow actinium in the Periodic Table (i.e., that have an atomic number greater than 89). Many actinides have radioactive *isotopes*.

addition reaction In organic chemistry, a reaction in which a new compound is formed by the addition of an atom or group of atoms to an existing compound (as opposed to a *substitution reaction*).

alcohol Any of a class of organic compounds in which a hydrogen atom (or atoms) of a hydrocarbon has been replaced by a hydroxyl (—OH) group (or groups); their names end in -ol. For example, replacing a hydrogen in methane, CH_4, produces methanol, CH_3OH (former name methyl alcohol). An alcohol with two hydroxyl groups is termed a diol; glycerol (1,2,3-propanetriol, $CH_2(OH).CH(OH).CH_2OH$) is a triol. Alcohols react with acids to form *esters*. Substitution of a hydroxyl group for a hydrogen atom in benzene or other aromatic compounds results in the formation of a *phenol*.

aldehyde Any of a class of organic compounds in which a hydrogen atom of a hydrocarbon has been replaced by an aldehyde (—CHO) group; their names end in -al. For example, replacing a hydrogen in methane, CH_4, produces ethanal, CH_3CHO (former name acetaldehyde). Aldehydes therefore have the general formula R.CHO, where R is an *alkyl* or *aryl* group. An exception to the above rules is formaldehyde, HCHO.

aliphatic Describing any organic compound that has a linear or branched chain of carbon atoms, or a ring or rings of completely bonded atoms (termed an alicyclic compound), as opposed to the closed rings of partly unsaturated atoms of *aromatic* compounds.

alkali A solution of a metal hydroxide, especially a hydroxide of an alkali metal such as potassium or sodium, or ammonium hydroxide. The presence of an alkali may be detected using an *indicator* such as litmus (which turns blue in the presence of an alkali). Alkalis produce hydroxyl (OH^-) ions in solution and the term is often extended to other compounds, such as hydrogen carbonate (bicarbonate) salts, which give an alkaline reaction in solution. Alkalis are a type of *base*.

alkane Any of a class of saturated hydrocarbons, formerly called paraffins. Their names end in -ane and they form a *homologous series* of general formula C_nH_{2n+2}, where n is a whole number. The first five members of the alkane series are methane (CH_4), ethane (C_2H_6), propane (C_3H_8), butane (C_4H_{10}) and pentane (C_5H_{12}).

alkene Any of a class of unsaturated hydrocarbons, formerly called olefins, characterized by the presence of one or more carbon-carbon double bonds. Their names end in -ene and they form a *homologous series* of general formula C_nH_{2n}, where $n = 2$ or more. The first four members of the alkene series are ethene (ethylene) C_2H_4, propene (propylene) C_3H_6, butene (butylene) C_4H_8 and pentene C_5H_{10}. An alkene with two double bonds is called a diene.

alkyl Any of a series of hydrocarbon *radicals* derived from the *alkanes* and having the general formula C_nH_{2n+1}. Examples include the methyl radical (CH_3—) and the ethyl radical (C_2H_5—).

alkyne Any of a class of unsaturated hydrocarbons, formerly called acetylenes, characterized by the presence of one or more carbon-carbon triple bonds. Their names end in -yne and they form a *homologous series* of general formula C_nH_{2n-2}, where $n = 2$ or more. The first four members of the alkyne series are ethyne (acetylene) C_2H_2, propyne C_3H_4, butyne C_4H_6 and pentyne C_5H_8.

alpha particle A positively charged particle consisting of a helium nucleus, He^{2+}; i.e., a combination of two *protons* and two *neutrons*. A stream of alpha particles is called an alpha ray.

amide Any of a class of organic compounds containing the grouping $-CONH_2$. The simplest is acetamide, CH_3CONH_2.

amine Any of a class of organic compounds containing one or more amino ($-NH_2$) groups. They can be considered as being formed by replacing one or more hydrogen atoms of ammonia (NH_3) by organic radicals such as *alkyl* or *aryl* groups. Substitution of one hydrogen results in a primary amine, general formula RHN_2 (e.g., aminomethane (methylamine) CN_3NH_2); di-substitution produces a secondary amine, R_2NH, and tri-substitution results in a tertiary amine, R_3N. A quaternary amine $(R_4N)^+$ is the organic analogue of the ammonium ion (NH_4^+).

amino acid Any of a series of *carboxylic acids* that contain one or more amino groups ($-NH_2$). There are more than 100 different amino acids, of which about 20 (called the alpha amino acids) are found - joined by *peptide* linkages - in *proteins*. These alpha amino acids have the general formula $RCH(NH_2)COOH$.

amphoteric Describing a chemical compound that reacts as a *base* with strong acids and as an *acid* with strong bases. For example, aluminium oxide is amphoteric; it forms aluminium salts with strong acids but forms aluminates with strong bases.

anion A negatively charged *ion*, such as chloride (Cl^-), sulphate (SO_4^{2-}) or phosphate (PO_4^{3-}). During *electrolysis*, anions migrate towards the (positively charged) *anode*. In ionic compounds such as salts, the charges of the anions are usually balanced by those of an appropriate number of *cations*.

anode The positive *electrode* in *electrolysis*, a *cell* (battery) or *discharge tube*. Current leaves the electrolyte and flows into the external circuit from, and *anions* are discharged at, the anode.

antibiotic A chemical substance, often used as a drug in medical treatment, that kills or prevents the growth of bacteria. Antibiotics are produced by fungi or bacteria, or they may be chemically synthesized.

aromatic Describing an organic compound that has one or more closed rings of atoms which are partly unsaturated and displays aromatic character as typified by benzene and its derivatives (as opposed to *aliphatic* compounds, which have open chains of carbon atoms or rings of completely bonded atoms).

aryl Any organic *radical* derived from an *aromatic* compound; e.g., the phenyl radical (C_6H_5-) is derived from benzene (C_6H_6).

association The grouping together of atoms or molecules, often in the vapour state or in solution, to form conglomerations of unexpectedly high molecular weight. See also *dissociation*.

atom The smallest particle of a chemical element that can have a free existence or take part in a chemical reaction. Atoms combine to form *molecules*.

atomic heat The product of *atomic weight* and specific heat (relative atomic mass and specific heat capacity). It is approximately constant for many solid elements and equal to 6 calories/gram atom/degree (25.2 joules/mole/K).

atomic number The number of *protons* in the nucleus of an atom, equal to the number of electrons orbiting the nucleus of the neutral atom. The atomic number gives a chemical element its identity; for example, an element may have several *isotopes* of different masses, but they all have the same atomic number.

atomic orbital A region in space occupied by an electron associated with the nucleus of an atom. Atomic orbitals have various shapes, depending on the *energy level* of the electron and the degree of *hybridization*. Atomic orbitals overlap to form molecular orbitals, or chemical bonds between atoms.

atomic radius The effective radius of an atom. Atomic radii vary periodically with atomic number, being largest for the alkali metals and smallest for the rare gases.

atomic volume The volume of one gram-atom of an element.

atomic weight The mass of an atom of an element compared with an atom of the common isotope of oxygen, which is assigned an atomic weight of 16.000. The modern term for this quantity is relative atomic mass. The gram atomic weight of an element is its atomic weight expressed in grams, e.g., the gram atomic weight of oxygen is 16.000 g.

base A substance that has a tendency to gain *protons* and forms *hydroxyl ions* in solution. A base reacts with (is neutralized by) an *acid* to form a *salt* and water. See also *alkali*.

battery A number of primary *cells* connected together to produce a higher voltage (cells in series) or a higher current capacity (cells in parallel). A set of secondary cells is called an accumulator. A single cell is commonly, but mistakenly, called a battery.

beta particle A fast-moving negatively charged particle consisting of an electron. A stream of beta particles, such as those emitted by radioactive substances, is called a beta ray.

biochemistry The branch of chemistry that is concerned with chemical processes that take place within living organisms.

bioluminescence The emission of light by an

organism as a result of chemical processes taking place within it.

biosynthesis The production of a substance by a physiological process (or series of processes) taking place within a living organism.

boiling point The temperature at which the saturated *vapour pressure* of a liquid is equal to atmospheric pressure. Standard boiling points are quoted for an atmospheric pressure of 760 mm of mercury. For a solution, the dissolved substance (solute) raises the boiling point of the solvent; such elevation of boiling point in dilute solutions may be used to determine the *molecular weight* of the solute.

bond A chemical bond, or valency bond, is the linkage that holds atoms together to form molecules. Most bonds involve a sharing or exchange of electrons. See *covalency*; *electrovalency*.

carbohydrate Any of a large group of biologically important organic compounds composed only of carbon, hydrogen and oxygen, with the general formula $C_n(H_2O)_n$. There are three main types of carbohydrates: monosaccharides (or simple sugars), which contain between three and nine carbon atoms, e.g., glucose, fructose and dextrose; disaccharides (also sugars), which consist of two monosaccharides linked together, e.g., sucrose (table sugar) consists of a molecule of glucose linked to a molecule of fructose; and polysaccharides, which consist of three or more (up to about 10,000) monosaccharides linked together, e.g., starch and cellulose.

carboxylic acid Any of a class of organic compounds that contain the carboxyl (—COOH) group. The acids' names end in -oic; the simplest are methanoic (formic) acid, HCOOH, and ethanoic (acetic) acid CH_3COOH.

catalyst A substance that brings about or accelerates a chemical reaction while remaining unchanged at the end of it; the phenomenon is called catalysis. An *enzyme* is a type of catalyst in biochemical reactions. A substance that slows or prevents a chemical reaction is called a negative catalyst.

cathode The negative *electrode* in *electrolysis*, a *cell* (battery) or *discharge tube*. Current enters the electrolyte from the external circuit and *cations* are discharged at the cathode.

cathode rays Fast-moving streams of electrons emitted by the *cathode* of an evacuated *discharge tube*. A tube made specifically for the production of cathode rays is called a cathode-ray tube, and is used for the visual display in computer equipment and in television and radar receivers.

cation A postively charged *ion*, such as a sodium ion (Na^+), ammonium (NH_4^+) or aluminium ion (Al^{3+}). During *electrolysis*, cations migrate towards the (negatively charged) *cathode*. In ionic compounds such as salts, the charges of the cations are usually balanced by those of an appropriate number of *anions*.

cell (electrolytic) A device in which a chemical reaction produces an electric current. It contains two *electrodes* (a cathode and an anode) in an *electrolyte*, usually consisting of an acid or a paste or solution of a salt. A potential difference (voltage) is set up between the electrodes. A primary cell uses an irreversible chemical reaction and cannot be recharged; in a secondary cell, the reaction can be reversed by applying an external voltage across its electrodes, so recharging the cell. A group of connected cells is called an accumulator or battery. In a *fuel cell*, the reaction is the oxidation of a fuel.

chain reaction In chemistry, a reaction consisting of a sequence of two or more reactions in which the product(s) of one becomes the reactant(s) of another. Such reactions can take place rapidly and, if they involve a branched chain reaction, may accelerate to explosive speeds. In nuclear physics, a chain reaction occurs during nuclear fission in a reactor or fission bomb. Neutrons produced by the disintegration of fissile material (such as isotopes of uranium or plutonium) initiate the distintegration of others, and the process rapidly accelerates, because the number of neutrons produced is greater than that required to initiate it.

chromatography A method of chemical analysis in which a solution of the mixture to be analysed is allowed to move through an absorbent material (such as a glass tube packed with powdered chalk or a strip or sheet of filter paper). The various components of the mixture move at different speeds and become separated into layers or bands along the column or paper.

cis- A prefix used in *stereochemistry* to distinguish an *isomer* that has two substituents or groupings on the same side of the main axis or plane of the molecule. The isomer with the two on opposite sides is denoted by the prefix *trans-*.

co-enzyme An organic compound that activates some *enzymes* to catalyse biochemical reactions. It is weakly attached to the enzyme and may be chemically changed in the reaction, during which it may act as a carrier. It is regenerated by further reactions.

colloid A substance that can occur in the colloidal state. Originally colloids in solution were distinguished from *crystalloids* by the fact that they cannot pass through a *semi-permeable membrane* (see *dialysis*). It was later found that most substances, even metals, can be prepared in the colloidal state.

combustion A chemical reaction accompanied by the evolution of heat and light. Usually the reaction is oxidation involving oxygen from air accompanied by flame – i.e., burning.

complex Any of a class of substances with a characteristic structure in which a central metal atom (often a *transition element*) is surrounded by – and bonded to – several non-metallic atoms or groups of atoms (*ligands*). Complexes are also called *co-ordination compounds*.

compound A substance consisting of two or more elements in chemical combination; it is made up of *molecules*. Unlike a mixture, it can be separated into its components only by undergoing one or more chemical reactions.

conductivity (electrical) A measure of the ease with which a material conducts electricity; the reciprocal of resistivity. The conductivity of an *electrolyte* depends on the presence of *ions*.

conjugation The presence in an organic compound of two carbon-carbon double bonds separated by a single bond. Such an arrangement favours certain addition reactions in which the double bonds become single, and the single bond becomes double.

co-ordination compound Any of a diverse group of complex compounds characterized by a structure in which several *ligands* surround – and are covalently bonded to – a central metal atom. Such compounds may be electrically neutral, or positive or negative ions. Similarly the central metal atom may be neutral, anionic or, rarely, cationic, but it is always one that is able to accept an electron pair(s) to form a co-ordinate bond(s). The total number of bonds between the central atom and the ligands is the co-ordination number which, in general, ranges from two to twelve; four and six are the most common.

co-ordination number. See *co-ordination compound.*

covalency A type of chemical bonding in which the bond involves the sharing of two electrons, one supplied by one of the combining atoms and one by the other. A two-electron molecular orbital is formed by the overlap of two one-electron *atomic orbitals*.

critical temperature The temperature above which a gas cannot be liquefied by the application of pressure alone.

crystalloid A substance which, when dissolved in a solvent, can pass through a *semi-permeable membrane* (as opposed to a *colloid*, which cannot).

dialysis A method of separating dissolved *colloids* from non-colloids (*crystalloids*) using a *semi-permeable membrane*, which does not allow the passage of colloids.

dielectric constant The capacitance of a capacitor (condenser) with a certain dielectric divided by the capacitance of the same capacitor with a vacuum (or, in practice, air) as a dielectric. It has also been called relative permittivity or specific inductive capacity.

diffusion The tendency of the molecules of a gas or mixture of gases to mix uniformly and spread to occupy evenly the whole of any vessel containing them. A gas diffuses through a porous substance at a rate that is inversely proportional to the square root of its density. Molecules or ions of a dissolved substance (the solute) also tend to diffuse through the solvent to produce a solution of uniform concentration.

dimorphism The property of a chemical substance that allows it to crystallize in two different forms.

discharge tube A device containing (usually two) electrodes and a vacuum or gas at low pressure; a (high) voltage applied to the electrodes causes an electric discharge to take place between them. A gas-filled tube (such as a neon tube) may emit visible light and other forms of radiation.

disproportionation The splitting of a molecule into two or more simpler molecules; it is also known as dismutation.

dissociation The reversible splitting of a molecule into two or more simpler portions. An ionic compound (such as a salt) dissociates in solution to form ions; this is termed electrolytic dissociation. If a compound splits into two others under the action of heat, the phenomenon is termed thermal dissociation.

electrochemical series A list of elements in order of their *electrode potentials* (with the highest negative electrode potentials at the top of the series). Any element (usually hydrogen is the only non-metallic element listed) will displace from solution all those elements below it. It is also known as the electromotive series.

electrochemistry The branch of chemistry that is concerned with chemical reactions that involve electricity. Electrical energy may initiate a chemical process (as in *electrolysis*) or a chemical reaction may generate electricity (as in a cell or battery).

electrode A conductor through which an electric current enters or leaves a liquid (as in *electrolysis* or in a cell or battery) or a gas (as in a *discharge tube*).

electrode potential The electric potential between an element and its ions in solution.

electrolysis A chemical reaction brought about

by an electric current passed between *electrodes* immersed in an *electrolyte*. The electrolyte (consisting of a solution of a substance, such as a salt, or a molten salt) contains electrically charged *ions*. Under the effect of a current, the positively charged cations migrate towards the negatively charged cathode, and the (negative) anions migrate towards the (positive) anode. At the electrodes, the ions are discharged and may be liberated (e.g., as a gas), deposited (e.g., as a metal), react with the electrode (as in the anoidizing of aluminium), or react with the solvent (e.g., sodium ions react with water to form sodium hydroxide).

electrolyte A substance that in the molten state or dissolved in a solvent consists of *ions* and can conduct an electric current. Typical electrolytes include acids, bases and salts; their melts or solutions are also termed electrolytes. When a current is passed between *electrodes* immersed in an electrolyte, *electrolysis* occurs. The electrical conductivity of an electrolyte depends on the presence of the ions. A strong electrolyte is completely dissociated into ions in solution; a weak electrolyte is only partly dissociated into ions.

electron A negatively charged fundamental particle found in the neutral atoms of all elements, where it orbits round the central nucleus. The combined charge of the orbiting electrons is balanced by the charge of an equal number of positively charged *protons* in the atomic nucleus. An electron is also the fundamental unit of electricity; an electric current consists of a flow of electrons along a conductor. Beta rays (see *beta particle*) and *cathode rays* consist of fast-moving streams of electrons.

electronegative Describing *radicals* that behave like negatively-charged ions. The electronegativity of a radical is a measure of its ability to attract an electron pair in a chemical bond. On Pauling's commonly used electronegativity scale, fluorine is the most electronegative element and caesium is the least.

electrophilic Describing a reagent that readily accepts electrons during a chemical reaction. Such reagents, therefore, typically react at centres of high electron density.

electrophoresis The movement of electrically-charged solute particles in a *colloid* towards the oppositely-charged electrode when a pair of electrodes is immersed in the colloidal solution and connected to an external source of direct-current electricity. It is used as an analytical technique similar to *chromatography*.

electropositive Possessing a positive electric charge. In chemistry, the term is used to describe *radicals* that behave like positive ions, i.e., radicals that tend to give up electrons in forming chemical bonds. There is no electropositivity scale; instead elements are classified according to their electronegativity because, at least in theory, any element (except those at the extremes of the scale) may be electropositive or *electronegative*, according to the electronegativity of the entity to which it is bonded.

electrovalency The power of an atom to form electrovalent bonds, which are formed by the transfer of electrons from one atom to another – in contrast to covalent bonds, which involve the sharing of a pair of electrons. In electrovalent bonding. the atom that gains an electron becomes a negative ion (*anion*), and the atom that loses an electron becomes a positive ion (*cation*). See also *valency*.

element A substance that is made up of atoms of the same *atomic number*; it cannot be converted chemically into any simpler substance. An element may, however, consist of a nixture of *isotopes* of different masses (see *atomic weight*).

elution The removal of material adsorbed on a surface by treatment with a solvent. It is a technique used in *chromatography*.

empirical formula The chemical formula of a substance in which only the relative proportions of each of its constituent elements are given. The empirical formula does not necessarily reflect a substance's *molecular formula* nor its structure. The empirical formula of benzene, for example, is CH, whereas its molecular formula is C_6H_6.

enantiomorph A compound that has two asymmetric structures, each a mirror image of the other. Enantiomorphs (also called antimers, optical antipodes or enantisomers), such as the optically-active forms of lactic acid, have identical chemical and physical properties, except in reactions with other enantiomorphs or in interactions with polarized light. See *optical isomerism*.

endothermic Describing a process or reaction that involves the absorption of external energy (usually in the form of heat). See also *exothermic*.

end-point The point during a *titration* when the two reagents involved are at exact equivalence, i.e., when all of each of the reagents has reacted and there is no excess of either.

energy levels (electronic) The series of specific, discrete energy states that electrons orbiting a nucleus can occupy. In certain processes an electron may absorb external energy and move to a higher energy level (in which case the electron is said to be excited) or it may release energy (usually in the form of light) and move to a lower energy level. Because the energy levels are discrete, these movements of electrons to different energy levels involve specific amounts (quanta) of energy. See *quantum theory*.

enthalpy That part of the energy change during a chemical reaction which can be measured as the absorption or emission of heat or light.

entropy A measure of the degree of disorder of a system. Together with the *enthalpy*, it makes up the *free energy*.

enzyme Any of a large number of *proteins* produced by living organisms that catalyse chemical reactions involved in various biological processes. Many enzymes require a non-protein *co-enzyme* in order to function.

equilibrium constant A numerical value that expresses the position of a chemical equilibrium at a given temperature and pressure. It is given by the product of the concentrations of the reactants divided by the product of the concentrations of the products.

equivalent weight The weight of a substance that exactly reacts with, or replaces, an arbitrarily fixed weight of another substance in a particular reaction. The combining proportions (by weight) of substances are in the ratio of their equivalent weights (or a multiple of that ratio) and a common standard has been adopted: for elements, the equivalent weight is the quantity that reacts with, or replaces, 1.00797 g of hydrogen or 7.9997 g of oxygen, or the weight of an element liberated during *electrolysis* by the passage of 1 faraday (96,500 coulombs) of electricity. The equivalent weight of an element is given by its gram *atomic weight* divided by its *valency*. For oxidizing and reducing agents, the equivalent weight is the gram *molecular weight* divided by the number of electrons gained or lost by each molecule. Some substances have several equivalent weights, depending on the specific reaction in which they are involved.

ester Any of a class of organic compounds in which a hydrogen atom of an acid has been replaced by an organic *radical* or group. Esters are considered as being derived from the reaction between a *carboxylic acid* (RCOOH) and an *alcohol* (R'OH) and have the general formula RCOOR'. Low molecular weight esters are liquids with pleasant odours and are widely used as flavouring essences. Most high molecular weight esters are solids and they include waxes and fats. *Hydrolysis* of an ester with an alkali yields a salt and the free alcohol. With long-chain esters this process is called saponofication, and its products are crude *soap* and glycerol.

ether Any of a class of organic compounds formed by the condensation of two *alcohol* molecules; they have the general formula ROR'. The compound commonly called ether is diethyl ether ($C_2H_5OC_2H_5$).

excited state (electronic) The condition of an electron that has absorbed external energy and, as a result, moved from its normal, *ground state* energy level to a higher energy level. The excitation energy is the difference in energy between the ground state and the excited state.

exothermic Describing a process or reaction that involves the release of energy (usually in the form of heat). Combustion, for example, is an exothermic reaction. See also *endothermic*.

fat Any of a class of organic compounds (collectively called *lipids*) that consist of *esters* of glycerol (glycerides) with various *fatty acids*. Fats, oils (excluding mineral oils, which are hydrocarbons) and waxes are chemically similar; the term fat is usually applied to lipids that are solid at and below 20°C, whereas oils are liquids at this temperature. Waxes are also solid but they are slick to the touch, rather than greasy, and consist of esters of longer-chain fatty acids. Fats and oils are used as energy-storage materials by plants and animals and are an essential part of the human diet.

fatty acid Any of a class of saturated, unsaturated or polyunsaturated monobasic aliphatic *carboxylic acids* having the general formula RCOOH. Saturated fatty acids contain no double bonds, unsaturated fatty acids contain one or two double bonds, and polyunsaturated fatty acid have three or more double bonds. The lower fatty acids are corrosive, pungent liquids, soluble in water; the intermediate members of the series are unpleasantly-smelling oily liquids, slightly soluble in water; and the higher members are mainly solids, insoluble in water but soluble in ethanol. Fatty acids occur widely in living organisms, usually in the form of glycerides in *fats* and oils.

fermentation A type of organic decomposition brought about by micro-organisms (such as yeast and bacteria) as a result of their *enzyme* action. The term is most often applied to the alcoholic fermentation of sugars using yeast to produce alcohol and carbon dioxide.

ferromagnetism A property of certain materials (principally iron, cobalt and nickel, and alloys of these elements) whereby they are capable of being relatively strongly magnetized by weak magnetic fields. Ferromagnetism results from unbalanced electron spin in the inner orbitals of the substances concerned, which gives the atom a magnetic moment. In ferromagnetic crystals, the ionic spacing is such that the individual magnetic moments of groups of atoms are arranged in magnetic domains. In an unmagnetized ferromagnetic material, these domains are oriented randomly; the application of an external magnetic field causes the magnetic axes of the domains to align, making the material strongly magnetic. A given ferromagnet loses its ferromagnetic properties at a specific temperature, called the Curie temperature. See also *paramagnetism*.

free energy The sum of *enthalpy* and *entropy*, i.e., the capacity of a system to perform work. The change in free energy accompanying a chemical reaction is a measure of its completeness.

freezing point The temperature at which there is equilibrium between the solid and liquid phases of a substance at standard pressure (760 mm of mercury); it is the same as the melting point of the solid. A solution freezes at a lower temperature than does the pure solvent, a phenomenon called depression of the freezing point. The amount of this depression is proportional to the number of *moles* of the solute dissolved in unit weight of the solvent.

fuel cell A type of cell that produces direct-current electricity by oxidation of a fuel. A simple fuel cell comprises gaseous hydrogen and oxygen brought together over catalytic *electrodes*; other fuel cells use ammonia, methanol or hydrazine to provide hydrogen. Fuel cells are recharged by adding more fuel, rather than by passing electricity through them. See also *cell*.

gamma rays A type of electromagnetic radiation similar to but of shorter wavelength than *X-rays*. Gamma rays are emitted in discrete units (photons) by the nuclei of radioactive atoms. See also *radioactivity*.

gel A colloidal solution (see *colloid*) that has set to a jelly-like consistency. The viscosity of gels is so high that they behave like solids in many respects, despite the fact that some gels may contain as little as 0.5% of solid matter.

ground state (electronic) The state of an electron in its lowest energy level. When all the electrons orbiting a nucleus are in their lowest energy levels, the atom as a whole has its minimum possible energy and is therefore in its most stable state.

halide Any compound (including organic compounds) of one of the *halogen* elements. Common salt - sodium chloride ($NaCl$) - is the best known metal halide. Most metal halides are ionic; most non-metal halides (e.g., chloroform, trichloromethane) are covalent.

halogen An element belonging to Group VII of the Periodic Table. There are five halogens - fluorine, chlorine, bromine, iodine and astatine, the last of which is the only halogen without a stable isotope (astatine's most stable isotope, $^{218}_{89}At$, has a half-life of only about 8.3 hours). All the halogens have one electron vacancy in the outer orbital and their main *oxidation state* is -1.

halogenoalkane Any of a group of organic compounds (formerly called alkyl halides) formed by the halogenation of (addition of a halogen to) an alkane. In the presence of ultraviolet light, alkanes react with halides by substitution. In the chlorination of methane, for example, one, two, three or all four of the methane's hydrogens may be substituted by chlorine - depending on how far the reaction is allowed to proceed - with the release of hydrogen chloride at each substitution; the resulting halogenoalkanes are chloromethane (methyl chloride, CH_3Cl), dichloromethane (methylene chloride, CH_2Cl_2), trichloromethane (chloroform, $CHCl_3$) and tetrachloromethane (carbon tetrachloride, CCl_4).

homologous series A series of organic compounds of the same chemical type, each member of which differs from its preceding member by having an additional $-CH_2$ group in its molecule; the *molecular weights* of members of a series therefore increase in steps of 14, and each series can be represented by a general formula. The members of a series show a gradual, regular change of physical properties with increasing molecular weight and have similar chemical properties. Examples of homologous series include the *alkanes, alkenes, alkynes* amd *alcohols*.

hormones Chemicals secreted by the endocrine (ductless) glands of animals and carried by the bloodstream to all parts of the body where they regulate many metabolic functions. Hormones may be *proteins* (e.g., insulin), *steroids* (e.g., cortisone) or relatively simple organic compounds (e.g., adrenaline). Originally obtaned from biological material, some hormones can now be synthesized.

hybridization The process by which two or more simple orbitals in the same quantum shell come together then redistribute themselves as an equal number of equivalent hybrid orbitals, this system possessing the optimum energy distribution for the molecule involved. For example, one *s* orbital and three *p* orbitals form four sp^3 orbitals; these hybrids can form *sigma bonds* with other atoms and are arranged so that the part of each hybrid orbital capable of bond formation is directed towards the corner of a regular tetrahedron. Similarly, one *s* and two *p* orbitals hybridize to form three sp^2 orbitals, which lie in a plane, the major axes of the orbitals being at 120° to each other. Thus hybrid orbitals are responsible for the basic geometry of the molecules in which they occur.

hybrid orbital See *hybridization*

hydration A special type of solvation in which water molecules are attached – either by electrostatic forces or by co-ordinate (covalent) bonds – to ions or molecules of a solute. Some salts, called hydrates, retain associated water molecules in the solid state (this water is called the water of crystallization); in solid copper (II) sulphate, for example, the hydrated ion is $[Cu(H_2O)_4]^{2+}$ or $[Cu(H_2O)_6]^{2+}$.

hydrogen bond A weak electrostatic bond that forms between covalently bonded hydrogen atoms and a strongly *electronegative* atom with a lone electron pair (e.g., oxygen, nitrogen and fluorine). Hydrogen bonds (denoted by a dashed line - - -) are of great importance in biochemical processes, particularly the N-H - - -H bond, which enables *proteins* and nucleic acids to form the three-dimensional structures necessary for their biological activity.

hydrogen ion concentration The number of grams of hydrogen ions per litre of solution; denoted by $[H^+]$. It is a measure of the acidity of a solution, in which context it is normally expressed in terms of *pH* values, given by $pH = \log_{10}(l/[H^+])$.

hydrolysis The chemical reaction of a compound with water, resulting in decomposition into two or more other compounds; the water itself is also decomposed. Hydrolysis occurs with salts of weak acids, weak bases or both. It also occurs with *esters* (the reverse of esterification) to produce an *alcohol* and an acid.

hydroxyl ion A hydroxyl group (−OH) with a negative charge, i.e., the OH⁻ ion. The presence of hydroxyl ions gives *alkalis* their characteristic chemical properties.

indicator A substance that indicates – usually by a sharp colour change – the completion of a chemical reaction. Indicators are often used to determine the *end-point* in titrations. Litmus, which is red in the presence of acids and blue with alkalis, is a commonly used indicator.

infra-red spectrum The part of the electromagnetic spectrum between the red end of the visible light spectrum and radio waves. Invisible to the human eye, infra-red radiation is perceived as heat. Infra-red spectroscopy is an important technique in analytical chemistry.

ion An electrically charged atom or group of atoms. Positively charged ions (*cations*) have fewer electrons than are needed for the atom or group of atoms to be electrically neutral;

negatively charged ions (*anions*) have more. Many crystalline substances are composed of ions held in regular lattice arrangements by the mutual attraction of oppositely charged particles. Ions migrate under the influence of electrical fields, and are the conductors of current in electrochemical reactions. See also *electrolysis*; *ionization*.

ionic bond (or electrostatic bond) A type of chemical bond based on the electrostatic attraction between oppositely charged *ions* in a compound. In the ionic compound sodium chloride, for example, the sodium atom loses one of its outer electrons to the chlorine atom (because of the greater *electronegativity* of chlorine), resulting in the formation of a sodium cation (Na^+) and a chloride anion (Cl^-), which are mutually attracted – and therefore form an ionic bond – because of their opposite charges.

ionic radius The effective radius of an ion. In positively-charged *cations*, the ionic radius is less than the *atomic radius* (because the electrons are more tightly bound); in *anions* the ionic radius is more than the atomic radius. Some elements, such as the transition metals, can have several different ionization states and their ionic radii vary according to the state involved.

ionization Any process by which an ion is formed. Ionization can occur in several ways: by the reaction of two neutral atoms, as occurs when sodium reacts with chlorine to form a sodium ion (Na^+) and a chloride ion (Cl^-) (ionically bonded as sodium chloride); by the combination of an already-existing ion with other particles, e.g., the addition of a hydrogen ion to an ammonia molecule to form an ammonium ion (NH_4^+); by the breaking of a covalent bond in such a way that each of the electrons of the bond is associated with one of the entities, e.g., the *dissociation* of a water molecule to form a hydrogen ion (H^+) and a hydroxyl ion (OH^-); and by the passage of energetic charged particles, electricity or radiant energy through gases, liquids, or solids, e.g., the passage of *X-rays*, *beta particles*, *gamma rays*, ultraviolet radiation or electric discharges through gases.

isomer See *isomerism*.

isomerism The existence of two or more different substances that have the same chemical compositions but different arrangements of their atoms. Butane, for example, has two isomers; each has the same molecular formula (C_4H_{10}) but one form is a straight, four-carbon chain whereas the other isomer consists of a three-carbon chain with a methyl (CH_3) group attached to the middle carbon. There are two main types of isomerism: structural isomerism (of which butane is an example), including *tautomerism*; and *stereoisomerism*, including optical isomerism and geometric isomerism. See also *cis-*; *trans-*; *enantiomorph*.

isomorphism The existence of identical or similar crystalline forms in different – although often chemically similar – compounds.

isotopes Species of the same chemical element (i.e. having the same *atomic number*) that differ in their mass numbers (and therefore in the number of *neutrons* in the atomic nucleus). An element's isotopes have identical chemical and physical properties, except those determined by the mass of the atom. Most elements have several isotopes, some of which (principally those of the elements with high atomic numbers) are radioactive. See *radioisotope*.

lanthanide (or lanthanon) Any of the group of rare metallic elements with atomic numbers from 57 (lanthanum) to 71 (lutetium) inclusive. The properties of all these elements are similar and resemble those of aluminium. The lanthanides constitute all but two of the elements that are commonly called the *Rare Earth* elements (the non-lanthanide Rare Earths are scandium and yttrium).

latent heat The amount of heat needed to change the state of a substance from solid to liquid (latent heat of fusion) or from liquid to vapour (latent heat of vaporization) without changing the substance's temperature. Each substance has characteristic latent heat values for each of its phase changes, corresponding to the amount of energy required to break the intermolecular attractions in the solid or liquid. In reversing the process (i.e. changing from vapour to liquid or from liquid to solid) heat is liberated, the amount being equal to the latent heat of vaporization or fusion, depending on the phase change involved.

ligand An atom or molecule attached to the central atom (usually a metallic element) in a complex or *co-ordination compound*. Most ligands are electron-pair donors in the bond formed with central atom, e.g., CN^-, Cl^- and OH^-. Occasionally they can be electron pair acceptors, e.g., NO^+ and $N_2H_5^+$. Other common ligands include H_2O, NH_3 and CO. Some organic compounds act as ligands with more than one point of attachment to the central atom.

lipid Any of a group of diverse organic compounds that are *esters* of *fatty acids*. Typically they are oily or greasy and insoluble in water (but soluble in ether, alcohol and other organic solvents). There are three main types; simple lipids, which are fatty-acid esters of glycerol and include oils, fats and waxes; compound lipids, which are fatty-acid esters of glycerol and phosphoric acid (or one of its derivatives) and include the phospholipids and glycolipids; and derived lipids, a group of complex lipids that includes the *steroids* (of which cholesterol is the best known example), carotenoids and lipoproteins. Lipids occur in all plant and animal cells and are essential to life – as an energy source, in biosynthesis and other metabolic processes, and as structural components.

macromolecule A very large molecule, typically with a diameter between about 10^{-8} m and 10^{-6} m (most ordinary molecules have diameters of less than about 10^{-9} m). *Polymers* – natural (e.g. cotton) and synthetic (e.g. plastics) – and many biologically important molecules, such as *proteins*, are macromolecules.

mass spectrograph An instrument for determining the masses of individual atoms by means of positive-ray analysis, which involves deflecting streams of positive *ions* using electric and magnetic fields. Ions with different masses are deflected by different amounts and can be detected (e.g., photographically) to produce a mass spectrum. *Isotopes* were first discovered in this way. A mass spectrometer is a similar instrument which measures the relative abundances of particles of each mass rather than their individual masses.

metabolism A general term for all the chemical processes that occur in living organisms. It can be divided into catabolism, the breaking down of complex substances into simpler ones (usually with the release of energy), and anabolism, the reverse process of building up complex substances. All metabolic processes are regulated by *enzymes*.

micelle (or association particle) A loosely-bound aggregation of tens or hundreds of atoms, ions or molecules in a continuous medium (usually a liquid), forming a colloidal particle.

mole (or mol) The *molecular weight* of a substance in grams; e.g., the molecular weight of oxygen is 31.9988, therefore one mole of oxygen equals 31.9988 g. The number of molecules in one mole is the same for all substances and is approximately 6.023×10^{23} (Avogadro's constant).

molarity The concentration of a solution expressed in terms of the number of *moles* of solute dissolved in one litre of solution. Thus a 0.5 molar solution of sodium chloride contains 29.22 g of NaCl (molecular weight 58.44) per litre of solution. Molality is the concentration of a solution expressed as the number of moles of solute dissolved in one kilogram of solvent.

molecular formula The formula of a chemical

compound showing the type and number of atoms of each type present in one molecule of that compound – in contrast to the *empirical formula*, which indicates only the relative proportions of each atom present. The molecular formula does not, however, show the structural arrangement of the constituent atoms.

molecular orbital A type of orbital resulting from the overlap of two *atomic orbitals*, forming a (usually covalent) chemical bond between the atoms involved.

molecular weight The mass of one molecule of a substance; it is the sum of the *atomic weights* of all its component atoms. A gram molecular weight is the molecular weight in grams, equal to one *mole*.

molecule The smallest unit of a substance capable of independent existence and retaining the properties of that substance. A molecule may consist of a single *atom*, as in a molecule of helium (He), or an aggregation of similar or dissimilar atoms held together by valence forces and acting as a single unit – oxygen (O_2) and water (H_2O), for example.

neutron A fundamental particle found in the atomic nuclei of all elements, except normal hydrogen (whose nucleus contains only a single *proton*). A neutron has no electrical charge and its mass is 1,838.65 times that of the *electron* – slightly greater than the mass of the *proton*. The mass number of an *isotope* of an element equals the number of neutrons plus the number of protons.

normality A measure of the concentration of a solution, expressed in terms of the number of gram equivalents (the *equivalent weight* in grams) of a reagent per litre of solution. For example, a solution that contains 2 gram equivalents per litre is a twice-normal (or 2N) solution.

nucleophilic Describing an atom, molecule or ion that seeks a positive centre (e.g., the atomic nucleus) during a chemical reaction. Nucleophiles react at centres of low electron density because they have electron pairs available for bonding. Common nucleophiles include the hydroxide ion (OH^-), ammonia (NH_3), water (H_2O) and halide anions. See also *electrophilic*.

nucleotide Any of a group of organic compounds consisting of a nitrogenous base (derived from pyrimidine or purine), a pentose sugar and a phosphate group. Nucleotides are of fundamental importance in living organisms: adenosine triphosphate (ATP), a compound essential for biological energy production, is a nucleotide, and polynucleotide chains make up nucleic acids, the carriers of genetic information.

nucleus (atomic) The positively-charged central core of an atom. Although relatively small in comparison to the volume of the entire atom, the nucleus has nearly all of the atom's mass. It comprises one or more positively-charged *protons* and (except in the case of hydrogen) one or more electrically-neutral *neutrons*. The number of protons in the nucleus is equal to the atomic number. The number of neutrons is given by the difference between the atomic number and the mass number.

occlusion The process by which some solids (mainly metals) absorb certain gases. It may occur in any of three main ways: by the formation of a chemical compound, by the condensation of the gas on the surface of the solid; or by the formation of a solid *solution* (a homogeneous mixture of two or more substances, the resultant substance being in the solid state).

oil See *fat*.

olefins The former name for the class of unsaturated hydrocarbons now called *alkenes*.

optical activity The property possessed by some substances (and solutions of these substances) of rotating the plane of vibration of plane-polarized light. A substance that rotates the light in a clockwise direction (as viewed facing the light source) is described as dextrorotatory and is prefixed by the symbol *d*; a substance that rotates the light in an anticlockwise direction is laevorotatory and is prefixed by *l*.

optical isomerism A type of *stereoisomerism* in which the isomers differ in their *optical activity* because of the different spatial arrangements of their atoms. *Enantiomorphs* (isomers with asymmetrical structures, each isomer being a mirror image of the other) are optical isomers.

orbital See *atomic orbital*; *molecular orbital*.

organometallic compound Any of a group of substances in which one or more organic *radicals* are chemically bonded to a metallic atom – excluding the ionic salts of metals and organic acids. A typical organometallic compound is tetraethyl lead, the "anti-knock" substance commonly added to petrol.

osmosis The spontaneous diffusion of a solvent (often water) through a *semi-permeable membrane* (i.e., one that permits the passage of solvents and crystalloids but not of colloids). If two solutions of unequal concentrations are separated by a semi-permeable membrane, there will be a net osmotic flow of solvent from the more dilute to the stronger solution, until the two solutions are of equal concentration. Osmosis is of fundamental importance in controlling the concentration of fluids within living cells. See also *osmotic pressure*.

osmotic pressure The pressure that must be applied to the more dilute of two solutions separated by a *semi-permeable membrane* in order to stop the osmotic flow of solvent from the weaker to the more concentrated solution. See also *osmosis*.

oxidation Any reaction in which oxygen is combined with another substance, hydrogen is removed from it, or in which an atom or group of atoms lose electrons. In the last case – an example of which is the change of a ferrous (iron(II)) ion (Fe^{2+}) to a ferric (iron(III)) ion (Fe^{3+}) – the electrons lost by the oxidized entity are taken up by another substance, which is thereby reduced; such combined oxidation and reduction reactions are called redox reactions. See also *reduction*.

oxidation state (or oxidation number) A value given to an element that represents the electrical charge on its atoms in a chemical compound; it equals the difference between the number of electrons associated with the element in the compound and the number associated with it in its pure form. A positive oxidation number indicates a relative electron deficiency; a negative number indicates a relative excess. An element's oxidation number is the same as its *valency* (although this latter is not given a positive or negative sign). In monatomic ions the oxidation number equals the electrical charge of the ion. In covalent compounds the shared electron pair is assigned to the atom with the greatest *electronegativity*. Some elements have the same oxidation number in different compounds whereas others, such as the *transition elements*, have different oxidation numbers depending on the precise compound concerned.

paraffins The former name for the class of saturated hydrocarbons now called *alkanes*.

paramagnetism A property of most elements and some compounds (but excluding the ferromagnetic substances – iron, cobalt, nickel and their alloys) whereby they are weakly magnetized by relatively strong magnetic fields. See also *ferromagnetism*.

peptide Any organic compound whose molecules are made up of *amino acids* joined by a peptide linkage (–NH–CO–) between the carbonyl group (–COOH) of one acid and the amino group (–NH_2) of the other. A long chain formed in this way is called a polypeptide. *Proteins* consist of one or more polypeptide chains cross-linked in various ways.

periodic law The generalization that there is a recurring pattern in the properties of elements when they are arranged in order of increasing atomic number. The law is most apparent when the elements are arranged in the *Periodic Table*, in which the elements in each vertical column (group) show similar properties.

Periodic Table An arrangement of the chemical elements in order of their *atomic numbers* such that each vertical column contains a group of elements with similar properties, i.e., the elements in each column demonstrate the *periodic law*. In the modern Periodic Table the elements in each group have the same number of electrons in their outer orbitals and therefore share the same *valency*, which accounts for the similarity of their chemical properties.

pH A measure of the acidity or alkalinity of a solution in terms of its *hydrogen ion concentration*. The pH of a solution is given by $pH = \log_{10}(1/[H^+])$, where $[H^+]$ is the hydrogen ion concentration. Pure water is neutral and has a pH of 7. Solutions with a pH of less than 7 are acidic, those with a pH of greater than 7 are alkaline.

phenols A class of *aromatic* compounds containing at least one hydroxyl group (–OH) attached directly to a benzene ring. The compound called phenol is the simplest of the phenols and has the formula C_6H_5OH.

phosphorescence A type of luminescence in which a substance exposed to radiation emits light, this emission continuing after the radiation has been removed.

phosphorylation The addition of a phosphoryl group (–PO_3^{2-}) to a compound. Phosphorylation is a very common step in numerous metabolic pathways, notably those concerned with energy storage, production and utilization.

photochemistry The study of chemical reactions that are initiated or accelerated by exposure to visible, ultraviolet or infra-red radiation. *Photosynthesis* is an example of a biological photochemical process.

photolysis The decomposition of a compound into smaller units as the result of exposure to light. Flash photolysis is an experimental technique used to study short-lived intermediates formed during many photochemical processes.

photosynthesis A metabolic process that takes place in green plants (those containing chlorophyll) by which they convert water and carbon dioxide into carbohydrates (such as sugars) and oxygen (a by-product).

poisoning (of a catalyst) The reduction in effectiveness of a *catalyst* as a result of it being contaminated by a reactant or a product of the reaction it catalyses. Although in theory a catalyst is unaffected by the reaction it catalyses, in practice particles ("poisons") accumulate on the surface of the catalyst and reduce its effectiveness.

polybasic Describing an *acid* that has more than two atoms of replacable acidic hydrogen in each of its molecules.

polymer A large molecule made up of (up to many thousands of) repeating units derived from a small number of simple molecules, called monomers. There are two main types: addition polymers, in which several identical monomer sub-units link to form a polymer which as the same *empirical formula* as the monomer; and condensation polymers, in which the monomers are joined during a condensation reaction (with the elimination of water or other simple compounds) to form a polymer with a different empirical formula to that of the monomer. Co-polymers are composed of two or more different types of monomers.

polymerization A reaction in which a number – generally not less than 10 and often 100 or more – of relatively small molecules (monomers) combine to produce a much larger molecule (a *polymer*).

polysaccharide Any naturally occurring large molecule consisting of many molecules of simple sugars (monosaccharides) joined together. Polysaccharides are one of the main types of *carbohydrates* and they play an important part in many biological processes; for example, starch is used as an energy store and cellulose is the main structural material of plants.

protein Any of a class of naturally-occurring *polymers* composed of hundreds or thousands of *amino acids* (carboxylic acids that contain the amino group $-NH_2$) joined together by *peptide* linkages ($-NH-CO-$) between the carboxyl group of one acid and the amino group of the adjacent one. Proteins have very high molecular weights – between about 18,000 and 10 million – and a variety of complex molecular shapes – helical in wool, for example, and globular in haemoglobin. About 20 different amino acids occur in proteins and most protein molecules contain all of them; it is the sequence of the amino acids and the type of cross-linkages between their strands that give the individual proteins their specific properties. Proteins are fundamental to life; in addition to forming the main structural components in most animal cells, they are also involved (as *enzymes*) in every metabolic pathway.

proton A stable subatomic particle with unit positive charge and a mass 1,836.12 times greater than that of the electron. The proton is a normal hydrogen nucleus (i.e., a hydrogen ion) and is a constituent of every atomic nucleus. In a neutral atom the number of protons equals the number of electrons and is the *atomic number* of the element concerned.

qualitative analysis The identification of the elements or groups of elements present in a sample, without taking into account the relative proportions of each of the sample's constituents.

quantitative analysis The determination of the amount or proportion of one or more constituents of a sample.

quantum theory A general mathematical theory based on Max Planck's discovery that radiant energy is quantized i.e., emitted in discrete quanta ("packets") of energy. The original theory has been extended to interpret a wide range of physical phenomena; e.g., quantum mechanics and wave mechanics are now extensively used to give quantitative accounts of the behaviour of small particles, such as electrons.

quaternary ammonium ion An ion in which the hydrogen atoms of the normal ammonium ion $(NH_4)^+$ have been replaced by organic *alkyl* or *aryl* radicals; it therefore has the formula $(NR_4)^+$.

racemic mixture A mixture of equal quantities of two *enantiomorphs* (isomers with mirror-image molecular structures). Because the *optical activity* of each component exactly cancels that of the other, the racemic mixture as a whole is optically inactive.

radical An atom or group of atoms containing an unpaired electron. Most radicals are incapable of independent existence (e.g., the ammonium radical NH_4- and the organic ethyl radical C_2H_5-) but maintain their identity during reactions that affect the rest of the molecule of which they are a part.

radioactive decay The process by which unstable atomic nuclei spontaneously lose some of their excess energy by disintegrating – accompanied by the emission of *alpha particles*, *beta particles* or *gamma rays* - into more stable nuclei. Several of the heavier radioactive elements, notably uranium and thorium, decay through a series of unstable *radioisotopes* before finally achieving a stable end-product, which is often an isotope of lead.

radioactivity The spontaneous disintegration undergone by certain unstable types of atomic nuclei; it is accompanied by the emission of *alpha particles*, *beta particles* or *gamma rays*. Alpha particles are emitted only by certain radioactive isotopes of the heavier elements (e.g. uranium 238); alpha emission results in the daughter nucleus having an atomic number two less than that of the parent nucleus and a mass number of four less. In beta emissions, the atomic number changes by one and the mass number remains the same. Gamma ray emission almost invariably accompanies alpha or beta emission and is therefore associated with the changes in atomic mass and/or number that these latter produce, although gamma-ray emission by itself affects neither of these quantities because it is merely electromagnetic radiation. Natural radioactivity is the disintegration of naturally occurring radioactive isotopes (such as those of uranium, actinium and thorium). Artificial radioactive isotopes of many elements can be prepared by bombarding them with high-energy particles.

radioisotope (or radioactive isotope) Any of several species (each with a different atomic mass) of the same chemical element whose atomic nuclei are unstable and radioactive. Every element has at least one radioisotope, although those of many elements can be obtained only by bombarding the elements with high-energy particles or in nuclear reactions.

Rare Earth elements A series of 17 elements whose compounds often occur together naturally and exhibit markedly similar chemical properties. The series comprises the 15 *lanthanide* elements (atomic numbers 57 to 71 inclusive) plus scandium (atomic number 21) and yttrium (atomic number 39).

reduction Any reaction in which oxygen is removed from a substance, hydrogen is added to it, or in which an atom or group of atoms gain electrons. In many reactions the reduction of one participant is accompanied by the *oxidation* of another; such combined oxidation and reduction reactions are called redox reactions.

resonance The concept that, in certain molecules, the electrons involved in linking the constituent atoms are not associated with a specific bond (or bonds) but oscillate between atoms. Thus such molecules are not represented by a single valence-bond structure but by two or more alternative structures; the molecule "resonates" between these alternative structures – i.e., its structure is a resonance hybrid of the alternatives. The best known example of resonance is benzene which, according to Kekulé's original formulation, resonated between two forms in which the double and single bonds were transposed. In Robinson's later modification, the six carbon atoms are linked by single bonds and the extra electrons are distributed equally among the carbon atoms, this being represented diagrammatically by a circle within the hexagonal carbon ring.

resonance hybrid See *resonance*.

respiration The metabolic process by which living organisms obtain energy by breaking down foodstuff molecules (e.g. *carbohydrates*) to simpler molecules (e.g. carbon dioxide and water). Most organisms require oxygen to respire (aerobic respiration) but some, chiefly micro-organisms such as bacteria, can respire without oxygen (anaerobic respiration). The term respiration is also applied to the way in which oxygen is transported from the atmosphere to the individual cells.

saccharide A little-used general term for any carbohydrate.

salt A compound formed when one or more hydrogen atoms of an acid are replaced by a metal atom(s) or by an *electropositive* ion such as ammonium. Most salts are crystalline ionic compounds; soluble salts dissociate into *ions* in solution.

saponification See *ester*.

semi-permeable membrane A membrane that allows certain substances in solution, such as *crystalloids*, to pass through it but is impervious to others, such as *colloids*. Semi-permeable membranes are used in *dialysis*.

sigma bond A type of chemical bond in which an electron pair (regarded as being shared by the two atoms involved in the bond) occupies a molecular orbital situated between the two atoms; the orbital is located along a hypothetical line linking the atoms' nuclei. See also *hybridization*.

silicone Any organosilicon *polymer* containing the -SiR_2O- group, in which R is an *alkyl* or *aryl* radical. The silicones are heat stable, chemically inert substances used as lubricants, hydraulic fluids, water repellants and synthetic rubbers.

smelting The extraction of a metal from its ore using heat. The process generally involves a reducing agent, such as carbon monoxide or carbon derived from coke or (historically) charcoal.

smoke A suspension of a solid in a gas; the solid is in the form of extremely small particles and the smoke may be a *colloid*.

soap An alkali metal salt of a high molecular weight *fatty acid*, typically the sodium or potassium salt of stearic or palmitic acid. Soaps are made by the *hydrolysis* (saponification) of fats (glyceryl *esters* of fatty acids) using caustic soda or potash, yielding glycerol as a by-product.

solute The dissolved substance in a *solution*, the liquid part of which is the *solvent*.

solution A homogeneous mixture of two or more substances, most commonly a gas or solid (the *solute*) in a liquid (the *solvent*). Liquids dissolved in liquids (i.e., any miscible liquids) and solids dissolved in solids (as in most alloys) are strictly also solutions. The components of a solution can be separated by physical means, such as evaporation and crystallization (solid in liquid), heating (gas in liquid) or distillation (liquid in liquid).

solvent The liquid part (or major component) of a *solution*, the other component of which is the *solute*. In solid solutions (as in most alloys) the solvent is taken to be the major component.

spectroscope An instrument that produces a spectrum for study or analysis. An object that produces radiation, such as a heated substance, forms an emission spectrum (see also *absorption spectrum*). Elements have characteristic spectra and spectroscopy is used in chemical analysis to identify the elements in a substance or mixture. Molecules or their constituent atoms or components of atoms can be made to absorb various types of energy in a characteristic way and give rise to such analytical techniques as infra-red, ultraviolet, X-ray and nuclear magnetic resonance spectroscopy. See also *mass spectroscope*.

statistical mechanics The branch of theoretical chemistry that deals with the properties and behaviour of atoms and molecules using mathematical analysis applied to the parameters that describe atoms and their component particles. It is an extension of *quantum theory*.

stereochemistry The branch of chemistry that is concerned with a study of the shapes of molecules.

stereoisomerism A type of *isomerism* in which two or more substances differ only in the way that the atoms of their molecules are oriented in space.

steroid Any of a class of naturally-occurring organic compounds that share a common basic structure based on the phenanthrene molecule and typified by the substance cholesterol. Steroids include such important compounds as the sex hormones and various plant poisons.

substitution reaction In organic chemistry, a general type of reaction in which a substance is formed by substituting a new atom or group of atoms for an atom or group in an existing compound (as opposed to an *addition reaction*).

sugar Any mono-, di- or polysaccharide (all of which are *carbohydrates*) that forms crystals and dissolves in water; solutions of sugars have a sweet taste. The common sugar extracted from sugar cane or sugar-beet is sucrose, a disaccharide.

tautomerism A type of *isomerism* in which a compound exists as a mixture of two readily interconvertible isomers in equilibrium. When one of the isomers is removed from the mixture, part of the other isomer converts so as to restore the equilibrium. Nevertheless, each of the

isomers can form a stable series of derivatives.

terpene Any of a class of organic compounds, originally derived from plant oils, that contain only carbon and hydrogen and are empirically regarded as derivatives of isoprene (C_5H_8). They are classified according to the number of isoprene units in the molecule – e.g., monoterpenes contain two isoprene units and have the formula $C_{10}H_{16}$, sesquiterpenes contain three units ($C_{15}H_{24}$), and diterpenes contain four units ($C_{20}H_{32}$). Turpentine consists of a mixture of several monoterpenes. Rubber is a polyterpene with between 1,000 and 5,000 isoprene units. Terpenoids are oxygenated derivatives of terpenes.

thermochemistry The branch of chemistry that deals with the heat changes that accompany chemical reactions.

thixotropy The property of a substance that enables it to form a jelly-like *colloid* that reverts to a liquid on mechanical agitation. Non-drip paints are common thixotropic materials.

titration A technique in *volumetric analysis* in which a liquid is added from a graduated burette to a precisely known volume of a second liquid until a chemical reaction between them is just complete (this *end-point* is usually detected using an *indicator*). From the volumes involved and the concentration of one of the solutions, the concentration of the second solution can be calculated.

tracer A radioactive isotope introduced into an experiment to follow the path of a chemical (often biochemical) reaction.

trans- A prefix used in *stereochemistry* to indicate that two groups or substituents lie on opposite sides of the main axis or plane of a molecule (as opposed to *cis-*, which indicates that they are on the same side).

transition element Any of a group of elements of similar physical and chemical properties that are characterized by having variable *valency* (*oxidation number*). They are grouped together at the centres of the long periods of the Periodic Table.

transuranium Describing any element beyond uranium in the Periodic Table (i.e., with an atomic number of greater than 92). Most isotopes of transuranium elements are man-made and radioactive.

valency (or valence) A number that describes the combining power of an atom or group of atoms in terms of the number of bonds it forms with hydrogen or its equivalent. Thus chlorine in hydrogen chloride (HCl) has a valency of 1; oxygen in water (H_2O) has a valency of 2; nitrogen in ammonia NH_3) has a valency of 3;

carbon in methane (CH_4) has a valency of 4; phosphorus in phosphorus pentoxide (P_2O_5) has a valency of 5; and so on. Increasingly the term valency is being replaced by *oxidation state*.

vapour density The density of a gas or vapour usually in terms of that of hydrogen (i.e., the weight of a given volume of the gas divided by the weight of an equal volume of hydrogen at the same temperature and pressure). The *molecular weight* of a gas is approximately equal to twice its vapour density.

vapour pressure The pressure exerted by a gas or vapour in an enclosed space. The saturated vapour pressure is the pressure of the vapour of a substance in contact with its liquid form; it varies with temperature.

vitamin An accessory food factor necessary for good health. Chemically, vitamins are complex organic compounds; many are referred to by letters of the alphabet (such as vitamin C), given to them before their chemical composition was determined. Many act as *co-enzymes*.

volumetric analysis Any method of chemical analysis that involves measuring volumes of liquids or gases (as opposed to gravimetric analysis, which involves mainly weighing). *Titration* is a common technique of volumetric analysis.

wax See *fat*.

X-rays Penetrating short-wavelength electromagnetic radiation produced when a stream of *cathode rays* (electrons) strike matter (such as the "target" in an X-ray tube). When X-rays strike a substance, it may emit secondary X-rays which are characteristic of the elements in it and so may be used as a method of analysis.

Index

The index entry in **bold** type will direct you to the main text entry in which the information you require is given.

169